14.50

Modern revolutions

an introduction to the analysis of
a political phenomenon

JOHN DUNN

Director of Studies in History
King's College, University of Cambridge

CAMBRIDGE
at the University Press 1972

Published by the Syndics of the Cambridge University Press
Bentley House, 200 Euston Road, London NW1 2DB
American Branch: 32 East 57th Street, New York, N.Y.10022

© Cambridge University Press 1972

Library of Congress Catalogue Card Number: 72-177942

ISBNS: 0 521 08441 5 (hard cover)
       0 521 09698 7 (paper)

Printed in Great Britain
by William Clowes & Sons, Limited
London, Beccles and Colchester

To the Memory of my Father

Contents

Preface

The title of this study is intended seriously. It is introductory in the limiting sense that reading it is not a proper basis for arriving at a firm opinion about the meaning of any modern revolution, let alone modern revolution as a whole. The enterprise to which it is offered as an introduction is the *study* of modern revolutions, the understanding of their character and of the causes of their occurrence. Insofar as any politically concerned person chooses to have reasons for their opinions, such study is plainly a necessary preliminary to any form of ideological assessment of revolutionary or other political phenomena. Revolution is a fiercely and an inevitably contentious topic. Indeed there are necessarily ascriptive as well as descriptive components even in the very identification of a set of events as constituting – or failing to constitute – a revolution. Hence it would be absurdly disingenuous and – in the light of the discussions which follow – implausible to the point of fatuity to pretend that this study does not embody the attitudes of the author. But it is not written in order to foist these off on the unsuspecting or indeed on the suspicious reader and the last response which it is intended to elicit is passive assent. Ideally what it hopes to provide is a sense of the necessary complexity of modern revolution and an understanding of why the bland professional claim of political scientists or political sociologists to aloof detachment in the face of these phenomena must be in such bad faith.

Much of the work consists of historical case studies, but it is not intended as a work of history and does not provide an adequate historical account of the occurrence of any revolution. Insofar as it belongs to any academic genre it is in intention a work of political theory. As such it is exploratory rather than conclusive in any respect. It takes two analytical traditions in the understanding of modern revolution, the ideological tradition of revolutionary action and the academic tradition of sociological analysis of revolutionary events, and attempts to show their evasiveness in the face of the actual character of a number of twentieth-century revolutions. In doing this it rests heavily for two reasons on a large body of predominantly historical literature. Were it not the case that some revolutions have actually occurred, any effort to explain the occurrence of revolutionary events would be otiose. Equally any effort to explain their occurrence which fails to explain what in fact occurred is something of a failure. History has an indefeasible role in the study of revolutionary phenomena. (Sociology may or may not be a game, but history was once life in earnest.) But in addition to its conceptual centrality, the tradition of historical analysis of concrete revolutionary phenomena happens in the case of modern revolutions to have reached levels of understanding which are incomparably superior, intellectually, to anything attained in any other discipline which has attempted their analysis. Historical writing on modern revolutions has at its best achieved a level which is both causally more sophisticated and morally more sensitive than any other writing on these themes, with the possible exception of a small number of works of literature. The proper concerns of political scientists and sociologists differ from those of historians; but the one dimension in which they can clearly not afford to be less sophisticated than the latter is in their understanding of causality. It is thus possible that the present work may make it slightly easier for sociologists or political scientists with an interest in revolutionary phenomena to develop greater delicacy in their grasp of the intricate problems of specifying precisely what aspects of what revolutions they wish to explain and thus of relating theoretical categories to historical social phenomena. But the present work is not designed with such a mildly presumptuous possibility in mind. Still less is it designed as a formal critique of any particular ideology or sociological analysis. What it aims to do is to assist anyone who wishes to think clearly, honestly and seriously about modern revolutions and who finds the conceptual and informational problems of beginning to do so slightly baffling.

The historical case studies were selected for a variety of

reasons. All are examples of the successful overturn of an existing governmental authority and the establishment of an alternative state power which has proved capable of maintaining itself in existence. Five have in some sense been Communist revolutions, though one, Cuba, very much in retrospect. All of these five have made manifest attempts to change pre-revolutionary patterns of social stratification and to augment production through state control of the economy. All involved substantial violent social conflict, Cuba again rather less than the others. The Russian and Chinese revolutions have been two of the key historical events of the twentieth century. No interpretation of the meaning of modern revolutionary phenomena could afford to ignore them. The three non-Communist revolutions all involved massive popular violence, all to some degree along ethnic lines, and all have been at one stage or another of their development affected by the success of some feature of the Communist revolutions. Decaying political orders to assault, mass violence and the advent of new and determined political elites are all features of all the revolutions taken. The revolutions in question were selected for possessing these characteristics, since these are here taken as the key indicators of what a revolution is. It is a common state of affairs for one or more of these characteristics to be found separately in a society at one time or another. Each can thus quite properly be studied separately in a universalist fashion: political decay, mass violence, the advent of novel and effective political elites. But the conceptual point of there being a separate category of revolution at all requires that the study of revolution focus on their coincidence in the history of particular societies, the conditions which make this possible, and the significance of the fact that they can coincide. Within these general constraints the bias of the examples selected here is towards the analysis of revolutions in which the post-revolutionary elites have attempted to establish an order of social relations inspired by the ideas of Karl Marx, or at least by what they took to be the ideas of Karl Marx. (The question of whether a revolution is a Marxist revolution is a question illuminating similar to the question of whether a society is a Christian society.) It is around these revolutions that the main concerns of the ideological tradition of interpretation, both sympathetic and hostile, cluster.

Inside the thought of Karl Marx himself the precise relationship between revolutionary political action and his general
theory of socio-economic development is optimistically vague.
It may well today be a totally trivial matter what the connection was supposed to be by Marx himself. But it is an
extremely practical question, as far as much of the world
today is concerned, what connection there turns out to be in
actual fact between revolutionary action to seize power and
post-revolutionary social change. The five cases of eventually
Communist revolutions studied here are thus taken in order
to disperse the spuriously unitary character of the category of
Communist revolution and substitute at least a more illuminating set of questions to ask about those which have taken
place.

In particular, the central conceptual issue on which all of
the case studies focus is the fact that all revolutions which
succeed in the twentieth century succeed by establishing a
government of a nation state in a world of other nation states.
This is a characteristic which Marxist revolutionary theory
is neither designed nor at all well equipped to explain. Marxist revolutionary theory revolves around the uniquely universalist role of the proletariat, a social grouping which was
universal precisely because it had escaped from any traditional status whatever.[1] The impending union of the 'Workers
of the World'[2] is a crucial element in Marxist optimism and
one which has not been rendered more plausible by the experience of twentieth-century revolution. Workers everywhere
continue to speak a particular language and to feel loyalties
to decidedly more particular collectivities than the world proletariat. Peasants, the great political resource of aspiring
revolutionaries in the second half of the twentieth century,
have, if anything, narrower and more rigid definitions of the
scope of allegiance, while those who control the state apparatuses in modern states seem behaviourally parochial, if not
always domestic, in what they select for the objects of their
devotion – Whoever would have guessed that the Ghegs and
Tosks of Albania would become tributaries within the new
Chinese World Order? But if the union of the world proletariat is at best a very distant aspiration, the union of great
masses of the populations of single countries, often against
alien ethnic domination, has been the key element of twen-

tieth-century revolutions. The significance of political revolution in the world historical process is a question the answer
to which is at present inscrutable, if indeed it can be considered a single question at all. But real revolutions, Marxist
or otherwise, take place in particular historical societies at
particular times. It is in terms of what they do or fail to do
for these societies, and of the geographical and ethnic definition which they succeed in giving of what these societies are,
that they must be understood and judged in the first instance.
Sub specie temporis these are the phenomena which require
explanation. How they will appear *sub specie aeternitatis,*
only eternity will have sufficient opportunity to know.

I wish once again to acknowledge with gratitude the generous
support given to my research by King's College, Cambridge,
and particularly in this instance by the Managers of the King's
College Research Centre. I have had the opportunity of as
much sympathetic and critical advice as anyone could wish,
first from the Revolution seminar in the King's Research
Centre organized by Dr Martin Bernal, then from the numerous distinguished scholars who attended the conference on
Revolution held by the Research Centre in the summer of
1969 and most recently from those studying for the paper on
Revolution in the first year of the Cambridge Social and
Political Sciences Tripos. If I have not made better use of
this assistance it is no one's fault but my own. I should like
particularly to express my gratitude to Quentin Skinner for
his continuing intellectual sympathy and encouragement and
to Michael Cook for saving me from many errors in my discussions of the Islamic world and for renewing a conviction
which he helped to generate for me over a decade ago that
in the study of politics history and sociology are activities
which are rendered absurd by being separated. I hope to
provide a more adequate return on these accumulated debts
by writing more formally about the theory of revolution in
the future.

Cambridge, May 1971   *John Dunn*

The pious say that faith can do great things, and, as the gospel tells us, even move mountains. The reason is that faith breeds obstinacy. To have faith means simply to believe firmly – to deem almost a certainty – things that are not reasonable; or, if they are reasonable, to believe them more firmly than reason warrants. A man of faith is stubborn in his beliefs; he goes his way, undaunted and resolute, disdaining hardship and danger, ready to suffer any extremity.

Now, since the affairs of the world are subject to chance and to a thousand and one different accidents, there are many ways in which the passage of time may bring unexpected help to those who persevere in their obstinacy. And since this obstinacy is the product of faith, it is then said that faith can do great things.

Francesco Guicciardini, *Ricordi*, Series C 1
(translated by Mario Domandi)

(=Francesco Guicciardini, *Maxims and Reflections of a Renaissance Statesman,* tr. Mario Domandi, Harper Torchbooks edn., N.Y. 1965, p. 39, reprinted by courtesy of Harper & Row)

Introduction: The ideological dilemmas of modern revolution and its analysts

Revolution is not a frivolous subject and revolutions are peculiarly unfrivolous events. What causes them to happen and what they mean are questions which cannot readily be separated from one another. They are also intensely political questions, questions at issue – today, at least – in every persisting order of power relations of any geographical scale and in every effort made to subvert such an order. The central issue which they raise is in the last resort rather a simple one – do human social conditions *have* to be as unequal and as unjust as everywhere they now are? But the answer which they give so far, if not obviously very encouraging, is also not a very clear one. But because the question which they raise is so profound, if in some respects so inscrutable, revolution is not a topic about which it is either possible or proper[1] to be neutral. This is not to say that in considering revolutions an analyst is properly liberated from the constraints of natural scientific criteria of truth or falsehood, let alone from more quotidian standards of veracity. Generous emotions may be unequivocally admirable in personal human encounters but in the study of revolution they have no privileged place. Responsibility to the truth is and must be absolute. Highly selective presentations of the meaning of revolution are commonplace and most of the general propositions which could be advanced about revolution in the effort to explain its occurrence are too tendentious to be true. This does not imply that anyone has to be either in favour of all revolutions or opposed to all revolutions – or, for that matter, unequivocally in favour of or opposed to *any* particular revolution. What needs emphasis is that to entertain any theory about the meaning of revolution – and it is not even possible to identify just what events do constitute revolutions, as will be shown later, without assuming *some* theory about the meaning of

I

revolution – is to assume a political posture. Indeed it may well be under some circumstances to commit oneself to an obligation to further certain political ends in the real world. Revolutionary theories, whether favourable or hostile, are major premises in a large range of hugely important practical syllogisms.[2] The value-free study of revolutions is a logical impossibility for those who live in the real world.[3]

Revolutions are very destructive and brutal affairs, but no revolution has ever failed to destroy much that is bad as well as much that is good. One may doubt that the great Russian Anarchist Bakunin was right to claim that the lust for destruction is a creative lust;[4] but there is certainly much social and political organization which is eminently in need of destruction in the world today. One very important characteristic of revolution is indicated by a paradoxical feature of Bakunin's claim. The appeal of destruction at a psychological level may be intrinsic to the act of destroying, but the justification of it cannot be so. Revolutions are either ventures in creativity or they are nothing – mere *jacqueries,* products of misery and devastation which lead only to greater misery and more pervasive devastation. As far as sheer destructive power is concerned, capacity for upheaval, the twentieth century has been the great century of revolution. But as far as sheer creativity is concerned, the general enhancement of freedom, perhaps the scope of its creativity is still a more open question. Revolution so far this century has exhibited highly rationalist pretensions, as, in its Marxist form, it might well be expected to do. It has claimed to establish more rational forms of order in the social world than have hitherto existed. Yet at the same time the rational coherence of the theories by which these actions are supposedly guided is no longer very impressive;[5] and much of the actual experience of twentieth-century revolution has a convulsive, essentially natural force to it which quite fails to suggest the dominance of human reason in any form. The revolutionaries of the twentieth century, even at their more successful, have seemed more to be riding the whirlwind than masterfully shaping the destinies of nations for the common good.

These disparities (not so much between theory and practice as between theory and experience – the world just will not keep still) suggest a fundamental dilemma in the analysis of revolution. The root of the metaphor of revolution is the field of natural science, specifically theoretical astronomy. In its early usage it was employed to refer to the ineluctably cyclical character of history, a gesture towards the revolutions of the spheres in Ptolemaic astronomy or the classical Polybian morphology of political order from primitive republican agrarian virtue to decadent despotic urban vice.[6] It suggested, as required, the reliable return to the proper course of organized political life[7] or the more or less purposeful disruption of the political order by those outside it. It was an elite perspective on a not wholly trustworthy political structure, an exercise in the exorcism of elite political anxiety, as perhaps in some uses it remains today. When the Duc de la Rochefoucauld-Liancourt replied famously to Louis XVI's plaint that the Fall of the Bastille was a revolt, 'No, Sire, it is a revolution', he was not exercising remarkable foresight.[8] What he wished to emphasize was the massive and essentially more than human, uncontrollable character of the forces at work. Mere men make revolts. But revolutions are to be traced to forces of a more cosmic scale.

Revolutions are facts of nature, analogous to physical processes, the release of enormous forces, moving vast masses through space. They are amoral, ineluctable. They crush all in their path. (The metaphors are insistently physical.) It is pointless to resist them and absurd, as Danton said, to put them on trial. This view, which was first worked out in detail as an interpretation of convulsive political and social transformation during the great French revolution, is crucial for an understanding of the determinist strand in Marxist revolutionism. The picture of *how* the social relations of production were to be transformed to accommodate themselves to the forces of production by a profound and essentially political upheaval was taken fairly directly from the experience of France during the great revolution.[9] In this way it became possible to think of violent political change as a motor for social transformation and revolutions at the right time came to seem like avalanches – easy to start, but impossible to stop until they had reached their appointed destination. In some ways this metaphor was a rather old elite viewpoint, a variant on *Après nous le déluge*. It suggests quite neatly the destructiveness of the process, the disparity between the numbers of those who initiate such processes and the scale of the forces which they unleash. It combines a useful accusatory device (it is moderately irresponsible to start avalanches) with an effective excuse for governmental failure (who can control the elements?).[10]

To understand revolutions in this way as natural events, initiated perhaps by a few foolhardy persons, but then rapidly eluding their control, makes it easy to see how there could be a theory of revolutions of a natural scientific type. It would be a distinctly complicated theory. Very possibly there does not exist such a specialized scientific topic as the theory of avalanches. But it is reasonably clear what sort of scientific inquiries are relevant to studying avalanches and the results of such investigations could in principle be constructed into a theory of avalanches in due course. But it would be likely that the abler natural scientists in the relevant fields (those interested in the systematic analysis of natural regularities) would not be greatly interested in organizing their analysis in these terms. Those most likely to attempt to reduce the relevant body of notions to a coherent order are those who most *need* to do so: those charged with the prevention of avalanches on a large scale or those with a strong interest in causing them. In this sense a theory of revolutions as illuminatingly resembling avalanches, as essentially unthought through natural events, is likely to be somewhat crudely pragmatic, whether the motive for compiling it has been revolutionary or counter-revolutionary.

There may be much revolutionary behaviour to which such a theory does justice and there might be much revolutionary behaviour which it successfully predicts, though it would hardly be correct to claim that there has been much thus far which it *has* successfully predicted. In any case, whatever the success of its predictive efforts, it is excessively likely – so likely as to be almost certain – to suppress the entire point of revolution as a unique type of social event. Much writing about revolution does take this form, both in the case of works with an informal historical approach and in those related to some types of general sociological theory, particularly to a sort of Parsonian functionalism.[11] Such analyses of evolution focus on necessary – or perhaps at best sufficient – conditions for the dramatic destruction of socio-political structures by mass violence. Revolution appears as a reasonably frequent type of social change, occurring intermittently throughout history and becoming rather more frequent in recent years.

It would be silly, plainly, to suppose that the social and political experience of earlier centuries is wholly discontinuous with that of the twentieth century – the industrial revolution, where it has in fact happened, cannot have made such a complete chasm between the present and the past. But it has undoubtedly made a number of very important differences to types of political relationship and nowhere has it made more of an impact than on the practice of revolution. In the past mass efforts to subvert the social order have almost always been either explicitly millenarian[12] (that is: largely transcendental, extra-terrestrial, in their understanding of how the social world was to be transformed) or else they have been explicitly preoccupied with the restoration of an ideal order in the past,[13] an order known to be *possible* at all simply because it had existed in the past. The guarantee of the possibility of a genuinely new order had to be essentially religious.[14] Any transformational effort which was not religious in its rationale was seen as conservative, not as innovative. In substance, of course, the Puritan dream of England's Saxon constitution before the Norman Yoke[15] was a dream of an order very different from anything which had in fact existed in the past. The dreams were revolutionary enough in their sense of what *was* possible. English radicalism remained cast in the mould of restored Anglo-Saxon equality even into the nineteenth century in the case of men like Cartwright.[16] But steadily throughout the later seventeenth and eighteenth centuries, the traditionalist ideologies of revolt became more adulterated with a quite different conception, a conception essentially based on the notion of progress.[17] It became possible to think of a revolt as potentially a prelude to decisive innovation, the creation of something *really* new under the sun. Instead of travelling cyclically from barbarism through civilization into decadence and renewed barbarism, unit by unit, it became possible to think of the human race progressing more or less steadily towards new heights of civilization. The place of the human race in history meant that a better, juster (perhaps richer) future lay ahead of it within the grasp of those with the nerve and the energy to reach out for it. The French revolution began as aristocratic reaction, the *révolte nobiliaire*,[18] but before it ended it had given birth to the first overt secular Communist conspiracy in history, the *Conjuration des Égaux* of Gracchus Babeuf.[19] It had also produced a document which epitomizes in its contents and in the circumstances of its production both the Utopian grandeur and the crude human degradation which characterize the process of revolution. The Marquis de Condorcet's *Outline of a Historical Picture of the Progress of the Human Mind* foresaw a future of expanding wealth and increasing economic and political equality generated above all by the expansion of educational opportunity and by a steady diminution in the hold of superstition at all levels of society. He saw existing inequality and poverty as a product of the manipulative egoism of elites which were prepared to keep the majority in a state of abject superstition in order to preserve their own political control. It was a very rationalist image. The guarantee of future progress and the mechanism of past progress was the rational progress of human thought. The model for the human race at large was the advancement of science, an additive process, as Condorcet conceived it and one without necessary boundaries. It was a strikingly serene picture to have come from a hunted man hidden away in an attic under the threat of the guillotine. But the serenity was firmly premised on the future. Condorcet's assessment of the present was balanced enough. 'We see that the labours of these last ages have done much for the progress of the human mind, but little for the perfection of the human species; much for the glory of man, something for his liberty, still almost nothing for his happiness.'[20] The spectacles of stupidity, slavery, extravagance and barbarism still persist in troubling the philosopher; indeed the only unmixed pleasure open to the friend of humanity comes in 'abandoning himself to the sweet hopes of the future'. Many men since Condorcet's day have won their serenity by abandoning themselves to the sweet hopes of the future and yet have seen this abandonment as a rational and a purely secular performance.

This rationalist construction is a necessary condition for envisaging the revolutionary career as both secular (to do with this world) *and* innovatory. But it is not a sufficient condition for seeing political action – and in particular violent political action – as the appropriate method for bringing about such a future. Indeed the very rationalist cast of this conception tends to suggest that violence must have a very subordinate and instrumental role in such a transformation and education, extension of human understanding, must hold an unchallenged central role. Implicitly such an image must be overwhelmingly elitist in the short run – even if its long-term implications are explicitly egalitarian. All men may be capable of understanding but at the moment in question only comparatively few have actually *understood*. The process of revolutionary change is one of instruction of the many by the few.

What made the picture of revolutionary action more egalitarian in its understanding of procedures and more preoccupied with violence in its methods was a profound structural change in society and economy which had only recently begun to make itself visible even in England by the time of Condorcet. The French revolution was the last great revolution to see political problems as the central problems of the revolution and economic demands and unrest as environmental distractions. The coming of industrialism made the structure of society and economy into the subject matter of revolution. It also provided the political support which the intellectuals needed if they were to challenge the existing holders of power. The role of the *sansculottes* in the French Revolution was an equivocal and muddled one.[21] The role of the proletariat in the revolutions of the future was advertised (though not, of course, advertised by themselves) as being altogether grander and more central. The old war between town and country which ran through the whole history of civilization[22] was to take a very different turn. Modern history, said Marx, is 'the urbanization of the countryside'.[23] In the Middle Ages all great risings against social injustice emanated from the country and remained totally ineffective because of the isolation and consequent crudity of the peasants.[24] The concentration of the proletariat and its organization in the very process of capitalist production created a politically educated mass – and a mass educated by its own situation, not merely by the grace of middle-class intellectuals. Some measure of equality of power was made possible even in the process of revolution because revolutionary understanding was not an elite prerogative. Marxist theory was an egalitarian theory of the revolutionary process, for all its blunt recognition of the centrality of violence in revolutionary action; it was by their *own* actions that men were to put an end to their alienation. Marxism was no longer a theory in which equality was as firmly a fact about the future as it had been in the standard Christian understanding of Heaven. It is true that this feature of Marxist revolutionary theory did not survive exposure to what was claimed to be the *success* of a Marxist revolution for very long. But it was a plausible inference from its failure to do so, as well as from a number of other features of the revolution in question, that it was not in fact a *Marxist* revolution at all, but something much more old fashioned, a *putsch* by a small group of intellectuals with a certain amount of tactically accumulated mass support, kept in power by the construction of a regime of authoritarian terror.

However, to look at Leninism in this way as simply a betrayal of the Marxian theory of the character of the revolutionary process itself is to ignore the extent to which it was a rather desperate effort, especially after 1914 amid the ruins of the Second International and the barbarism of the First World War, to rescue the central Marxist theory of social development, the inevitable triumph of socialist over capitalist production. The theory of the revolutionary process in Marx's own thought was a sort of political rationalism. Its egalitarianism came from the shared exposure of the proletariat to the rationale of their social situation. The general Marxist theory of social development was also rationalist, but its rationalism was economic, rather than political. The mechanism of social transformation was the contradiction between the forces of production and the social relations of production, issuing in massive crises of over-production. Marxist economic rationalism implied that future production must in due course be rationally organized, just as Condorcet's more epistemological rationalism implied that human thought – and with it all the social and political structures in which men lived – must in due course become rational. Both identified a logic of the future, a path to which history must in the end conform. Neither was exactly a determinist theory (though Marxism at times sounded much more like one),[25] because neither was based on the analysis of causal regularities and their critical identification as natural uniformities. Both began with what was desirable[26] and attempted to show why it must come about, rather than beginning with the actual and showing how, over a restricted period, it was most likely to develop. Both struggled to elicit a desirably logical structure from the future, rather than submitting blandly to reckoning the odds from a probabilistic social science. Revolution was still a reaching out for necessity, for uniformity – though it was an exceedingly assured sort of reaching. But the assurance came from grasping the logic of a set of categories, not from isolating the most predictable features of a natural environment.

To put this point in a slightly different way: the revolutionary theories of Condorcet and of Marx were essentially philosophies of history, not, as natural science itself attempts to be, philosophies of nature. Both Marx and Condorcet did, of course, hold philosophies of nature and Marxian historical materialism purports to be a general philosophy of nature, though it is not clear how seriously Marx himself took it in this guise. In any case, whatever his personal attitude to its scope, there is no doubt that the structure of historical materialism as a theory is very different from the structure of materialism as a philosophical position. When Engels spoke at the graveside of Marx in Highgate Cemetery in 1883 he called Marx 'before all else a revolutionist', a man whose 'real mission in life was to contribute in one way or another to the overthrow of capitalist society and of the state institutions which it had brought into being, to contribute to the liberation of the modern proletariat which he was the first to make conscious of its own position and its needs, conscious of the conditions of its emancipation'.[27] Marxian historical materialism is above all else a theory of revolution, a theory of the creative intervention of human action within the opportunities afforded by the historical evolution of human societies. 'Men make their own history, but they do not make it just as they please, under circumstances chosen by themselves, but (rather) under conditions immediately encountered, given and transmitted from the past. The tradition of all the dead generations weighs like a nightmare on the brains of the living.'[28] Marxism is a theory of *how* to make a better sort of history, a theory of the conditions of revolutionary possibility. It is in many ways a very Utopian theory, in the sense that it is predicated on the arrival of a very different order of human existence, the beginning of truly human history. But it is also in ambition, if not perhaps in performance, a very toughly anti-Utopian theory, contemptuous of the wishful thinking of bourgeois liberals and the weakness of those who think that the world can be made better by loving-kindness. Marx, like Machiavelli, scorned above all the enfeeblement of will which came from putting concern for one's own spiritual condition above the need to master the world. Revolution was a historical necessity because it was a precondition for the establishment of Socialism.[29] As such it was a Socialist's prime duty to be a revolutionary and to confront the imperatives of this role without flinching. The role was highly authoritarian in one respect. A revolution, said Engels, 'is certainly the most authoritarian thing there is; it is the act whereby one part of the population imposes its will upon the other part by means of rifles, bayonets and cannon, authoritarian means, if such there be at all, and if the victorious party does not want to have fought in vain, it must maintain this rule by the terror which its arms inspire in the reactionaries'.[30]

But if revolution in the real social world was a tough and in many ways rather ugly performance, its necessity (a rather abstract feature of it) was reassuringly elegant. Marxists, like Hegelians, saw the present as in many ways a cross and, again like the Hegelians, they adapted themselves to this *via crucis* by concentrating on those aspects under which the present was aptly seen as rational. For Marxists, as for Hegelians, there was, in Hegel's phrase, 'a rose in the cross of the present';[31] but for Marxists the rose was an attribute of the future. It was the reality of the changed world, not the rational consciousness of the philosopher, where the evils of the present could be transcended. Revolution was to be central to the process in which the ideally rational could become actual. Marxism is in this aspect a necessarily inegalitarian doctrine (like Condorcet's) in its epistemological dimension. Lenin consequently drew a legitimate inference from its structure (though a very partial and a necessarily destructive inference) when he saw that it could serve as essentially a legitimating theory for an elite. Marxism could come to be seen as a theory for those who had broken the code of modern society, a code which only cryptographers of high intelligence were in practice capable of breaking. In breaking this code Marxists learnt not only much useful practical guidance on how to garner power in such a social order, they also learnt the esoteric wisdom which *entitled* them to juggle with destinies of nations, for tiny groups of men to seize vast power over the lives of millions of other men. The mechanism by which they contrive to seize power is not, at least within the theory itself – and in a rather different sense in the real world also, as shown later – purely *arbitrary*. But it is clearly not as a result of noncoercive lessons in formally logical reasoning. It may in Catholic theology be 'the last temptation and the greatest treason to do the right deed for the wrong reason', but in Leninist theory the proletariat is essentially given precisely that opportunity in the process of revolution.[32] The intuitive consciousness of the proletariat is concerned with economic provision in the here and now, the present – and the past. It takes an intellectual to keep both eyes firmly fixed on the future. So indeed it might be expected to be, taking account of class structure and social experience. The future is the slave of thought. It marches and countermarches to the orchestration of ideas. It does the bidding of diverse intellectuals with equally endless docility. It is marvellously plastic. But the present – and to a lesser extent the recent past – are no one's prisoners. The masses of men know what life is like, however nasty it may be, and they do not readily bet such painfully won security as they have mustered on the chicly-cut elegance of the dreams of intellectuals. Revolutionary theories in consequence may be both neat and subtle. They may follow pleasant developmental pathways into pretty futures with the utmost assurance. But in revolutionary facts, as Engels noted, the prettiness must generally be dispensed with – and often, unfortunately, it turns out that the future must be dispensed with too.

Revolution, like the doors of the Temple of Janus, has two faces. One is an elegant, abstract, and humanitarian face, an idyllic face, the dream of revolution,[33] its meaning under the calm distancing of eternity. The other is crude, violent and very concrete, rather nightmarish, with the hypnotic power of nightmare and the loss of perspective and breadth of understanding which you might expect to go with this. Most general accounts of revolution concentrate on one of the two visages, because they essentially require such very different efforts of understanding and because each is sufficiently uncomfortable for many to contemplate on its own to make their joint confrontation distinctly too much of a strain for most, both intellectually and emotionally. The very naturalistic accounts of revolution as mass social violence plainly concentrate on the second and, in doing so, they plainly take a conservative ideological stance. The general body of *gauchiste* writing concentrates predominantly on the first, the fantasy life of revolutionaries and its sanctioning theology, an equally ideological stance. As it stands, this division is slightly simpliste. Some revolutionary enthusiasm – particularly that of certain sorts of anarchists,[34] but on occasion such orthodox Marxists as Karl Marx himself – clearly reflects a straightforwardly sadistic pleasure at the destructive power of revolution – there is no incompatibility between self-righteousness and sadism. By contrast the deepest, subtlest and in some respects the most honest interpretation of any great revolution – the writings of Alexis de Tocqueville on the French revolution – arose from a real hatred for what the revolution was in fact like, balanced by an inability to deny the force of the values in whose name it was undertaken.[35]

What are the main – and very crude – conclusions which follow from such an attempt to characterize what revolutions are? What does it suggest that one should be attempting to explain? Revolutions are a form of massive, violent and rapid social change. They are also attempts to embody a set of values in a new or at least a renovated social order. Because these ideas are articulated in a sophisticated way by comparatively small elites and because revolutions in actual fact represent, or have so far represented, the seizure of power by these elites, it is necessary to understand what exactly the ideas were and why they seemed persuasive to the elites in question. We have to understand what being a revolutionary meant at particular times and in particular places and why there were revolutionaries of that particular sort there and then. Because post-revolutionary elites attempt to determine many aspects of post-revolutionary societies – and because they sometimes have great power to determine some of them, it is a central question about the revolutionary process what the revolutionaries think they are trying to do. But because revolution in order to take place in any form must eventually mobilize the energies of large numbers of men, whether for destructive or for constructive purposes, it is equally necessary to understand why it is the case (if indeed it *is* the case) that the purposes which the revolutionaries advertise seem to these large numbers of people to be likely to favour their interests so markedly more than the existing social arrangements that it is worth their while creating chaos to give the revolutionaries their chance. It is hardly surprising that this process of conviction is difficult to bring off in 'normal' times by purely rational procedures. Hence it is not surprising that the revolutions which have happened in this century have mostly happened in conditions in which a large measure of chaos already existed from the viewpoint of the greater part of the population, above all in conditions of military defeat and of invasion. Nor is it surprising that revolutionaries denied these facilities by history or the competence of existing ruling classes have increasingly taken on the assignment of attempting to create the chaos by their own efforts. But it is also unsurprising that their behaviour has come to seem to the majorities of the working classes in advanced industrial societies on the whole not so much a matter of swimming masterfully with the tide as of stirring up the mud. 'What childish innocence it is to present impatience as a theoretically convincing argument', as Engels once aptly observed.[36]

However, it is no easy matter to identify the conditions of revolutionary possibility. All revolutions are definitionally failures of political control by an existing ruling elite. But there are very many more ruling classes which fail to maintain political control than there are successful revolutions which take place. To consider the conditions of revolutionary success is to consider under what circumstances failing ruling classes get their just deserts, what types of failure endanger them, rather than merely injuring their subject populations. The best statement of the centrality of this question in the analysis (or indeed the practice) of revolution comes in a rather late work of Lenin's, written at the time when the interests of the world revolution and of the foreign policy of the Soviet state were just beginning to come into embarrassing conflict, a work entitled *'Left-Wing' Communism, an Infantile Disorder*. It makes clear just why the failure of social control is such a central factor in the explanation of revolution and why it is a much wider issue than merely one of police power. 'Revolutions are made, at moments of particular upsurge and the exertion of all human capacities, by the class consciousness, will, passion and imagination of tens of millions, spurred on by a most acute struggle of classes.'[37] In itself this is a reasonably orthodox Marxist view – and hardly a delicate anticipation of the course of, for example, the Cuban revolution. It makes clear only that Lenin did not see himself as a mere Blanquist, a believer in the revolutionary sufficiency of a quick *putsch* by a handful of well-drilled conspirators. But it has to be read in conjunction with a more extended passage.

The fundamental law of revolution, which has been confirmed by all revolutions, and particularly by all three Russian revolutions in the twentieth century, is as follows: it is not enough for revolution that the exploited and oppressed masses should understand the impossibility of living in the old way and demand changes, it is essential for revolution that the exploiters should not be able to live and rule in the old way. Only when the *'lower classes' do not want* the old way, and when the 'upper classes' *cannot carry on in the old way* – only then can revolution triumph. This truth may be expressed in other words: revolution is impossible without a nation-wide crisis (affecting both the exploited and the exploiters). It follows that for revolution it is essential, first, that a majority of the workers (or at least a majority of the class-conscious, thinking, politically active workers)[38] should fully understand that revolution is necessary and be ready to sacrifice their lives for it: secondly, that the ruling classes should be passing through a government crisis, which draws even the most backward masses into politics (a symptom of every real revolution is a rapid, tenfold and even hundredfold increase in the number of members of the toiling and oppressed masses – hitherto

apathetic – who are capable of waging the political struggle), weakens the government and makes it possible for
the revolutionaries to overthrow it rapidly.[39]

A revolution happens, then, when a set of revolutionaries
with quite complex ideas succeed in arousing in vast masses
of men already deeply discontented with the prevailing order
a sufficient sense of their own superior political and moral
capacity to justify the masses in struggling to destroy the prevailing political (and to some degree social) order and to replace it with the political control of the revolutionaries. A
revolution happens, though, only if this process of political
struggle does lead to the collapse of social control by the
existing political elite. This is a tautological observation (if
it does not, what takes place is not a revolution); but it is of
rather more than tautological significance. For in the event
of this sort of struggle not resulting in the collapse of social
control, what tends to happen instead is the deaths of very
large numbers of people. Revolutionaries, whatever their
theories, have political responsibilities like any other contenders for political power. If what they bring about turns
out to be extended massacres, they end up with much blood
on their hands. In the morality of politics consequences have
weight as much as do intentions. The responsibility of revolutionaries, the making, to put it tendentiously, of a 'real'
revolution, extends, too, substantially further than to the
destruction of the political power of the existing political
elites. For a revolution to be a *real* revolution it is necessary
for the revolutionaries who seize power to be genuinely more
capable of handling the problems of the society in which
they win power than were their immediate predecessors – and
above all it is necessary that it should not turn out that the
only problem which they are capable of handling more deftly
than those whom they replace is the single problem of social
control. The legitimacy of revolutionary elites in the process
of struggle comes from their claim to be able to solve (or go
some distance towards solving) some of the problems of their
societies. It is a legitimacy which can only survive their success intact if they do contrive to solve some of these.

This is why the sociology of revolution, if there is to be
such a subject at all, is such a very distinctive segment of a

general theory of collective behaviour, social unrest or rapid social change. There are many respects in which great revolutions resemble primitive millenarian movements or cargo cults[40] – and they all contain some behaviour which is strictly analogous to cargo-cult behaviour. Some revolutionary leaders nourish expectations about a fairly imminent post-revolutionary condition, such as those expressed by Lenin in *The State and Revolution*, which are so Utopian as to be quite aptly characterized as millenarian. Certainly the gap between the political conditions which Lenin there describes as the dictatorship of the proletariat and the realities of the present-day Soviet Union is as cataclysmic as that between the ideology of primitive Christianity and the realities of the pre-reformation Catholic Church. Mao, at least in 1938, looked forward to not just temporary but perpetual peace, not just in one country but throughout the world and attainable by joint struggle in several decades.[41] It is true that this millenarian flavour does often change rather sharply during the process of revolution – Mao has recently looked forward to a struggle for transformation within China itself which is to last for a number of centuries, a perspective in which the Maoist understanding of human perfectibility has entered on a time perspective which seems similar to that of bourgeois liberals. It is essentially this transformation – what one might in the case of the Russian revolution, though clearly not yet in the case of the Chinese revolution, speak of as the *embourgeoisement* of the revolutionary leaders – which makes the issue of how to begin to analyse revolutions such a very intractable one.

It has been argued so far that there is an inescapable necessity in all revolutions for both mass action and responsible and effective political leadership. But there is an unavoidable element of stipulative definition[42] in any such insistence. Others have at times made very different stipulations. The Cuban revolution, now a supposedly very Marxist affair, did not really involve very enthusiastic mass participation in the destruction of the existing power structure – which is not to say that the great majority of Cubans were not even initially delighted to see the last of Batista. Some events of a still more dubiously Marxist inspiration like the Egyptian revolution under Neguib and Nasser did not really involve mass parti-

cipation at all: merely a brusque little military coup. Whatever was revolutionary in any social sense about the two events
was rigidly separated from the conditions in which power was
seized – indeed it was largely a consequence of the identity
of the men who did seize power and the way in which they
were led to handle the problems which confronted them. So
there can be revolutions – of a sort – without much mass
participation except at the level of minimal post-revolutionary
cooperation; and there clearly cannot be political regimes
of any efficacy of *any* ideological colouration without the
minimal cooperation of substantial numbers of their subjects.
By contrast, it is also the case that there can be massive struggles involving huge numbers of people and effectively displac-
ing pre-existing governments without generating political
elites which are in any way capable of coping with the chaos
which ensues, or, more commonly, without any capacity to use
the power which they enjoy in the subsequent political order
which does emerge to surmount the problems which face that
society. This has very obviously been true of the Republic of
Indonesia in the period from 1945 to 1965.[43] It is at least arguably true at the moment of the state of India and it is quite
likely to be true of any recently post-colonial state. That is to
say, many of the problems which such governments are faced
with are not so much problems generated by the process of
political revolution or by the inadequately revolutionary character of this process,[44] (though both of these aspects can generate many problems), as they are simply consequences of these
states being post-colonial states. There is more in common
between the political problems of Algeria and those of, for
example, Tunisia than there is between those of Algeria and
Cuba, despite Algeria's substantially greater ideological sympathy with Cuba than with Tunisia. All post-revolutionary
governments do considerable damage. It is very difficult to
govern a country in the aftermath of a revolution and political talent is a scarce commodity. Moreover, even if the experience of twentieth-century revolution has provided a rather
ribald commentary on Professor Oakeshott's view of politics,[45]
it remains true, as the Cuban leaders, for instance, have freely
acknowledged, that there is a wide gap between the skills
needed to exercise governmental power and the skills needed
to gain it and that the public expense of the new rulers'

education on the job may be great. Since revolution is a project offered by revolutionaries to the populace at large, it makes good sense to assess the quality of the offer by attempting to assess the quality of the services eventually rendered. Even for the revolutionary, disruption *tout court* is no achievement. The only revolutionary achievement is the creation of a new order.

Some revolutionaries in the twentieth century have seized power in their societies and created a very different social order. For the first time in history such very different and unremittingly secular (non-sacred) social orders have shown themselves militarily capable of survival in the international environment. It is no longer possible to imagine the military triumph of international reaction, in the sense of the forcible suppression of all the revolutionary states. The very existence of internationally viable revolutionary states has altered the conditions of survival for other initially successful revolutionary states in a decisive way. Since there are real revolutionary ruling elites in the world today, it is no longer possible to think seriously about revolution without assessing the credentials of revolutionaries as contenders for and users of political power and authority. Something novel and, for better or worse, enormously important has happened to the experience of revolution in the twentieth century and it requires to be studied as what it is – face-on – not just squinted at as an array of segments of other worthy topics in sociology, political science or social engineering (collective behaviour, the mechanisms of the *coup d'état,* or the theory of counter-insurgency).

There are, then, strong historical reasons in the face of twentieth-century political experience for stipulating a definition of revolution which does examine it as a process of accumulating political power and putting it to the end of promoting a distinctive social transformation. But it is essential to be clear that stipulating such a definition does do violence to one aspect of the phenomenon. It is a central aspect of Marxist theory (and although the time scale involved becomes evasively indeterminate, it remains a central aspect of Leninist theory too) that the Socialist revolution should lead to the destruction of the vast inequalities of power which characterize the societies of industrial capitalism. The administration of things might be an exceedingly complex process technically but it was to cease in the future to be a process which involved the domination of most men by small groups of other men. The state as a hierarchy of oppressive power was to wither away. This aspect of Marxism was, if anything, accentuated rather than suppressed in some of the explicit doctrines of Lenin. *The State and Revolution* was written to counter the reformist practices and democratic scruples of western European Social Democracy, as set out most elaborately by Karl Kautsky.[46] But for all its vivid and uncompromising insistence on the need for violence and destruction as a prelude to the creation of the new order, the detailed picture which Lenin gives of what the new political order would in fact be like is Utopian to a degree unmatched in the writings of Marx himself. Leninism is a strategic doctrine for a revolutionary elite and, as such, in the pre-revolutionary period it is highly authoritarian and quite consistently so. But as a charter for a post-revolutionary autocracy (particularly more than fifty years later) it simply does not exist.[47] The postrevolutionary society advertised by Lenin was advertised as no very distant goal and it was advertised as egalitarian, *politically* egalitarian through and through. There is no Marxist theory of what twentieth-century revolutions are in fact like and what they mean. There are no Marxist political leaders whose revolutionary pretensions are matched by their postrevolutionary performances because the post-revolutionary society which they promise is a society which will not be produced merely by the sorts of events which twentieth-century revolutions have so far been or which we have any good reason to expect them to become in the future, and indeed is a sort of society which it *may* in fact not be possible to produce by any means at all. Marxism as a theory, a coherent body of doctrine, is false. It is perhaps unfortunate that it is false, in the same way that it is unfortunate that Christianity is false. How nice it would be if either were true. How nice it would be if any theory were true which promised access to a kingdom in which the lion will lie down with the lamb and no one hurt nor destroy. But as yet, sadly, there is no reason to believe that any such theory is true. The history of twentieth-century revolution, in many ways a great history, is still a commentary on the falsity of the Marxism which has inspired so much of it in the same sense as the history of mediaeval Europe is a commentary on the falsity of Christianity. In stipulating that a revolution be considered as the forcible seizure of power by an elite which attempts to face the problems of its society in a way altogether bolder than its predecessors have done, it is assumed that Marxism, a doctrine which implies that a true revolution *cannot* represent the seizure of power by an elite, is false. Freedom for the great majority is not an elegant adornment of a Marxist revolution which can be added on decades later as an afterthought, a pretty finishing touch. It is central to what a Marxist revolution is, to what Marx conceived the act of Socialist revolution to mean. Lenin knew this clearly enough when he was writing *The State and Revolution,* even if he had to suppress the knowledge rather thoroughly in the next few years. If a defence is needed for assuming the falsity of Marxism in this way, it seems sufficient to point out that the assumption appears from their actions to have been shared by those Marxist leaders who have actually acquired political power. That is the way the world is.

In some ways this is a most uncomfortable perspective. Revolutions must be taken seriously because they represent (or may represent) profoundly important and in some ways distinctively successful attempts to improve the human social condition – at particular times and in particular places. But there are no revolutions without revolutionaries. And it seems a consequence of the previous argument that revolutionaries must *not* be taken too seriously, because they are intellectuals or lumpen-intellectuals committed to theories which are for the most part intrinsically and not merely accidentally mistaken. De Tocqueville in the middle of the nineteenth century wrote bitterly of the new and terrible thing which had come into the world, an immense new sort of revolution whose toughest agents are the least literate and most vulgar classes, while they are incited and their laws written by intellectuals.[48] It expressed, perhaps, a rather naively aristocratic prejudice to see the matter this way (though numerous scholars with less elevated pedigrees have since shown little hesitation in adopting the same perspective). But even from de Tocqueville's own point of view what was terrible was the success which the *intellectuals* attained in inciting 'the most vulgar classes'. It was a success which they attained because the existing ruling elites had failed so utterly to offer these classes a viable community. The process of democratization, a process which de Tocqueville understood in general in a most imaginative way, had meant that political elites could no longer rely on the docility of their subjects, unless they could make such an offer. De Tocqueville hated revolutionary intellectuals because he saw them as claiming arrogantly to be able to provide a measure of community which they did not necessarily have the least capacity to provide.

The experience of twentieth-century revolution has done little to show up this distaste as simply misplaced, but it has perhaps shown up the degree of anxiety behind it as slightly silly. Advanced capitalist societies are still in many ways very ugly communities – the claim that, where they are formally democratic, they represent 'the good society itself in operation'[49] is one which even Professor Lipset might hesitate to advance today. But in many ways the same is true of such countries as have thus far come to call themselves Socialist. What is ugly about them naturally differs substantially in some respects, though by no means in all. But there is enough which is ugly about both to make it an unappealing prospect for the masses of the people to risk their lives to produce the other, unless conditions have already become very disturbed indeed. Those countries in which the masses do come to listen to the siren songs of Socialist ideologues are countries in which there is no viable form of social order and in which existing elites are blatantly incapable of handling the problems of the society. There are in the world today a great many countries which do endure the domination of elites which are in this sense (though not necessarily in their capacity for maintaining social control) appallingly ineffectual. Some of such countries have had Marxist-inspired revolutions in the past. Others will have them in the future. The creation of the world economy, an important component of Marx's own theory, though hardly in itself the central focus of his interest, has subjected all the state-structures of the weaker and poorer powers to a series of shifting strains. Often these are violent enough to make the incumbent political elites virtually paralysed with fear. The spread of secularization has shaken the providential aura which for long clung around all concen-

trated power. All political elites today in the world are subject to some measure of challenge for sheer incompetence,
though many countries including the U.S.A. and the U.S.S.R.
possess reasonably effective ways of removing the incumbents
without endangering the political system itself.[50] No doubt
they are somewhat more stable for having devised such
methods of succession, but there is abundant continuing evidence that the methods are far from foolproof. It is *conceivable* in the future, though not in a future which anyone has
yet imagined in a very plausible way, that the political systems of these societies too may be destroyed because of their
inability to serve the needs of their societies. But there may
well be little reason to look forward to such an event. The
level of devastation in an advanced industrial society which
would be necessary to make such a collapse possible is so
great that no post-revolutionary regime could compensate for
it for some little time. Both of these states and a large number
of their more immediate satellites are too powerful and not
oppressive enough for there to be any serious prospect of
revolution within an imaginable future. This is partly because there is no serious need for a revolution in these societies within an imaginable future, not because both of these
societies do not have many dreadful features (often features
from which the rest of the world suffers more directly than
the inhabitants of the society in question), but because the
defects which they do display inside their borders are not the
sort of defects which revolutions have yet shown any capacity
to cure. Revolutionaries do have something to offer politically
(as potential rulers) to many societies in the world today, even
though what they have to offer may be rather distantly related to what they advertise themselves as offering and even
though very many societies in the world may well never take
up their offers. The real revolutionary ideologies in the world
today are primitivist in inspiration (the villages of the world
surrounding its cities) because the real revolutionary situations in the world today are primitive in character.

Partly as a consequence, revolution is not authoritarian in
manner, as Engels proclaimed and liberating in effect. It is
authoritarian in manner and authoritarian in effect. It does
not come as Marx saw it, as a decisive summit of the development of civilization, the coming of real equality to a society

which need no longer suffer from real political problems and thus can be organized without needing to be hierarchical. Rather it comes in countries which have heard that material civilization is possible, but which feel that their leaders are failing to bring it. It comes as a transfer of authority to those who set themselves to solve the extraordinarily acute problem of how to bring it and to those who have the moral nerve (to use a deliberately ambiguous phrase) to subordinate all other ends to this single end. It is not really clear yet how much specific expertise Socialist revolutionaries have in promoting economic development in this way.[51] What they assuredly have and have in abundance is the will, the courage and the ruthlessness to sacrifice all other values to the attempt.[52]

I *Russia*

The revolutions analysed in this work are merely a sample of the revolutions which the twentieth century has seen, but they are some distance from being a random sample. Russia, China, Vietnam, Yugoslavia and Cuba all experienced revolutions which were in a conventional (though rather extended) sense 'Marxist' revolutions, though even in this sense of the word only that of Russia was explicitly Marxist in inspiration and leadership from start to finish.[1] The remaining three revolutions were decidedly more heterogeneous. Mexico, Turkey and Algeria were none of them especially Marxist in the initial orientation of their revolutions and two of them, Mexico and even more Turkey, are now rather close allies of the leading anti-revolutionary power in the world today, the United States. The revolutionary regimes in Russia, Mexico and Turkey have held power for long enough for it to be possible to judge their capacity to cope with the problems of their country (though all in fact continue to trespass on the charity of their adherents by pinning their legitimacy firmly on the less than immediate future). The other revolutions, with the possible exception of Yugoslavia have either been successful for too short a time or else have so extended their objectives since their initial achievement of power that it is still hard to make out what sort of impact they are eventually going to have had on the condition of their peoples. In important respects half at least of these revolutions are still incomplete and from one perspective all of them are still incomplete. From the viewpoint of revolutionary Marxism it was perfectly appropriate for the late Isaac Deutscher to title the Russian revolution the 'unfinished revolution',[2] in that it is still some way from realizing the promises of the theory under whose auspices it was originally carried out. But from other more prosaic viewpoints it seems clear enough that the

Russian revolution *is* finished.[3] Anything less revolutionary in character than the day-to-day working of the Soviet state it would be difficult to imagine. Electrification today has come in abundance, as Lenin promised – even if the Soviets are hardly what they were. The leaders of the Communist Party of the Soviet Union preside over an empire of impressive stability and undeniable achievement. But 'preside' over is the appropriate verb. One does not preside over a revolution.

The revolution which Lenin and his followers made in Petrograd and Moscow in October 1917 was an attempt, as all Lenin's thought had been since the beginning of the twentieth century to answer two very different questions. The first question was a question entirely within the tradition of revolutionary Marxism: how can the European revolution at large be caused to happen? It had been made considerably more urgent around the turn of the century by the suggestion put about by Eduard Bernstein, that perhaps it *could* not be made to happen at all.[4] Bernstein, a leading member of the German Social Democratic party and a former secretary to Marx's coadjutor Friedrich Engels, had drawn attention to the growing disparity between Marx's socio-economic expectations and the character of social and economic development in the advanced societies of western Europe.[5] As he put it tartly in a note scribbled on an envelope: 'Peasants do not sink; middle class does not disappear; crises do not grow ever larger; misery and serfdom do not increase.'[6] Since society was not dividing ever more sharply into the two hostile groupings – the exploiters and the exploited – it no longer in his view made sense to expect a violent revolution as the pathway to Socialism. Furthermore the growing constitutionally legitimate power of the party of the working class made this crude method of political progress eminently dispensable. Revisionism promised Socialism (in the fullness of time) without the tears of revolution. In his polemic against Revisionism in *What is to be Done?* and in later writings Lenin was facing not merely a set of tactical precepts which implied a long and gloomy future for Socialists with the misfortune to be born Russians, but more importantly, as he saw it, a betrayal of the ideals of western Socialism as a whole, an abandonment of the transformational struggle by parts of the most advanced portion of the working-class movement. Revisionism, viewed parochially, was a threat to the Russian revolutionary movements but viewed more broadly, as Lenin did view it for far the greater part of his active political life, in the context of Socialism's international prospects, it seemed to him to threaten not just the prospective success of the Russian movement but the entire meaning of its struggle. Lenin's intellectual and political energies were devoted to confronting these twin threats. Eventually he succeeded in meeting the parochial challenge and triumphing over it, but the ecumenical challenge was one he never contrived to meet – and despite Mr Deutscher's resolute optimism this failure continues to call into question the meaning of that struggle. The revolution whose occurrence in Russia it is here attempted to explain is the revolution which *did* take place in Russia, a finished revolution, a revolution in one country which became very much a revolution *for* one country, a nationalist and anti-capitalist revolution, a revolution in the cant phrase of 'modernization'.

In October 1917[7] quite a small group of men seized power in a great, if crumbling, empire. One feature of the revolution which must be explained is *why* it was possible for quite a small group of men to seize power in these conditions. Another feature, perhaps harder to assess fairly, is simply why it was, given that a small group of men could seize power in a great empire at that time, this was the small group of men which did do so. A third feature which requires explanation is how such a small group of men could *keep* power. None of these questions has much to do with classical Marxism which is a theory in which small groups of men do not seize power from the controllers of the bourgeois or pre-bourgeois state apparatus, let alone hang onto it indefinitely after they have done so. There are, plainly, many other questions which arise in any attempt to understand what happened. The question, for example, of why the Russian empire did reach such a point of disintegration in the course of 1917 is a very complex question of historical development and one which, unlike the question of the immediate preconditions for the seizure of power, can hardly be answered effectively within a short space.[8] Even given that the Bolsheviks did succeed in seizing power, it remains equally necessary to explain why they put it to the sort of use which they did. The extreme ambiguity and the obvious political delicacy of this last question make it particularly tricky to handle. In the course of more than fifty years many different Bolsheviks have put that power to many different uses and for exceedingly diverse reasons. The collectivization of the peasantry might have been expected in due course from any Marxist government (in itself a slightly paradoxical category) which had had the nerve to take power in a peasant country, though the methods and eventually the speed with which it was carried out were much more specifically chosen by the ruling elite. By contrast certain features of the purges[9] were clearly irrelevant to any rational set of ends served by the Bolshevik regime and in no way contributed to such continuing efficacy as it succeeded in displaying. However, insofar as the question of why the Bolsheviks used their power as they did can be answered at any level of generality, be answered by anything more schematic than a history of all that they proceeded to do or even an entire history of modern Russia, it seems plausible that this answer is implied in the answer to the second and third of the questions indicated. That is to say: what the Bolsheviks did with power was a product of the characteristics which distinguished them as a group which *could* seize power, when confronted with the difficulties involved in retaining it in the conditions in which they had to make the attempt to retain it. Very abstractly this view is much the same as that of Soviet historiography (unlike the interpretation of the first question, the question of why it was possible for such a small group of men to seize power in the circumstances). More concretely, it is also the explanation of the Soviet Union's thus far decisive abandonment of the liberating promise of Marxism, of why it is so difficult to imagine a future for it which is more than Marxism with the politics left out, the material abundance which industrialism really can bring, even if it has not quite done so yet.

It is simplest to begin with the crumbling empire and its problems: all revolutions which do take place take place in particular locations. Vast in scale but ethnically heterogeneous, administratively chaotic, economically backward and politically riven, the empire presented a formidable array of challenges to anyone who attempted to rule it, still more to change it in any extended fashion. With many nations, many languages and a populace largely illiterate, the marvel, as Sergei Witte remarked in 1905 in the aftermath of the disastrous Russo-Japanese war, was that the country could be held together even by autocracy. 'If the Tsar's government falls you will see absolute chaos in Russia and it will be many a long year before you see another government able to control the mixture which makes up the Russian nation.'[10] The geographical control of the Tsarist government had increased greatly over the preceding hundred years – the Russian empire had never been so massive as it was in 1900. But its political viability both internally and externally was becoming increasingly questionable.[11] In a sense the reasons for these difficulties were mostly external to it – outside its direct control. But they posed problems which were very much within it and which it proved increasingly incapable of solving. Historically Russian culture had been obsessively introverted, a world sufficient unto itself, the Third Rome, and even in the nineteenth century there were men of imagination and energy determined that it should remain so. Frequently the Tsar's government was in the hands of men of this persuasion dedicated above all to the preservation of the traditionalist autocracy. But the rest of the world would not stand still. The Tsars were happy to use the most advanced military and communications facilities in their expansionist efforts, as they had been since the days of Peter the Great. But the progress of industrialization and modernization made it increasingly difficult to detach these technical developments from much broader changes in social training and attitudes. Guns could be purchased abroad; even armaments factories could be purchased abroad. But modern armies could only be developed at home and armaments factories could not be operated without a disciplined industrial labour force. As the Russo-Japanese war showed all too clearly the Russian state could not organize effectively for the stern disciplines of modern warfare without extensive transformations in Russian society. These transformations, industrial, educational.[12] agrarian, did not readily harmonize with the crudity of the prevailing system of social control,[13] though as the experience of both Germany and Japan had already shown and as the Bolsheviks themselves were to show in due course, autocracy and rapid industrialization were not in themselves by any means incompatible.

Both industrialization and educational expansion were in the end attempted, but both contributed to the weakening of the structure of social control. In the aftermath of the revolution of 1905 an attempt was made belatedly at transformation even in the agrarian field under Stolypin;[14] but it was still in its early stages when the outbreak of war subjected the entire social fabric of Russia to strains which it proved quite unable to bear.

Throughout the nineteenth century the Russian government wavered between the determination to modernize Russian society in order that the Russian state should be able to compete effectively with the other great world powers and the conflicting determination to maintain intact the autocratic structure of social control. But the initial scale on which the energies of the government had to be deployed meant that these twin objectives encroached violently upon one another. The autocracy was too traditionalist, too dedicated to its own perpetuation in detail, to be prepared to buy off the opposition of the educated classes through political reforms. At the same time it was too preoccupied with dynastic ambitions of expansion to avoid the necessity of making some efforts at modernization. Russia was, as Witte then Minister of Finance observed in 1899 in a memorandum to the Tsar,[15] in a relationship to the European economies which precisely paralleled that between colonial countries and their metropolises. It imported western manufactures and exported primary products. But there was one radical difference between the position of Russia and that of a colony: Russia was a politically independent and mighty power. It wanted to be a metropolis itself. Applying the ideas of Friedrich List, the theorist of the autarkic German industrialization, Witte set himself to industrialize the empire. For a time he enjoyed dramatic success. But eventually the economic crisis of the turn of the century, aggravated by the savage pressure on the purchasing power of the peasantry led to Witte's own downfall and subsequently to a vast peasant revolt. In due course it was to be a peasant revolt on an even vaster scale and at a point in time when huge masses of peasants in uniform with weapons in their hands had in large measure replaced the relatively disciplined professional army of the empire which made it possible for the Bolsheviks to use their support among the proletariats of

Moscow and Petrograd to take power. It was three factors taken in conjunction, peasant insurrection, proletarian revolt and military collapse which caused the empire to crumble. Peasant insurrection and proletarian revolt had both been impressively evident in 1905. Together they had forced the Tsar into making a rather exiguous set of constitutional concessions. But despite their fervour and geographical extent, their power was eventually destroyed with remarkable ease by the rifle fire of the soldiery. As long as the army remained loyal, liberal constitutionalists could hardly hope to be conceded full political power and revolutionaries had certainly not the least chance of seizing it. A correct understanding of this point leads historians sympathetic to the old regime like George Katkov[16] to see the fall of the empire as a ghastly but largely accidental drama, the product of cowardice, stupidity and personal ambition distributed among crucial members of the elite (valiantly assisted by the machinations of the German intelligence service). Historians sympathetic to the revolution by contrast are reduced either to assuming the First World War as an intrinsic aspect of the internal development of Russia or as an inevitable consequence of the character of international capitalism. The latter view, where held theologically, is no doubt irrefutable. But it is certainly not a very deft articulation of the present state of historical knowledge about the circumstances in which the war broke out. There is, however, one perspective which avoids the more desperate of these shifts with reasonable completeness. It was assuredly *not* a mere accident that the Tsarist empire was involved in the First World War and it was surely not a mere accident that after three years of unrelenting struggle against the armies of imperial Germany Russian military, political, economic and social organization should all have been savagely scarred. The Tsarist empire had neither the will nor, in the face of the German threat, the capacity to retire from the strains of international power competition. It lacked the level of social integration and economic modernity necessary to support the costs of this competition in a modern war. It was not a viable modern state in the final test of a modern state's viability. To see this weakness, though, as fitting it particularly for a Marxist revolution would be to espouse an extreme version of the heresy which Lenin himself most abhorred: Defensism. The military weakness of the Russian state stemmed from its economic and social backwardness. It made it in the aftermath of massive defeat liable to proletarian revolution, but it assuredly did not make it in Marxist terms *fit* for it. Military efficacy turned out in the circumstances of the First World War, perhaps rather unsurprisingly, to be a product of advanced – and thus at the time of advanced capitalist – industrialization. The existence of a proletariat sufficiently hostile to the nation state to be prepared to tear it apart even in the face of enemy invasion (together with a much greater liability to military collapse) turned out to be a product of a much earlier stage of industrialization.

The total size of the Russian proletariat was not large at the time of the revolution when compared with the proletariats of other great world powers and it was even less large as a proportion of the total working population.[17] Russia remained a predominantly peasant country. The proletariat was, however, highly concentrated geographically and in terms of units of employment.[18] The Putilov works in Petrograd was the largest in the world and the proportion of the proletariat employed in really large factories was the highest in the world. Marx had pointed in *Das Kapital* itself to the importance of concentration of production in increasing the strength of the working-class movement, but he had seen its main importance perhaps in the disciplined and organized character imparted to it by this experience, in a sense a genuinely civilizing process, if a highly coercive one.[19] The Russian proletariat had not, however, on the whole benefited from this aspect of its concentration.[20] It had grown in size too rapidly and in too coercive conditions to display the intuitive commitment to industrial society as a going concern which western European Marxists had come to assume in it, the expectation which is made overt, for instance, in Engels's discussion of authority and which lies behind much of Lenin's own argument in *The State and Revolution*.[21] It was this largely anarchic quality which made the post-revolutionary situation so grossly chaotic and it explains the frenzied tone of many of Lenin's statements during the heroic period in which he began to reimpose order on the chaos.

The proletariat had grown most rapidly in two periods, the

first from the early 1890s to the turn of the century during
Witte's efforts at forced industrialization, the second starting
around 1910 during a boom which was, from a purely economic point of view, rather better balanced than the first.
The proletariat which had been created in the 1890s had not
on the whole been organized into a labour movement under
Socalist leadership, though the Jewish workers in the Pale
had begun to be.[22] The most effective union movement in this
early period was started and indeed largely controlled by a
secret police official, Zubatov; and the first great workers'
demonstration in 1905 was led by a priest, Gapon.[23] But during the 1905 revolution large sections of the proletariat, particularly in Petrograd itself, had come under the sway of the
Social Democrat movement. In the aftermath of the revolution this control was naturally extensively disrupted. The vast
and increasingly politically orchestrated strike movements fell
away to nothing. At the same time the near common front of
all elements hostile to the absolutist regime which had appeared briefly during the revolution came to an end which
proved to be permanent; and the splits in the Social Democratic movement itself widened alarmingly once again. When
industrial activity expanded sharply from 1910 onwards and
the proletariat grew rapidly in size with it, the development
of a disciplined and politically responsive Russian labour
movement of a western European type which it had been the
ambition of the Menshevik section of the Social Democratic
movement to create[24] became more and more obviously a
mirage. From the mass shootings in the Lena goldfields in
1912 onwards there was a steadily increasing swell of strikes
in which political and economic demands were inextricably
entwined and which broke out erratically, often without dis-
cernible purpose.[25] At the same time larger and larger numbers of peasants, many of them possibly driven out of their
villages by the impact of the Stolypin land reforms,[26] were
recruited into the proletariat, increasing both its size and its
touchy belligerency towards the rest of the society. Some of
the resulting strikes were definitely led by the Bolsheviks, and
Bolshevik influence in general spread rapidly in the union
movement at the expense of the Mensheviks.[27] Increasingly
the working class turned its back on the rest of society in
bitterness and struck out more or less blindly at the immedi-

ate symbols of authority in its daily environment. A large proportion of the proletariat remained semi-migrant in attitude, far from fully integrated into urban society and culture and some of the dynamic hostility of the working class in this period clearly came from such men. But Bolshevik influence was far from confined to these most immature sections of the working class. In this period the party even came to control the union of the most advanced workers in Russia, the pride and hope of the Mensheviks, the Metal Workers' Union.[28] So while there was, if anything, increasing disunion among elite sections of the society hostile to the Tsar, and while the government remained in the hands of men who were for the most part mediocre as well as bigoted, the proletariat was becoming increasingly overt in the violence of its opposition to the autocracy and insofar as it was under any sort of leadership increasingly under the leadership of the most autocratic and extremist section of the hostile elites, the Bolshevik party. It was not a particularly glorious phase for the Bolsheviks – their leading member inside Russia had just been exposed as a police spy and Lenin himself was the only major intellectual figure still to belong to them, but there does seem much reason to suppose that the outbreak of war did avoid a major proletarian uprising and one in which the Bolsheviks would undoubtedly have enjoyed something of a leading position.[29] But there is not much reason to suppose that this would have enabled the Bolsheviks to seize power. The Tsarist regular army could have shot down the workers in 1914 or 1915 or 1916 as readily as it had in 1905 or 1906. If it had done so, it is even possible that the Mensheviks would have enjoyed something of a revival. The fear of military repression constituted the most immediate and in some ways the most conclusive argument for the virtues of the Menshevik view of proper proletarian strategy. The experience of military repression might have discredited the Bolsheviks as the Blanquist adventurers which their opponents saw them as being. Whether or not a proletarian revolt would have occurred spontaneously in this way and been duly repressed, had the First World War not broken out in 1914 (an idle question in any case), there is little reason to suppose that the future of Russia would have been liberal democratic. The Russian road to modernity would have been a hard road, whether or not the Bolsheviks had contrived to seize power in 1917. The liberal democratic interlude in Russian history ran from February to October 1917. It was a brief and inglorious interlude, lauded since only by participants like Kerensky and to a lesser extent Miliukov[30] and scorned both by the men who destroyed it and their inheritors and by the admirers of the autocracy who saw the Provisional Government as founded upon treachery. It was assuredly not a fair test of the merits of liberal democracy nor even perhaps of its capacity as a system of rule to handle the problems of Russia. But it was the only test which history permitted and its outcome gave a clear and rather icy answer to a question which had been central to the interpretation of Russian society and its problems for more than a century: did Russian development, political, economic and social, have to parallel the development of western Europe, the heartland of advanced capitalism, stage by stage?

It was a question which Marx himself had been asked directly and had attempted to answer.[31] It was also a question which his writings had raised for many Russian thinkers in a particularly acute form.[32] Indeed, in the closing decades of the nineteenth century and from 1900 on, the controversy over the opportunities for and constraints on the social and economic development of Russia revolved essentially around Marx's own theories. Leading populist thinkers like Mikhailovsky and Danielson drew their understanding of the meaning of capitalist development from Marx's works; indeed Danielson went so far as to translate *Das Kapital* into Russian. The notion that Russia might enjoy a distinctive mode of development was widespread among the intelligentsia, going back as far as gentry radicals like Herzen.[33] The confrontation with Marx's analysis of capitalism made the appeals of such an idiosyncratic route still more obvious, at the same time as it made it still more difficult to identify any alternative route as being plausibly open. The threat faced by Russian society in the later nineteenth century was, from the point of view of the most penetrating of the Populist analysts a twin threat. In addition to the proletarianization of the peasantry as a class, an inevitable concomitant in some of its aspects of *all* industrialization on a simple reading of Marx and certainly an inevitable concomitant of capitalist industrialization on any reading of his works, there was considerable risk of the proletarianization of the Russian nation as a whole. Russian industrialization had to be carried out, if carried out at all, in the teeth of the advanced industrial competition of other capitalist powers. Unlike the first industrializing nations Russia could not rely on a large and uncompetitive foreign market for its industry. Instead it had to face in the early stages of industrialization severe competition in its own home market from foreign products.[34] In their analysis of these difficulties in the particular form in which they confronted Russia, Populist thinkers achieved at times a highly sophisticated analysis of the distinctive problems of Russian social development. But they failed to develop any particularly cogent solution to these problems, either at a theoretical level or in the domain of practical politics. In terms of political strategy they wavered between the attempt to educate and lead the peasantry in revolt against the autocracy and the attempt to use autocratic power to govern the country on behalf of the peasantry. Their tactical alignment towards the end of the nineteenth or the beginning of the twentieth century led them to espouse essentially democratic goals as far as the protection of peasant interests was concerned. They defended the rather battered institutions of peasant communalism against the efforts of the autocracy to speed the development of rural capitalism. Even in 1909 Lenin saw their espousal of essentially 'petty-bourgeois' capitalist ends as progressive in the Russian context: 'American capitalism', he called it, as opposed to the 'Prussian capitalism' of the autocracy.[35] Marx himself had agreed earlier with some of the theorists of the People's Will in seeing the possibilities of preserving the peasant commune as a component of a non-capitalist road to modernization. He had indeed written with savage scorn of the absurdity of assuming a necessarily uniform developmental process in all societies as later Russian Marxists like Struve or even Plekhanov were in effect to do.[36] Mikhailovsky, Marx complained, felt 'himself obliged to metamorphose my historical sketch of the genesis of capitalism in western Europe into an historic-philosophic theory of the *marche générale* imposed by fate upon every people, whatever the historic circumstances in which it finds itself...'.[37] One will never attain scientific understanding of particular instances of social evolution 'by using as one's master key a general historico-philosophical theory, the supreme virtue of which consists in being super-historical'.[38] Most of the Populists' social policies were developed for purely defensive purposes, to protect the peasantry from the worst strains of processes to which it was already being subjected. It is not surprising in consequence that they can hardly be claimed to have charted a bold and realistic plan for the future social development of Russia. They saw the tragic dilemmas of Russian development more clearly than most of their Marxist opponents, but ironically their only legacy to Russia today was a style of political action which could be —and was – used to further a form of social transformation which would probably have seemed to them, given their peasant allegiances, infinitely more appalling than the worst tragedies of British or French or German industrialization on the capitalist model. After the gentry conspiracy of the Decembrists in 1825 all major Russian political reform movements in the nineteenth century were largely Populist in inspiration and membership. Though the Social Democratic Party at the turn of the century was conceivably the largest and certainly the most dynamic mass political movement, it was easily surpassed in the scale of its appeal, eventually, by the recrudescent Populism of the Social Revolutionaries.[39] It could hardly have been otherwise in an overwhelmingly peasant country. The tactics espoused by Populists at different stages varied enormously. Some, like Lavrov, saw the essential goal of Populist activity as a massive educational effort which would haul Russian society out of its barbaric backwardness into the light of modern civilization. The political endeavours which went with such a view were often touchingly naive. Going to the People was as inscrutable as a project from the viewpoint of the peasantry into whose villages the bright-eyed students came, as it was risible as a political threat to the autocratic government.[40] It was hardly surprising that sharply contrasting styles of political action, better adapted to face the repressive capacities of the government, should have gained in appeal as a result of the fiascoes of more liberal Populist ventures. Elite bands of terrorists, autocratic in organization and autocratic in their intended political impact on society were formed on several occasions. Men like Chernyshevsky

dreamed of the slow growth of civilization in a Russia in
which total power had been seized by a small revolutionary
elite, though later, when in prison himself, he did come to
believe that personal freedom was a necessary condition for
civilization to develop.[41] Conspiratorial organization and ter-
rorist activity of the sort in which Lenin's elder brother took
part were a natural response to the political climate of the
autocracy; but they were also politically ineffective, as Lenin
himself very early realized.[42] Conspiratorial organization was
indispensable before (and it turned out to some degree after)
the seizure of power, but terror had better be postponed until
after power had been safely seized. It was too capricious in its
incidence and, even in Russia, stuck in too many people's
throats. It made more enemies for the revolutionaries than it
won friends.

Lenin adopted a form of conspiratorial organization which
had been to some degree pioneered by earlier Russian revolutionary elitists like Tkachev. Like Marx himself, Lenin
had great admiration for the extent to which many of the
earlier Populist revolutionaries had taken revolution seriously. Some of the technical problems which they faced were
necessarily still problems which any serious revolutionary in
Tsarist Russia was equally bound to face. But the elitist
stamp which he gave to his party was a product also of his
characteristically rationalist and dogmatic view of Marxism,
at a time when it was threatened internationally by the canker
of Revisionism.[43] It was however also a response to a crisis
which had begun to appear throughout Russian Social
Democracy.

Russian Social Democracy, like all European Socialist parties, was a party of intellectuals and workers. The major opposition to the autocracy throughout the second half of the
nineteenth century had come from intellectuals and above
all from students. The Populist students had been paladins
for a peasantry whose capacity for political action did not rise
above (or indeed until 1917 reach) the level of the *jacqueries*
of Stenka Razin or Pugachev. The appearance on the Russian
political scene of a nascent industrial working class provided
the student and intellectuals with long overdue mass support, but in doing so they also raised problems. The peasantry from one point of view posed few problems for their

intellectual protagonists, simply because they betrayed for the
most part not the least flicker of interest in these protagonists.
The workers proved not only more interested – and hence
more responsive to intellectual political initiatives – but also
much more specifically recalcitrant. Because Social Democracy was a real social and political movement, its purposes
and organization provided something real to argue about. The
structural character of worker – intellectual conflict within
the early Social Democratic movement has recently been sug-
gestively explored[44] and it has become clear that Lenin's organizational programme of 1902 presented in *What is to be
Done?* was in fact common in several respects to nearly all
sectors of the *intellectual* wing of the movement. The conditions in which the movement operated were such that frequent strike action often on directly political grounds was
inevitable. Much of the behaviour of the Social Democratic
movement would have remained more or less unaltered
whichever of the two main currents of Economism or revolutionary agitation had gained the ascendancy. But the way
in which the movement was organized and consequently the
uses to which it could be put in the event of revolution, as
Lenin clearly saw, would be decided largely by which of these
currents prevailed. The first impact of Socialist intellectuals
on the labour movement had created a body of educated and
articulate working men committed to the steady organization of the movement for economic action in the factories
and for the spread of Socialist understanding. The product
of this method of organization would have been a steady increase in the ascendancy of working-class militants[45] inside
the movement at the expense of intellectuals, the development of a measure of 'trade-union consciousness', an increased
stress on economic gains and disciplined action to secure
these, in brief to the development of the party as an adaptive
organization for accommodating proletariat and factory more
comfortably to one another. The worker elite dedicated to the
spread of Socialist education amongst the proletariat at large
and to the parochial concerns of the factory clashed repeatedly
with the intellectuals over the control of funds and tactics,
offended at being, as they thought, ignored by the intellectuals, and distrustful of them as men whose own interests were
not involved in day to day industrial conflict and whom they

suspected (in a sense correctly, if without undue dishonour to either party) of wishing to manipulate the workers for their own ends. Lenin was concerned above all else, as many Populist revolutionaries had been before, with the struggle against the autocracy. He saw quite correctly that the autonomous development of a workers' movement as a defensive organization was likely in the long run to damp down the explosive potentialities of the most revolutionary section of the Russian population. The 1905 revolution, occurring at a time when the Bolsheviks had had little impact in Russia, established that Economism was not in the short run a severe threat to the revolutionary energies of the proletariat. But the repression in the aftermath of the revolution gave the most advanced sectors of the working class good reasons for retiring to lick their wounds. Menshevik tactics which demanded, as soon as political conditions permitted this, the emergence of a disciplined, democratic and open mass working-class movement on the western European model might have had some appeal had this sort of interlude continued for some time, and the Bolsheviks were in fact extensively discredited at this stage. But as the Russian economy began to expand once more in 1910, as peasants flooded into the factories and industrial and political unrest increased sharply, the exotic character of the Menshevik ambition became increasingly obvious.

Russian industrialization was taking place in a highly autocratic and prodigiously inefficient administrative setting. This long-standing pattern of autocracy and incompetence had developed a powerful tradition of violent resistance, above all among the belatedly much expanded student population.[46] The combination of massively alienated half-peasant, half-proletarians in increasing numbers and the final collapse of the autocracy in February 1917 gave the Bolsheviks their chance to make a bid for power. They appear to have done nothing to bring on the revolution of February 1917 and in the defensist climate of the war, their power even to make trouble was initially minimal. In the preceding month of January 1917, Lenin himself had said gloomily at the end of a lecture: 'We of the older generation may not see the decisive battles of this coming revolution.'[47] Even after the fall of the autocracy in February the Bolshevik triumph was very far from being a foregone conclusion. It required a far more complete collapse of the armies at the front, together with a massive peasant insurrection, before power could be seized; and, above all, it required the return of Lenin. It required him partly, as Trotsky said, because the party could fulfil its mission only after understanding it, and for this Lenin was needed.[48] But more importantly perhaps it required him simply in order to exploit the full possibilities of the revolutionary situation.[49] Indeed for those who view the party's mission as extending beyond the seizure of power there is an obvious sense in which the party could hardly have afforded to understand its mission, if it was indeed to fulfil it. But the extraordinary skill and tenacity which characterized Lenin's leadership in the period leading up to the seizure of power was clearly a necessary condition for the party to have the least chance of success. The programme which Lenin advanced, Peace and Bread, Peace and Land, was from a long-term point of view opportunist. It marked a precise reversal of the classic proposals of the *Communist Manifesto,* the distribution of land to the peasantry and the nationalization of industry, in place of the nationalization of land and the government supervision of capitalist industry.[50] But if it was opportunist in motivation it was also supremely successful in effect, simply from the viewpoint of seizing power. Lenin was determined to seize and to keep power and he did precisely what was necessary in order to do so. By the time that the Bolsheviks moved, not only the provisional Kerensky government but all other political forces had discredited themselves by their inability to confront the imperatives of the situation. The Bolsheviks succeeded in capturing the Petrograd Soviet politically and Trosky used it as a political cover for the insurrection. It was the Military Revolutionary Committee of the Petrograd Soviet which formally led the revolution. It was possible for the Bolsheviks to employ it for this purpose because of Lenin's political triumph in defining the situation as a choice between Bolshevik dictatorship and counter-revolution and in offering as a reward of Bolshevik dictatorship, the only programme which could cope with the chaos: armistice and distribution of land. Lenin remained in power, as Dietrich Geyer has said, 'because he dared to do what had become a necessity'.[51] The Bolsheviks took power because power, by October 1917, was there for the taking and they were the only group with the nerve to take power on the terms on which alone it could be taken. In themselves these terms did not represent bold initiatives. The efforts to obtain an armistice and the acceptance of peasant seizure of land both merely required a surrender before what were already *faits accomplis* The detailed study of the collapse of the Tsarist armies is still in its infancy but the broad reasons for it were intrinsic to the character of the Russian regime: its social backwardness, its chaotic administration and its largely preindustrial economy, all subjected to the massive impact of the imperial German armies. Lenin's acceptance of the sheer necessity for peace was genuinely in the context a response to national need and not solely to agitational convenience. But from the perspective of today it is possible to see how heavy were the costs of this decision. It was not merely that the inglorious annexationist terms of the peace of Brest-Litovsk came as a disagreeable shock to many of the leading Bolsheviks who had assumed that German insistence on such crude truncation of Russian soil would be met by a recourse to a revolutionary war of national liberation.[52] Nor was it merely that the bitterness of conflict within the Bolshevik party itself and between it and the other Socialist parties over this issue provided the occasion, if hardly the excuse, for the erosion of such remnants of Socialist democracy as still survived.[53] The most important cost was the loss of the only opportunity which a proletarian movement in a predominantly peasant country can have to establish itself unequivocally in the eyes of the majority of the population as the legitimate representative of the nation. Defensism, the decision of the great European Socialist parties to put the military requirements of their fatherlands above the cause of international Socialism was, in Lenin's eyes, the vilest of all vile heresies within the Socialist movement – and Lenin's sensitivity in detecting, and virulence in assailing, heresy would have done credit to Torquemada. But since 1917 such Communist revolutions as have been made have been made as wars of national liberation and the legitimacy which this has given to them has been of enormous importance in their subsequent careers. It has been 'People's War', to use the cant phrase, which has made the Communist Party into a national party in Yugoslavia, in China, in Vietnam. The rejection of a war of national liberation by Lenin, a leader who was genuinely cosmopolitan in vision and sympathy as perhaps no successful Communist revolutionary leader since has been, kept the Russian regime as the dictatorship of a party over a largely hostile or indifferent people for decades.[54] It was not really until the second German invasion, in 1941, that the Bolshevik government clearly established itself as a genuinely national government. It was Stalingrad which belatedly gave national legitimacy to the Bolshevik rule. By then the costs of the nervy dictatorship of the party had become appallingly heavy.[55] In practical terms Lenin was plainly correct in rejecting the possibility of fighting a revolutionary war. The Bolshevik rule would have been most unlikely to survive such an enterprise. But the very fact that from his point of view he was so *obviously* right to do so exposes still more clearly the extreme ideological fragility of the regime which he established.

This regime had become a dictatorship over the working class quickly enough, but the class over which its power was exerted most strenuously and with most ghastly results was clearly the peasantry.[56] The Bolsheviks were able to take power because they were prepared to give the peasants their land (or, more accurately, to accept temporarily the fact that the peasants had taken their land). They used power eventually to take all the land back again and in doing so they crushed the peasantry without pity. The reason why the Bolshevik regime was victorious in the civil war and hence was in due course in a position to reappropriate the land was the extent to which the peasantry preferred them to the white armies which threatened to reappropriate it at once. This preference, which had been rendered precarious by the systematic pillaging of the villages for food supplies for the cities in the period of war Communism, was reinforced by the reversion to a comparatively free market in agricultural produce in the New Economic Policy – in fact to what Maxim Gorky insisted on referring to as the 'Old Economic Policy'.[57] The Bolsheviks were able to take power because they accepted, as the imperial regime and the other Socialist parties did not, the peasant seizure of lands. They kept it because they were prepared, when the choice came, to accept the real obstructive power of the peasantry and to make terms with it for as long as proved necessary. There was little sympathy either way between Bolsheviks and peasantry; the peasants, other things being equal, would often no doubt have gladly massacred the urban revolutionaries. The forces of the country in the old war between town and country had served in altogether more advanced countries like France to keep the revolutionaries in their place. The purpose of the Stolypin land reforms had been to establish a more contented and stable basis of peasant support for the autocracy. It was the failure of these reforms which in the chaotic circumstances of 1917 produced a peasant revolt which toppled the autocracy.[58]

The Russian agrarian problem under the old regime was extraordinarily intricate and even now many aspects of it are not well understood.[59] The situation of the peasantry in 1917 derived from a system of serfdom, of labour tied to land. The Russian nobility had been converted into a service nobility by the Tsars in the effort to face the military threats of Mongol, Lithuanian and other invaders. In return for their military and administrative services the nobles received land rights. In order to make these land rights of some economic use to their beneficiaries and in order to consolidate the defence of the empire, the free peasantry were barred from the seductions of the open land frontier and tied down to given units of land. They cultivated this land in return for labour services on the manorial demesnes or for fixed payments in money or kind. The system favoured depended upon the fertility of the soil. In the rich black-earth lands of the south labour services predominated. In the poorer soils to the north, fixed payments were normally required. In both, the state serfs, rather under half of the total around 1800, owed fixed payments at a relatively moderate level. Besides the tenurial role of the serf, another set of institutional relations, those of the peasant commune, the *mir,* determined the economic and social position of the peasants. The greater part of the lands in European Russia were held in repartitional tenure. The *mir* did not merely control the methods of exploitation of the largely unconsolidated family plots; it also redivided the land at intervals and retained a general right to control the peasants' sale, mortgage or inheritance of land. The emancipation of 1861 may well on the whole have worsened the economic

position of the peasants, despite the legal improvement in
their status, decreasing their individual holdings in the fertile
black-soil areas where there were rich returns on the investment of labour.[60] It burdened the former serfs as a whole with
a level of repayments for their lands which forced them
steadily further and further into arrears as the century wore
on. The government retained and strengthened the commune
as an instrument of social control. Yields remained extremely
low and technology remained backward; only one peasant
holding out of two even had an iron plough as late as 1917.[61]
Social relations inside the villages worsened under increasing
pressure of population. The general problem of peasant in-
debtedness grew more severe and skilful peasant exploiters,
'eaters of the *mir*',[62] manipulated the communes in the service of their own interests. Rumours of a possible second
emancipation swept the villages at intervals and archaic
memories of a time when land was not yet private property
recurred insistently. There was a growing surge of peasant
unrest in the first years of the new century, culminating in
the massive uprisings of 1905–6. These movements were semi-
millenarian in character, as was natural in a peasantry which
lived in near isolation from both Orthodox Church and State,
practising its own semi-pagan rituals or drawn into strange
and multifarious sects. But the final cause of the uprising was
simply the massive economic failure of Russian agriculture.[63]
Certainly it was little affected by revolutionary agitation. As
a peasant said in 1902 to an examining magistrate who was
inquiring into one of the outbreaks of that year: 'No rumours
came to me about any little books. I think that if we lived
better, the little books would not be important, no matter
what was written in them. What's terrible is not the little
books but this: that there isn't enough to eat.'[64] Terrified by
the scope of the 1905 uprisings, the Tsarist government under
Stolypin set itself to destroy the *mir*, which had shown itself
a seedbed of revolution, rather than an effective instrument
of control. The new policy was avowedly a wager on the
strong.[65] It encouraged consolidation of holdings and a general
development of capitalist relations in the countryside in a
system of private landholdings. The peasants were not given
the land – indeed some millions of the poorer of them seem
to have been eased out of the villages into the once again ex-

panding factories from 1910 on. What Stolypin hoped to do was to develop a sense of private property in the peasantry, to teach then not to *take* the land.[66] Despite this purposeful dissolution of the communes, under a quarter of the peasant allotments had been consolidated in 1914.[67] Individual consolidation was not confined to any economic level of the peasantry, certainly not to the richest sections of it, but nowhere had it gone very far by the outbreak of the war. In the conditions of 1917, especially from February to October, as the army split up, the strike movement spread and peasant soldiers began to trickle back to their villages, the peasant communes reconstituted themselves and took back not just the lands of the nobility (which had in fact already shrunk extensively since the emancipation)[68] but those of many of the separators. While the Provisional Government wavered and the Bolsheviks seized power, built up the Red Army and held power against the white armies, the villages of Russia realized their ancient dream and became once again a world sufficient unto themselves, virtually independent of the state. The Tsarist government was broken by the last and greatest of Russian peasant risings. It was replaced in due course by a government which succeeded in subjecting the peasantry to the control of the state to an extent no Tsar had dreamed of, though the peasantry to some degree have taken their revenge by keeping Russian agriculture drastically the least successful sector of Soviet production.

Lenin had realized as early as 1907 that the Russian revolution could only come with a peasant agrarian revolution.[69] But he had still assumed, in *Two Tactics of Social Democracy*, in 1905, that the post-revolutionary government would be what he called a democratic, not a Socialist, dictatorship. It would not 'extend beyond the scope of bourgeois social and economic relationships'.[70] It would carry the revolutionary conflagration to western Europe and the socialization of the economies of advanced capitalist societies in the west would enable Russian social and economic development to proceed in conditions of unique ease. But Russian industrialization would still be in essence capitalist in character. The theory of permanent revolution developed by the German Marxist Parvus[71] and extended by Trotsky as a response to 1905 implied that a revolutionary dictatorship of the proletariat with the aid of the peasantry, if it contrived to seize power, would be able to consolidate its power and eventually to pass over to a Socialist regime, as a result of the 'direct state support of the European proletariat'.[72] Lenin, seeing as Marx and Engels had clearly before him, the services to international revolution that a Russian revolution could bring, preserved a relatively modest view of the internal social advantages which the revolution could bring to Russia itself. Trotsky, a decidedly more prominent actor in the conditions of 1905, concentrated more on the distinctive opportunities for a seizure of political power by the proletariat led by Socialist intellectuals which Russia offered. When Lenin in his April Theses announced his programme for Bolshevik seizure of power to set up a revolutionary dictatorship of proletariat and peasantry, with the slogan 'All power to the Soviets', a Menshevik bystander shouted out, 'But this is nonsense: insane nonsense.'[73] Four years later when the European revolution had clearly fizzled out, Lenin took a more sober view of what he had brought about. 'It was a fantastic idea for a Communist to dream that in three years you could drastically change the economic structure of our country; ... let us confess our sins: there were many such fantasy-makers in our midst. But how can you begin a Socialist revolution in our country without fantasy-makers?'[74] How indeed? Lenin could scarcely be blamed for the error in his prediction of a Socialist revolution in western Europe, but in itself the fantasy that industrialization could come blithely to Russia under the egalitarian rule of a vigilant proletariat and as a result of a generous foreign-aid programme from a Socialist World Bank must rank among the most *outré* fantasies of this or any other century.

The adventure of the Bolshevik regime has been a great adventure, a great and in some ways a terrible one. The change in the atmosphere in Petrograd, as indeed the whole history of the Bolshevik Party, made it evident that, whatever happened in Russia, without Lenin and indeed without his return in 1917, there would have been no Bolshevik revolution.[75] Even Kerensky in a sense grasped this when he told a meeting of the Provisional Government hysterically in March: 'Just wait. Lenin himself is coming. Then the real thing will start.'[76] Lenin made the Russian Revolution. No one else would have quite had the nerve. But, as might be expected from a revolution dependent on the daring of one man, it was not a very Marxist revolution which he made. The dictatorship of a party over a backward country has provided a political elite like many other political elites, autocratic, ruthless, supremely dishonest. It has certainly had great achievements to its credit, but it still displays in the light of the Marxian heritage what Lenin himself identified in 1922 as 'our main deficiencies: lack of culture and that we really do not know how to rule'.[77]

2 *Mexico*

There may be much dispute about why the Russian revolution happened and even more about what it means that it happened; but there is at least merciful unanimity as to *when* it happened.[1] When it comes to the Mexican revolution, matters are not so simple. From some points of view it is plausible to argue that there has still not been a real revolution in Mexico. But, on the other hand, it is at least intelligible, if not perhaps terribly sensible, to ask as the title of a recent American work implicitly does[2] whether the revolution is *yet* dead? The title of the single governing party in the country, the Institutional Revolutionary Party (P.R.I.), displays a nice ambivalence. Clearly in itself such a title would not preclude the government from being the inheritor of a genuine revolution. It would in many ways be no bad title for the Soviet Communist Party itself. But it does emphasize one sharp contrast between the two events. The Russian revolution identifies itself, tendentiously enough, as an instance of a general theory of history and society. It is supremely universalist in its pretensions. In *ideological* stance, except for the most gloomily and temporarily tactical of reasons under Stalin, it was Communist first and Russian second. When the German Communist Paul Levi suggested in all innocence as a motto for the Comintern 'Russia expects everyone to do his duty',[3] he meant that the duty was a duty to the historical future of humanity, not merely one to the political conveniences of the Soviet fatherland. The political inheritors of the Mexican revolution are in no position to identify their government with a universalist label. They cannot claim, however tendentiously, that it is the necessary history of the world as a whole which offers them their legitimacy. Their pretensions are prudently parochial. They are the heirs, even in their own eyes, of a single if very complex historical event in one

48

country, not the apotheosis of a global historical process. It was a historical event, too, which is extremely hard to characterize in terms of the theory which the Russian revolution claimed to exemplify. Clearly not a socialist revolution, it has presumably to be relegated to the less impressive status of 'bourgeois-democratic revolution'. But it is in many ways problematic even as a member of this category. The present political structure in Mexico with its single governing party and its local bosses is, from any point of view, less than perfectly democratic.[4] While it depends constitutionally for its legitimacy on regular elections, the same could have been said for the protracted dictatorship of Porfirio Diaz, with its Positivist *Cientificos* and ideology of advance under the Comtean banner of *Order and Progress,* which gave rise to the revolution. Equally, if it was not dramatically more democratic after the revolution in its political procedures, it would also be difficult to argue that it was much more bourgeois in the scope of its social and economic relationships. It would be hard to argue that the revolution in any of its more revolutionary phases gave a decisive impetus to the development of capitalism in Mexico, though it certainly accentuated Mexican economic nationalism at various points.

The distinctive character of the revolutionary events can be highlighted by considering the roles played in them by proletariat and peasantry. To a very considerable extent what was revolutionary about the Mexican revolution was of agrarian, rather than of industrial origin. A peasant revolt in the most advanced area of Mexican agriculture, the sugar lands of Morelos near the capital, was the most persistent and remarkable focus of revolutionary energies and its leader Emiliano Zapata was the greatest hero of the Mexican revolution. It was a highly traditionalist revolt in inspiration and its legacy on the national level, the *ejido*, has not proved an economic success in the competitive environment of a capitalist agriculture. The Russian revolution was made possible by a peasant revolt; but the revolutionary regime which it established was committed in due course to transforming the traditional peasant communities which the peasant revolt had briefly strengthened. The only *revolutionary* long-term impact of the Mexican revolution was the preservation of traditional agrarian communities which were being destroyed by the advance of agrarian capitalism. The contrast is equally striking when it comes to the role played by the proletariat. The Russian revolution may have ended up as the dictatorship of a party over the proletariat almost as much as over any other class; but it could certainly never have begun, if the Bolsheviks had not been able to muster much proletarian support and support in a form more demanding than that of the vote. In Mexico there was a rather small proletariat at the time of the outbreak of the revolution and much of what proletariat there was supported, or at best made no effort actively to oppose, the least revolutionary forces. There were worker military units, the Red Battalions, which took part in the protracted civil war which made the revolution; but they fought not for the revolutionary agrarian armies of Zapata or even Pancho Villa but for the repressive regime of the Constitutionalist leader Carranza, a former provincial governor under the dictatorship of Porfirio Diaz.

The key point about these idiosyncrasies is not that the Mexican revolution was somehow a *purely* nativist and localist phenomenon. There was for a time a genuine anarcho-syndicalist organization among the workers, with an irreproachably internationalist orientation, linked with the United States I.W.W., the 'Wobblies', and possessing in its ranks quite a number of accredited foreign revolutionaries including many Spanish refugees and even a Frenchman who had allegedly taken part in the Commune.[5] The ideas held by the more vocal revolutionaries were universal ideas, taken from the mainstream of western social, economic and political development, just as the *ideas* sanctioning the Diaz regime had been. But the most revolutionary segment of the revolution, the stubborn peasant infantry of Zapata, were led by a man with few ideas and those of a very local reference. The Mexican revolutionary intellectuals in discussing the meaning of the revolution and its proper course were fingering through a universalist rhetoric.[6] But what they succeeded in finding was not a world-historical destiny for it to realize, but simply a local identity for it to assume. Thus the Mexican government today looks back for its legitimacy to a past historical event of which it claims to be the heir while the Russian government looks forward for its legitimacy to a future – world communism – which it still proposes, at least verbally, to do its utmost to create.

The Mexican was the first great revolution of the twentieth century to begin. It had been in progress for seven consecutive years by 1917 and its outbreak was in all essential respects totally unexpected. No one planned it. No party led it. Indeed the only party intimately associated with it was literally created by it and *for* it, created to administer its outcome, rather than promote its occurrence. It was begun almost by accident and it is extremely hard to hit upon a point at which it may reasonably be said to have ended. As late as 1934, more than twenty years after the outbreak of the revolution and long after a stable political control had been established and perpetuated by the leaders of the victorious armies, the most distinctive outcome of the revolution had still had very little impact. The Presidency of Lázaro Cárdenas from 1934 to 1940 formed the period in which the character of the revolution was finally established.[7] Up to that stage it was still possible to consider the revolution as a vast and meaningless turmoil of classically Latin-American style, full of grand abstract nouns and purposeful individual enrichment, a modern replica of the *Porfiriato,* the dictatorship of Porfirio Diaz. There are indeed still many who believe that this is just what it has become since the retirement of Cárdenas. Since Mexico did not have a proper 'socialist revolution' (and whatever that may be, it is certainly clear that Mexico did not have it), the revolution must have been a meaningless and regressive *jacquerie,* a mere hiatus in the development of a modern capitalist Mexico. In this perspective, all that requires explanation in the case of Mexico is why it was so unfortunate as to suffer such extended disruption and why even such extended disruption came to such little good effect. It would be necessary to show why as widespread revolt took place in the different rural areas in which it did take place, and why the Mexican proletariat failed to put itself at the head of the revolts that did take place. The occasion for these puzzlements is very much *ex post facto.* It can be illuminatingly, if ungenerously summarized as the question of why the Mexican revolution was not led by a Communist Party. In 1910 such a question would scarcely have been intelligible there being no such thing as a 'Communist Party' anywhere in the world, let alone in Mexico. Even in 1920 by which time the main part of the shooting was virtually over, it could hardly have seemed a very puzzling problem. Only the success of the Chinese revolution has lent substance to the teleology which really makes it seem a question at all. The reason why it did not happen like *that* in Mexico was simply that it never occurred to anyone that it might.

But if we abandon this particular tendentious and essentially anachronistic puzzle, we are left with the question of why agrarian uprisings did take place on the scale on which they did, with why the Mexican proletariat, such as it was, proved less than sympathetic to these uprisings and why, partly in consequence, the victors of the civil war came from the groups opposed to the agrarian revolutionaries. But if the Mexican revolution is taken in its own terms and not as an inadequate replica of something else, it is also necessary to provide an explanation of why the heirs of the victorious generals should in the end have implemented a large proportion of the proposals of the agrarian and urban revolutionaries, even if they can scarcely be asserted to have realized many of their goals. This last question is extremely difficult, perhaps even impossible, to answer by anything except a detailed political history. But, from different points of view, the very extent of the upheaval itself provided both moral occasion and pragmatic motive for the belated commitment of the Cárdenas years.

To answer the other, rather simpler questions, it is necessary first to consider a number of general facts about Mexico. The Indian peasantry of Mexico after three centuries of Spanish colonial rule had revolted massively in 1810 against their local masters and the colonial rulers. The revolt had originated in an extensive conspiracy among the local population of Spanish origins, the creoles, against the domination of the colonial state structures by the metropolitan members of the royal administration, the peninsulars. But its leader, a creole parish priest, Father Miguel Hidalgo y Costilla, proved incapable of imposing any form of discipline or organization upon his Indian followers and the rising took the form of a communal blood bath, rapidly alienating the majority of the creoles, landowners with their private militias and churchmen, as well as government employees.[8] Only in the south did the revolt acquire a leader of real moral force and political imagination. Jose Maria Morelos was also a parish priest and one furthermore whose record in his parish was not entirely above reproach from a moral or religious point of view.[9] But at one point in his remarkable military and political odyssey, he set out a programme of reforms which in many respects prefigured the endeavours of Mexican revolutionaries in the present century. Slavery was to be abolished, large landed properties (including those of the Church) were to be confiscated and divided up or used to finance the revolutionary armies, wealth was to be redistributed in such a way as to treat both urban and rural dwellers with equity, government records were to be burnt, and local production for the world market, tobacco, sugar and mining, was to be systematically destroyed.[10] Agrarian reform may have been very much instrumental for Morelos to the destruction of the colonial government,[11] but it is hardly surprising that the creoles were as eager to close ranks against his disciplined revolutionary determination as they were against the chaotic massacres unleashed by Hidalgo. Morelos was duly executed in 1815. But the advent of a liberal anti-clerical government in Spain itself[12] drove the creole elite and the Church to resume the struggle for independence in earnest. In 1821 Mexico became an independent state. The ensuing decades were not a happy time for the new nation. Shorn of half its territory by the United States after a disastrous war, its internal condition was if anything more parlous still. The intricate corporate character of Spanish colonial society left behind it, as in Spain itself, a legacy of virulent conflict between centre and periphery, making the country almost ungovernable. Upon this endless struggle between federalists and centralists was superimposed, again as in Spain itself, an equally virulent war between anti-clericals and the Church. In its time this struggle led to the French intervention, eventually crushed by Juarez and to a vast weight of governmental debt. When one of Juarez's most effective generals, Porfirio Diaz, succeeded at length to his power in 1876 by a coup, four years after Juarez's own death, the country was still in an unenviable condition. Paradoxically the thirty-four-year dictatorship of Diaz which eventually produced the

revolution was in many ways marked by considerable progress, and even by some measure of its approved Comtean
accompaniment, order. There was much foreign investment,
especially in the north and in the sisal industry of Yucatan by
United States interests, and there was substantial capital
growth, though at heavy social cost. Railways, a particular
favourite of Diaz's *Cientifico* advisers, were built on a grand
scale – even though they did tend to be sited in such a way as
to promote the economic integration of the country itself less
effectively than they did the funnelling of goods into and out
of the American market.[13] Just as Russian industrialization
had been funded largely by European loans, particularly
from France, so Mexican economic development, the establishment of an infrastructure and the development of mining,
sugar and sisal production was largely financed by American
capital.[14] In both countries there was certainly occasion for
resistance to these processes on grounds of economic nationalism; but in both the local bourgeoisie, even if they were often
in an essentially comprador relationship with the world
economy, were enjoying sufficiently generous side benefits for
the most part for them not to object too vehemently. However, in Mexico the capital was not entering to the same
degree as it was in Russia in the form of loans to the government; and, partly as a consequence, it was not being used to
nearly the same extent to develop manufacturing production.[15] Much, as in Russia, went into mining; but in the
Mexican case the production was overwhelmingly exported.[16]
Substantial amounts went into really large-scale capitalist
agriculture. In contrast to Russia, where the revolution,
although made possible by a peasant revolt, had nothing in
fact to do with the aspirations of the peasantry, in Mexico the
revolution was in effect constituted by the massive peasant
revolt and merely made possible by the unbalanced character
of the capitalist development of the economy. In both
countries the occurrence of peasant revolt was a consequence
of the persistence in a drastically changed environment of
residual traditional institutions of communal action. In both
countries these communal structures had survived because of
their convenience to the rulers of the country. In neither
country had they proved economically very effective from the
viewpoint of those inside them. But whereas in Russia such

pressure as the *mirs* were under economically speaking came at least as much from within them, from rising population and individual enterprise, as they did from outside, in Mexico the economic situation of the Indian communities was being systematically eroded from the outside. In Russia between emancipation and revolution the total amount of land available to the peasantry, quite apart from the vast increments furnished by the colonization of Siberia, increased substantially.[17] In Mexico Indian village lands were extensively expropriated throughout the ninety years of Mexican statehood before 1910, as they had been indeed during the centuries of colonial rule.[18] The land had been divided during the colonial period between the Indian village communities, recognized as independent legal corporations, and the great haciendas of church or private owners. The relationship between the two forms of landholding was to some degree symbiotic. The labour force of the haciendas was supplied partly by landless peons working permanently on the haciendas and partly by semi-coercive, semi-contractual relationships between hacienda and community, such as temporary debt bondage.[19] The increasing monetization of the rural economy and the ending of the formal status of slavery if anything worsened the exploitative character of these relationships. The rapid expansion of capitalist production in agriculture in the closing period of the Porfiriato generated a still more dynamic demand for both land and labour, a demand satisfied in the corrupt and autocratic conditions of the oligarchy in a way which was unscrupulous and often brutal. The Russian government had (intermittently) been rather sharply aware that it faced an agrarian problem. The Emperor Alexander II himself had commended the emancipation of the serfs because it was better that revolution should come from above, rather than below.[20] The Stolypin land reforms came too late to save the Tsardom but they were at least a purposeful *attempt* to remove its greatest and most intractable weakness. But in Mexico the bland Comtean apologists of Porfirio Diaz's regime did not even know that they possessed an agrarian problem. Indeed it was precisely the agricultural sectors in which they took the greatest pride, the most advanced sectors of capitalist agriculture in Mexico, which unleashed the revolution which convulsed the country

for the ensuing decade. If it had not been for the archaic
Zapatista uprising in the rich sugar lands of Morelos, the
mild constitutionalist initiatives of the lawyer Francisco
Madero might have put paid to the tenure of Diaz himself,
but they would scarcely have eventuated in anything more
remarkable than a restored regime of a more or less in-
distinguishable type.

The manner in which the rural revolt developed in
northern and northern-central Mexico differed markedly
from that in the vicinity of Mexico city and the south, a
difference which was to have dramatic consequences. The
Zapatista armies from Morelos and neighbouring southern
states had little but a rural background in common with the
cowboy troops of Pancho Villa from the north.[21] It was not
difficult for the Constitutionalist armies under Carranza and
Obregon to split the two forces and subdue them separately.
The Villa forces were less tied to a particular base and less
serried in their loyalty than those of Zapata. They were more
individualist in attitude and decidedly easier to buy off. The
huge open ranchlands of northern and north-central Mexico,
with their irregular rainfall and sparse population had developed a social structure very unlike that of the fertile and
densely settled areas of the south.[22] Opened up originally
largely because of its mineral wealth, the north had attracted
an influx of population from many sources, mulattoes,
déraciné Indians and Spaniards. The indigenous Indian
populations were still nomadic,[23] unlike the settled communities of cultivators established in the south. The lands of
the north were divided up into huge haciendas, raising cattle
and sheep and constituting virtually independent political
units under the autocratic control of their seigneurs. The
constant threat of Indian raids turned these great ranches into
veritable fortresses and led their owners to encourage an influx of marginal cultivators and stock-raisers without land-
rights of their own, in order to augment the defensive
resources of the hacienda. The development of substantial
population settlements inside the seigneurial franchises led
in the late eighteenth and above all in the nineteenth century
to attempts by officials of the central government to establish
independent communities in many places in the midst of the
haciendas.[24] Such communities facilitated control of the popu-

lation by the central government, perhaps ultimately for tax purposes;[25] but since they necessitated the appropriation of substantial amounts of hacienda land to the community to endow it with the mandatory communal lands, the process of establishing communal lands in this way met with extensive opposition from the hacienda-owners. Well over half medium-sized landholdings in Mexico had been created after 1854;[26] and a large proportion of these had come not from the communal lands of the threatened villages, but from this process of encroachment upon the northern haciendas. The balance of opportunity, individualism and restriction which arose out of this long struggle for municipal autonomy and emancipation from the tyranny of the hacienda helps to explain both the extent and the impermanence of Villa's hard-riding armies and the extent to which areas of the north later supported the counter-revolutionary Catholic revolt of the Cristeros.[27] Villa confiscated a number of great haciendas and announced that they were to be run for the benefit of the state[28] and he espoused the Zapatista agrarian reform programme in a gingerly manner in 1914;[29] but the shifting and heterogeneous communities of the northern haciendas had no resource to offer to the rest of Mexico apart from the ability to disrupt the central government. They produced dashing military leaders in profusion,[30] but not men with sufficient understanding of the modern international political and economic structures within which the future of Mexico had to be constructed to enable them to build stable political coalitions amid the fierce stresses of the civil war. At the Convention of Aguascalientes in March 1915 the Villista delegates resisted the attack of the Zapatistas on the inadequacy of liberal property rights.[31] But in doing so these representatives of an essentially bandit regime showed not their reluctant acceptance of the stern constraints of economic modernity, but merely their lack of a past worth defending. If the only rural component of the Mexican revolution had been Villa's armies, the revolution might still have cost hundreds of thousands, possibly even millions of lives[32] and it might certainly have produced, as it did in fact in any case, a national economy which was essentially capitalist in structure. But it would hardly have transcended the categories of the usual Latin American caudillo-led Populist putsch with

its autocratic violence and economic nationalism. Villa and
the ranchlands of Chihuahua had neither a memory nor a
dream to offer the people of Mexico. Zapata and his men had
only a memory: not enough to win power (or even *wish* to
win power) and unite a nation. But the dream behind the
Mexican revolution, as it was eventually to be delineated in
due course, was a fairly commonplace one. What marks the
Mexican revolution out among the endlessly botched pseudo-
revolutions of Latin America was not this banal dream of
economic nationalism in a capitalist framework, successful in
many ways though this has in the end proved.[33] It is not this
rather drab vision which made the Mexican revolution distinctive. Instead, it was a memory: the memory of a community, the ancient pueblos of Morelos which the progress
of agricultural capitalism had almost contrived to obliterate.

Morelos was far from being the most archaic sector of
Mexican rural society. It was close to the colonial and national
capital of Mexico City, and its people were of somewhat mixed
origins. The agents of the rural revolution in Morelos were
the traditional village communities. But they were no longer
in cultural terms essentially Indian communities.[34] In 1910
less than 10 per cent of the population of the province of
Morelos spoke Nahuatl, the regional Indian language.[35]
Emiliano Zapata himself was not a pure Indian.[36] When in
1909 he was studying the ancient land titles of his village of
Anenecuilco whose leader he had been elected, he was obliged
to send his secretary to another village to secure translations
from the Nahuatl because he himself knew none of it.[37] Only
once in the history of the Zapatista rising did the revolutionaries issue proclamations in Nahuatl – to a few Tlaxcalan
and Pueblan villages; and this was very late in the history of
the rebellion, in March 1918,[38] when Zapata in despair was
looking for assistance even to Felix Diaz, the United States-
based nephew of the former dictator, in his struggle against
Carranza. The pueblos of Morelos which stood by Zapata
through thick and thin till his death in 1919 were not the
culturally entrenched Indian pueblos of many areas of
southern Mexico which in the end perhaps benefited most
directly from the revolution. Although the inhabitants of
Anenecuilco preserved many features of the culture of their
distant ancestors,[39] they had lost others beyond recall. It was

the political element of these communal traditions, in part recreated and in part strengthened by their recent experiences, which was to prove crucial. They did not think of themselves as Indians. It was true that it was the clause of Madero's Plan of San Luis Potosí which offered redress to illegally expropriated smallholders, 'in their majority Indians', which had first led Zapata and his followers to throw in their lot late in 1910 with the revolutionary regime. But, as John Womack nicely remarks, they knew that Indian was only what city people called country people.[40]

It may seem superficially surprising that an agrarian radical should have been happy to throw in his political lot with a political figure like Madero, a lawyer who had taken his stand against Diaz on the letter of the constitution and who came from a family with major industrial interests[41] including ownership of the only independent smelter for Mexican ores left to compete with the subsidiary of the giant American Smelting and Refining Company. Madero was in many ways an implausible revolutionary.[42] Indeed he had refused, a mere four years before the revolution, to provide arms for a rising against Diaz on the grounds that the dictator was not really a tyrant and in any case that he himself had a horror of bloodshed and would never lend aid in making a revolution.[43] At the time Zapata knew little enough about Madero, and in due course he and his men learnt all too clearly that this frock-coated revolutionary could not furnish them with what they needed. When the centralist armies of General Victoriano Huerta, supposedly under the control of Madero's government, drove into Morelos in 1911, laying the countryside waste and decimating the population, while Madero fluttered agitatedly from one side to the other in the effort to propitiate their incompatible demands, it became obvious to all that he had little to offer to the people of Morelos.[44] But although Zapata was obliged in the end to learn in this painful way the limits of Madero's political utility, it was not merely the extent of his and of other local leaders' ignorance about the man Madero himself which explained their initial rallying to the Maderista camp. Madero had taken his stand upon the letter of the Constitution of 1857. Zapata and his followers also took their stand on legality, the letter of the law. The rights which they attempted to defend were rights which they believed to belong to them, often correctly, under the law. The story of the Zapatista struggle is the story of how they learnt how much else had to be changed, socially and politically, before the letter of the law could become social and economic fact once again.

The haciendas of Morelos had been run largely as sugar plantations for some little time by 1910. They had developed, as had most of the great Mexican haciendas, as social and political structures directed less to the maximization of purely economic returns than to the realization of status. They had established considerable leverage, economically and socially, over the local village communities, but they showed no great tendency to erode these. Since they were run, as Womack puts it, 'more as symbols than as businesses',[45] it was possible for different types of community to co-exist. But from the 1880s onwards these tolerant, if not always comfortable, relationships altered decisively. The availability of better techniques of sugar extraction from cane and the climate of high investment and rapid economic growth provided by the Porfiriato encouraged the planters of Morelos into a rapid expansion of production. The large estates became virtual company towns with populations of thousands. Machinery and methods of cultivation were both drastically modernized. Some planters even established laboratories for research.[46] Concentration of rural property increased sharply. In the thuggish patronage system of the dictatorship, it was a goal which presented few problems for those with the money to spend. Village after village found that lands which had belonged to them for centuries, often the most fertile of their lands, too, had been seized by the great haciendas. The courts seldom provided any redress. The towns became ringed in by the spread of the haciendas and the village lands shrank steadily back. After the turn of the twentieth century matters became even more alarming. The lands of Morelos were subject to the risk of soil exhaustion as early as 1910, unless they were heavily fertilized.[47] The industry was already producing more than the Mexican domestic consumption of sugar and several Morelos planters had entered the giddily risky export trade as early as 1905. Even on the domestic market, and after securing effective tariffs against sugar imports, the planters of Morelos faced threats on at least two other fronts. The possibilities for the development of beet sugar production were thought good, particularly by landowners in the northern province of Sonora, and large concessions had been offered to an American company for growing beet much closer to Mexico City.[48] At the same time American companies had begun to produce cane sugar on a large scale in the tropical gulf islands around Vera Cruz where yields per acre were some 30 per cent higher than in Morelos.[49] The pressures of competition on the great haciendas were heavy and insistent. The bigger ones invested sums ranging up to hundreds of thousands of dollars in a number of cases in cane-crushing and other equipment. The rates of return on these huge investments could only remain favourable, if the supplies of cane for milling were constantly increased. Hence the pressure upon land supplies became even more insistent and the assault upon the lands of the pueblos even more virulent. In 1908 the twenty-four mills of Morelos produced a third of Mexico's total sugar production. 'After Hawaii and Puerto Rico, Morelos was the most productive cane sugar region in the world.'[50] The planter aristocracy of Morelos grew richer, more ruthless and more confident. It might face dangers in the turbulent sugar markets of the world, but inside Morelos, with the ready backing of the dictatorship ever at hand, it was hard to imagine how anyone could stand against them. When Emiliano Zapata was elected council president of his own pueblo Anenecuilco in the late summer of 1909, the day of the free village community living under its own laws, off its own lands and according to its own customs, seemed almost ended. It is true that when an opposition candidate had run for governor against the official Diaz candidate earlier in the year, popular hostility in town and countryside to the steady destruction of local autonomy had exploded into a savage riot.[51] But there had been little difficulty in repressing the riot: as long as the Diaz regime lasted, and virtually no one in the summer of 1909 expected it to come to a speedy end, the sporadic resistance of local communities to a legally cloaked expropriation was destined to remain futile.

Morelos was not a big state: about 5,000 square kilometres in area and with a population of 180,000 in 1910 in a country of 2 million square kilometres with 15 million inhabitants.[52] But it was very rich because of its sugar plantations and thus not initially an area which, as competitors for national power, the centralist government were at all ready to abandon. Not only was it too rich to abandon in a hurry, it was also, even after the Huerta or Robles armies had done their damage and the haciendas were in ruins and the fields laid waste, too close to the capital Mexico City and too well placed for descents upon it to be left alone. Had it been some impoverished and above all outlying province, the central government might well have decided to leave ill alone and to ignore its archaic defiance. But, situated where it was, the governments of Madero, Huerta and Carranza had no alternative, within their own political assumptions, but to seek to crush it utterly. And crushing it proved no easy task. Long after a more or less viable central government with its modern armies had been re-established in Mexico City and its authority extended into the remoter areas of the country, long after the cowboy hordes of Pancho Villa had melted away and Villa himself become a fugitive, even after Carranza had been recognized in 1917 by the United States, the Zapatistas struggled on. As Zapata himself said proudly but sadly in February 1914, 'Revolutions will come and revolutions will go, but I will continue with mine.'[53] The Zapatista armies shrank in size from the 70,000 who had entered Mexico City in 1915 to 30,000 in 1916, 15,000 in 1917–18, to 10,000 in 1919.[54] In 1919 Zapata himself was shot down in a treacherous and skilful coup. But although he did not himself live to see victory, by this time the victory had virtually been won. The more radical General Obregon from the north-western province of Sonora was on the point of supplanting the former Porfirian dignitary Carranza. Obregon, who was sympathetic to the agrarian ideas of the Zapatistas and eager to restore a more genuine measure of national unity (especially if it could be under his own leadership) gladly made peace with the surviving Zapatista forces under Zapata's elected successor, General Magaña.[55]

There had been an intimate link from the first between the fighting morale of the Zapatista forces and the social structure which they were struggling to preserve. The village in arms fought to preserve the village at plough in the maize fields, fought to preserve a form of social and economic organization which stretched back in time to the *calpulli*, the

village community under the Aztecs.[56] It had been the rather
perfunctory agrarian plank of Madero's proclamation of 1910
which led the people of Morelos to rise against the dictator.
But they did not fight for long under someone else's banner.
In November 1911 Zapata drew up with the guidance of the
schoolmaster Montaño, his famous Plan of Ayala,[57] which remained the watchword of the Zapatistas up till his death and
which they insisted must be accepted *in toto* before they
would make peace with the central government. It provided
for the armed seizure and defence of their rightful properties
by communities or individuals whose lands or woods or
waters had been purloined from them.[58] It also provided, in
defiance of the liberal laws of 1856–7 aimed at the destruction
of the church estates, for the establishment of communal
holdings for villages which lacked them, through the
appropriation of a third of the area of great neighbouring
estates, with indemnities to the estate owners.[59] It provided,
too, for the nationalization of the properties of owners who
opposed the Plan and the application of the residual two thirds
of their properties to cover the costs of war and to furnish
pensions for the families of those who were killed in the
struggle.[60] In 1914 and 1915 with the encouragement of a
radical intellectual and lawyer from Madero's state, Antonio
Diaz Soto y Gama,[61] and the assistance of a group of young
agronomists, the legal and administrative character of this
agrarian reform became more definite in outline.[62] Inalienable
individual and communal landholdings were surveyed and
registered all over Morelos, institutions of rural credit were
established, and the provisions of the reform extended even
to parts of the provinces bordering on Morelos.[63] Even Carranza
came to realize the necessity, if the villages were ever to know
peace again, of promising some sort of agrarian reform. In
January 1915 he in turn issued a law, drafted in part by a
brilliant constitutional lawyer, which put the bucolic phrasing
of the Plan of Ayala elegantly in its place.[64] But the sophistication of its drafting was matched neatly by the leisurely character of its implementation and the negligible scale of its
effect.[65] Five years later a mere 50,000 people had benefited
from it. The urgency and the scale of the issue were never
really grasped by Carranza. It took the advent to power of
Obregon, an entrepreneur and son of a ruined rancher in the

United States-dominated north-west of the country, before agrarian reform became accepted as a prerequisite for the establishment of lasting peace and prosperity. Obregon's ideological proclivities were in no real sense Socialist,[66] but his own chequered career had given him some sympathy with the demands of both peasantry and proletariat. He was prepared to make peace with Morelos by simply accepting most of the Zapatista demands locally. Nationally, he set himself to implement the programme which had been formally accepted and embodied in the Constitution of 1917 under Carranza: extensive labour-protective legislation, land reform and provision for the expansion of secular education.[67] Carranza had explicitly excluded radicals of Villista or Zapatista persuasion from the Constitutional Convention. But despite these exclusions, the tone of the Convention's decisions showed distinctly the prevalence of a certain corporatist radicalism throughout the country. Carranza himself took little notice of its provisions; but they were in practice a reasonable summary of the conditions under which peace and effective central government could be re-established in Mexico. The realization that this was so made Obregon glad to accept them. In 1920 he sanctioned the use of the word '*ejido*' in application to inalienable holdings, communal and individual, in the villages.[68] But governments from Obregon to Calles, for the next fourteen years, continued to assume the existence of large private holdings, in effect of haciendas, which represented to them the imperatives of economic rationality; and they regarded the *ejidos* as essentially temporary defensive institutions, designed to ease the transition to a thriving rural capitalism. It was not until the presidency of the first post-revolutionary President from the populous south of Mexico, Lázaro Cárdenas from Michoacan, that agrarian aspirations were fully accepted and the present highly distinctive Mexican land tenure system established. Under Cárdenas, from 1934 to 1940, three times as many acres were handed over, with definitive deeds, to ejidal tenure than had been under all previous presidencies added together; and for the first time irrigated haciendas on some of the richest land were transformed into collective *ejidos*.[69] By 1940 the *ejidos* owned more than half of the high-yield irrigated land in Mexico. At the same time ejidal members were organized into a wing of the national ruling party, as a peasant trade union, the C.N.C. This has duly kept them under the control of the government; but it has also, as Chevalier argues, effectively kept the government attentive to peasant interests.[70] There do still remain huge estates in Mexico, but they are situated in arid and sparsely populated zones suitable only for extensive stock raising. There are also substantial areas of high-yield farmland under private ownership, especially in the richly irrigated northern provinces producing for the American market. The precise extent of private control of the best agricultural land is hard to estimate because it is often of dubious legality and it is never politically convenient for it to be widely known. Rapid increases in agricultural production have come largely from this private sector and from a relatively small number of wealthy *ejidos*. The majority of the *ejidos* have enjoyed little investment, private or public, and are situated on land on which profitable capitalist (or for that matter co-operative) farming is scarcely possible.[71] Mexico, like other largely pre-industrial countries, has suffered from very rapid population growth. The main effect of the *ejidos* has been to absorb the greater part of this growth into a semi-subsistence farming sector, while providing a labour force for fairly rapid industrial expansion and permitting to individuals a minimal measure of capital accumulation through the remittances from largely illegal *bracero* labour in the United States. It is an authoritarian, and in many ways extremely corrupt, political and social structure, and it leaves a large proportion of the population in a decidedly marginal situation, as far as participation in the national society is concerned.[72] In terms of modernization of the rural areas in general its achievements are rather slender when set against those, for example, of the Soviet Union; but Mexican resources were decidedly more exiguous than those of Russia in 1910. The *ejido* has certainly not proved a means for promoting the dramatic economic modernization of the countryside. But its provisions against private land sales have prevented the degree of concentration of holdings which, in a country so uneven in its social development, would have inevitably followed from the free play of capitalist forces.[73] Any rapid growth of the majority's standard of living in the rural areas would have required massive movements of population from the over-populated and over-farmed plateau areas on which much of it has been settled for centuries onto lands where there would be significant returns on inputs of capital.[74] The *ejido* has not, for the most part, brought the fruits of modernity to the peasantry of Mexico. But then it was not for the fruits of modernity that the pueblos of Morelos struggled for ten years and sacrificed a third of their inhabitants.[75] The Mexican revolution was a revolution which the peasants won and won for themselves. The *ejido* is the fruits of their victory, what they struggled for, the preservation of a form of social life, of a community. This is why the revolution, for all the approved internationalist rhetoric offered by its intellectual mouthpieces, was such an intensely localist affair. It was – less than any other revolution – a revolution about what men said. Its triumph was the defence of a locality and its ways, not the realization of any set of theoretical ideas. It was determinedly a subsistence revolution, not an export commodity.

The issue remains, however, of *why* it was only a peasant revolution, why in 1915 the worker 'Red Battalions' should have fought on behalf of the Constitutionalists Carranza and Obregon and why the mass of the Mexican labour movement ever since has been essentially a dependent, and usually a rather submissive dependent, of the government. It is not a particularly difficult question to answer;[76] but the answer to it has many implications for an understanding of what has on the whole actually happened in twentieth-century revolutions, what twentieth-century revolutions have been like. In the year 1910 the industrial workers of Mexico numbered some 195,000, rather more than four times their total in 1873. In addition some 79,000 were employed in mining. By contrast there were some 516,000 artisans, almost twice as many as could possibly by any stretch of the statistical categories be assigned to the industrial working class.[77] Apart from the miners and a very restricted number of metal workers, the only significant unit-concentration of production was among the 33,000 textile workers of the provinces of Vera Cruz and Puebla. Industry was very localized. Apart from the mines the only substantial concentrations of industrial activity besides those of the textile mills were in the capital, Mexico City, and the town of Monterrey whose population of 15,000 was stationary between 1910 and 1930. By the first years of the century the rapid economic expansion generated by massive inputs of American capital, especially in the mines and the railway network, had also led to an extensive distribution of fairly radical ideas and produced in the rapidly growing labour force widespread unrest which broke out in large-scale strikes, a number of which were brutally repressed.[78] The fact that it was largely American – and to a lesser extent British – capital which had created this labour force and created by direct investment, not, as in Russia, by the roundabout route of governmental loans, was to have very important effects. Even before 1910 a number of labour-protective measures had been implemented by local officials of the Porfirian government, something which could hardly have happened in the case of the rural labour force. In due course, after 1921 particularly, this relationship was to have the effect of making the proletariat more anti-foreign than anti-capitalist and to lead to the débâcle of the apparently foreign-led I.W.W. and Communist Party labour organizations. The labour movement which developed between 1880 and 1910, with the assistance of Americans and Spaniards in particular, was not only very local and very discontinuous in organization; it was also, despite the rhetoric of its leaders, mostly very reformist in orientation. Half the strikes between 1881 and 1910 took place in the capital, most of them over wages. Only one section of the working class in this period, the railway workers, unionized between 1887 and 1904, retained their independence and their anarcho-syndicalist ideas throughout. They supported the anarcho-syndicalist Flores Magon rather than Madero; they refused to join the Red Battalions and even in 1923 supported the purportedly (though very dubiously) radical De La Huerta rising against Obregon.[79]

The Casa del Obrero Mundial which was organized in 1912 on a basis of anarcho-syndicalist principles[80] drew its main support from the city trades in Mexico City, rather than the industrial proletariat. In 1913 unions even went so far as to declare their support of the reactionary General Victoriano Huerta when he was threatened with American intervention. At the end of 1914 when Carranza and Obregon had abandoned the Convention of Aguascalientes to the Villa and Zapata deputies[81] and had been forced back to the seaport of

Vera Cruz and the railway lines from Vera Cruz to Puebla, the Constitutionalists were desperately short of manpower. The access to supplies provided by the port and the mobility provided by the railway in the end enabled them to reconquer the country; but to do so what they needed above all else was *men*. It was under these circumstances that Obregon succeeded in drawing up a pact between Carranza and the Casa del Obrero Mundial for official recognition of the latter in return for its provision of worker units, the Red Battalions. Obregon had some reputation with the workers because he had established minimum wage laws in a number of states under his control the preceding year. But it was still a bizarre alliance for the revolutionary proletariat and it was too much for some segments of the latter to stomach: the railworkers, the oil workers under I.W.W. influence, and the radical textile workers of Puebla and Vera Cruz, especially in the area of the tragic Río Blanco strike of 1906–7.[82] Carranza himself broke the power of the Casa a year later, when the military situation had improved, by threatening with capital punishment, in the face of a strike, anyone who attempted to disrupt public services by strike action. It duly collapsed without a struggle.

An official Mexican labour movement, the C.R.O.M., was brought into existence in 1918 after a conference summoned by a State Governor in which the delegates' expenses were paid out of public funds. In August 1919 the C.R.O.M. made a secret pact with Obregon against Carranza. Under the Presidency of Obregon from 1920 onwards the C.R.O.M. was integrated firmly into the regime and favoured systematically against the much smaller dissident C.G.T. In return it provided military assistance for the government against intermittent military challenges from left or right to its authority. It has been a pillar of the regime ever since and had much influence over government policy. Under Cárdenas its pressure even produced the nationalization of the oil industry and the railways,[83] the boldest gestures of economic nationalism in Latin America before the Cuban Revolution and one which earned Cárdenas at the time an American reputation almost as diabolic as that of Castro himself. There is no doubt that organized labour remains politically powerful in Mexico. There is equally little doubt that it is conservative politically, passively wedded to capitalist organization and unrevolutionary to a degree. When the peasant armies of Zapata challenged the Constitutionalist government in 1914-15, the organized working class were either neutral or favoured the government against what seemed to them reactionary hordes. Like all good anarcho-syndicalists, especially of Spanish derivation, they were virulently anti-clerical. The soldiers of Carranza stabled their horses in churches and the Red Battalions sacked them. The Zapatistas were mostly devout and saw the Constitutionalist armies as the ranks of the ungodly. The working class, such as it was, showed little class-consciousness, following leaders rather than concepts of social organization, the antithesis of Zapata's followers. The workers fought for the cities and civilization[84] against the countryside, bigotry and the threat of a catholic labour movement. Those of the workers, often the most advanced sectors, who could not stomach alliance with Carranza, simply stood aside from the conflict. There could be nothing in common between peasants organized for and by themselves and a proletariat most of which was at least as anti-foreign or anti-clerical as it was anti-capitalist. So the Mexican working class in the face of revolution decided in the great majority to accept being bought off for the largest amount they could get and for the most part they have stuck to their choice ever since. Mexico remains in consequence today a country divided sociologically but united politically (at least so far)[85] by the success of one revolution, a peasant revolution and the failure to take place of another revolution, a proletarian revolution.

3 *China*

In terms of the numbers of human beings which it
involved – and perhaps ultimately in terms of its significance
for mankind at large – the Chinese revolution has been the
greatest so far of all the revolutions of the twentieth century.
It began – as did the Russian revolution – within the structures of an autocratic empire toying with the idea of introducing representative institutions into its governmental
structure and, unlike the Russian revolution, it required a
vast and long-drawn out military struggle for the revolutionaries to acquire power. Unlike the Russian revolution,
also, it is still even now very far from having ended. It began
in humiliation more extreme than anything that the history
of Russia can show and the way in which it developed
throughout was heavily affected by the struggle to escape from
this humiliation. The Chinese revolution was supremely a
nationalist revolution, a revolution in which highly civilized
elites set themselves to vindicate the battered pride of a great
civilization and in the end in part succeeded in doing so. But
it was also a social revolution, a revolution not merely made
possible but actually carried out by and for the peasantry
and, although it was directed by its leaders to exorcising the
shame of national impotence, it did not produce, as the
Mexican revolution appears to have done, a society divided
sharply into a peasantry with its face resolutely set towards
the past and the perpetuation of its communal traditions
(partly because of the comparative weakness of communal
traditions in China)[1] and an industrial sector following the
capitalist way but keeping a determined eye on its national
independence. In China the revolutionaries who went to the
peasantry, as the bright-eyed Populist students in nineteenth
century Russia did, were not (at least in their own conception)

70

Populists: they were, or soon in most cases became, members of the Communist Party. The Mexican revolution was a peasant revolution which served to strengthen localism among the peasantry and economic nationalism within the industrial sector: a revolution which turned inwards and backwards. The Chinese revolution was a peasant revolution which not merely rescued a severely battered national pride but gave to the elite who led it, a grandly universal message. The *Analects* of Confucius were the rubric of a civilization which turned in upon itself. The *Analects* of Chairman Mao in their red plastic covers offer, more vulgarly, a message to the whole world. In this, its most accessible form, the message may be hardly worth the listener's attention and its proponents can often be parochial to the point of insanity. The heroic defence of the Chinese embassy in London with meat cleavers and dustbin lids against the menace of press photography suggests that in some respects the Chinese revolution has not altogether left behind the distant days when the Boxers laid siege to the Foreign Devils in Peking. The proud consciousness of possessing a genuinely universal message and the uncomfortable sense of still being scorned by the rich, confident great powers of the world both stem from the character and motivation of the elite which seized power in the Chinese revolution and of the changes which this elite has subsequently undergone.

The national component of the revolution, the response to external political pressure has the longest history. Even as a political organization in its decrepitude the empire was attempting to recover control over its destinies.[2] The threat of being partitioned among the European powers, of becoming 'another Annam'[3] evoked the most urgent responses both in the government and in society at large. In the field of power politics Chinese political pressure in the first decade of the twentieth century to extend the formal recognition of their control into all the loosely-secured semi-independent areas on the frontiers, into Sikkim, Tibet and Burma, became vigorous and in many areas successful.[4] The treaty right to import opium was attacked and the European powers were forced into making a number of concessions about its enforcement.[5] New departments of the imperial government were set up in the effort to recapture control over Chinese foreign trade[6] and the army was greatly improved.[7] But the government itself was extremely badly placed to re-establish its control. Chronically in arrears in its debt-repayments to European creditors, its revenues were in effect pledged before they were collected and, so far from being able to repudiate the debts, it was even forced to take out additional loans at high interest rates and secured on the last remaining Chinese assets.[8] Military weakness and fiscal disaster severely restricted its capacity to carry out any policy which challenged the rapacity of western interests. More persistent (though naturally not particularly effective) initiatives emanated from private individuals and associations, the overseas Chinese communities, students, even gentry and local officials.[9] Some of these were by necessity organized and systematic: fund-raising exercises to buy back, for instance, the railways which had been constructed by foreign capital.[10] Others were more sudden and reflex in character: massive anti-foreign riots, especially around the Concessions, political strikes by the new labour unions or individual suicides over the latest national disgrace.[11]

It is hardly surprising that there should have been such a pervasive sense of humiliation. The Russian empire, too, was a great power which, in the Russo-Japanese war, had shown itself incapable of defending its interests effectively against a modern military challenge. For almost a century its intellectuals had either mocked it as hopelessly backward or attempted to knock up a eulogistic self-image out of its own distinctive features. It too had been in a virtually colonial relationship with expansive western capitalism and had had to be bailed out of fiscal difficulties by an enormous European loan.[12] But the extent of humiliation was different on both dimensions. The cultural depth of Chinese civilization reduced the cultural pretensions of Russians, whether westernizers or Panslavists, to near absurdity. The Chinese empire had been civilized for millennia when Russia was still a barbarian kingdom. It was an avowedly universal civilization and it admitted no legitimate rivals. It was power and power alone which challenged its viability and self-sufficiency: the massive incidence of what was felt to be totally hostile power on the central political structures of the empire. Western European capital might control much of Russian industry, but western governments did not possess in Russia as they did in China large enclaves of land protected by armed guards in which their citizens, as traders, could live virtually outside the law of the empire. They did not possess in Russia as they did in China the right to import into the country a substance which they themselves admitted to be noxious in effect. During an official campaign of the Chinese imperial government to stamp out the consumption or growing of opium, the British Consul-General at Shanghai intervened with a gunboat to prevent the governor of Anhwei from destroying opium stocks owned by British merchants at Anking.[13] The first Chinese revolution, the revolution of 1911 which led to the establishment of the Republic, was a large-scale national uprising against the increasingly insistent humiliations to which the Chinese state in its imperial form had been subjected. It failed essentially because it failed to produce any ruling group capable of outlining a way in which these humiliations could be better avoided in the future.

There were many reasons for the absence of such leadership. By 1911 the project of gouging western intrusion out of the Chinese economy and indeed simply of evicting it forcibly from its territorial appropriations, required the accumulation of enormous and very controlled military and economic power by a Chinese government. But the development of great military and economic power required a firm and uninterrupted control of national resources within the boundaries of the state itself – required, that is to say, precisely the sort of independence which the Chinese empire had already hopelessly lost and which it was seeking so desperately to recover. The Meiji restoration in Japan could be an effective revolution from above and a successful feat of modernization – at the purely military and industrial level[14] – because it represented the seizure of power by determined modernizers in a country in which power could be seized *inside* the country, because power – and power of initiative, not merely power of repression – did still lie inside the archipelago and had not been elaborately damaged by western intrusion. There were, of course, other advantages which Japan possessed and which most or all of China did not share – most notably the availability of very high returns on investment in irrigated land which, together with significant technical progress in wet-rice cultivation, enabled the Japanese to generate both a rapidly growing agricultural surplus and an expanding industrial proletariat out of a demographic increase which in China came close to destroying the viability of existing agrarian structures.[15] In the short run the combination of these political and economic advantages turned Japan into an expansive industrial and military power in the Far East, one which in its expansive pressures greatly weakened first the Chinese and then the Russian empires between 1890 and 1910, and which between 1927 and 1945 in effect forced the Chinese revolution into the most radical of paths and made possible the general disintegration of western imperial control in the Far East. Japanese wealth and power were accumulated largely under traditional, or increasingly as the time went by, pseudo-traditional, auspices; and they were conceived by Japanese elites as instrumental to the preservation of traditional values. The crisis of Chinese society and polity was a much more profound cultural crisis. To re-establish the political viability of the traditional Chinese state in the face of its external aggressors and despite its desperate internal economic straits required a fundamental and explicit transformation of Chinese values. It might begin instrumentally enough with the construction of the Kiangnan arsenal and Foochow shipyards and with the establishment of a School of Western Studies,[16] in a manner reminiscent of the modernizing efforts of Peter the Great or the Ottoman empire, as well as of Japan. There was certainly, too, no inevitability to the denouements to which it has led, to the Communist revolution, let alone the Cultural Revolution. Indeed, the extent of sheer economic chaos, the helpless dependence of the central government on foreign support for most of the period from the turn of the twentieth century or earlier to 1949, and the near anarchy in the time of the warlords, all make it very clear that the empire – its territorial limits – might simply have fallen apart. There is no Ottoman state today. There might well have been a number of different states, nations, within the area of what is now China. The fact that there is today, despite the legalistic absurdities of the United Nations, *one* Chinese nation, and a nation which has lost more of its territory to a client state of Russia than to those of America, is due to the extraordinary political achievements of the Chinese Communist Party and its changing leadership. No one could have achieved this feat of national consolidation in geographical and military terms without being able to provide for the disintegrating fabric of Chinese rural society a very clear and direct set of services and without in consequence being able to draw enormous power from precisely the most helpless sections of Chinese society. And no elite could have drawn this strength or provided these services without being able to face at least the prospect of the challenges of modernity without blinking. In the early twentieth century the cultural heritage of China became a heavy burden to the Chinese elite in search of power and painfully or agreeably aware that power was no longer to be had without wealth. Joseph Levenson catches the nervy quality of surviving Chinese traditionalism with great delicacy: 'Compulsion to preserve the gifts of the Chinese past was psychological now, from an emotional sense of threat to special identity; it was not philosophical, as of old, from an intellectual conviction of the general value of Chinese classic experience.'[17] Confucianism, even under the Manchus, had been very much more than an official ideology for the empire, carefully inculcated into the subservient peasantry in public lectures.[18] It was more, too, than a professional ideology of the mandarinate, the literati scholar-officials, who operated the bureaucratic structures of the empire. A philosophy with genuinely universalist pretensions, it held together the complex and shifting elements which made up Chinese civilization. The structures of Chinese state and society were structures of power, like those of other states and societies, and they changed drastically over time. What gave them a common continuing core of meaning was less linguistic or geographical or ethnic than it was explicitly cultural, the heritage of Confucianism. Without Confucianism the bureaucracy might have become more drastically feudalized or it might have become more effectively subservient to the imperial will. What it could not have done was to make such exquisite sense out of the balance of instrumentality and independence which it enjoyed. It was not that there were not ideological rivals to the Confucianism of the literati: Buddhism above all among the populace and the Legalist authoritarian and manipulative doctrines which on occasion emanated from the imperial court itself. Without Confucianism the imperial government might still have been able to restrain the gentry from the permanent feudalization of bureaucratic roles; but from the point of view of the gentry themselves these roles could have been nothing more than the way in which their class made its big money.[19] As it was, the cultural pretensions of the role, the conscientious amateurism which justified its often resolute independence of imperial control, derived directly from its service to values which transcended (in the eyes of its exponents) the sordidly political. The mandarins were very professional amateurs; blue at all costs, rather than expert. Entry to their ranks was notionally and to a considerable extent actually through a series of exceedingly difficult examinations; but the examinations were examinations in cultural mastery, not in techniques which could be directly applied to the world. Yen Fu, in the first decade of the twentieth century, looking at them through the eyes of Montesquieu whom he was then engaged in translating, saw them as genuinely a *pouvoir intermédiaire*, with a cohesion bred of their own distinctive *esprit*, defenders of the liberty of the people.[20] Determinedly secular and tied firmly, at least at an ideological level, to the duties of their station, they were perhaps more promising seedbeds than the *noblesse de robe* for a modernizing ruling elite.[21] But since it was not the heirs of the *thèse nobiliaire* who were given the opportunity of presiding over the modernization of France, it is hardly surprising that only the most ruthless centralizers should have succeeded in restoring viability to the Chinese state in the face of the challenges of modernity. The Chinese revolution had to take the form of a war of national liberation (and this quite apart from the issue of whether or not, as Chalmers Johnson argues, the Japanese occupation was a necessary condition for the success of the Chinese communist movement).[22] It had to be a war of national liberation because China as a nation was deeply unfree. From the first, national liberation as an overwhelming ambition involved a dedication to the accumulation of power and a distinctive purity of will, not the dispassionate disengagement of the austere (or self-indulgent) mandarin, but the fierce self-dedication of the revolutionary whose proudest boast is to reduce himself utterly to instrumentality. Even the millenarian Taipings were in effect ruthless exponents of the Chinese *thèse royale.*[23] The successful revolutionaries unsurprisingly retained the secularism and ethical self-consciousness of the Confucian elite from whom they were extensively recruited; but they discarded the disengagement for a passionate commitment to changing the world in a very concrete fashion. In doing so they abandoned of necessity the universal import of Chinese civilization and reduced it to a role in world history shared with other and culturally distinctly less imposing national societies.

Marxism, then, was a new ideology of the literati, which could sanction the heroic efforts needed to rescue the people of China from the disintegrating impact of the imperialist world economy (and of internal demographic strain), sacrificing the universal meaning of a civilization in order to recapture the particular reality of a nation and endowing the latter again with a universal significance by placing it within a universal history. But it was not only this metaphysical self-image for a new ruling elite which Marxism offered to the people of China, but also, perhaps rather despite itself, something more, a clue to how to generate the power necessary in order to establish the control of this revolutionary elite. It was only a clue, not by any means positive guidance. Such positive guidance as Marxism itself or the world Marxist movement in all its branches did give to Chinese Marxists has famously done them decidedly more damage than it has brought them assistance.[24] But the clue, though abstract in the extreme in the form in which it was offered, was crucial to the success of any nationalist elite in China. The power to defend China against the ravages of the world market had to be derived from the damage which these had already done inside the country. Only from the disruption of economic relations inside China could the power be generated to recover control over the Chinese economy for the Chinese. The liberation of China had to be autarkic because it could only be carried to its conclusion in the face of the power of industrial nations by a national government whose own power was in no way dependent on the world economy.

There were three main stages in which this realization of the necessarily autarkic character of the revolution was reached. They correspond crudely to the period leading up

to the revolution of 1911, the period of the Kuomintang
regime, and the period of Communist rise to mastery. None
of these periods were homogeneous politically or ideologically
and they overlapped by substantial periods of time. But it is
illuminating to look upon them in this way as a deepening of
political understanding by segments of the national political
elite. The first stage was almost entirely ideological – the
political component of the 1911 revolution being highly confused and disorganized. A particularly elaborate exploration
of its ideological problems can be found in the work of Yen
Fu, translator of Herbert Spencer, Huxley, John Stuart Mill,
Montesquieu and Adam Smith. Yen Fu attempted to trans-
pose the intellectual traditions of western liberalism to the
Chinese setting, explaining the political, military and
economic weakness of the Chinese empire by the absence of
the liberal democratic institutions and ideas which had lent
such expansive dynamism to the nations of the west.[25] Liberal
values were commended as instrumental to the increase of
national power and no very drastic distinction was made
within the structure of capitalist industrialization between
the English and German (or Japanese) paths to modernity.
Any preference for the more democratic English approach
was effectively erased by the experience of the First World
War in which, Yen Fu sneered, three hundred years of European progress had brought only 'profit self and kill others,
diminish incorruptibility and banish shame'.[26] His support for
Yuan Shih'kai's pastiche of a restored empire and his insistence that in the face of the challenge of modern warfare
the more libertarian aspects of western political experience
had become simply irrelevant showed a painfully acquired
realization that wealth and power were not to be attained by
the crumbling nations of Asia by following the precepts of
John Stuart Mill. Sadly in the aftermath of the war he observed 'As for the various doctrines of equality, liberty, and
people's rights which have been considered a second gospel
during the last hundred years, their limitations are now
apparent.'[27] The way ahead was clearly the Japanese way,
industrial certainly, but authoritarian in a pseudo-traditional
manner, bureaucratic and above all military, as far as could
be from the spirit of Mill or even of Spencer. The next stage
of intellectual and political adaptation to the impact of

modernity is harder to identify neatly. The Kuomintang was an exceedingly heterogeneous movement which lasted, in name, over a long period of time (indeed in some sense is still with us in a geographically truncated form). It changed in character substantially during that time. Ideology, too, was not its strong point, particularly after Chiang Kai-shek's crushing of the Communists and the left Kuomintang in 1927. Chiang himself was no intellectual. A soldier, strongly influenced by his period of study in Japan in the aftermath of the Sino-Japanese war, he was a great admirer of the Japanese notion of *bushido*.[28] The supposedly reforming arm of the K.M.T., the New Life Movement bore the impress of this eminently military conception of virtue. It was difficult enough to get the Chinese armed forces to behave in a disciplined or loyal fashion even when they were being paid to do so. Hence the notion that the greater part of the Chinese population in conditions often of great economic distress might care to form themselves into a disciplined army for the greater glory of Chiang Kai-shek was optimistic.[29] Military organization as such was less than appealing as a value in the midst of warlord anarchy; and the K.M.T. began with too many initial disadvantages to be able to establish its own effectiveness even at national defence: the least that an army can reasonably be relied on to do for the national society which maintains it. Most importantly it was too internally disorganized and too divided in purpose to care to contemplate closely and to set out to cope with the terrible social and economic problems which confronted China. All large-scale human organizations, political parties no less than business corporations, are in practice affected in their operations by the efforts of their members to draw direct benefits from the way in which they operate. Political parties are perhaps peculiarly likely to be deflected from the achievement of difficult governmental purposes by the urge to service these particular interests. The K.M.T. was overwhelmingly a vehicle for the private interests of its more powerful members. The scale of the problems which confronted it and the dispersed quality of the attention which it was able, as an organization, to devote to solving these problems made its failure to solve them hardly surprising. The challenge which the Chinese Communist Party was in the end able to offer to it made this failure fatal to the K.M.T. regime.

In order to understand how the Communists were able to create such a powerful military challenge, it is necessary first of all to grasp the sheer enormity of the problems which were facing Chinese society and economy in July 1921 when the Communist Party first came into existence. The most important consideration in understanding these problems was simply demographic. China's population was around 150 million in 1700 according to the most reliable recent student;[30] and at this point its land/labour ratio was economically extremely favourable with prevailing techniques of cultivation. But by 1794 it had more than doubled, reaching some 313 million, and, by 1850, it totalled some 430 million. In this period techniques of cultivation had mostly changed little, if at all, and the situation of the population in many areas had become critical. It is against this background that the vast social convulsions of the third quarter of the nineteenth century must be seen: the Taiping rising with its fourteen years of consequent war and death toll of at least 20 millions, the Nien wars and the Moslem rebellion in Shensi and Kansu.[31] The devastation produced by these civil wars did plainly halt the expansion of population in some areas and the regular recurrence of internal war helped to keep the crude numerical land/labour relation from reaching the point at which permanent famine was demographically inevitable.[32] But unsurprisingly they also had many effects more purely damaging from an economic point of view. The appalling state of the communications system in particular, which meant that most peasant production was confined to a very narrow market for its outlet,[33] was extensively aggravated by the internal political disruption, while major flood control and irrigation works were severely damaged. From the most traditional to the most modern, the instruments by which the Chinese populace maintained its control of the physical environment were disrupted by political and military chaos and by the private war or semi-official brigandage which went with them. 'A general with a railway is like a monkey with a watch', observed R. H. Tawney tartly in his 1931 report to the Institute of Pacific Relations on the economic problems of China.[34] Precisely those modern tech-

niques which were most necessary in order to reduce the
enormous cost of transport in a country in which a large
proportion of agricultural produce was still carried to market
on the backs of men, were the most frequently diverted to
the largely destructive purposes of military rivalry.

Tawney's study, *Land and Labour in China*, remains a
marvellously lucid introduction to rural economic relations
in China in the first half of this century. It makes it easy to
understand how rural revolution could come to China and
why, when it did come, it was in Tawney's own words of 1931
'perhaps not undeserved'.[35] The particular form which these
problems took varied from one zone of the huge country to
another, but broadly, with the exception of the zones of
colonization like Manchuria which permitted a certain degree
of mechanization, they fell into two main categories: those of
tenancy and debt. The average size of holdings varied widely
from the arid uplands of the north and west to the rich river
deltas of the south and east, and the proportions of cultivator–
ownership varied with it. In the north-eastern provinces average holdings were between 15 and 20 acres and up to 70 per
cent of holdings were cultivated by their owners. In the
southern provinces *average* holdings ranged between 1 and
1½ acres (which, of course, means that many were substantially smaller) and only some 25–30 per cent of holdings were
cultivated by their owners. Yields on the smaller holdings,
particularly of rice, were quite high, though distinctly lower
on average than in Japan. But it was not the yield per unit of
land which really mattered, so much as yield per unit of
labour and this was in the vast majority of holdings extraordinarily low. Prosperity, as Tawney observed, is a condition
not of acres but of human beings.[36]

Concentration of holdings was not on the whole the crucial
problem, though wherever it was to be found it was naturally
bitterly resented and provided the main dynamic of Communist advance in the later stages of the revolutionary process.[37] The real problem was the growing subdivision of
holdings in the face of sustained population pressure and the
increasing exploitation of peasant labour, either through rack-
renting or through usury which this pressure made possible.
Prevailing techniques of cultivation made it virtually impossible to produce a substantial surplus after rents and credit

repayments had been met. The Marxian doctrine of the im-
miseration of the proletariat, whatever its theoretical status,
has never sounded very convincing as a description of the
tendency of proletarian income in an industrial society, but
in rural China in the first half of the present century it must
often have seemed a sober image of daily economic reality.
Massive increases in productivity or massive diversions of
labour into non-agricultural work might have broken the exploitative chain, but as labour was the only plentiful factor
of production and existing techniques of cultivation remained
more or less constant, those with initial capital at their disposal in the form of land or credit supplies could continue to
expropriate virtually the entire surplus of others – and very
often more than the entire *surplus*. The rate of exploitation
was often sufficient to force adults into starvation or into sell-
ing their children into debt-bondage. There were, as Tawney
said, whole districts 'in which the position of the rural population is that of a man standing up to the neck in water, so
that even a ripple is sufficient to drown him'.[38] Even under
normal conditions the character of Chinese agriculture was
painfully intricate, almost a kind of gardening, characterized
by 'economy of space, economy of materials, economy of im-
plements, economy of fodder, economy of fuel, economy of
waste products, economy of everything except of forests which
have been plundered with prodigal recklessness to the ruin
of the soil, and of the labour of human beings whom social
habits have made abundant and abundance cheap'.[39] Increasingly inequitable tenurial conditions in the south and west
and the growing burden of peasant debt everywhere were
tearing apart the traditional structure of Chinese rural society
and brutalizing social relations in village after village. Since
China was a poor country with a colossal population, we can
have no direct knowledge of the extent of misery over most
of the country for most of the time, but the main colours and
contours of the picture are so crude that agrarian revolution,
or at least the *jacquerie*, seems an almost inevitable response
to them. Even the K.M.T. government was hazily aware of
this; Tawney in 1931 noted noncommittally that as far as
programmes were concerned, all the agrarian reforms carried
out in other parts of the world in the course of the preceding
century were by now part of the official policy of the K.M.T.

government.[40] In 1933 Madame Chiang Kai-shek in her efforts
to devise effective pacification techniques for the reconquered
areas of Kiangsi even considered supplementing the use of the
American missionaries in a programme of rural reconstruction by getting another American, Professor Buck, the leading
academic expert on Chinese agriculture, to devise an agrarian
reform scheme for the area.[41] It was a pattern of manipulative
concern which, at least in its secular dimension, was to recur
later in the American relationship with the peasantry of Asia
and their uneasy rulers. The eventual military débâcle of
Mao's Kiangsi Soviet, which in many respects had been a
surprising venture for a Communist Party in itself, might
easily have put paid to the future of Marxist revolution in
China itself. The Chinese people might never have found
their Mao – just as the Russian people might never have
found their Lenin. It is thus very important to be clear that
the excellence of the K.M.T. agrarian *programmes* does not
necessarily (or even at all plausibly) imply that, but for the
military strength of the Communist movement in 1945 or
1949, the K.M.T. government could have been expected to
devote itself successfully to coping with the enormous social
and economic problems of China's rural heritage. It is, of
course, a highly contentious question how far the Chinese
Communist Party has contrived to do this;[42] but, whatever
may be thought of Mao's political prudence in unleashing the
Cultural Revolution, there can hardly be any justifiable doubt
that the Communist Party as a government of China, and
even before it attained that position, has set itself systematically to alleviate the dense and essentially capricious weight
of human oppression to which the ordinary Chinese villager
had come to feel himself subjected. Nor is there much doubt
that in a social structure as intricately oppressive as the
Chinese village had become by the 1930s, dramatic alleviation
of this condition could only come from fairly brutal struggle
inside the village and could not have been simply imposed
from the government downwards. This would have continued
to be true in all probability even if the K.M.T. had by some
sociological miracle ceased to be the party of the gentry and
the urban capitalists, the direct or indirect beneficiaries of
the greater part of this exploitation, and been transformed
into the responsive instrument of an estimable agronomist

like Professor Buck. The Chinese villages, unlike those of Mexico, could not be in effect sealed off and left to their own communal resources, because they were, far more than the villages of Mexico, firmly integrated into a money economy, because their taxes furnished a significant part of the national revenue. But more important even than this economic significance, though this was no doubt the cause of the government's determination to maintain its direct control, was the fact that the most bitterly resented and the most salient aspects of the human exploitation were often internal to the village itself. Mexican villages were preserved as communities by their shared hostility to the haciendas. Chinese villages were torn apart by the bitterness of the economic conflicts in their own midst.[43] There is much reason to see the initial military triumph of the Communists as deriving from their success in recreating some real communal solidarity against the shared threats from marauding K.M.T. and Japanese soldiery. Later, though, this solidarity was deliberately broken down and, after the most savage internal conflict, a solidarity among a smaller proportion of the village, more reliable because more directly dependent, re-established in its place.

Whether or not this final stage of reconstitution of the village community was a political precondition for attending to the economic problems of the country and whether or not, in the aftermath of the Cultural Revolution, attending to the economic problems of the country is again going to become the assignment in terms of which the Communist Party is happy to measure its progress, it is worth exploring further the question of why the K.M.T. could not have provided at least the first stage of the Communist offering, security and peace, or, if this was unavailable, a measure of communal solidarity in facing those who destroyed such village security. In part, of course the answer was simply one of military weakness. The K.M.T. government was simply unable to control the numerous local military commanders because it had effective monopolies neither of military supplies nor of men. But this is to restate the question, not to answer it. Military insubordination was no new problem for a Chinese government to have to face and Chiang Kai-shek made considerable progress in the decade from 1927 to 1937 in the restoration of central military and political control. The organized ban-

ditry of the warlord armies was often a terrible scourge; but
it was one which a K.M.T. government under ideal conditions might have gone some distance towards eradicating.
The same, however, hardly holds good for the extent of social
and economic oppression inside the village. A reasonable
measure of political control and social and economic harmony
in traditional Chinese society had been a direct result of the
control exerted by the central government over the gentry
through the institution of the mandarinate. The extent of
social oppression inside the village was not in itself a direct
result of the breakdown of this control – the mandarin was
no ombudsman.[44] It came rather from the sheer demographic
pressure of the preceding century. But what made it virtually
impossible for the government to begin to alleviate this oppression was that the social group which benefited most
directly from the demographic pressure, the gentry or the
groups of large landowners in general, were precisely the
groups over which governmental control had broken down.

Traditional Chinese government involved the exercise of
central bureaucratic control over very large areas by the
selection of an elite service group with very high status and
economic rewards by highly formalized public competition
among a very much larger group, the gentry, which controlled
a very large proportion of agricultural land. The rewards of
the literati career and the stern disciplines upon which access to it officially depended[45] gave the imperial court powerful leverage over the gentry as a whole when affairs were
going well. The weapon of withdrawing the right to hold
examinations in a particular area, for example, so impaired
the mobility prospects of the gentry of that province that the
enticements of local separatist adventures had little chance
of outweighing it.[46] Consequently the abolition of the examination system with its traditional eight-legged essay in 1905[47]
not only left the gentry as a class more explicitly to what it
could get out of the economy, formally sundering a very
special relationship indeed and one with heavy, if not always
very precise, moral overtones, but also removed it fairly effectively as a class from control by the central government, however pure the latter's intentions might be. Individual gentry,
of course, continued to make their careers in the government
service, as bureaucrats or doctors, or in the almost officially

sanctioned banditry of the military role. Other gentry, by contrast, adopted the values of the revolutionaries. The symmetry of career structure, moral ideology and central political authority was replaced by increasing disparities between moral theories, social roles and economic opportunities. Traditional Confucian values offered in this new context no social opportunities in return for such inhibition of individualist economic rapacity as they demanded.[48] The government might wish to protect the villages from banditry, whether of a populist or a warlord variety, and it might prefer the gentry to be less exploitative than their market opportunities permitted. But it had no means of making such decorum of advantage to the gentry and little capacity to inspire them collectively to exhibit a virtue which had to be its own reward. One way of describing and in part of explaining – (a necessary condition) the grounds of Communist success – one understandably much favoured by the Communists themselves – is simply that they did succeed in establishing the plausibility among their membership at large, in the conditions of struggle, of minimally decent behaviour. Such behaviour in the long run was very far from having to be its own reward. Indeed it led to the establishment of Communist power in China – and that power has since been used, as power tends to be used, in ways which are often needlessly brutal and sometimes as pointless as they are ugly. The Chinese revolution at any stage was no vicarage tea party. But, in the civilization which had continued to exemplify, however partially, for the longest continuous period of time in world history, a single coherent social ethic as a standard by which to judge the holders of power, it would be inept, as the first-hand testimony makes endlessly clear,[49] to ignore the massive impact of the practical demonstration of how power could again be used for good ends. Agrarian revolution came *deservedly* to China, as Tawney said it might,[50] but it came not, as he seems to have expected, as a *jacquerie*. Instead by its coming it brought power to the Communist Party of China and it brought power to them in the last resort because to tens of millions of harassed peasants they alone seemed any longer to deserve power.

It had not, naturally enough, been initially supposed by anyone, least of all by the Comintern advisers who arrived to assist the K.M.T., that the Communist Party, if and when it won power in China would do so as the party of the peasantry. Even today there is substantial ideological sheepishness over the fact that the road to power was so severely rural for a party which was allegedly proletarian. Mao himself has fidgeted extensively since with his initial ascription of 70 per cent of Chinese revolutionary achievement to the peasantry.[51] It is, too, still a contentious issue how far any other route to power for the party was simply out of the question. In particular, in the disastrous aftermath of the Comintern-sponsored collaboration between the supposedly national-revolutionary K.M.T. and the Communist Party, it was vociferously argued by Trotsky and his followers that a classical urban proletarian revolution led by an independent Communist Party had been a real historical possibility and one which had proved abortive only because of the flabby conservatism of Stalin's insight into the revolutionary potential of China and the egotistic ruthlessness with which he was prepared to subordinate the interests of the Chinese people to the foreign policy gains of the Russian state.[52] This view[53] may be in part justified in its assessment of Comintern objectives, but it is not in general at all convincing. The Chinese proletariat was not only very concentrated geographically and thus very easy to suppress militarily, when the suppression came, as Chiang Kai-shek showed all too graphically in 1927. It was also the product of a very much less developed and, in proportion to national income or total population, a much smaller industrial sector than had existed in Russia by 1914.[54] K.M.T. armies might not be efficient and disciplined enough in the long run to suppress massive rural insurrection under modern leadership (a very difficult military assignment for the most modern of societies to attempt, as recent history has shown). But, even without the Whampoa Military Acadamy and other fruits of the Comintern's organizational assistance, there is no reason to believe that these armies could not have suppressed urban risings, if required to do so. Such Chinese industrial proletariat as did exist, largely confined to the great coastal cities and the foreign concession areas inside these, had much with which to be discontented. Chinese industrial production was vastly inefficient and, even in the larger factories, working conditions were appalling. Child labour and very extended working hours were particularly prevalent abuses. Much of the proletariat was still only partially distinguished from the peasantry. It was a volatile basis for political protest, particularly protest against foreign economic interests. Although it was unstable and disunited, it was hardly more so, as Jean Chesneaux its most systematic western student has said, than were all other social classes in China at the time.[55] Its crucial weakness was its incapacity to defend itself militarily against the K.M.T. or indeed against other warlord armies. After the massacre of Shanghai, the Communist Party made further efforts to lead proletarian insurrection, notably in the Canton Commune of December 1927 and in the period of the Li Li-San line in the late 1920s and the beginning of 1930. But the efforts were in all cases crushed with ease and it is difficult to see how a proletarian party could have consolidated a defensible military position in the cities at any time. Even if it had done so, the subsequent history of the Chinese revolution might well have been less rather than more edifying for its success. The peasantry, instead of furnishing an indispensable revolutionary resource to the party might well have come to seem at best a passive spectator in the short run, and in the long run perhaps even, as in Russia, a deadly enemy, to be ruthlessly and uncomprehendingly forced into collectives from above. The techniques of social control which the Chinese party evolved in the course of its revolutionary experience are, if anything, even more disquieting to those raised in the liberal west than anything which successive Russian regimes have dreamed up;[56] but, in the Chinese countryside at least, they are certainly based upon a vastly more sophisticated understanding of the material upon which they are attempting to act than the urban bureaucratic experience of the Russian rulers has made available to them.[57]

As a result of the repeated suppression of its urban insurrectionary efforts the Communist Party was forced gradually back to the adoption of a completely different and an altogether novel revolutionary strategy based upon the peasantry. Even during the period of collaboration with the K.M.T. the extent of peasant unrest had facilitated their organization into massive peasant leagues. Mao Tse-tung himself had first worked at organizing peasants in 1925. Early in 1927 in the province of Hunan he came to realize the enormous revolutionary potential of the peasantry as a class and wrote a famous report on his observations to the Kuomintang, which in effect called for extended peasant revolution.[58] Even his own organizational efforts in the countryside in the aftermath of the K.M.T./Communist Party split had an exceedingly chequered career. It took a number of years before the Chinese Communist Party as an organization accepted without equivocation that its road to power must lie through the villages. In the eighteen years between the Shanghai massacre of 1927 and the beginning of the final struggle against Chiang Kai-shek, Mao and his associates tried out many different tactics for mobilizing peasant support and establishing Communist control over areas of the countryside. The Hunan report itself was as much concerned with the eradication of archaic social customs, such as those which reflected the subordination of women, as it was with the systematic exploitation of class conflict in the villages. Throughout the period of its rural consolidation, the party experimented with the optimal techniques for mobilizing peasant support, manipulating a battery of devices from rent-restriction ordinances to straightforward expropriation and even to execution of those designated by a variety of economic or military criteria as class enemies. But although on occasion they certainly pursued the class war in the villages with greater energy than their immediate military situation made expedient, it does not seem that the deftness of these programmes was the crucial factor in the movement's eventual success. An American scholar, Roy Hofheinz, has recently unleashed the full panoply of American behavioral science on the attempt to explain the 'ecology of communist success',[59] the environmental factors in social relations which explain why the movement proved effective in some areas and ineffective in others. Little that is noteworthy in practice emerges from the not always very perceptively conducted investigation: his main conclusion that what really mattered was how vigorously and skilfully led the Communist Party was in particular regions could well have been reached by a shorter route. What he does establish, on the way, is how far the success of the Communist enterprise had to be a military success and how tangential were considerations of the precise degree of exploitation prevalent in a particular county. Chinese rural society as a whole in the anarchic conditions of the 1920s, 1930s and even 1940s was massively oppressive and exploitative. For hundreds of millions of the population, security and ease of life were permanently absent. Even the most backbreaking toil and the most unhesitating servility offered little assurance of survival and usually no hope whatever of even modest prosperity. The social reward which the Communists succeeded in the end in offering to the villages was at first merely minimal security and a certain decency, for the most part, in the exercise of power. No one else offered as much, certainly not the marauding warlord armies or the Japanese invaders forced back onto the precept of the 'Three Alls' – Kill all. Burn all. Destroy all.[60] When the choice was reduced to these terms, it is scarcely surprising that the Communists should have attained the measure of support which they did. But to reduce the choice to these terms was a very considerable feat and one which for its effect required the supplementation of K.M.T. brigandage and of Japanese military pressure. The former can be crudely but fairly seen as a consequence of the social situation inside China itself, but the precise weight of the latter, the Japanese impact, requires some comment. The purely military feat of consolidating base areas against the K.M.T. up to 1937 was in itself no easy task. The rates of increase in membership recorded by the party, a very crude measure of its success, were quite impressive for the period from 1931 to 1934, as impressive indeed as in the period picked out by Chalmers Johnson as deciding its triumph, the Japanese occupation.[61] But most of the soviets established in the early 1930s proved quite unable to defend themselves against the armies of the central government and in 1934, in the last of five successive campaigns of encirclement, the K.M.T. armies succeeded in crushing the Kiangsi Soviet itself and in forcing the remnants of the party's military units over much of south and central China to set out on the Long March to Yenan.[62]

At that point the Communists had not demonstrated a capacity to protect the peasantry under their control against direct military attack. It was this purely military failure, failure at the same type of power enterprise as that in which the warlords of different areas were engaged[63] which threatened their prospects for eventual triumph. Whether or not at that point they had alienated too large a proportion of the peasantry in the areas which they controlled for the remainder to provide a firm base in guerrilla warfare or whether they had not as yet learnt how to incorporate secret society or indeed former K.M.T. units into an effective military sub-ordination, is not of great significance. What was clearly established was that they were not yet able to guarantee the service which in the end enabled them to win over the villages. They were not yet able to play the warlord's own game with such effect that they could defeat the warlords at it. Even after the establishment of the Yenan base area at the end of the Long March, a much more readily defensible geographical complex than the Kiangsi base, it is not easy to be sure whether even the survival of the Communists as a major military and political power was guaranteed. Yenan could not readily be encircled and blockaded like Kiangsi; but it was economically an excessively backward area, of little importance, unlike Kiangsi, to the central government of China and scarcely capable of maintaining a modern army and an intensive level of politicization out of its own resources indefinitely.[64] Chiang Kai-shek could afford to ignore it, as he could not afford to ignore Kiangsi, while attending to the task of bringing to heel the warlord forces which controlled more economically or strategically significant areas.

But, whether or not the Communist forces could have maintained their position in Yenan indefinitely, had the military forces inside China been operating in a vacuum, is in any case an idle question. The initial basis of Chiang Kai-shek's following and the source of his most dramatic successes, in particular of the Northern March, was his claim to represent Chinese national interests against the pressures of the imperialist power, most especially Japan. It was true that Chiang, through his family, was as closely associated with American initiatives in the Far East, as he was for instance with the bankers and secret societies of the great entrepot city of Shanghai. But American investment in China at the time was only a tenth of total foreign investment in China and only some 6 per cent of U.S. foreign investment as a whole, so that even if the pattern of American concern in China in many ways strikingly anticipated its later involvement throughout the Far East and South-East Asia, it did not at the time greatly damage Chiang's credentials inside China.[65] The domestic economic performance of the K.M.T. in addition was deeply unimpressive. Reluctance to tax the gentry and heavy expenditure on the maintenance of military units (45 per cent of the budget was devoted to 'national defence') prevented the extraction of an economic surplus from the rural sector to facilitate industrialization.[66] Industrial production stagnated and the government was forced into wild deficit financing by short-term high-interest loans. Private investment went into real estate in the east-coast cities, and corporate investment into high interest government loans. Industry and agriculture, in fact all forms of productive enterprise, were alike starved of capital. But in themselves it was neither the equivocal foreign entanglements nor the woeful internal economic performance of the Chiang government which served in elite Chinese eyes to erode its title to represent the national interest, so much as simply its weakness as an instrument of national defence. Each fresh Japanese invasion was greeted with massive student demonstrations and steady K.M.T. complaisance. In January 1936 there were large-scale propaganda exercises among the peasantry in areas near the university centres of Peiping and Tientsin in an endeavour to spread the nationalist concerns of the enraged students to the peasantry. The campaigns were not terribly successful; the attitude of the peasants was assessed as 95 per cent curious, 5 per cent sympathetic. Most of them had heard vaguely of Japan, but few knew even the name of Manchuria, the locus of Japanese aggression, the nearest part of which was less than 100 miles away.[67] One farmer pointed out to the students that the present government seemed all right; their taxes were lower than before. Student leadership of the peasantry on a purely nationalist platform was assuredly no way to power; certainly not before the Japanese had arrived in person and made their presence felt in no uncertain terms. Many of the thousands of student demonstrators learnt this lesson over the years and their support naturally accrued to those who had from the start espoused the economic interests of the peasantry as vehemently and systematically as they had the national interests of China as a whole. The weakness of the K.M.T. government made it attempt at all costs to avoid a military confrontation with the Japanese. By the time of the final break in 1937 between Japan and the K.M.T. government, something like a third of the university students of

China, according to a survey done at the time, seem to have been pro-Communist in orientation.[68] The Sian incident in which Chiang Kai-shek was seized and then forced, partly at the Communist Party's behest, to form a serious United Front against Japanese aggression made clear the breadth of anti-Japanese feeling in the country at the elite level. The conduct of the K.M.T. between 1931 and 1936 and later during the Japanese invasion established in the minds of the most vigorous and socially sensitive nationalists among the young Chinese elites its unfitness to defend the nation. Large numbers of the most enterprising of these young men duly made their way to the areas in which Communist forces were operating and became revolutionary cadres. The quality of leadership provided by the Communists was described eloquently by a small number of journalist observers at the time,[69] and its importance is becoming increasingly salient in the academic analysis of the revolutionary process in China, as this proceeds.[70] One main reason, hence, why the Chinese Communist Party was in the end successful was that it was the residuary legatee, as a result of the brutal pressure of Japanese imperialism, not so much of the wartime peasant nationalism identified by Chalmers Johnson, as of the student nationalism of the period from 4 May 1919 to the outbreak of war in 1937. It was the allegiance of so many of the ablest, the most passionate and the most determined of the young Chinese elites which made it possible for the Communist Party to lead the peasantry against the Japanese army and go on leading them despite appalling losses (the population of the Communist-controlled areas in northern China fell in the 1941–2 period by over 40 per cent),[71] while the K.M.T. armies tried with increasing desperation to keep their forces intact by more and more elaborate evasive action. The massive mobilizing effects of the struggle against the Japanese armies described by Johnson may well have assisted the establishment of Communist control over large areas. But from the point of view of the villages these effects did not derive from the *nationality* of the invading forces. Japanese destructive enthusiasm against villages under Communist control scarcely exceeded that of the K.M.T. armies. It was not the uninhibited character of their respective behaviour but simply in its efficiency and its thoroughness that the Japanese out-

matched the K.M.T. Whether or not the Communists could
have mobilized the villages for self-defence in this way without the allegiance of the patriotic elite youth of the country
and against the K.M.T. armies is an idle, if difficult, question.
By the 1940s the party had become so manifestly the most
authentic representative of the national interest that its able
young nationalist cadres were as much committed to defending it against K.M.T. repression as against Japanese invasion.
It was plausibly 'having the German army to expel' which
made the Yugoslav revolution; but Chalmers Johnson seems
to have been misled in his comparison of the two revolutions.[72]
The Japanese played a vital role in the dynamics of the
Chinese revolution, but they played it, essentially, largely off
stage. It was not 'having a Japanese army of occupation to
expel' which made the Chinese revolution. Rather it was the
readiness to accept any humiliation rather than risk invasion
by Japan which discredited the K.M.T. government. The
sense of overwhelming and self-reliant achievement which
their ensuing victory gave to the Chinese Communist Party
and their legendary leader left them with an astonishing assurance. It reinforced insights (from which its leaders had
started out) into the total corruption of entrenched social
power throughout the greater part of the world; and these
conceptions have been further reinforced since by the actions
of the Russian as well as the American governments. Proud,
fierce, Puritan, resolutely uncomprehending, the government
which Mao himself, supposedly a Marxist, calls 'the dictatorship of the people', pledges itself in all purity of will to lead
the forces of light against the forces of darkness, the villages
of the world against its cities.

From the bare uplands of Yenan to the intricate and
densely-crowded cities of the industrial west is too far for the
political imagination of the Chinese rulers to carry. China
itself has been torn apart in Mao's efforts to preserve the
simple purities of those uplands; and, when set against the
outside world, the foreign cities are still very rich and powerful and the Chinese villages are still very poor and still,
against certain assaults, quite without defence. The international vision of the Chinese political leadership is one of
highly abstract projective hostility; all foreigners with any
trace of social power still aspire to the condition of devils.

The Chinese regime is sanctioned by Marxism, a universal theory; but it is guided, insofar as it is rationally controlled at all, by Maoism, a highly particular disposition, and one which owes more to the history of the Concessions and the Opium Treaties than to the sophisticated theories of the potential liberations of industrialism formulated by Karl Marx. The tensions between these universal and particularist elements has been much discussed, most brilliantly perhaps by Franz Schurmann.[73] It is hard to imagine how they can be resolved or to assess where they are likely to lead. Both the grandeur of the political achievements of the Chinese Communists and the schematic absurdity of much of the vision which it has reinforced arise out of the conditions of an embattled cultural world. It is too soon even to guess with assurance what convulsive surges of creation or destruction, what ornate Asiatic splendour or what final *jacquerie*, may yet come out of this combination.

4 *Yugoslavia*

The Chinese revolution produced a regime which has been in attitude and in power highly independent in its performance. In itself, there is nothing very surprising about this; the Chinese revolution was very much made by the Chinese themselves and, although it was very much a Communist revolution, it was one made in a way which owed nothing to the theoretical or practical guidance of the titular agency of Communist internationalism, the Comintern. The precise degree of deviance displayed by Mao Tse-tung at different stages of his career is still a matter of fierce scholastic dispute, but no one has yet suggested that the path along which he led the Chinese Communist movement was in its essentials and throughout its course a product of the theoretical inspiration of the Comintern. In the late 1950s and early 1960s as the Sino-Soviet dispute was beginning to become public, the first efforts were made to distinguish the character of the Chinese regime from that of other prevailing Communist regimes in order to explain the distinctive attitude towards the Soviet Union which the Chinese exhibited. At first sight this explanation was a simple enough matter. The Chinese revolutionary regime, unlike the Communist regimes of the eastern European countries was not a direct product of the tanks of the Red Army or of the massive Russian diplomatic and political pressures on a militarily defenceless nation which brought Czechoslovakia into the Soviet camp. The Chinese regime could be independent because it was not a mere facade for Soviet military power. The Russian revolution had happened a relatively long time ago and the Stalinist political style, unappealing though it might be in other respects, was at least reasonably predictable in its international demeanour. The Communist regimes of eastern Europe were simply a product of Soviet military power in the classic idiom of power politics. Even Winston Churchill, a luxuriantly old-fashioned statesman who might have found direct confrontation with Lenin or Trotsky a trifle baffling, knew rather accurately where he was with Stalin. The Chinese state was disquieting by contrast in two separate ways: it was disquieting because of how it might behave, because of the unpredictability of its actions in the international arena;[1] and it was disquieting too because of how it had arisen, because its very presence there on the map showed uncompromisingly that internal revolution remained a real possibility. In a valiant effort to lay both ghosts at once, the American political scientist Chalmers Johnson advanced a theory of the causation of the Chinese revolution which suggested that even if revolutions did remain a real possibility, their occurrence did not imply the growing power of international Communism.[2] It was in many ways a tricky problem in classical Marxism to explain how the Chinese revolution could have come about as a Communist revolution (a problem which Russian ideologists such as Kuusinen have recently been reduced to solving by the argument that the Chinese revolution did not establish a proper Communist state).[3] The revolution had indisputably been a peasant revolution (the majority of the soldiers of the Red Armies had been peasants) and it had undoubtedly been a national revolution (it had had the effect and been *intended* to have the effect of re-establishing a unitary national government in an area subjected to intensive foreign encroachment and eventually occupation). Chalmers Johnson argued that it had been successful and had secured massive peasant support (plainly a necessary condition for its success) *because* it had been a national revolution. Peasant nationalism had generated Communist power: peasant nationalism not in the sense of a generalized allegiance to symbols of independent political sovereignty or national power, but simply in the sense of reflex communal solidarity in the face of the Tacitean thoroughness of the Japanese style of pacification.[4] The Chinese peasantry had discovered their national identity at the hands of the Japanese and their self-discovery gave dramatic impetus to the Communists' claims to represent the interests of the Chinese nation. The uncompromisingly national basis for their attainment of power naturally both encouraged and assisted them to make use of this power to advance the interests of the nation.

This interpretation of the basis of the independence and of the origins of Communist power in China was reinforced for Chalmers Johnson by a comparison with the only other Communist regime which had at that period showed a marked independence of the Soviet Union.[5] Yugoslavia, like China, was won for Communism by a guerrilla war of national liberation waged almost entirely in the rural areas and largely in the more remote parts of these areas against a highly efficient and ruthless modern army of occupation. In Yugoslavia, as in China, the resistance forces were by necessity largely peasant or mountaineer in composition and the intensity of indigenous hostility to the occupying forces, the depth of their 'national' feelings, was a product of the savage repressive diligence of the invaders. It was plausibly once again peasant nationalism in this rather specific operational definition which had generated Communist power in Yugoslavia as well as in China. However, even in reference to China, Chalmers Johnson's thesis is, as shown earlier, defective as an explanation of the revolution.[6] It misrepresents the basis of peasant support for the Communist leadership by tying it so closely to the resistance to Japan, and even if it is correct in seeing that the revolution was a national revolution in its outcome, it fails to make clear how far it was in its essence a national revolution throughout. The source of the Communists' peasant support was not directly their leadership against the Japanese armies, convenient though the opportunity which this gave them for extending their territorial impact may eventually have proved. If anything, it was the initial breadth of their peasant support in the areas which they already controlled which made them, unlike the K.M.T. armies, ready and able to provoke Japanese reprisals without the fear of immediate military disintegration and collapse. Instead, the basis of their peasant support in areas which they controlled came from the moral purpose and political competence which enabled them uniquely among Chinese political elites of the time to provide the peasant villages with a modicum of security and economic equity. At the same time, the basis of their role as representatives of the nation, while it was certainly vindicated during the struggle against the Japanese occupying forces, derived from their performance over a much longer period than that of the occupation and from the steady increments of elite cadres of high ability which this performance had brought them. Over the preceding fifteen years the Communist Party had attracted growing numbers of the most nationally conscious, determined and socially sensitive members of the student generations and these recruits had enabled them to provide vastly better government in the backlands than the K.M.T. succeeded in offering even in the vicinity of the great cities.

Chalmers Johnson was obviously right in seeing the tremendous mobilizing effects of the Japanese and German occupations on the rural areas in China and Yugoslavia as critical in the speed and effectiveness of the Communist triumph with peasant forces and by strictly military means. Wars of national liberation have been fought since 1945, sometimes with great success as in Vietnam and Indonesia, and the possibility of uniting a nation by leading a peasant-based guerrilla movement is now a commonplace of political calculation on the part of dissident elites of widely varying persuasions. It may be that Chalmers Johnson gravely misjudged the importance of this particular phase in the explanation of the Chinese revolution, but he was undoubtedly right in supposing that it must take a great deal of the weight in explaining the Yugoslav revolution. For one thing, the sense in which there was a nation within which to make a revolution was altogether more elusive in the Yugoslav than in the Chinese case. China had by 1937 been subjected to extensive political and indeed military segmentation over the preceding thirty years; indeed it had suffered in some measure from substantial centrifugal forces throughout its history. But although there were many in the 1930s, from warlords downwards, who might be glad enough in practice that this was how it was, there was virtually no political group with the ideological effrontery to pretend that this was how it *ought* to be. In Yugoslavia, by contrast, the major weight of political energies both popular and elite had gone in the years between 1918 and 1941 into the vindication of the ideological claims of a plethora of local nationalisms. The basis of mass parties and the content of elite ideologies were both overwhelmingly to be found in the national identifications of the variety of linguistic and ethnic groupings which made up the Yugoslav kingdom. Even today some eight million Serbs, four million Croats, one and a half million Slovenes, a million Macedonians, almost a million Moslems, nine hundred thousand Albanians and half a million Montenegrins, to say nothing of sundry other dribs and drabs of ethnic groupings find it far from comfortable to have to share a single nation state.[7] The individual ethnic nationalisms of many of these groupings long preceded the emergence of any real sense of Yugoslav national identity. At the time at which the Yugoslav state was formed as a geographical and political unit in the aftermath of the First World War the extent of these national separatist feelings was in effect recognized in its official title, the Kingdom of the Serbs, Croats and Slovenes;[8] and, although with the suspension of parliamentary government in 1929 determined efforts were made to check the process of political fragmentation by replacing the recognition of national groupings by a single Yugoslav group, by 1939 this policy had manifestly failed and the government had been forced into granting substantial political autonomy and a formal recognition of their national status to the Croats. The Communist Party itself had not escaped entanglement in these sectional struggles. It contrived eventually to emerge as the first genuinely national Yugoslav party; but this emergence came at the end of a career chequered with a multitude of separatist enthusiasms. Macedonian separatism, for instance, was heavily involved with the national ambitions of Bulgaria, and local sections of the Yugoslav Communist Party became associated with the political interests of the Bulgarian state, a development which caused great annoyance to the central organization of the party, especially during the time that this was firmly in Serbian hands.[9] The official policy of the Comintern in the 1920s of fishing around determinedly for support among dissident peasant nationalists was extremely unwelcome to the central party leadership under the Serb Sima Marković. It led in practice to the formation of alliances, like that with the Croat peasant party, which were not merely bizarre in ideological terms, but also disastrous in their political effect.[10] It would be hard to exaggerate the difficulties of constructing a firmly national political organization in the teeth of these separatist feelings. Linguistic differences and political traditions posed problems enough. When supplemented, as they were, by the overwhelming cultural and religious division between the Catholic areas of the north, largely Croat and Slovene in population, ruled for centuries by Austria-Hungary and Venice, powers with a Latin culture and an orientation towards western Europe, and on the other hand the Orthodox regions of the south, Serb, Montenegrin and Macedonian, for centuries part of the Ottoman empire, they seemed almost insurmountable.[11] The hostility in particular between Orthodox Serbs and Catholic Croats, the two largest ethnic groupings, formed the central theme of Yugoslav national politics in the interwar years and during the war itself it erupted into a series of massacres of rare ferocity. Had one been peering round the map of Europe in 1940 for a united nation to liberate itself by disciplined struggle from alien occupation, if such occupation ever came, Yugoslavia would have been about the *last* nation one would have picked upon. If the Yugoslav revolution means simply the accession to power of a Communist government in Yugoslavia, it can be said with some assurance that it was having a German army of occupation to get rid of which made the Yugoslav revolution. If ever a revolution was *made* (and not merely its success facilitated) by a war of national liberation, the Yugoslav revolution was so made. What is perhaps more remarkable and what requires a more elaborate explanation is that to some degree it was the German army of occupation which made the Yugoslav *nation*. However such a sense of cultural identity was mediated and whichever social strata it was located in, there is little surprising in the fact that centuries of imperialist pressures *should* at length have transformed Chinese cultural autonomy into Chinese political nationalism. It is not remarkable that in their very different ways, both Comintern and Chinese Communist Party should have seen the Communist road to power in China as lying through service to the goals of political nationalism and it is equally unsurprising that so many of the ablest Communist leaders should have described their accession to the ranks of the party in terms of its eligibility for essentially nationalist purposes. In Yugoslavia by contrast the effort of the Communist Party to assume the role of a legitimate national political elite was an intrinsically more precarious project. Indeed it was not at all

obvious that there *could* be such a group as a national political elite enjoying nationwide legitimacy.

In China both the policy of the Comintern and initially the
policy of the local Communist leadership focussed on the
large cities[12] and on the temporary unity of bourgeoisie and
proletariat in promoting a bourgeois national revolution. The
Whampoa Military Academy, so important in the training of
the K.M.T. officer corps, was specifically modelled on Trotsky's training programme for the Red Army and the military
organization of the K.M.T. armies as a whole was heavily indebted to the assistance of a Soviet military mission.[13] The
eventual success of Mao's policy of going to the peasants
among the Communist Party's leadership was predominantly
a consequence of the K.M.T. liquidation of Communist organization and power in the cities. As a policy, it had little
initial appeal to the Comintern experts and its capture of the
party leadership's assent was plainly very much *faute de
mieux*. Even in 1945 Stalin's enthusiasm for Mao's road to
power was glacial in its moderation. Soviet attitudes to China
revolved around a solid core of purposeful great-power politics
throughout. In Yugoslavia, unlike China, the Soviet government was never in much of a position to imagine itself exercising powerful political leverage on the existing national
government. It enjoyed no special relationship with the monarchy and had no need to be restrained by any considerations
of tactical diplomatic advantage in fishing expansively for
whatever revolutionary forces it could discover. In this quest
it was perforce largely to the peasantry that it was compelled
to look. What ends it imagined itself to be furthering in the
particular strategies favoured owed more to the internal political conflicts of the Soviet Union than to the distinctive characteristics of Yugoslavia or, for that matter, of any other
eastern European country. In consequence it was frequently
the case that policies which made eminently good sense in
terms of the world revolutionary hopes of the Soviet Union
made rather little sense in terms of the organizational problems or long-run political intentions of the local parties. Such
a tension between the international vision of the world 'socialist' camp, at that time located, as Stalin pointed out, in one
country, and the perspective of 'socialist' forces in other
countries was perhaps inevitable. Many of the tactical

initiatives of the Comintern, rational enough from the
perspective of Moscow, were bizarre to the point of absurdity
at their points of local incidence. But it was equally plain
that the political interests in the national setting of the
organizational elites of local Communist parties would not
necessarily add up to the most effective possible collective
impulse towards world revolution. Furthermore it was
extremely likely, and indeed to some extent happened in
the Yugoslav Communist Party under Sima Marković, that
in a polyethnic state like Yugoslav, the party would become
excessively associated with one dominant nationality. The
tension between centralism and federalism in Yugoslav politics, a tension in which the Serbs, the largest ethnic grouping,
were naturally firmly on the side of centralism, was one in
which short-term political gains and net long-term political
effect might well be in direct conflict. Marković was inclined
to accept at a theoretical level the implications of the major
Marxist treatment of the nationality problem, that set out in
the Austrian Otto Bauer's, *The National Question and Social
Democracy*, published in 1907.[14] This favoured the granting
of autonomous status to different nationalities within the
state, but opposed strongly the systematic dismantling of polyethnic states and the making of propaganda for political self-
determination which would be likely to have this effect. It was
a policy conceived firmly in the traditions of western European Marxism, an effort to establish how in the long run
social progress and cultural freedom could be most effectively
promoted within existing state structures, and it was rather
firmly democratic in conception. The actual political proposals could be argued for without embarrassment in public.
Marković's sympathy with this point of view was infelicitous
in the context of Comintern politics, since Joseph Stalin's first
major piece of theoretical writing had been a wholesale rejection of Bauer's position in favour of a more explicitly op-
portunistic approach, the encouragement of ethnic separatism
in a specifically political form as a means of attacking the
political control of existing governments.[15] In view of this it
is not surprising that Marković should in due course have
been compelled to abandon his initial stance. In the short run
the Comintern alternative did the Yugoslav Communist Party

little political good. But it did have the incidental effect of decisively lessening Serbian dominance of the party and enable it, in the event of the war, to adapt itself to a more genuinely national role than would plausibly have been open to it, had it remained as firmly in Serbian hands throughout its history. The hegemony of the Serbs has been, at least subjectively, a recurring threat in Yugoslav politics even since Tito's triumph. While it may be difficult to estimate its precise weight, for instance, in the grouping around Ranković in the early 1960s, it would be silly to assume that it had no weight at all.[16] Thus the Comintern's addiction to fostering localist dissident, less than sensitive though it may have been in its political motivation and very much less than deft though it certainly was in its immediate effects,[17] did offer some service to Yugoslav nationalism, besides simply training Tito himself, by detaching the party for some decades rather thoroughly from the tentacles of Serbian nationalism.

Many of the complaints directed at the Serbian leadership of the party were in practice quite unjustified. The Serbian Social Democrats had traditionally been very muted in the assertion of nationalist goals; they were the only Social Democrat Party in continental Europe to refuse to vote war credits in 1914.[18] The accusation by the Croat peasant leader Radić during his 1924 visit to Moscow that the leadership of the Yugoslav Communist Party was in the hands of Serbian Communists who were violent and severe centralists and who stood for the same point of view as the Serb militarists, especially on the national and administrative questions, was far from the truth.[19] But the Serbs did form the largest single ethnic component of the Yugoslav population and it was for instance not until 1928 that a non-Serb was chosen as Secretary of the Party.[20] The 'left' section of the party in the 1920s which favoured a more extensive measure of local autonomy and a more revolutionary orientation was of more varied national composition than the largely Serbian 'right' faction of Marković. During the 'left's' periods of dominance the Party Central Council was less predominantly Serb than it had been before. It was not easy in principle to elude the complexities of the national issue. The problems which it poses for the Communist Party have persisted through the latter's successive strategic transformations from blithe participant in the prospective post-1918 triumph of world revolution to the manipulative ethnic hell-raising of the Comintern, the National Front against German and Italian occupation and the responsible applicant of the insights of Socialism in one Country to the economic problems of a genuinely independent Communist state. In some measure the problems posed by the national issue to the Yugoslav government still remain the most formidable challenge that it has to face. They are also a challenge for which – just because it *is* genuinely independent – it cannot very well pass off the blame onto Soviet interferences. As debts go, the Yugoslav debt to the Comintern and its nationality problem is a very refracted one; but in the aftermath of the failure of widespread revolution to take place in Europe, the proper function of a Communist Party in a predominantly peasant country with a distinctly independent national government did not exactly leap to the eye. The Comintern in its efforts to recapture rationality for the world revolutionary movement may have foisted off on the Y.C.P. some exceedingly peculiar projects, but until the coming of the war and the German invasion, indigenous resources also had hardly succeeded in devising any plausibly effective long-term strategy.

It is convenient to begin considering the varying effectiveness of the party by examining the shifting role for which the Comintern, its rather interfering mentor, cast it. In the immediate aftermath of the creation of the Yugoslav state, at the time for instance of the revolutionary Béla Kun government in Hungary,[21] the Comintern's expectations of the possibility of a Europe-wide revolution were still extremely strong. These expectations derived naturally from the success of the revolution in Russia, but they were not explicitly conceived at first as a matter of Russian dominance of Europe as a whole. In the area which had become Yugoslavia, these pan-European prospects were more specifically focussed on the role of Russia and were none the less plausible or emotive for being so focussed. Communist victory in Budapest came in March 1919 and a month later there followed the first Congress of the Yugoslav Communist Party, a union of the Social Democratic Parties of a number of previously separate areas of Yugoslavia. This new party was weakest in the area of most elaborate Socialist organization during the war, Croatia and

Slovenia where, alone in Yugoslavia, the leader of the Social Democrats succeeded in establishing a sizable Socialist Party in opposition to the Communists.[22] It was the general pattern of Communist success in eastern Europe, as Burks points out,[23] that the Communist Party should be successful more or less inversely in proportion to the degree of industrialization, because where there was a significant urban working class, it was likely to be extensively organized by Socialist parties which were able to retain the allegiance of their intellectual and proletarian supporters in the face of the appeals of Communism.

It was unsurprising from this point of view that Croatia, one of the more industrialized parts of the country and one with centuries of participation in western cultural traditions as a privileged province of the Austro-Hungarian empire should have provided the only base in Yugoslavia for a western-type Socialist party of modest dimensions. The Yugoslav Communist Party was largely peasant in membership – and, where not peasant, frequently middle-class from peasant backgrounds. Its most effective electoral support came in the national elections of November 1920 (after the fall of the Béla Kun government in Hungary) from the areas of Macedonia and Montenegro, the most backward economically and the most unrelievedly peasant areas of the country.[24] In these two places the Communists won as much as a third of the votes. Overall, Yugoslavia was one of the least industrialized and the most overpopulated countries, even in the under-industrialized and overpopulated zone of eastern Europe,[25] and the electoral appeal of Communism proved strongest in the most archaic areas of the country. It is clear that this electoral appeal cannot have been based upon widespread electoral insight into and appreciation for the Communist Party's unique grasp of the problems of a semi-colonial economy and of the way in which these problems could be surmounted. For one thing, the Communists had not as yet developed any very elaborate theory of how the problems *could* be met, and such suggestions of a theory which might have been seriously intended to cope with these problems as had initially come to mind would certainly not have enhanced their electoral appeal among even the less prosperous of the peasantry. Comintern policy up to 1929 continued to lay great emphasis on the political significance of the peasantry,[26] a point which in itself might have been a markedly more helpful guide to political strategy in an overwhelmingly peasant and rather poor country, than it was likely to be, for instance, in that other focus of Comintern peasantist optimism, the Democratic Farmer-Labour Party in the United States,[27] a group whose supreme political artefact was to prove in the fullness of time to be Hubert Humphrey. But although the social locus of the emphasis on the peasantry was appropriate enough, the sense which informed it of what could be gained politically was considerably less unerring. At first the Comintern simply hoped for widespread peasant revolt, more or less hazily on the Russian model, and it encouraged a variety of fairly adventurist strategies in the effort to evoke this response. This perspective survived in Zinoviev's management of the Comintern for some time after it had lost plausibility among the men most influential in shaping the internal development of the Soviet Union and its economy and even longer after it had had the incidental effect in Yugoslavia itself of getting the party banned by law.[28] Zinoviev's faith in the imminence of massive peasant revolt, whether on nationalist or on purely economic grounds, was proof against a multitude of disappointments. Other reservoirs of revolutionary possibility appeared well and truly dry by the time of Lenin's stroke in 1922. If the peasants could not muster some revolutionary energy, the situation of the Soviet Union was ideologically and practically gloomy in the extreme. It was under the auspices of Zinoviev that the Comintern created its own Red Peasant International, the Krestintern, and admitted a former coalition party in the Yugoslav national government, Radić's Croat Peasant Party, to a rather fleeting membership in it. Radić was back in the Yugoslav government within eight months, and he succeeded in exacting some remarkable conditions from the Krestintern for the term of his brief membership.[29] The eclipse of Zinoviev and the ascendancy of Bukharin offered a more reassuring basis for cooperation with peasant parties. A policy of very slow capital accumulation in the Soviet Union itself, through an alliance with the middle peasants, might make Russian industrialization seem a gloomily protracted process,[30] but at least it meant that peasant support elsewhere could be angled for in direct terms and without the need for painful discretion over what lay in store for the peasants in the event of Communist victory. It was widely known and indeed explicitly noted on occasion by the leaders of peasant parties[31] that the Communist plan for their eventual socialist order held no place for a prosperous independent peasantry, owning their own land. If Bukharin had had his way, their eventual social order might have been distant enough in time to seem irrelevant to most; and the threat of immediate and compulsory collectivization in the Stalinist style would never have arisen to cement the hostility of the leaders of European peasant movements. The victory of Stalin over Bukharin inside the Soviet Union and the policy of rapid industrialization financed by the extraction of large surpluses from the peasantry, a supposedly 'left' line, however contingent the circumstances under which it was actually adopted initially, led to Comintern sponsorship of distinctly more putschist tactics, attempted insurrection anywhere in the world because of the possible returns on such activity to the interests of the Soviet government. Even in China these tactics had some deleterious effects, in the form of Comintern sponsorship of the disastrous Li Li-San line.[32] In Yugoslavia where the party was extremely depleted in scale, and despite the creation of a legal front organization, obliged to operate in an essentially undercover fashion,[33] the effects of a serious attempt to apply such tactics might have been disastrous. Even as it was, in the more difficult operating conditions of King Alexander's dictatorship from January 1929 onwards, the party organizational Secretary Djaković was killed attempting to escape from the police and some thirty party militants were killed after assaults upon police posts.[34] Party membership figures are extremely controversial; but it is possible to have a rough sense of the fortunes of the party at different stages in its response to the Comintern line by comparing estimates of membership at these points.[35] From between 40,000 and 80,000 in the years of full legality, 1919 and 1920, it fell away to less than 1,000 with the first banning of the party in 1921, recovered to some 2,500–3,000 from 1925 to the beginning of the dictatorship in January 1929, and then shrank again to less than 1,000 in the period referred to euphemistically as the period of 'armed insurrection'. At that stage prospects for the Yugoslav party did not appear exactly glowing. What served essentially to resuscitate them was the Nazi threat and the party's acquisition, in the face of this threat, of two groups of cadres, veterans of the Spanish Civil War and students from the University of Belgrade, who were to play a vital role in the Partisan fighting which eventually gave national leadership and, in the aftermath of the war, effective political control to the party. It is hard to imagine that the party could have presented an effective challenge for national power without the unique opportunities offered by the war. In the circumstances of the war itself it was partly the simple organizational skills of the core party leadership with their decades of highly professional experience of clandestine work which enabled the party to take the opportunities offered to them. But there was one other factor besides their purely organizational skills and their strong commitment to the struggle which was clearly a necessary condition for their emergence as leaders of an army of national liberation. This factor was rather subtly related to the depth of commitment to the struggle which they did maintain. Alone among the local political forces, the Yugoslav Communist Party was emotionally committed to liberating the *Yugoslav* nation: not just the Serbs, not just the Croats, not just the Slavo-Macedonians or the Bosniaks or the Slovenians or the Montenegrins, but *all* the peoples of the Yugoslav state and the state itself as a national entity. It showed remarkable political intelligence and even more nerve and discipline to adhere to this policy amid the competitive massacres and counter-massacres of one ethnic group by another. It was the will to do so which gave to the Communists, as it notably failed to give to the remnants of the royal army and their supporters, to the Četniks under Colonel Mihailović, extremely strong motives for involving themselves continuously in the battle. Mihailović expected, reasonably enough, that the Axis powers would in due course be defeated, and that the preservation of his own forces as a unit would at that point serve to ensure the restoration of the monarchy and the perpetuation of effective Serbian control at least over Serbia itself and hopefully over the whole territory of Yugoslavia. The policy of skulking in the forests as far as possible from the German army of occupation, in itself perfectly rational in the light of these preoccupations, discredited the Četniks with non-Serb sections of the population and eventually also with allied purveyors of military assistance, as leaders of a national resistance movement.[36] At the beginning of the occupation Yugoslavia was split up into a variety of occupation zones on combined historical, ethnic and strategic criteria. The determined effort to organize a nation-wide resistance and the military success which this effort won for the Partisans were the product of their *inclination* to organize a nation-wide resistance, an inclination which they were alone in feeling with any energy. Had they not felt it, there might well be today no unitary state of Yugoslavia and it is virtually certain that there would not be a unitary *Communist* state of Yugoslavia.

This national preoccupation did not, as seen earlier, spring fully grown from the minds of the founding leadership of the party, either the slightly Serbian-centralist right wing of the party or the more national-separatist left wing. Still less did it arise out of any mechanical acceptance, coerced or voluntary, of Comintern doctrines on the matter. The Comintern directives, as seen earlier, did play some part at an ideological level – the same directives which assisted the disintegration of the Yugoslav Communist Party as a mass political party did in the end erode the assurance of the more insensitively centralist Serbian elements. But a much more important reason for this eventual capture of the national mantle was simply that the Yugoslav party had been in a number of ways the least ethnically tendentious Yugoslav national party throughout its existence. In the Yugoslav national election of 1920, 'the only free election in the entire history of Yugoslavia', as Burks tartly calls it,[37] the Communist Party secured some $12\frac{1}{2}$ per cent of the votes nationally, a reasonable showing, considering that it had only been founded as a party the year before. What was much more important in this context than the size of the figure or even its geographical distribution was the fact that it was distributed *throughout* the national territory. Thirty-five political parties contested this election and thirty-two of them were explicitly ethnic groupings. There were only two other parties whose vote was distributed throughout the nation, the Radicals and the Democrats, and both of these drew more than a third of their total votes from the Kingdom of Serbia and a large part of the remainder from the *prechani*, the ethnic Serbs resident in other parts of the country.[38] The Communist party did not draw a substantial proportion of its votes from Serbia and, as Burks shows, there is no significant correlation between the scale of its vote in different areas and the distribution of *prechani*, of Serbs outside Serbia. The Communist Party was the only national political party not identified by the distribution of its electoral support as an instrument of Serbian nationalism. The Communist vote varied from over 30 per cent in Montenegro and Macedonia, through some 10–15 per cent in Dalmatia, Serbia and Slovenia, down to some 5–7 per cent in Croatia and Bosnia.[39] It was clearly largely peasant in composition and the party was least effective where, as in Croatia, there was both a Socialist party to compete against for intellectual and worker support and a vigorous peasant party to articulate local ethnic particularism. Initially the situation of the party was not an easy one, relying as it did for its support on the vaguely putschist flavour which clung around most Communist parties in the immediate aftermath of the war and yet necessarily risking by this very reliance a fairly speedy legal repression, as it duly suffered in 1921. Its position was not made easier by the fact that although Yugoslavia was an overwhelmingly peasant country with nearly 80 per cent of her population engaged in agriculture in 1920, it was one which despite heavy rural overpopulation and a distribution of holdings which was more inequitable than that in Bulgaria, though less severe than that in Rumania or Poland,[40] was not characterized by really dramatic agrarian exploitation. Yugoslav agriculture was of very low productivity, only one area of the overwhelmingly rural country being even a net food exporter,[41] and there were significant areas of residual near-subsistence agriculture. But the problems of the peasantry, distressing though they were, did not, in the absence in most areas of real large-scale land-holdings, like those of Hungary, lend themselves to projective personalization in the way that the social relations of Chinese villages in the twenties and thirties came to do. During the democratic period of the Yugoslav state before 1929 there was a series of unstable coalition governments which made little real impact upon the economic problems of the country. But all the coalition partners were, at least in pretension, peasant parties. Land reform of a rather mild type was carried out; and although the problems of the economy were little affected by this and although the government's motives in carrying it out were clearly supplemented by anxiety over the events in Russia, it did serve to increase the plausibility of the government's peasantist claims. Even the royal dictatorship from 1929 on was hard to present as the immediate source of the pressing economic problems of the villages, even though as Tomasevich points out[42] the tax revenue raised from the peasantry was almost all spent on government administration and national defence. The state as constituted, was plainly, as the events of 1941 showed, not worth fighting for in the eyes of the majority of the peasant population. But it was also, while in working order, insufficiently oppressive for large masses of men to take the substantial risks of fighting against it. Above all in the villages, as perhaps in the capital, it was obvious that the overwhelming economic problem of Yugoslavia was less exploitation, than it was simply overproduction of children and underproduction of food.

In many ways the problems of the preponderant agrarian sector of Yugoslav society persist until today, mitigated only by the fact that Tito's government has succeeded in promoting fairly rapid industrial growth. There have been further land reforms, cutting the maximum of private landownership to a point at which significant individual capitalist enterprise in agriculture is not much easier to carry out than it is in industry. But the main consequence of this has not been a rapid increase in participation in well-capitalized and efficiently equipped agrarian cooperatives, but a steady continuation of the trend towards fragmentation of holdings and an increased measure of production for consumption within the household. This has inhibited the growth of a true proletariat despite the expansion of industry. About 12 million of the population of $18\frac{1}{2}$ million in 1961 drew their income wholly or partly from agriculture and at that time 85 per cent of the agricultural land was still cultivated in family farms.[43] Hopes, common among intellectuals in the interwar period, that the *zadruga,* the traditional peasant extended-family residential and productive unit, might form a natural basis for the transition to collective agrarian production have proved abortive. The same forces in terms of problems of incentives on the market for nuclear families within the *zadruga* which served to break it down two or three generations ago, also weaken the appeal of the agriculturally more efficient and economically more prosperous cooperatives.[44] Partible inheritance led to widespread fragmentation of holdings in the transitional phase between *zadruga* and the present day and this process has certainly not been decisively checked, nor has the efficient consolidation of holdings been much advanced. Under the first Five Year plan from 1947 to 1951 some effort was made to promote compulsory collectivization. But, with the open split with the Soviet Union and the extensive resistance which collectivization received, this policy was abandoned and has not been resumed since. The absence of dynamic revolutionary forces in Yugoslav peasant society has been revealed as clearly by the extremely restricted purchase on agrarian socioeconomic structures which the Communist government has been reduced to accepting, as it was by the absence of massive peasant challenge to the interwar governments. The Communist Party has provided a reasonably efficient and comparatively delicate administration, decidedly less tyrannical than most Communist regimes and with a certain refreshing organizational originality;[45] but it is still difficult to tell whether its net modernizing effect will or will not prove less effective as well as more humane than those of parties which have adopted more draconic strategies. It is reasonably clear that the cause of its adoption of this less coercive approach was the need to transform itself without Russian military and political backing, after having asserted its independence of the Cominform. Tito could scarcely have asserted his independence in this way – or in any case not until about two decades later – if the Yugoslav party had not led its own national struggle for liberation, though it would be foolish to suppose that its success in this struggle somehow compelled him to assert his independence of the Cominform.

The Communist Party of Yugoslavia, then, has achieved such social transformation as it has brought about, in the rather more populist style of administration which it has developed, because it succeeded in leading to victory the Partisan resistance to Axis occupation and to the political dissolution of Yugoslavia as a state which this occupation produced. To round out this explanation, we need to know just what made it possible for this rather small political sect to gain the leadership of the Partisan resistance and just what made it possible for the resistance to defeat the Axis forces. The first question is in some ways easier to answer, partly a question of personnel and partly one, as suggested before, of the uniquely nation-wide scope of the party's concerns. The party leadership had demonstrated a variety of political and organizational skills simply in surviving to this time. Tito, a Croat peasant by origin,[46] who returned to the country in 1937 to be organizational and later General Secretary of the Party[47] had contrived to survive the purges which removed most of the other Y.C.P. cadres in Russia, and he and the local leadership had managed to maintain more effective propaganda and organizational activities, magazines, trade unions and so on, than the other political parties succeeded in doing under the dictatorship.[48] The organizational skill and dedication of the Communist Party cadres gave them a central role in most of the European resistance movements and in Yugoslavia with its varied heritage of local brigand tradition it had rich material with which to work.[49] By the time of the German invasion in 1941 the Communist Party had expanded to several times its 1938 membership, picking up extensive student support. It also at the outbreak of war or shortly afterwards had at its disposal the military experience of some hundreds of Yugoslav veterans of the Spanish Civil War.[50] More than a thousand Yugoslavs fought on the Republican side, the majority recruited in western Europe, particularly France, and about half of them party members. They suffered heavy casualties, but nearly 500 escaped and many eventually made their way back to Yugoslavia and took a prominent part in organizing the resistance. The other (and in terms of numbers the more important) source of highly effective party cadres in the period from 1937 to 1941 was the student body of the University of Belgrade. Communist appeal in student circles had been fairly strong throughout the party's history. The Communists were the strongest political group at Belgrade University in 1920 for example, though by 1923 they had diminished to being only the third strongest.[51] By 1940, despite the disastrous impact of the Comintern's putschist tactics a decade earlier, the Communists were once again the largest and most effective political grouping at the University. Partly this resulted sim-

ply from the impact of world events on the students. The
growing menace of Fascism encouraged belated United Front
tactics throughout Europe. The scale of Communist success
in Yugoslavia was not particularly outstanding by comparison
with other and richer European countries at the time: as
Avakumović points out, the percentage of party members
among the student body was lower at Belgrade University than
it was in Cambridge at the time.[52] University autonomy provided particularly favourable opportunities for organization
during the period of the dictatorship. Total party membership may never have reached very elevated figures: Dedijer
claims that it never exceeded 200 at Belgrade University.[53] But
even in Zagreb which had a higher than usual proportion of
industrial workers among party workers, student membership
at the University of Zagreb always exceeded worker membership until 1940. Total membership of the party expanded
under Tito's control from some 1,500 in the autumn of 1937
to 12,000 in the spring of 1941.[54] The increasing threat of Axis
pressure on Yugoslavia and the residual Popular Front orientation of the Communist Party enabled it to take full advantage of elite nationalist anxieties. It was more than a little
embarrassed, it is true, by the Nazi–Soviet pact and party
discipline in this period was severely disrupted.[55] Croat Communists in large numbers went over to the support of a government which had at last granted them autonomy and Tito
was obliged to purge the Central Committee of the Croat
Party in order to re-establish control.[56] The party organized
strikes in defence industries and demonstrations against involvement in the war. In Montenegro it even resisted mobilization into the army.[57] These exploits did as much in the short
run to weaken the appeal of the Communists as a national
political elite as any of their earlier tactical ventures, even
including their collaboration with the Croat Fascists under
Pavelić in the 1930s.[58]

However, by the spring of 1941 it had become clear to the
Yugoslav party that the German threat to both Yugoslavia and
Russia was imminent and that no sensible purpose could be
served by distinguishing the two. Serbian national feelings in
particular were inflamed by the crudity of Axis pressures;
and, when Cvetković's government finally acceded to Hitler's
Tripartite Pact late in March, a group of mainly Serbian offi-

cers under the air force commander General Simović chose to
seize power and begin talks with the British.[59] Hitler was taken
by surprise by these developments. Anxious to protect his
communications with Greece, he responded by ordering an
immediate occupation of Yugoslavia. On 6 April Nazi forces
entered the country and Belgrade was subjected to heavy
aerial bombardment, killing 10,000 people. The Yugoslav
army offered little effective resistance and ten days later capitulation was signed. The Communist Party played little active
part in these events. But, two months later, in June, Hitler
invaded the Soviet Union, making the situation of the Yugoslav Communists once again mercifully free from ambiguity.
Stalin himself called early in July for guerrilla struggle behind the German lines. The liberation of Yugoslavia and the
defence of the homeland of Socialism, the Soviet Union, had
become identical ventures for all practical purposes. They
were not to diverge drastically again until the Yugoslav Communists had secured their power in Yugoslavia too thoroughly
for anyone to be willing to pay the price necessary to dislodge
them.

At the time of the German invasion, there were in most
parts of Yugoslavia entrenched nationalist parties whose existence had indeed been a major reason for the Communist
Party's lack of political success in the interwar period. Few
elements greeted the invasion with any great delight. Even
the dismemberment of the Yugoslav state between a German
puppet regime in Serbia, Italian, Bulgarian and Albanian
occupation and a semi-autonomous Croat Fascist state, headed
by the former Communist collaborator Pavelić, under Italian
protection, won little local enthusiasm. Guerrilla resistance
might have seemed admirable in the abstract to many in all
parts of the country. General Simović himself, in the course
of his argument with the Regent, Prince Paul, over the prospective pact with the Axis powers, had indeed noted the
suitability of the terrain for such resistance even before the
invasion.[60] But he had envisaged guerrilla resistance as a supplement to operations by the regular forces (he *was* the commander of the air force). The Serbian soldiery under Colonel
Mihailović who set out to continue resistance in the aftermath
of the capitulation of the regular army soon discovered how
very unabstract a matter resistance to Nazi occupation was

certain to prove. Mass risings against the Germans in Serbia and against the Italians in Montenegro in July 1941 gave some indication of the potential for popular resistance. But the savagery of German reprisals led Mihailović to decide to keep his Četniks in future as far as possible out of the struggle. Even in Montenegro where the populace rose en masse against the Italians and briefly succeeded in driving them out of the country, except for two garrison towns, the resistance encountered some disturbing difficulties. The half-million Montenegrins, traditionally bellicose and pro-Russian, showed themselves to be highly effective at mountain warfare. But the savagery of their behaviour proved quite beyond the control of Djilas and his Communist cadres and resulted in wholesale massacre of neutral elements. There was abundant primitive ferocity for the resistance to utilize here, as elsewhere in the country; but it was no easy task to use these atavistic feelings without in practice venting them on other groups inside the society with whom communal tensions had a vastly greater historical depth and a more emotionally focussed character than they were likely at first to have towards German or Italian armies of occupation. The massacres of Jews, Gipsies and Orthodox Serbs by Pavelić's Fascist Ustaši led to counter-massacres by Mihailović's Četniks of Croats. Other ethnic groupings, like the Moslem Bosniaks suffered heavily. Most Yugoslav ethnic groups provided some military units which served as auxiliaries for the occupying powers. In consequence, pretences for communal massacre were readily available to all resistance forces. Even in the later stages of fighting Communist units were often seen by villages as occupying forces belonging to alien ethnic groupings, not least because on many occasions that was indeed essentially how they behaved. Initially the membership of large Communist units (except in Montenegro) was predominantly Serb. The first substantial area of Communist control was in Serbia and the first really dramatic recruitment of Partisan forces came from the Serb *prechani* in Croat areas, under the threat of communal massacres.[61] But their policy throughout was to organize the occupation of territory by units as much as possible ethnically homogeneous with the local population and, after the mediocre early results of a strategy, favoured by Djilas, of provoking German reprisals,[62] they made determined efforts to offer themselves to local peasantry as effective guarantors of security. Their success in this venture was necessarily limited:[63] for the first two years of the uprising they were harried from one end of the Dinaric mountain chain to the other, from Serbia to Bosnia to Montenegro and back again. During this time, they enjoyed virtually no military support from outside the country and had to rely for their arms largely on what they could capture from the enemy. The effort to establish significant liberated areas which could be defended successfully against German attack was not effective in this period. But in many parts of the country, the beginnings of a structure of local administration had been established, at least briefly, and the occupying forces been subjected to extensive harassment.

By contrast Mihailović kept his mind resolutely on the post-war situation. As time went by, he not only devoted more and more of his men's energies to attacking the Partisans, but actually cooperated frequently with the German occupying forces in these ventures.[64] Although he continued to receive allied military support for several years, the relative military contributions of Četniks and Partisans did eventually percolate through to Allied military leaders. With the partial exception of Stalin, none of the Allied military leaders viewed with unalloyed pleasure the prospect of a Communist government in post-war Yugoslavia. But there was a war going on and Churchill in particular had little difficulty, once the information did reach him, in choosing between royalist Serb collaborators and Communist-led resistance forces. Substantial British, and some Russian, military support and the supplies provided by the surrendered Italian army enabled the Partisans to increase their forces to a total of some 300,000 fighting troops by the end of the war and enabled them, as the German armies retreated, to occupy effectively virtually the whole of Yugoslavia.

The scale of this final success owed much to geopolitical factors, the mutual advantages for the Partisans and the western allies of cooperating against German occupation forces. Until the advent of really substantial military assistance from the west, the surrender of Italy, and the really heavy allied military pressure on the Germans on the eastern front, in Greece and in Italy, the Partisans contrived to survive as the most plausible organized focus of resistance on a nationwide basis. They developed an apparatus which *could,* under the highly favourable circumstances of the closing stages of the war, take and hold state power. The Axis occupying forces had been strong enough to hold onto a country as ethnically riven as Yugoslavia more or less indefinitely, if resistance had had to be constructed from purely internal resources. But they were entirely insufficient for the complete suppression of guerrilla resistance, particularly when this was backed, as it now was, by foreign military assistance. It was specifically recognized by German military authorities at the beginning of their occupation that their forces were (as the Japanese forces in China had been) only sufficient to protect major communication links.[65] Accordingly, again as with the Japanese in China, they determined from the beginning to use terror, in the form of mass reprisals, deliberately in an attempt to stamp out overt resistance.

The occupation, then, gave the Yugoslav Communist Party a unique opportunity. It was an opportunity which Tito and his followers took with both hands and there is some reason to associate the courage and purposefulness with which they took it with the use to which they have since put it. In the aftermath of the war other political elites in Yugoslavia were too discredited for many to be prepared to die on their behalf. The initial moves, both economic and political, of the victorious Partisans were fairly orthodox by Comintern standards. Domestically they devised a five-year plan to spur on industrial development and gave rather brusque encouragement to the peasantry to enter cooperatives or collectivize. Internationally, however, elated by their unique military achievements, they behaved less respectably in Russian eyes. Efforts to establish a Balkan federation with Bulgaria, Greece and Albania in which Yugoslavia would clearly have been the major partner earned general suspicion outside the country.[66] But when Stalin eventually decided that he had exercised his patience for long enough, the Yugoslav party showed that its credentials as a national political elite could no longer be revoked from abroad. The ensuing struggle forced the government into a number of substantial deviations from the versions of Socialist orthodoxy purveyed from Moscow. Some of these, such as the acceptance of substantial foreign capitalist investment, were very much an accommodation to external economic constraints. The Yugoslav economy was in no position to promote forced industrialization out of its own resources. But others, particularly at the level of institutions for political expression and corporate economic control of units of production by their workers, may in the end prove more useful innovations and may do more to establish the standing of the Yugoslav Communists internationally as revolutionary innovators.[67] Nationally their title as legitimate political elite seems better established than that of the rulers of any other Balkan country. Perhaps this is not the grandest world-historical claim; but all revolutions take place in particular countries. To have made as much as they have of the political heritage of *Yugoslavia* is no small political feat.

5 *Vietnam*

In the Yugoslav revolution the Yugoslav Communist Party, a small elite political organization, contrived to amass both power and to some extent legitimacy by providing successful leadership in a war of national liberation. The reason why it was successful in this struggle was partly geopolitical. The Communist Parties of France and Italy, for example, played prominent roles in their respective resistance movements and the relative absence of success of these movements was due to the concentration of German military force, the density of military occupation to which the countries were subjected and to the difficulty of providing really massive assistance to resistance forces under these circumstances. It was also, no doubt, due in part to the terrain in the first instance. Yugoslavia was particularly favourable geographically as an area in which to *begin* widespread guerrilla resistance. But if it was geopolitical considerations which helped to explain the military success of the resistance in Yugoslavia and if the organizational skills and determination of Communist cadres were a factor common to all three countries, there were clearly rather different sorts of reasons for the comparative dominance of the Communists in the Yugoslav resistance. Some of these are rather obvious. Charles de Gaulle was no Mihailović. Far from being, as Yugoslavia was, a semi-colonial economy, France belonged to the core countries of developed capitalism. Unlike Yugoslavia, France was no longer a synthetic political unit, but one with a core historical identity reaching back for more than half a millennium. France had a real national bourgeoisie and a military tradition strongly maintained among higher status groups, a nation to be liberated and core sectors of society committed by interest and by socially learnt disposition to attempt its liberation. There were

technical *military* reasons why the resistance was less successful in France than it was in Yugoslavia. There were profound
social reasons why the Communist Party in France could not
come to dominate the French resistance as the Yugoslav Communists had come to dominate the Yugoslav resistance. Fighting a war of national liberation might enhance the power of a
revolutionary elite where the nation due for liberation was
not a developed capitalist society and perhaps where it was
not superabundantly apparent that it was a nation at all in
the first place. Quite a large proportion of the nations which
now exist in the world were not only colonial economies in
1940, but also legally colonies as such, dependent non-
sovereign political units. Some of them, Morocco, Vietnam,
large-areas of India for example, had been in a sense nations
before they became colonies. Most had not. Today, more than
thirty years later, the formal western empires have shrunk
dramatically. Few acknowledged colonies of any scale exist as
such in the world today and the ones which do are depend-
encies of some of the more ailing powers on the international
scene, most notably Portugal. The same factor which moti-
vated the creation of these empires, the development of the
world economy, has rather severely restricted the liberating
effects of their rapid contraction. But contracted they certainly
have and in some, though not overwhelmingly many, cases, as
a direct result of armed conflict. Decolonization has been
marked by many quite virulent struggles for what, from
today's perspective, must be titled national liberation, since
the colonies are now nations in international law, if not always in social fact. In some cases it has been marked by what
can genuinely be titled *wars* of national liberation: Vietnam,
Burma, Indonesia, Algeria, Portuguese Guinea perhaps. All of
these governments (or prospective governments in the case of
Portuguese Guinea) tend to use the word 'revolutionary' of
themselves with some frequency. In only one of them, in
Vietnam, is it even broadly true that the war of national liberation was led by a Communist Party. There is an assumption,
shared as much by anti-Communists as by Communists,[1] that
the acquisition of power in a country by a Communist Party,
at any rate where it is acquired by their own efforts, is a sort
of package deal in which efficacy of a sort is traded for the
acceptance of autocracy. Both the efficacy and the autocracy

come supposedly from the application of the Leninist programme to the economic and social conditions of the nation.
What comes after must in significant respects be drastically
different from what comes before. In some ways this is a very
naive view. Russia, China and Yugoslavia set side by side suggest how very unhomogeneous the application of the Leninist
heritage to widely diverse social and political situations is
likely to turn out in fact. Even quite cursory inspection of
their recent histories, particularly in a reasonably causally
sophisticated mood, throws some doubt on the notion that
there is such a thing as a unitary Leninist heritage which
could in principle be applied to such diverse socio-economic
contexts. However, at a less sceptical level, there are a number of features which do mark out Leninist elites as more
desirable political inheritors than numbers of their more
likely alternatives. For one thing, their possession of a fairly
plausible metaphysic justifying the seizure of power appears
to enable them to preserve considerable assurance in the face
of a political and economic environment which provides scant
occasion for assurance. A good measure of autocracy, of enthusiasm for pushing people around, certainly accompanies this
assurance. But in the countries in which they are at all likely
to contrive to acquire power by military action, alternative
governments would be apt to be at least equally autocratic
and very probably decidedly less effective into the bargain.
Besides this simple possession of the nerve to attempt to make
some constructive use of the power which they have gained,
Communist parties do possess at least a generalized sense of
just what it is that is problematic about the economic situation of these countries. Construing their problems in terms
of their situation within the world economy is at least a minimal necessary condition for discharging national political responsibility in the dependent economies. It makes sense to
suppose that in acquiring a Communist political leadership
North Vietnam and perhaps in the fullness of time South
Vietnam too have incurred a political elite with a governmental style which will bring them some distinctive advantages, as well as a number of perhaps equally distinctive, if
currently less pressing costs. What the net balance of these is
likely to be over time no one is in much position to guess. But
that it is *not* likely to resemble that current in, for instance.

Indonesia or Burma, is perhaps now tolerably clear. The North Vietnamese revolution was a revolution in that it was a forcible instance of decolonization and one in which the colonized people won by 1954 a decided military victory in a large part of the country. Indonesia, too, experienced a revolution in this sense – and the military struggle there was substantially shorter. But, unlike in Vietnam, the Indonesian revolution was not led by a Communist Party[2] and, again unlike in Vietnam, the Indonesian regime which derived from the revolution proved itself in the long run quite unfit to discharge the responsibilities of national rulership. This is not a purely accidental conjunction of differences. The North Vietnamese nationalist movement was captured by a Communist Party, just as the Chinese nationalist movement was captured by a Communist Party. There was more to Vietnamese nationalism than linguistic community, hostility to the French and the disruptions of the world economy; while, in the case of Indonesia, there was not much more to Indonesian nationalism than linguistic community (of a rather artificial and precarious type) and hostility to the Dutch and the disruptions of the world economy.[3] The North Vietnamese revolution was contingently anti-colonial (The French came back) and national in essence. The Indonesian revolution was contingently national (Indonesia had to be a nation for Soekarno to rule it), but it was anti-colonial in essence. The Indonesian revolution was, it turned out, virtually over when the Dutch left. The Vietnamese revolution will not be over until Vietnam is independent, united and prosperous. Anti-colonialism in Vietnam has been a protracted political necessity, frequently in the short run inimical to the economic interests of the *soi-disant* liberated area of the country. But in Indonesia anti-colonialism became a whole way of political life.[4] The sole public goal of the Indonesian state for a number of years was to be anti-colonial, to mess around in Malaysia or foster the extensive foregatherings of the leaders of international neutralism.

It is, then, more than a little important to understand why wars of national liberation in colonial countries should bring about one of these results rather than the other. Anti-colonialism is a natural and in many parts of the world an eminently rational political emotion, but it is strikingly threadbare as a way of political life. During the colonial period itself, this exiguous provision may represent no material disadvantage: while the colonialists are there, being against them may provide guidance enough as to how to act. It is when they are gone that the poverty of the political vision begins to become apparent. But it is also, of course, true in contemporary geopolitical conditions – and it was even more so in those of ten or twenty years ago – that acquiring a Communist Party as a national government meant acquiring severe disadvantages as well as manifest gains. Just being anti-colonial the western powers (with the exception on occasion of the colonizing nation in question) could learn to put up with, if not necessarily actually to *enjoy*; but being Communist was a less acceptable political option. This is not a trivial matter. Marxism is a serious causal theory about how the world can become better. If acquiring a Communist government means consistently, in the American vernacular, to be bombed into the stone age (or in Professor Huntington's odd usage 'urbanized'), acquiring a Communist government is not a project one could recommend with confidence to any country. But in practice of course although the North Vietnamese population has paid a crippling price for this venture, the price has not quite reached the level of a return to the stone age. It seems likely, too, that its preparedness to pay the price it has (or perhaps one should say the preparedness of its *government* to pay this price) may well have done something to diminish the price that other countries will have to pay for the privilege, if they choose to try to acquire it.

The Communist Party came to power in North Vietnam through its leadership in a war of national liberation against French colonial reconquest. The forces which it was able to draw on in this struggle were those which in the case of China and Yugoslavia have been called forces of peasant nationalism. In Vietnam, as in both China and Yugoslavia, it is appropriate to divide these categories along elite/mass lines. The peasantry were anti-colonial, anti-French, because over a rather long time, the French colonial occupation had been a disagreeable experience as felt in the villages.[5] A large proportion of the peasantry might have preferred, as peasants are apt to do, not to take sides. But the vitality of the Communist struggle has forced a great many to do so. Faced with the choice between the Vietnamese Communist Parties in their nationalist guises, the Vietminh or the Vietcong, and the French or, as it later was, the Americans, it is scarcely surprising that the Vietnamese Communists should have seemed comparatively appealing. The response of the peasantry to Communist initiatives, peasant anti-colonialism, was a fairly reflex matter and it was clearly a much denser and more focussed emotional response, being the product of many decades of experience, than the reflex anti-foreign sentiment on which the Yugoslav or Chinese Communists were able to draw in their confrontation with Axis or Japanese occupying forces. It is easy to explain the development of the Vietnamese revolution in terms of this solidly available peasant (and, of course, industrial working class and plantation labour) hostility to the colonial power and its local personifications and there is no doubt that this does go far to explain the failure of the war of colonial reconquest. A great many colonies were predominantly peasant economies, with the greater part of their populations engaged in agricultural-commodity production. Such societies had obvious mechanisms for arousing peasant discontent of foreign rulers who affected the novel range of constraints upon their working lives in an often apparently whimsical fashion. When such a colony escaped completely, as Vietnam did towards the end of the Japanese occupation, from the structure of colonial social control for even a brief period and when it acquired a determined indigenous political leadership it was not an easy feat to return it to a structure of colonial social control. All this explains why Vietnam is no longer a French colony. But it would also explain why Indonesia is no longer a Dutch colony and why Algeria, for instance, is no longer a French colony and other cases too. However, not only is it not quite *true* as an explanation of why Algeria is no longer a French colony – the French were not defeated militarily in Algeria as they were in Indochina – but it fails also to explain why the Indonesian revolution and even the Algerian revolution were such different affairs in their consequences when compared with the Vietnamese revolution; why, to present the issue more simply, the Vietnamese Communists should have won a comparatively effortless control of the movement for national liberation, while both the Indonesian and Algerian Communist Parties elaborately failed to do so. In Yugoslavia, the Communist Party in effect secured such control under in many ways radically less promising circumstances simply because it alone made a serious attempt to bring about in a nationwide and ethnically egalitarian fashion the liberation of Yugoslavia as such. The only other contender for securing national liberation, Mihailović's Serbian units, were discredited as liberators of a united nation in a variety of eyes by their evident disinclination actually to *do* anything much in the way of liberation and by their association with the dominant ethnic group in the national territory over the last twenty years.

The national component of peasant nationalism in these revolutionary movements is necessarily in crucial respects an elite contribution, an identification of the boundaries of the national group designated for national liberation,[6] that is minimally for eventual recognition under international law as a sovereign political unit with an effective government. The Yugoslav Communist Party generated sufficient military power out of its impartial mobilization of peasant resentment against invasion throughout Yugoslavia, in the effort to liberate Yuogslavia as a whole, for it to earn extensive foreign support for its effort. The combination of foreign military support and nationwide potential for resistance gave it in due course national power. No equally neat explanation of the Vietnamese Communists's capture of Vietnamese nationalism as an elite posture can be provided. Other Vietnamese nationalists may have been to some extent discredited in some circles; but they were in no position to be as discredited as Mihailović necessarily was in numerous areas of Yugoslavia before the liberation struggle even began, simply because Mihailović was seen as the representative of a highly ethnically discriminatory government. The Popular Front character of nationalist struggle lasted much longer in Vietnam than it did in Yugoslavia, and in an important sense it persists today in South Vietnam. The achievement and even the maintenance of Communist dominance under these conditions is an elaborate business, very much a matter of superior skill at the more lethal forms of political infighting. In any attempt to estimate how far other contenders for a nationalist mantle were discredited, it would be prudent to bear in mind, for example, Ho Chi Minh's preparedness as late as 1947 to keep the former emperor Bao Dai as honorific Supreme Adviser to the Republican Government,[7] not a role which it is easy to imagine Tito proffering to King Peter of Yugoslavia. Ho clearly had a fairly cautious assessment of the degree to which even traditional authorities in Vietnam should be considered as discredited. The Communist Party did win control of Vietnamese nationalism and other contenders for its control may have been in part discredited. But it would be rash to assume that it was only because the other contenders were in part discredited that the Communists won control. This is particularly important because it marks off the Vietnamese revolution from the Chinese, otherwise an obvious model, in one decisive way. The Chinese Communists led a war of national liberation because they had amassed a great deal of power, even before the Japanese invaded by proving themselves locally an equitable government. Their military success arose out of their capacity to confront the ineluctable problems of Chinese rural society at least locally. Their nationalist opponents, the Kuomintang, had shown themselves incapable of the latter and reluctant to say the least to make much of an effort at leading a war of national liberation. The Vietnamese Communists like the Chinese, had nationalist opponents, the V.N.Q.D.D., and these closely resembled, and indeed were in alliance with, the K.M.T. But the Vietnamese Communists' triumph over these opponents, even if it is arguably likely to be to the eventual net advantage of the Vietnamese population, did not as it had done in China, result from the demonstrated political ineptitude or irresponsibility of these opponents, since the latter had never had the opportunity to show whether or not they did deserve power.

There were in fact a substantial number of differences between the Indonesian and Vietnamese cases, one of them simply being the very heavy taxation of Vietnamese rice-cultivators.[8] A large part of Indonesian anti-colonial dissidence outside the cities and the ranks of the elites came from labour employed on the large-scale plantations, while the Vietnamese insurrection was able in the long run to call on massive *peasant* support. Another important difference was the obviously much greater strength of the national factor in Vietnam than in Indonesia. A third difference was the Islamic character of much Indonesian mass organization: on the whole inimical to Communist control.[9] But probably the most important single contrast came in the circumstances in which power had to be seized by the nationalist movement, a contrast in some ways of a highly contingent character, having to do with the comparative time-scale and intensity of the Japanese occupation,[10] the fact that the French Vichy government was supposedly not hostile to the Japanese, while Indonesia was in fact simply treated like a conquered province, though it was not described as such. By the time that the Japanese control of Indonesia could be broken, a very broad nationalist movement, large sections of which had been organized under Japanese tutelage had come into existence. Dutch colonial social control had been disrupted for years. Hence when a war of colonial reconquest could at last be undertaken, the broadly-based and highly syncretistic nationalist government enjoyed too wide support for it to be crushed by military means at any level economically acceptable to the Dutch. In Vietnam, because of the Vichy government's status,[11] the structure of colonial social control was disrupted by the Japanese over a very much shorter time-scale. Furthermore no large organizations of Vietnamese were recruited by the Japanese to assist their military control and no set of members of the Vietnamese elite were employed by them as prominent agents in civil administration. In Indonesia the nationalist movement in effect simply inherited power from the Japanese masters whom many of them had been engaged at least for a time in serving, though they were obliged eventually to fight extensively to defend their inherited power against the return of their former Dutch masters. Formally it might seem that something similar might have been true in Vietnam since, in Hanoi at least, the Japanese did surrender their arms to the Vietminh. But in substance the situation was very different. The Vietminh had not collaborated with the Japanese, as the majority of Indonesian nationalists had done.[12] It was the French colonists who had collaborated with the Japanese in Vietnam, while the Vietminh had been the sole group to attempt any very concerted and long-drawn-out resistance.[13] They had acquired certain minor advantages from this obduracy even during the belated Japanese occupation, in the shape of very modest American military assistance in return for help in recovering shot-down American

pilots. But they had operated almost entirely in areas very
remote from major population centres. Their crucial advantage was that they were the only organized and effective
nationalist force in operation and they had the nerve, as Lenin
had had in October 1917, to take power at a time that no one
else among either the Vietnamese nationalists or the colonial
forces was in a position to do so, and the nerve too to hang
on after they had taken power.

The Vietnamese revolution was in the first instance simply
a *putsch*, though a *putsch* conducted in a temporary total
vacuum of authority. But in Vietnam, unlike Russia, it was
a *putsch* the results of which had to be defended overwhelmingly against power from outside the society rather than
against power from within it. It was a *putsch* which became
a war of national liberation because of the massive initial
success of the French war of colonial reconquest. The first
part of this war lasted until 1954[14] and in the second part of it,
still in a refracted way a struggle against colonial reconquest,
the end is even now not yet in sight. As protracted wars go,
it has already lasted under the Communist banner longer
than the military phase of the Chinese revolution and no one
knows yet when it will come to a finish. In this period in the
north, and in many ways in the south too, the Vietnamese
Communists contrived to win and hold the leadership in a
war of national liberation. Those who wished to win independence for Vietnam more than they wished not to be ruled
by a Communist government joined the Vietminh and fought
for them. Once the war of colonial reconquest had begun,
quite large sections of Vietnamese society even in the villages
were forced more or less actively to choose between these alternatives. Most Vietnamese had some reason to prefer the
French gone and initially the Vietminh took some pains to
see that few had strong reasons for disliking being ruled by
Communists and that, of those who did have such reasons at
an elite level, they took even more pains to see that a fair
number of them ended up dead. In this context it was important, as it was for instance in Yugoslavia, that the groups
which did have strong reason for not wishing to be ruled in
due course by Communists were for a variety of reasons not
at all well-placed to assume leadership of a Vietnamese
national movement. The Catholics in the ecclesiastical fiefs

of the north in the Red River valley, some of the ethnically non-Vietnamese mountain tribes,[15] much of the membership of the sects in the South, the Cao Dai and the Hoa Hao,[16] viewed the prospect of Communist success at times with severe misgivings; but all of them were in some measure extrinsic to the main body of Vietnamese society, village-based, lowland, rice-growing, syncretistically Confucian/Buddhist, ethnically and linguistically Vietnamese.

Vietnam had been a cultural and even intermittently a political entity for nearly a millennium.[17] There was a Vietnamese nation to liberate, though French administrative structures had attempted to break it up and French cultural policies to erode its identity. It had, to be sure, as the British or the French nations themselves had, a number of excrescences from the viewpoint of the core nationality. There were abundant potential separatisms for the colonial power (or as it later became the neocolonial power) to exploit in the effort to restore its political and military domination. But the only symbolically effective competitor with the Vietminh for national representation, the traditional authorities of Vietnam, in effect conceded the struggle before open conflict even began when the emperor Bao Dai abdicated in favour of Ho Chi Minh's provisional government.[18] Partly because Vietnam was a colony and China was not, the Chinese revolution was more involved with internal class struggle throughout its course than the Vietnamese struggle was to be, at least until victory had been won. There was little in the way of a Vietnamese bourgeoisie. Bourgeois economic roles were filled mostly by nationals of the colonial power and by Chinese. There was a modern educated class, what could be politely called an intelligentsia; but this had more extensive reasons as a class for hating the French than for distrusting the Communists; indeed it was the main source of their cadres for the Communists. Even large-scale Vietnamese landowners were not necessarily more favourable to the French than to the Vietminh. Even in China crucial elite segments were in the end forced to choose between the short-run interests of the class, very broadly the land-owning gentry, from which they came and the interests of the Chinese nation. It was a protracted choice precisely because it was in many respects such a stark one. But in Vietnam the internal tensions of

Vietnamese society were initially, and are to some degree still today, less salient than the conflict between foreign economic or geopolitical interests and the unity and independence of the Vietnamese nation. By establishing a national government in place of the French colonial state and by fighting to defend it against French efforts at colonial reconquest, the Vietminh, who were in effect, despite the fact that the Indochinese Communist Party had been formally disbanded,[19] simply the Vietnamese Communists, inherited the Vietnamese national allegiance. This is not to say that the majority of the Vietnamese population would necessarily have identified themselves in 1945 or 1954 or perhaps even today with such an entity as 'the Vietnamese nation', still less that they would cheerfully die for it. Even in the developed industrial countries with democratic constitutions, real wars have to be fought by conscript armies, a coercive rather than voluntaristic mode of recruiting. In national insurrections against alien states, there is necessarily much that is brutally coercive about the recruitment procedures adopted. But in terms of available quantitative brutality, the modern armies of the French and later of the United States necessarily have access to a level of pure coercion which the terror of Vietminh or Vietcong could hardly match except in a very intermittent fashion. The reason why the coercion applied by the insurgents has been so much more effective is that pure coercion is necessarily less effective than coercion exercised on behalf of intelligible moral solidarities. No doubt one should not present too roseate a view of the intimate moral solidarity sensed between bemused peasantry and harassed guerrilla organizer. But it hardly seems surprising that in bulk the notion should seem more plausible along lines of ethnic identity than when stretched to the French or the Americans. And if the relationship between touted moral solidarity and lethal revenge seems disquietingly close, it is worth remembering that touting for moral solidarities in occupied countries is a necessarily emotionally taut activity, as the fate of tens of thousands of 'collaborators' in western Europe in the closing stages of the last war shows very clearly. Given that the Vietminh, as the only organized group in a position to do so, *did* assert the interests of the Vietnamese nation in 1945, it is not surprising that they contrived to win over to their side most of those with a strong allegiance to Vietnamese national independence, and that nothing but a variety of separatisms was in the end left over to augment the energies of the French and later the Americans. If the bulk of the population remained as neutral as they could, as far as active participation and willing acceptance of risk was concerned, the balance of energies between ideologically devoted partisans of a united independent Vietnam and essentially defensive separatist interests was likely over time to be an unequal one. Recently it has taken a uniquely massive weight of foreign firepower to keep the balance from tipping decisively once again, as it did at Dienbienphu.[20]

The Vietnamese revolution, the assumption of power by a Communist government in North Vietnam in 1954 (as perhaps its eventual extension to South Vietnam will do), happened because there was a Vietnamese nation to liberate from French colonial control. But liberating a nation from French colonial control – and even now completing its liberation from neocolonial control has not been a simple matter. The relationship between national independence and revolutionary success is more intricate than this glib equation suggests. For one thing, it is still almost as opaque for Vietnam as it is for China what the Vietnamese revolution means, apart from the simple attainment of national independence by a Communist government. Even the latter struggle is far from complete and the effort to extend Chinese formalizations of the class struggle into North Vietnamese villages after the acquisition of national power created quite large-scale peasant revolt in the traditionally most revolutionary province of Vietnam, the birthplace of Ho Chi Minh.[21] What Communist rule is likely to mean in a country which could not in principle undertake fully autarkic industrialization, despite already possessing substantial industry, and which has a historically uneasy relationship with its great neighbour, China,[22] is still unclear. The evidence suggests that the North Vietnamese leadership might have been quite pleased to be left to work out an answer to this question; but Diem's attempt to establish a Latin Kingdom of Saigon in the South led the Vietminh's southern residue to involve the North once again in active attempts to reunite the country.[23]

A further intricacy to the relationship between national

independence and revolutionary success lies in the ethnic makeup of the population of the land area which now consists of North and South Vietnam. For, if Vietnam is now fighting a classic war of liberation against colonial rule and its neocolonial replacement, the greater part of the history of Vietnam is a history of successful imperialism in the classic pre-capitalist mode.[24] Much of the land area of Vietnam, particularly the Mekong valley and Cochin China in general was only conquered by Vietnam in the mid-eighteenth century, while Vietnamese control over Cambodia, also a component of French Indochina, was not fully established until the nineteenth century. The area of Vietnam designated for liberation was never as extensive as the area of the former Vietnamese empire. It included the three French provinces of Cochin China, Annam and Tonking, but excluded Cambodia and Laos, parts of which had belonged to the empire. Even inside the three ethnically Vietnamese provinces, the extent of Vietnamese ethnic domination reflects the decisive impact of the Vietnamese's own colonization process. In 1962 the total Vietnamese population was estimated at $30\frac{1}{2}$ million. Of these only some 15 per cent were estimated to be ethnically non-Vietnamese: some $3\frac{1}{2}$ million hill tribesmen in North and South, Thai, Meo, Muong, about a million Chinese and some half-million Khmers.[25] In the area which the Vietnamese Communists set themselves to liberate, the core of Vietnamese nationality was heavily demographically preponderant. There is no doubt that a reconstitution of a Vietnamese state was potentially highly unwelcome to some of the non-Vietnamese groups: the feelings of Khmers in Cambodia itself, for instance, have recently been made very tragically evident. But the relative weights of numbers involved made it far easier in Vietnam to consolidate national feeling around a political identity taken from a core nationality. By contrast in Yugoslavia the core nationality, the Serbs, constituted a relatively small proportion of the total Yugoslav population. Both Vietnam and Serbia were peasant warrior kingdoms whose political control had come to extend over alien ethnic groups. When it came to competition for liberating populations from alien occupation Serbian political dominance proved too recent and too extensive for its own good. Too many Yugoslavs had reasons for disliking the Serbs because of their recent control of state power. Vietnamese ethnic assertiveness was much older and had been much more thorough. It was also desirably detached from recent exercise of state power. Thus when the formal representative of the Vietnamese nation, the emperor, recognized the incapacity of his office to take on the real political responsibilities of power and abdicated, there was a national identity with wide symbolic plausibility in elite circles and with numerically restricted counterbalancing disadvantages at a mass level for his successors to assume. This serves to explain the national component of the victorious war of national liberation, why Vietnamese ethnic identity (at least as counterposed to French or American) should have formed an effective focus for mass military and political mobilization. But it does not explain why the Vietnamese Communists contrived to lead the movement or why the movement was to such a degree successful. To complete this sketch of an explanation of why the Vietnamese revolution has taken place as it has, it is necessary to understand three matters: why the impact of French colonialism had been sufficiently traumatic to arouse large numbers of people to fight against its return, why it was that the Vietnamese elites did not contrive to create any alternative viable political organization or ideology of resistance in the period leading up to the Vietminh revolt, and why it was that the Vietminh *did* manage to establish a provisional government in 1945 which did not simply collapse in the face of French reconquest. It is really only the second of these three issues which presents particularly intractable problems. The continuous corporate integration of the Vietnamese village formed a powerful instrument for the organization of a national liberation movement and the impact of the world economy had been sufficiently disruptive in effect and coercive in style for it to maintain fairly steady anti-colonial resistance throughout the French occupation: the tradition of anti-colonial rebellion never waned for long in Vietnam from the invasion of Cochin China onwards.[26] Equally the process by which Ho contrived during the wartime to develop a political equipe capable of seizing power, despite its largely clandestine character and its undoubted tactical intricacy is not essentially puzzling in outline.[27] But the answer to the second question, why it was that Vietnamese elites failed to produce any effective alternative political organization or ideology of resistance to compete against the Vietminh in 1945, is not so easy to pronounce with any confidence. There had in fact been a whole range of nationalist revolts reaching back virtually to the beginning of the French occupation. As early as 1862, only three years after the French invasion of Cochin China, a placard was found by the French near a village which threatened them with ceaseless resistance: 'We fear your valour, but we fear Heaven more than your power. We swear to fight on for ever, and without relaxing. When we have no other resources left, we shall take branches of trees and make them into banners and sticks to arm our soldiers. How then will you be able to live among us?'[28]

Pacification in Annam was not completed until the Muong tribesmen handed over the refugee child-king Ham-Nghi, in 1888 and in Tonking the delta was pacified only in 1892 and the mountains by 1900. Between 1900 and 1930 resistance was sporadic and local. But in 1930 the nationalist party, the V.N.Q.D.D., provoked a revolt of Vietnamese soldiers at Yen Bay, the Communists organized soviets among the peasantry of Nghe-An, and there was widespread peasant and industrial unrest.[29] It was estimated that there were 10,000 political prisoners in the major jails in 1932.[30] Both Communists and Trotskyists achieved a certain amount of overt popular support during the interlude of participatory opportunity provided by the relative leniency of the Popular Front government in France itself.[31] The Marxist groups made more attempt than others to amalgamate nationalist political demands and general agitation about social and economic conditions. Particularly among the mining and industrial labour force this approach proved effective, though the industrial labour force (especially under conditions of externally undisturbed colonial control) was in no position to head a successful struggle for national liberation. The contrast with Algeria is instructive. The Algerian example shows clearly that to acquire leadership in an eventually successful struggle for national liberation does not necessarily demand that an elite group should have any clear idea at all about how to handle the problems of the nation it will create in the event of victory. It also suggests that relationships between a metropolitan and a colonial Communist Party may have very strong

effects on the prospects for success of the colonial party. Insofar as there was an Algerian proletariat it was largely resident in France and it was largely organized in a working-class
movement, the *Étoile Nord-Africaine* of Messali Hadj which
was in the end to prove hostile not only to Communism but
also to the Algerian revolution itself. In the case of Algeria
the French Communist Party acted in effect as the advocate
of French national economic interests and indeed political
interests in the 1930s during the Popular Front period,
Thorez for instance maintaining the position that Algeria
was an integral part of France.[32] Consequently the *Étoile
Nord-Africaine* became anti-Communist and on occasion
pro-Fascist. Perhaps equally important, Algeria was a Muslim
country and mass feeling, as to some degree in Indonesia, was
apt to be exceedingly uneasy at being co-opted by an avowedly atheist political movement like Communism. In Vietnam the French Communist Party was not injudicious enough
to take up very specific positions about its ideal future political status while the colonial regime was effectively entrenched and its subsequent (from the Vietnamese point of
view extremely disappointing) response to the beginnings of
the Vietminh struggle for independence came too late to
have much effect on the Vietminh in nationalist eyes.[33] The
Étoile Nord-Africaine was a strongly Islamic and an ideologically rather unsophisticated organization. Its elite appeal in
Algeria was exiguous; but its capacity to reach the masses,
where made accessible by their participation in industrial
production, was beyond doubt. How far in contrast it may
have helped the Vietnamese Communists to attract the support of the mass of the Vietnamese population that Vietnamese religious values were for the most part Confucian or
Buddhist or vaguely syncretistic (or even possibly just that
they were *not* Islamic), it is not easy to say. But it does seem
plausible that folk-Islamic beliefs widely accepted provide
some impediment to the mobilization of large bodies of
people behind an overtly secular nationalist leadership. To
put the point differently, in an Islamic society, intellectuals
with an Islamic accreditation, whether traditionalist or modernist, are better placed to communicate effectively the existence of a broad national interest to the mass of the population
than any strictly secular competitor could be. Arguably, the

construction of solidarities by Islamic elites in Islamic societies has not yet proved anywhere a very effective manner of
providing for a government capable of carrying out a social
revolution of a modernizing sort. It is not clear that this has
to continue to be true; but it has plausibly been so thus far.
At an elite level in Vietnam, Chesneaux among others has
argued,[34] the Confucian heritage provides an emotionally
comfortable and conceptually accessible entry for the militantly secular and socially responsible doctrines of Communism. At a mass level the point seems more a negative than a
positive one. Vietnamese mass social behaviour is certainly
historically concerned with accepting the political authority
of an intelligentsia and many of the Vietminh cadres were
recruited from these social roles. And the variety of popular
religious beliefs, being for the most part quasi-magical and
localist in reference or heavily transcendental in character, do
not provide any particularly strong reasons for mass rejection
of Communist authority as such.[35] The extent to which
effective challenge to the Communists' national pretensions
has come from the comparatively small religious group of
Catholics suggests that the facilitating role of traditional religious attitudes may be of some importance in explaining the
possibility of Communist triumph.

Pursuing a more rationalist tack in the effort to explain the
extent of Marxist influence in the colonial resistance movements after 1930, it may be illuminating to consider the
possible ideological repertoire open to the traditional elites of
Vietnam in the more modern roles which their abler children
were given the opportunity to assume. Vietnamese elite civilization was Confucian in its essential character, but it was
also linguistically and thus in some respects culturally non-
Chinese. Confucianism was the operational ideology of
Chinese civilization. Vietnamese history revolved around the
effort to escape Chinese domination.[36] For China Vietnam was
Annam, the pacified South, an insubordinate and successfully insubordinate province masquerading as an independent empire. For Vietnam China was a millennial political
and military threat. Confucianism was a universalist ideology, but its presence in Vietnam was causally associated with
Chinese imperial power. From the point of view of the political elite the Vietnamese nation as an ethnic and linguistic

entity with more than a millennium of its own history could be detached from Confucianism the ideology which sanctioned mandarin roles, with an ease which could hardly be matched in China itself. In China, as Levenson has shown in his study of Liang Ch'i-Ch'ao,[37] the choice between culturalism, the preservation of the universal status of Confucian civilization, and nationalism, the preservation of the political viability of the Chinese state, was one of terrifying bleakness. In Vietnam a decidedly more tactical eye could safely be cultivated. The first modernist protagonist of Vietnamese nationalism, Phan Boi Chau, went to Japan in 1904 to study how Asian countries could learn to cope with modernity, there being at the time nowhere else to go.[38] He visited the Chinese scholars, Liang Ch'i-Ch'ao and K'ang Yu-Wei, smuggled into exile by the Japanese government in the wake of an unsuccessful Chinese reform movement. A year later Phan returned to Tokyo with a member of the Vietnamese royal family and founded an elite League for the Modernization of Vietnam.[39] This organization never had any very dramatic impact in Vietnam, though some of its members joined the first significantly Communist-influenced Vietnamese nationalist movement, the Revolutionary League of Annamite Youth, two decades later. Ideologically the appeal of Japan was unlikely to prove very lasting despite the extent of its industrial success. Its efficacy against European imperialism was rather soon offset by its aptness to prove even more imperialist on its own behalf. Liang Ch'i-Ch'ao for example had come to see by 1915 that Japan was probably more of a threat to the viability of the Chinese state than any western power.[40]

The next ideological and organizational focus for Vietnamese nationalism, the V.N.Q.D.D., was modelled on the Kuomintang. Its combination of modernist militarization and protection of traditional interests under a nationalist banner exerted some appeal, particularly, naturally enough, among the colonial armed forces.[41] But developments in China from 1927 onwards hardly enhanced its mass appeal, and in many respects its attractions even to the more prosperous in a fully colonial situation were necessarily less than they were in the peculiar conditions of China itself. The slightly painful pseudo-traditionalism of the Kuomintang[42] lacked in Vietnam the residual point which it possessed in China of maintaining

the illusion of cultural continuity. Only the remaining employees of the imperial court at Hue had any direct group
motive in terms of their own interests for preserving a traditionalist interpretation of the existing situation or a traditionalist solution for its discontents. The modernist elites and
sub-elites had many reasons for wanting the liberation of
Vietnam from colonial rule, but they had little need for it to
remain Confucian in its liberated condition. The key point
was made rather cruelly by Liang Ch'i-Ch'ao, a *Chinese*
thinker, when he explained the conquest of Annam by the
extent to which its national culture had become too heavily
contaminated by Chinese elements for its integrity to escape
destruction.[43] What had once to Chinese eyes seemed the victorious march of universal (that is: Chinese, Confucian)
civilization into a territory in which Chinese political control
had lapsed became to the eyes of a modern nationalist (even
a Chinese nationalist) a disastrous instance of cultural mis-
cegenation. It required a long, painful and noisy debate in
the laboratory of imperialist pressure to separate Confucian
culturalism from Chinese nationalism in China itself. In
Vietnam even a Chinaman could see the artificiality of the
conjunction and in effect could *blame* the conjunction for the
sorry fate of the Pacified South. If in 1900 Vietnam was an
awful warning to China and its aspirant nationalist rescuers,
by 1937 China had contrived to become an awful warning to
Vietnam and to the protagonists of the effort to recapture its
national independence. This effect was particularly important in determining the eventual allegiance of the Vietnamese
nationalist movement because of the particular impact of
French colonialism on Vietnamese economic relations.

Very heavy colonial taxation in the effort to make the colonial administration self-sufficient, and extensive French
land-appropriation in Cochin China, the first area colonized
by France,[44] had dragged the great majority of the non-
mountain population, however reluctantly, into commodity
production for the world market. Rice had been a traditional
food crop, but little of it was exported – less than 60,000 tons
a year in 1860, before the French occupation. By 1937 $1\frac{1}{2}$
million tons were exported annually.[45] The stability of the
Vietnamese currency, pegged to silver in the aftermath of the
First World War, encouraged heavy French capital invest-

ment, particularly in mining and in industrial production in the north and in rubber plantations in the south.[46] Highly coercive methods of labour recruiting in addition to the massive tax burden and to the concentration of landholdings, particularly in the south, created rumbling agrarian discontent, and, in the urban and industrial areas, a labour force rapid in turnover and extremely restive in disposition. The V.N.Q.D.D. made little systematic effort to exploit this agrarian and urban discontent; but the various groups of Marxist-inspired nationalists, both Communists and Trotskyists, addressed themselves to doing so with considerable effect and their efforts were at times significantly facilitated by changes in French domestic politics, particularly in the period of the Popular Front.[47] The French colonial administration found it easy to maintain control over this largely urban movement focussed on the modern sector of the economy, just as the K.M.T. government had managed to do in China. Furthermore, as long as the structure of colonial social control was not challenged externally by force of arms, the effort to establish liberated areas in the countryside of any significance was necessarily doomed to failure.[48] But if the largely urban or elite base of the movement restricted its effectiveness as long as French colonial rule continued unimpaired, it is scarcely surprising that the K.M.T. model of nationalism did not greatly appeal to it. The fact that the K.M.T. government could and did control the Chinese proletariat with ease could not be expected to recommend a K.M.T. interpretation of the proper contours of Vietnamese nationalism to the Vietnamese proletariat.

The elements of the explanation are now available. Vietnam was a colony of an effective modern state, the French Republic. For there to be any Vietnamese revolution, any successful rising against the colonial state structure, there had first to be some external challenge to this state structure. This is plainly a contentious judgement – the case of Algeria in particular might be thought to tell against it. But there seems strong reason to argue that it does not do so and that indeed the French military defeat in Vietnam may well have been a necessary condition for the success of the Algerian revolution.[49] The invasion of the French colony by the Japanese and their eventual disposal of French authority in the colony in

March 1945 gave the various Vietnamese nationalist groups
inside the country, in practice the Vietminh and the Trotskyists, the opportunity to organize extensively for resistance.[50]
Two months after the Japanese seizure of the government, in
May 1945, the Vietminh announced slightly grandiosely the
establishment of a liberated area in six provinces north of the
Red River running up to the mountains on the Chinese
border.[51] In August Bao Dai, reacting to a demand from the
Hanoi General Association of Students under a former
Trotskyist leader, abdicated in favour of the Vietminh. It
took another nine years of energetic political activity and
intermittent heavy fighting before the Vietminh consolidated
its control of North Vietnam and it has taken already another
eighteen years since the Geneva agreements of 1954 for the
movement for a reunification of Vietnam under Communist
auspices to reach its present dimensions. Throughout the first,
the pre-1954, war the determination and skill, political and
military, of the Vietnamese Communist leadership under Ho
Chi Minh was a prerequisite for success.[52] There is a direct
link between the qualities displayed in this triumph and the
constraints which have forced the North Vietnamese leadership into a continuation of the struggle in the effort to promote reunification. The ability and ruthlessness of the
Communist leadership enabled them to seize control of Vietnamese nationalist energies, of the urge to re-establish a
united and independent Vietnam, and to win for these
energies an impressive level of victory. But in the aftermath
of the Geneva agreement and the application of the counter-
vailing energies of the Catholic Ngo Dinh Diem, the force of
the energies for national reunification which they had canal-
ized drove the North Vietnamese leadership out of the comfortable routines of building a Communist nation in North
Vietnam into the in many ways reckless national adventure
of liberating the whole Vietnamese nation. What had enabled
the Communists to establish in the first place an *équipe*
capable of seizing control of Vietnamese nationalist energies
is a subtle and in some ways still rather inscrutable question.
It is true that the Vietminh was the only group to maintain
any level of systematic hostility to the Japanese throughout
the occupation, because of the continued existence of a Vichy
colonial regime for most of the war.[53] But the circumstances

in which the Vietminh had to maintain their organizational identity in even rather restricted conflict with the Japanese forces were highly disadvantageous in many respects. Ho Chi Minh was obliged to organize the Vietminh largely from southern China in association with the K.M.T. government, in particular with the general who controlled Kwangsi province and Yunnan.[54] He was forced for a time to work through an organization which included elements of the V.N.Q.D.D. which had gone into exile after the failure of the Yen Bay mutiny in 1930. He was even jailed at one point by the Chinese authorities because of their fear of Communist influence in the nationalist movement.[55] But the Vietminh were considerably the most effective elements among the nationalists, because of their greatly superior contacts inside Vietnam and the Chinese eventually decided to release Ho, because of the comparative ineffectiveness of their own supporters.[56] The superior discipline and external organizational linkages of the Communists enabled them over time to out-manoeuvre their Trotskyist contenders for leadership of the nationalist movement inside Vietnam itself, and their access to significant popular support in Vietnam itself as a result of their leadership in protests on economic and social issues before the war enabled them to out-manoeuvre their V.N.Q.D.D. opponents, even when it came to cooperating with the K.M.T. government.

But the key component of the explanation must be an account of what they had succeeded in co-opting in gaining control of the movement for Vietnamese national reunification and independence. It would be a considerable mistake to adopt a simplistically causal account of the Vietnamese revolution in which the character of the Vietnamese national heritage and of the Vietnamese colonial experience was *bound* to produce a national elite capable of leading Vietnam to victory first against the French and in the long run to some degree perhaps even against the Americans. Other nationalists at other points in time might have led such a movement with very different prospects of success. It was not a necessary consequence of the internal development of French colonial society or of the heritage of the Vietnamese nation that Vietnam was invaded by the Japanese (still less that metropolitan France had to submit to the Vichy government). Had the

Japanese invasion happened some fifteen years earlier it is quite possible that a V.N.Q.D.D.-type party might have led the struggle; and it is equally possible that under these circumstances the anti-colonial movement might not have resulted in military victory. Vietnam would never have been a country, for example, in which for *Indonesian* nationalists to lead a revolution. The Communists were well-placed to provide leadership in 1945 and the leadership which they did provide over the succeeding years was both heroic and effective. Its efficacy depended upon the heroism and upon the extent of the support which this succeeded in winning from Vietnamese society at large. It remains to consider why it did succeed in winning such support. Vietnam as a unit ceased to exist (not for the first time) between 1858 and 1883 with the French conquests, becoming simply a number of components of French Indochina, the colony of Cochin China and the protectorates of Annam and Tonking.[57] The name itself ceased to be used. The first modernist Vietnamese nationalist Phan Boi Chau revived it in 1905 in the title of his League for the Modernization of Vietnam[58] and it recurred more prominently from the 1920s onwards in the titles of nationalist organizations. The Vietnamese traditional elite, the custodians of more than a millennium of distinctive Vietnamese national history, were a mandarin elite. Access to public office both in the imperial court at Hue and in the provinces was through competition in public examinations. The ideology sanctioning the political structure as a whole was Confucian. The mandarins were recruited in practice largely from the more prosperous landholders and the rewards of public office served to maintain the economic position of wealthier land-holding families. Not all Confucian scholars wished to enter, let alone succeeded in entering, the mandarin ranks. Much of the resistance in the early stages of French colonial conquest was led by such scholars living relatively modestly in the villages, after centralized resistance from the imperial bureaucracy had lapsed.[59] Over the decades the rural gentry of Vietnam adapted themselves with varying enthusiasm to the changes in the economy produced by the French. Sporadic tax revolt continued in the villages, but nationalism became increasingly focused on the towns and particularly on the educated groups in these. Confucian education was replaced by modern education as a mode of access to remunerative employment and the universalism of modern scientific and democratic attitudes replaced that of Confucianism among the educated. The Vietnamese Communist Party in a colonial context had no difficulty in addressing itself to the feelings of the urban young in readily intelligible accents. Ho Chi Minh as a national leader had a cosmopolitan breadth of experience and a familiarity with the operating character of the Communist movement in several different countries which could be matched among Chinese Communist leaders perhaps only by Chou En-Lai. In many respects, too, the crudity of colonial exploitation gave to the vulgar presentation of Marxist categories a psychological immediacy and a depth of conviction which in the complicated and anomic disarray of Kuomintang China it was more difficult for them to attain. Vietnam never wholly lost a national elite preoccupied with the necessity for its renewal. It was always clear, too, that renewal minimally required the regaining of national autonomy. Communism was merely the clearest and most purposeful and most rhetorically effective presentation of the universalist status of this goal in the modernist idiom to come their way. They had little motive as a group to hesitate over adopting it and it fitted admirably with the peasants' (rather accurate) sense of the historical misuse to which the colonial regime had subjected them. In these several ways Communism was an ideal ideology to sanction the renewal of the Vietnamese nation. Rather more contingently, it was also the ideology adopted by the best organized militant group in a position to bid for national power at the beginning of 1945. Rather less contingently, its adoption lent the Vietnamese drive for national liberation a determination and a solidity in the teeth of massive military opposition which are unique in modern history.

6 *Algeria*

In 1954 the first stage of the Vietnamese revolution came to an end with the establishment of the Democratic Republic of Vietnam. The French had suffered an overwhelming military defeat at Dienbienphu and it was clear that their chances of contriving to bring off a reconquest of the whole of Indochina at any remotely tolerable cost had simply ceased to exist. The liquidation of French assets in Indochina, the acceptance of the loss of plantations, factories, mines and rice-production was an economic blow, but one which, with the prospect of access to a unitary western European market, many French political leaders could accept with equanimity. The national humiliation of failure in a war of colonial reconquest, though real enough in the ranks of the regular officer corps of the army, was not supplemented by any intolerable level of economic loss for the French nation as a whole. The total number of Frenchmen involved in the colonial presence in Indochina had never been enormous except specifically in the military effort at colonial reconquest. Moreover the commitment to this reconquest on the part of sections of the regular officer corps was hardly matched throughout the ranks of the army, particularly among the many conscripts. While only a few Frenchmen remained for long in the independent state of North Vietnam, much of the *colon* population had always resided in the former province of Cochin China, an area which was entirely inside the territory of the state which was established in the south as a result of the way in which the Geneva agreements of 1954 were implemented. Naturally enough under these circumstances much of the former *colon* population continued to reside there. In sum, the liquidation of French colonial control in Indochina was hardly a crippling disaster for the metropolitan country. Its retrospective painlessness (as opposed to the vague continuing distress evoked by the manner in which it had been brought about) helped accordingly to facilitate a slightly lighter touch in the process of decolonization in many other parts of the former French empire in due course. But while 1954 saw the end of French colonial repression in Vietnam and the acceptance by France of the independence of both parts of a divided Vietnam, it also saw the beginning of an armed struggle for independence in another portion of the empire in which metropolitan acquiescence was politically far more difficult to concede. The revolt unleashed, largely in the Aurès mountains, in 1954 by the Revolutionary Committee for Unity and Action, the future F.L.N., was initially a feeble affair involving only a few hundred men and with an armament perhaps restricted to several dozen obsolete shotguns.[1] But it grew in scale and impact with some rapidity and the strains in the French body politic created by the effort to repress it in the end brought down the Fourth Republic and then created a large-scale military revolt against its Gaullist successor. The Algerian revolution was successful, insofar as it was so at all, not because of the extent of its military triumph which even after seven-and-a-half years of fighting was exiguous, but because the internal divisions of France and the vast cost to the metropolitan country which the struggle had meant simply made its continuation intolerable. In many ways the economic relationship between the French and Algerian economies has been until very recently little impaired from the French point of view by the independence of Algeria. The end product of vast military and economic effort in a war of colonial repression, viewed in the light of hindsight, has not proved strikingly different in Algeria from what it did in Vietnam. Hence *one* aspect of a war for national liberation in Algeria which was in the end politically successful, even if it was never militarily a clear victory, which may seem puzzling is simply why it was necessary at all: why in 1954 France was prepared to face going the whole way through the script all over again. In order to begin to understand why Algerian national liberation could only come by military means – though it could not come by military means only – which is also to begin to understand what the Algerian revolution was, it is necessary to revert to the perspective of 1954. At that time the idea that the petty brigand attacks in the Aurès meant the beginning of a national movement which would lead France to the brink of civil war and force it to decide to abandon its substantial European colonial population in Algeria, would have seemed extravagantly far-fetched. Algeria was formally a part of Metropolitan France. The French presence in Algeria went back slightly further in time than in Vietnam and it was also demographically far more extensive than it had been in Vietnam. Algerian agricultural production, particularly production of the major cash crop, wine grapes, was heavily dependent on the protected French domestic market. Several hundred thousand Algerian proletarians worked in the industries of metropolitan France and, particularly in the Kabyle mountains,[2] their remittances home had become a necessary component for bare subsistence among substantial portions of the population. The intimacy of the legal tie between Algeria and France, the degree of dependence of the Algerian on the French economy and the bulk of the French and other European population permanently resident in the territory all militated against speedy decolonization. Indeed the intimacy of the legal tie in effect affirmed that decolonization was not so much unlikely or undesirable as impossible, since Algeria was not in fact a colony at all. Both ideologically and politically metropolitan France was in no position to retire gracefully from the scene. It was also not clear just what Algeria as such stood to gain economically from a sundering of the carefully complementary French and Algerian economies, since at this point no one's eyes were on the control of the Saharan oil deposits, which has formed the basis for most of the improvement of the relative positions of the two economies which the Algerian independent government has set itself to bring about. To put the point very crudely; it was easy enough to see what members of Algerian elites might hope to gain from anti-colonial insurrection – roughly, the roles currently occupied by the *colons* – but it was nothing like as easy to see what the majority of the Algerian population could hope to gain from the change. It was also perfectly clear that only very extensive popular support for the rebels was at all likely to threaten French control to any significant degree. How could any group of the Algerian population hope to elicit the necessary level of support?

It is around the answer to this question that any explanation of the character of the present Algerian regime, the product of the revolution, and of the degree of military and political success enjoyed by the revolutionary forces, any explanation of what the Algerian revolution has turned out to be and of why it happened at all, must be arranged. As phrased, it is plainly a slightly artificial dilemma. The mass component of anti-colonial revolution is likely to be of a largely reflex character and most unlikely to be predicated on any particularly clear picture of the regime which it is hoped will supplant the colonial regime. Colonial populations most commonly know what they do not like – an immediately given experience – but they are seldom in any position to know what they would like among such regimes as remain real possibilities in the post-colonial situation. It is minimally necessary that the regime which it is hoped will supplant the colonial regime should seem more available as a vehicle for ethnic identification than the regime which it hopes to replace; but certainly anything very elaborate in the way of social and economic programmes for the future is apt to be supererogatory once the fighting has begun. It was a historical accident that the greater part of the colonies in the world at the time of the Second World War were regimes in which one ethnic group dominated another racial group: as Marx noted, the creation of the world economy was largely an achievement of the European bourgeoisie, and the great colonial empires of the twentieth century had resulted largely from this achievement. However, if the racial component of anti-colonialism in mass terms is a historical accident, though plainly one which facilitates the process of ethnic identification with anti-colonial rebels against the colonial state, there is a quasi-definitional characteristic of anti-colonialism which is of some importance in thinking about the explanation of any anti-colonial revolution. A colony may or may not represent the domination of one race over another – it necessarily represents perhaps only the domination of one *nation* over large numbers of those who are not members of it. But it must represent such domination in a fairly continuous fashion over a reasonably long time. What distinguishes an invasion from the establishment of a colony is how long the invasion persists. The Germans invaded Norway, Holland, France, Yugoslavia. They established many quisling governments and used a number of already established governments as instruments for maintaining political control. The colonial structure known as the protectorate, a form of colonial rule which existed for example in much of French Indochina and French North Africa, is in effect often a form of quisling rule. The German invasions lasted a few years, the Germans being defeated, though not usually by those over whom the protectorates had been established. The French invasions lasted many decades. Algeria and Vietnam in the end fought wars of national liberation against the French invaders, as did Dutchmen, Yugoslavs and Frenchmen against the German invaders. But, in fighting wars of national liberation in colonial countries, the Vietnamese and Algerian revolutionaries were fighting against something very different from what the French or Dutch or even Yugoslav Resistances were opposing. In the cases of France and Holland, of course, though less so in the case of Yugoslavia, they were also fighting *for* something very different from what the Algerians and Vietnamese were fighting for. The French and Dutch had continuing national identities which it was natural for their citizens to continue to identify *with* as against the German invaders. The Yugoslavs, as indicated earlier, did not have anything very convincing in the way of a unitary national identity with which to identify and this lack was part of the explanation of why the resistance of the Yugoslav nation was not in the end conducted under the auspices of the representatives of the previously existing Yugoslav state. For the members of a long-standing national unit to continue to resist enemy invasions for some years is scarcely remarkable. Most colonies contrived to resist the initial invasions of their colonizing powers for some time, at least sporadically, whether or not they had previously constituted national units of any great historical depth or any great geographical extent. Localist resistance over time might indeed represent as effective a challenge to the establishment of colonial hegemony as a more unified national resistance which might be conclusively broken in pitched battle or by the seizure of the decisive focus of national unity, a royal family, capital city or ancestral shrine. But whereas the initial stage of colonial conquest might be much hindered by localist resistance because of the difficulties which this presented in consolidating any reliable degree of central control, once the colonial state structure had been fully established, the situation was very different. To destroy a colonial state structure it was necessary to oppose it effectively at the level of the colony as a whole and to develop a political elite capable of re-establishing political authority at that level, at the very least as a plausible symbol, before victory is won. Colonial state structures are protected by modern armies of some sophistication; and no permanent degree of political reconstruction can be achieved by an insurgent movement until the colonial army has in effect abandoned the struggle. However, if and when the colonial army (or its masters) is prepared to recognize that it cannot effectively and permanently pacify the insurgent population or the metropolitan society decides that it is no longer prepared to meet the wage-bill and suffer the odium of the colonial army's efforts to do so, many different factors facilitate the establishment of a successor elite capable of serving as a militarily viable government of the country. An elaborate nexus of international institutions today bolster the most crumbling state structure, and arms and administrative facilities to preserve the residue of the colonial state are readily available, in order for it to preside over the relationship between the ex-colony and the world economy. Just whom they will be available *from* depends on what sort of political intentions the successor government exhibits and on whether it has any significant products to dispose of on the world market, from the proceeds of which it will be able to pay for the weapons. But there are few central governments in the world today so grossly bankrupt or universally politically abhorrent that they cannot get their apparatus of military repression serviced by someone. Even President Duvalier was perfectly capable of keeping up a well-armed coercive force. Once the state apparatus has been handed over to a local elite (however recruited) by the departing colonial powers, it is not difficult to grasp how they can keep the machinery operational for some time. That this opportunity should not prove universally distasteful to prospective insurgent elites is not surprising. That it should not prove abhorrent to the colonial masses insofar as they participate in insurrection is equally unsurprising, though for rather different reasons: the great majority plainly lacking the information, or the habit of systematic reflection on political issues, which would have been necessary to get any clear idea of how the political future of the country was in practice likely to turn out. Once the situation had been made to come to an armed struggle, an achievement which in 1954 required only a trivial level of initial force, the weight of the French colonial presence in Algeria established the insurgents as more appealing subjects for identification than the *colons* or their metropolitan military protectors.

Furthermore the fact that, as is structurally probable in colonial situations, this process of identification was not impeded by any actual experience of what the F.L.N. leaders would be like (or had been like) as an alternative government, made it a plausible vehicle for quite Utopian dreams. Even at an elite level this is easy to see in the pages of Frantz Fanon. At a mass level and in an Islamic culture it is scarcely remarkable that the aspirations should on occasion have been even more messianic. But, for the bulk of those involved, the rationality of the rebellion was as much expressive of historically deep structures of feeling as it was instrumental in terms of clearly designated political ends. Few of the F.L.N. fighters appear to have had much idea of the long-term character of the successor regime which they wished to create. If it was true that the leaders of the rebellion were not for the most part widely known or clearly labelled in ideological affiliation, this was not in itself a particularly crippling disadvantage. If there was nothing much known in their favour, there was also – unlike the representatives of the Serbian monarchy in Yugoslavia during the last war – nothing at all known against them. The one thing which was *clearly* known about them was the fact that they were engaged in fighting the French colonial regime and, against this, much of a very specific kind was necessarily known to all. Leading resistance against a fairly massively invasive colonial regime with a large settler population, like that of Algeria, just as leading resistance against the foreign invasion of a modern territorial state, requires less in the way of intrinsic political appeal than it does of organizational effectiveness from a purely military point of view. The invasive nature of the French regime in Algerian eyes resulted directly from the scale of the *colon* population and the degree to which this had contrived to control the political and economic development of the colony. The weight of the regime was experienced most crudely in the control of land. By 1919 the non-European population of Algeria owned less than two thirds of the agricultural land and they had lost control of the greater part of the most fertile land.[3] Even inside the *colon* population landownership was very highly concentrated and production was extremely specialized – production of wine grapes being particularly highly developed.[4] The laws governing indigenous property-holding were overtly devised to facilitate expropriation of indigenous landholders in favour of European colonists, particularly in the wake of the Moqrani revolt of 1871.[5] The President of the Algiers court stated in 1871 that the essential point of a property law was to provide native land for purchase by Frenchmen.[6] In nineteenth-century conditions the only form of significant development of the colonial territory available was agricultural, and, in the eyes of European peasant colonists, the vast, open, unhedged lands of the Algerian coastal plains and hills seemed absurdly undeveloped. The existing largely pastoral economy with its complex patterns of transhumance appeared strikingly wasteful in the light of conditions of painstaking peasant cultivation in Provence or Southern Spain from which many of the *colons* derived.[7] The great majority of the *colons* would not have been much interested in understanding – and virtually none did in fact contrive to understand – the categories of property in land in traditional and Islamic law. Indeed the precise structure of legal rights involved was in some ways the subject of intrinsic dispute. A palimpsest of claims balanced between a form of collective property resting in the tribal group and at least an attempt to establish a right of eminent domain in the imperial authority was not easy to decipher even in the pre-colonial period;[8] and the colonial legal authorities had less obvious motives for attempting to decipher it accurately than they had for converting it into a simpler and more convenient array of categories. In any case the massive array of sequestrations resulting from the suppression of Moqrani's revolt released large supplies of land onto the market. The combined effects of sequestration and a law of landed property designed to favour European interests produced over time an extremely large *colon* population. By 1954 this group was no longer largely rural – a clear majority of its 850,000 members lived and worked in commercial or industrial roles in towns or cities. But it had been the availability of land which had provided the initial and necessary motive for establishing a substantial *colon* population in Algeria.

Even in 1954 *colons* still controlled almost seven million acres of the most fertile land in Algeria – at a time when the Algerian peasant population had greatly increased in numbers[9] – and the larger *colon* landowners remained among the most politically influential members of the *colon* community. Before the rebellion of El Moqrani in 1871 it was widely assumed by the Muslim population that the French were likely to disappear reasonably soon. Money was even frequently borrowed in the form of a loan repayable on the day of the French departure.[10] A revolt in 1864 took the form of a *jacquerie* led by the religious brotherhoods. In 1871, emboldened by French defeats in the Franco-Prussian war, the great tribal leaders whose position had been severely damaged by the administrative reforms of 1868, led a tribal insurrection under the *bach-agha* El Moqrani.[11] Within a month it had been joined by the leader of one of the major religious brotherhoods, the Rahmâniyâ, who declared a *jihad*, a classic Islamic holy war, at which point the Kabyle tribes also joined in the rising. El Moqrani himself, and his brother who succeeded to the leadership of the revolt after his death, took the traditional title of *emir* of the *moujahidin*, leader of the holy warriors.[12] The thoroughness with which this traditionalist revolt was crushed was undoubtedly responsible for the comparative absence of large-scale organized resistance for the next seventy or so years. The French colonial presence had demonstrated a highly effective repressive capacity. But the manner of the repression itself was far from endearing; certainly it was not calculated to win the emotional allegiance of the Algerian populace. Some seventy years later, in the next war in which the French were conclusively defeated militarily by the Germans, the notion that Algeria might succeed militarily in throwing off the chains of French domination recovered a degree of popular plausibility. But the apparatus of colonial social control was never effectively disrupted by the war in the way in which it was in fact disrupted in Vietnam. The combination of entrenched communal animosity and raised hopes of independence produced a violent popular demonstration against the colonial regime at Sétif which had repercussions all over the territory, and which was suppressed by the authorities at the cost of many thousand lives.[13] Up to this point political activity designed to enhance the status and protect the interests of the indigenous population of Algeria had been extensively focussed on the formal political institutions established by the French or had taken a largely cultural or religious form. After the Sétif massacre it was, in retrospect at least, easy to see that a military rising was in the end more or less inevitable. However, it was still true that the conditions in which such a rising had to take place were in many respects drastically less favourable to the insurgents than they were, for instance, in Vietnam. It is likely that the revolt might have broken out substantially *later* and, perhaps, certain that it would not have succeeded eventually to even the degree to which it did succeed eventually, had there not been a number of changes in the character of the colonial commitment of the western powers at large over the nine years between 1945 and 1954. By 1954 an Arab nationalist government of a strongly anti-colonial character had been established in Egypt and the protectorates of Morocco and Tunisia, the two states bordering on Algeria, were within two years of attaining their independence.[14] All three of these states lent substantial military and political assistance to the rebellion virtually throughout its course, Tunisia and Morocco in fact supporting quite large rebel armies on their territories for much of the war. The movement of decolonization in many areas had reached substantial dimensions; a number of former colonies had already liberated themselves, or else were well on the way towards doing so, from colonial control – notably Indonesia and Vietnam itself. The international environment was drastically more favourable to the Algerian rebels in 1954 than it had been in 1945; moreover, during the next few years, with the rise in the diplomatic status and organizational effectiveness of the non-aligned powers, it was to improve still further. From the perspective of the Algerian elites it appeared that a largely Muslim indigenous population in Algeria was increasingly being left behind in the renaissance of national independence among colonial countries, for one reason and one reason only; that the territory of Algeria had been subject to much heavier European settlement than other Arab countries (and indeed than the great bulk of other colonial territories in general). The Vietnamese had had to fight a war of national liberation because a determined elite group had made a bid for independence at a time at which colonial powers had not as yet accepted the idea that colonial rule was an outdated project. Indeed the Vietnamese had helped to no small extent to establish in the mind of colonial powers the notion that colonial structures based upon military repression might no longer be at all an economical way of protecting their interests abroad. The Algerians nevertheless had to fight a war of national liberation because there were permanently or semi-permanently resident on their territory about 850,000 Europeans. From the elite point of view, the consequences of this state of affairs in terms of economic development provided additional incentives to revolt. The prize of victory would certainly include actual Algerian access to (as opposed to at best formal Algerian eligibility for) a large number of highly attractive elite positions. At the same time the extent of European presence had a decisive impact on the attitudes towards revolt of the mass of the Algerian population at large. In terms of social and economic relations, the French colonial presence in Algeria was as obtrusive and as provocative as any European colonial presence anywhere. The resentment which it evoked at elite and at mass levels naturally varied in ideological expression. But there was little ambiguity or variation in what exactly the resentment was directed against: the *colons*. In a very real sense the extent of colonial settlement in Algeria was what has created such of an Algerian nation as does yet exist. What brought such unity to the Algerians as they attained in the course of the war, given the Islamic culture in terms of which they understood their struggle, was simply the French whom they had to get rid of – one reason for the internecine bloodbath which accompanied their victory. The same reasons which made it difficult for the French to abandon their colonial control made the Algerians, both elite and mass, eager to compel them to relinquish it. Once the war had begun, too, the only reason which particularly increased the French government's eagerness to retain control over Algeria, the Saharan oil deposits, naturally served to increase the insurgents' expectations of the desirable consequences which would result from their triumph.

However, in looking at the context of revolt in this way, one aspect of the French colonial presence which was certainly of great ideological weight to the French themselves has been determinedly ignored: the fact that from a constitutional point of view Algeria was supposedly not a colony, but, rather, a part of metropolitan France. It was ideologically simple, if emotionally painful for France to abandon explicitly colonial territories or protectorates, the cost of defending which had become prohibitive. It disturbed the French colonial armies; but most Frenchmen could learn to live with it without undue emotional unease. But it was not such a simple matter when it came to a territory supposedly integrated into France itself in a comprehensive fashion. The French colonial doctrine of assimilation was directly and intractably at issue in Algeria and it was at issue in the persons and livelihoods of large numbers of persons, the *colons*, who were indubitably of French nationality, whatever their forebears had been. It is still possible to analyse the colonial history of Algeria and the relationship of metropolitan France to it in terms of the ideology of assimilation and the causes of its failures. In the pages of the *Revue Historique*, the leading French historical periodical, for January and April 1970, two of the most distinguished historians of modern Algeria, Agéron and Yacono, were still engaged in debating whether the record of French assimilationist policy in Algeria between 1871 and 1919 had proved a failure because of the intrinsic absurdity of attempting to create an integrated nation out of Arab and Berber Muslims and European Christians, or whether it turned on the incapacity of the French national government to resist the reactionary pressures of the *colon* leaders against the integration of Algerian Muslims fully into the French body politic:[15] whether, that is, the policy of assimilation failed in Algeria because it was necessarily absurd in a colonial situation, or because the effort actually to put it into effect was never really made because of the weakness of French national governments in the face of *colon* pressure. That there would have been powerful *colon* pressure against any serious attempt to impose an assimilationist policy is evident enough. There was, indeed, extensive and effective resistance to numerous initiatives, either legal or administrative, which would have enhanced the status of the Muslim population, throughout the period of French colonial rule. Napoleon III's comparatively sympathetic attitude to the Muslim population earned him the contemptuous title of *Sultan* from the *colons*,[16] and under the Fourth Republic supposedly Socialist governments executed policies determined more or less exclusively by *colon* interests. It is undisputed that the policy of assimilation was for the greater part not applied, or applied extremely narrowly, at all stages between 1830, the French conquest of Algiers, and 1954. Since assimilation was, and had been from the time of the French revolution, the legitimatory theory of French colonialism, legal and constitutional categories predicated on assimilationist values appeared throughout much of the period of French control; and particular projects, especially in the realm of education, which would have had the effect of improving the situation of the indigenous population were devised by metropolitan politicians and justified by them in terms of these values. Leading French politicians, like Jules Ferry,[17] appear on occasion in Algerian history defending the application of such values. It is thus perfectly legitimate – in that the participants would have understood clearly what you meant – to describe the French colonial venture in Algeria in terms of the effort to make Algerians Frenchmen and to explain the failure of the venture by the extent to which French metropolitan politicians and their local administrative representatives failed on crucial occasions to fight effectively on behalf of these values against entrenched *colon* opposition. The vast gaps in wealth, education and political power between European *colons* and native Algerians in 1954 show the extent of the failure, but they cannot in principle demonstrate that no such struggle was ever in question. It is largely the story of this struggle which Professor Agéron tells in the 1250 pages of his *thèse* on the Algerian Muslims and France and it would take a more than Pyrrhonian scepticism to deny that the themes which he treats possess historical content.[18] However, it remains perfectly possible that however necessary to explain the actions of numerous people on particular occasions between 1830 and 1962, the ideology of assimilation which characterized virtually all French colonial policy is of quite exiguous importance in explaining why it was that Algeria eventually became independent again after 130 years of French occupation. From the point of view of the actual relationship between the metropolitan society and the territory of Algeria, especially after large-scale European settlement had taken place in Algeria, assimilation was a quite contingent feature of the public rhetoric in which the relationship was described inside the metropolitan society itself. French colonial policy was assimilationist in its teleological self-justification because universalist natural rights were central to the constitutional tradition and the language of political aspiration of French politicians from the time of the revolution and of Napoleon onwards. All men in the state of culture in which they were actually to be found were not, regrettably, equal; but by being judiciously civilized, gallicized, they could be generously enabled to become so. That this language should be reflected in metropolitan relations with Algeria was inevitable and that it should be recognizable in the contours of the actual political institutions on occasion was equally so, whether in constitutional trivialities like the status of an Islamic territory, Algeria, as a number of *départements* of metropolitan France, or on more pragmatically important occasions, such as the conscription of 173,000 Algerian soldiers to fight in the French armies during the First World War[19] and the large-scale transport of labour to metropolitan France at the same time to replace the French industrial proletariat in the factories. Where it did not matter to the *colon* population or where it certainly mattered very much to metropolitan France, the assimilationist categories might become operative. But for the most part, as Professor Yacono argues, it makes little sense to consider the outcome of Algerian political processes in these terms at all.[20]

The great bulk of French metropolitan politicians showed virtually no interest whatever in the political arrangements in Algeria. Few members of either House of the legislature even bothered to attend debates on the subject.[21] Metropolitan administrators despatched to Algeria found themselves insistently and effectively besieged by the political demands of the *colons*. Most, particularly after the 1871 revolt, succumbed to the *colon* interpretation of proper administrative values without much resistance. In a position in which they were subjected to endless harassment locally if they did resist and in which they could in general rely on little assistance and indeed rather little innovative *interest* on the part of their metropolitan superiors in the event of their resistance, it is not surprising that few did put up much resistance. Nor is it altogether realistic to suppose that most of them would necessarily have felt much initial eagerness to resist the values of the *colons,* even if they had been left entirely unpressured to make up their own minds. Universalist values are not necessarily, psychologically speaking, heavy baggage with which to travel. Algeria was a conquest society in which the conquered population had been engaged largely in subsistence agriculture[22] subject only to the obligation to pay some sort of tribute to a titular superior, ultimately to the Turkish representative, the Bey at Algiers. It was a society heavily settled by colonists drawn from the same ethnic grouping as the conquerors and already fully participant in the economic structures of capitalist production for the market. It comprised a society, Arab or Berber in ethnic identity, largely Arabic and Islamic in religious culture, conquered and dominated by a society made up of European Christians. It was also a society in which indigenous resistance under various tribal leaders, most notably Abd-el-Kader, had assumed formidable proportions. A limited number of French military officials engaged in the French equivalent of Native Administration became over time strongly identified with the values of the indigenous culture and their preservation. They were hardly likely to favour the sort of syncretistic cultural and social development necessary to make assimilation a real possibility over time. They liked their Arabs – or, as it more frequently was, Berbers – pure. For the majority of the administrators, the cultural gap between themselves and the *colon* population, uncouth though the latter might be from some points of view, as so much narrower than the gulf between them and the great mass of the Algerian population that the defensive and self-righteous stance of the *colons* in their ruthless pursuit of their own interests could hardly fail to touch a number of answering chords. Wherever universalist values came up against the serried hostilities and intractable inequalities which made up

Algerian society, one or the other had to give ground extremely sharply. It is hardly surprising, particularly when we consider how many men the two forces were respectively incarnated in over time, that universalist values should have proved so much more pliable than Algerian society. Only a steady and overwhelming commitment of political power from outside the society could have lent sufficient impetus to the small number of liberal administrators or *colon* professional men and intellectuals who wished to advance the goal of assimilation for them to win much ground against the great majority of the *colons*. Among the metropolitan French political class few had sufficient interest to care much either way about the outcome of this struggle; and of those who did fewer still had the inclination to lend real political support to furthering assimilationist values.

Furthermore, even if the French state had been unflinchingly committed to the contriving of an integrated Franco-Algerian nation at whatever cost it proved necessary to pay, and even given that it did in practice succeed in winning the allegiance of a number of Algerians, both ideologically among the elites and practically among the masses, it is not at all clear that the venture could ever have been successful. As Bernard Lewis points out, the revolution's most common slogan in daily propaganda was not *'Algérie Arabe' or 'Algérie Algérienne'*, but *'Algérie Musulmane'*.[23] Algeria was an Islamic society. It was the common tie of Islam under the pressure of colonial occupation which united Arab and Kabyle, tribesman and city-dweller in their rejection of the path of assimilation. The *colons* might secure by their insistent political pressures that the liberal initiatives of metropolitan statesmen should regularly prove abortive. Demographic change and colonial land law might mean that the gap between an increasingly wealthy *colon* population and the great mass of an increasingly impoverished indigenous population widened consistently. Taken together, they made it certain that the path of assimilation should have been one which the vast majority had no possibility of taking. But it was the massively Islamic culture of the population as a whole which meant that for the greater part they were even more devoid of the will to take the path of assimilation than they were of the ability. In 1936 when the Popular Front

government came to power in Paris, there were 7,817 naturalized Arab or Berber Algerians who had benefited from the
more liberal provisions of the law of 1919, passed in the aftermath of Algerian participation in the First World War.[24]
Even the law of 1919 explicitly required that, in order to
become a naturalized French citizen it was necessary for an
Algerian Muslim to abandon his Koranic status, the legal
rights which he enjoyed and the legal obligations to which
he was subject under Islamic law. Only those prepared symbolically to desert the Islamic community for the secular
ideology of their conquerors were given the opportunity of
becoming full citizens in their own land. It was no easy
psychological feat for an Algerian to conceive this transition
in classic historicist style as an abandonment of primitive
superstition for a mature secular rationalism, when the greatest mosque in Algiers had been turned into a Christian
cathedral by the secular conquerors.[25] More popularly accessible contexts in which the members of the indigenous population could associate themselves with the colonial power,
military service in particular, carried bitter emotional overtones. Algerians who fought in the French colonial armies
turned the epithet 'volunteer' into a term of violent abuse;[26]
and the threat of introducing conscription to assist in the
suppression of their co-religionists in Morocco revived the
traditional symbolic protest of emigration when the Mufti of
Tlemcen in 1911 led more than a thousand of its inhabitants
away to Syria.[27] In these circumstances the choice between a
legal status under French law, the *indigénat,* which deprived
them of most rights available to Frenchmen but allowed
them to retain their Koranic status and thus their full symbolic participation in a religious community, and on the
other hand the full enjoyment of French citizenship combined with an explicit abjuring of their status under Islamic
law and thus their membership in a religious community,
was not a choice which most found difficult. Paradoxically a
great many Algerians, traditional tribal leaders or *marabouts,*
holy men, to say nothing of the large numbers of Algerians
serving in the French army, all of whom were heavily involved with the French colonial presence and drew direct
benefits from it, were quite untouched by the appeals of the
official ideology sanctioning the French regime. There were

during the Algerian war of national liberation, as there no longer were in Vietnam by the end of the French colonial regime,[28] at least as many of the indigenous population fighting with the French colours on a voluntary basis, as there were fighting against the French. Indeed a number of traditional areas in Algeria especially in the Kabyle mountains had in effect established enduring ties of mutual advantage with the colonial regime. In many respects even up to the 1950s the colonial regime retained an extremely stable structure of social control. But this stability, such as it was, had virtually nothing to do with any success of the professed policy of assimilation. In 1936 the Popular Front government put forward a proposed law, the Blum–Viollette provisions, which attempted to resolve the severe tensions between cultural identity and modernist social mobility presented by the colonial structure by making it possible for many categories of Algerians to enjoy the status of naturalized French citizen while retaining their status under Islamic law and by in addition increasing the political representation of Algeria in the French legislature. The failure of this law to pass the Assembly because of the vigour of *colon* opposition is conventionally taken by French historians today as the death knell of a French Algeria. But it would be unrealistic to suppose that its passage would necessarily have avoided a major military confrontation. As Le Tourneau points out, only some 20–25,000 Algerians would have been in a position to benefit from the law, even had they chosen to do so;[29] and it is hard to see the gap between the two introverted, culturally arrogant and mutually suspicious societies, with the growing disparities in their respective wealth being reliably bridged in such a fashion. As late as 1951, though by then many tens of thousands had undergone some French education, the number of the active French-educated elite was estimated at about a thousand.[30] Assimilation, to be at all effective, required not merely the possibility in principle of social mobility for a tiny minority, but some actual mutual accommodation of two totally different social structures, structures which in practice continued relentlessly to diverge. A number of the earlier Algerian anti-colonialist leaders came from the most *évolué* groups, accepted the ideology of assimilation and struggled for the more real implementation of assimilationist values.

But the possibility of their retaining indefinite control of any movement with mass support directed against the interests of the *colons* was clearly remote. Ferhat Abbas was honest and disarming in admitting before the war, in 1938, that he could not be an Algerian nationalist because there had never been, and certainly did not then exist, any such entity as an Algerian nation. Even in the past there had merely been a Muslim empire to which Algeria belonged and which was now as much extinct as the Roman or the mediaeval Christian empires.[31] This was clearly no populist rallying cry. But sixteen years later when the revolution began and significant numbers of Algerians started to struggle against the colonial regime, it was a logical culmination of even Ferbat Abbas's political career that he should think again and decide eventually, in 1956, to join the rebellion and become President of the Provisional Government.[32]

Assimilationist values had been adopted by the first modernist political leaders to appear in Algeria, the Young Algerians before the First World War, who demanded the abolition of the *indigénat* in return for acceptance of the principle of conscription, an issue which provoked the more traditional response of the Tlemcen exodus at about the same time. But the forms of political or cultural opposition which attracted more extensive support throughout were always more unequivocally anti-French and usually more archaic in symbolic identification. The Emir Khaled, a descendant of Abd-el-Kader, was alleged in 1922 to have been the first Algerian to suggest in public in the twentieth century that the French occupation might at some point come to an end.[33] Somewhat in contrast, both of the first two major movements of organized nationalism were in stronger tension with traditional organization inside the country. One the reformist *Ulema*, led by Ben Badis, were part of a universalist Islamic revival which had an impact throughout the Islamic world.[34] The other, the *Étoile Nord-Africaine* established by Messali Hadj was largely confined to those Algerians most radically removed from the colonial context, the Algerians resident in metropolitan France. The *Ulema* were a religious reform movement, inspired in the first instance by the ideas of Mohammed 'Abduh, who had visited Algeria in 1903,[35] and dedicated to reversing what they saw as the reason for the collapse of Islamic power in the face of western Christendom, the spiritual degeneration of Islam, by the recreation of a strict Islamic culture. Algerian Islam, like the Islam of most of the Maghrib littoral, was highly syncretistic and, by orthodox standards, superstitious. Furthermore local *marabouts* and the leaders of the religious fraternities were not only doctrinally unorthodox, they were also heavily involved in collaborating with the French administration. The reformist *Ulema* were based largely on the traditional bourgeoisie of the ancient cities. They devoted themselves to the expansion of Muslim education, the proliferation of Koranic schools and the encouragement of all components of orthodox piety consciously conceiving these measures as prerequisites for the regeneration of a national culture. As a specifically political grouping they did not address themselves much to the issues of *colon* politics, though Ben Badis, their most prominent leader, was prepared to associate himself tactically with more assimilationist leaders in the unsuccessful struggle to secure the passage of the Blum–Viollette law.[36]

The second major movement of organized opposition to the colonial regime, the proletarian *Étoile Nord-Africaine* of Messali Hadj, was necessarily still more detached from the groupings of traditional Algerian society. Its initial organization in Paris was greatly assisted by the French Communist Party, but it did not remain long under these universalist auspices. Conceived from the first by Messali as a secular nationalist movement, it was later transformed in 1936 under the influence of a Druze pan-Arabist leader, Shakib Arslan, resident at the time in Geneva, into a militantly pan-Islamic and populist grouping in total opposition to the colonial system. Even as early as 1924, two years before the foundation of the *Étoile*, there were 100,000 Algerians working in industry in France itself.[37] Their proletarian situation made them easy to organize at the purely practical level, accessible to organization in a way in which the predominantly rural population under the repressive colonial structure of social control simply were not accessible. The conditions under which they worked, still a topic for major national scandal at times in France today, and the huge cultural gap between them and the surrounding European society, equally combined to make them emotionally susceptible to the appeals of militant Islamic opposition to the assimilationist project. Messali was an effective agitator and a skilful organizer whose exertions were rewarded by a number of lengthy spells in French jails. His movement was suppressed on several occasions; but it responded merely by resurrecting itself under other names. It was a token of its more overtly political flavour and modernist political style that it should have specifically opposed the Blum–Viollette proposals.[38] It was also perhaps an indication of the futility of the assimilationist project that the first mass political movement of Algerians of inescapably modern status should have been even more hostile to the promise of assimilation into the French nation than the reformist *Ulema* themselves. It was hardly surprising that a movement whose main social basis of support lay in traditional strata of Algerian society, the bourgeoisie of the ancient cities, and whose ideological purpose was specifically a restoration of the purity and orthodoxy of the traditional religious culture should have felt slightly equivocal at the offer of absorption into the laic universalism of the French nation. But although Messali Hadj himself had come from firmly traditional origins – he was the son of a Tlemcen artisan – his movement was indubitably proletarian in composition. Karl Marx, at the very inception of his theory, had seen the potential salvation of the proletariat as lying in the fact that its situation deprived it of every traditional status and left it as a consequence only with the universal status of being human.[39] Appropriately enough, too, the *Étoile Nord-Africaine* had at first been organized largely with the assistance of the French Communist Party. When even the members of the *Étoile* discovered that their identity still tied them closer to the Islamic culture from which they came than it did to the secular universalism of the French political tradition, the future of French Algeria appeared bleak indeed. This is not to say that the precise contours of the Algerian revolution, let alone its success, were somehow determined by the late 1930s. Indeed during the revolution itself Messali Hadj's followers were overt opponents of the F.L.N. and fought a private civil war against them throughout most of the fighting, a war which in metropolitan France where the prize of controlling the wage packets of the Algerian labour force was extremely rich took the lives of many hundreds. What the character of the *Étoile* perhaps did serve to determine was that the Algerian revolution was not to be led by a Communist party. Partly no doubt this was the fault of the French Communist Party's tactics. As early as 1928, two years after the foundation of the *Étoile*, the French Communist Party were criticized at the Comintern Congress for having failed to establish independent Communist parties in the Maghrib countries;[40] and as late as 1946, as the Chinese pointed out acidly in 1963,[41] Maurice Thorez, the French Communist leader, was prepared to proclaim Algeria as an inalienable part of France and to dilate upon the economic benefits to the French domestic economy which this relationship provided. But the main reason for the failure of the Communists to maintain leadership of a proletarian movement in Algeria dedicated to Algerian independence went further than such ambivalence about the officially assimilationist purposes of French colonialism. In France the Algerians might be classical proletarians; but in Algeria the same men were often the most effective traditionalists in the Algerian population. Germaine Tillion, a French anthropologist, argued against Algerian independence during the war on the grounds that some sections of Algerian society, particularly the Kabyle mountain tribes, were economically dependent for their very subsistence on the returns from migrant wage labour in France.[42] This was perfectly true; indeed it remains true today and serves to point up the in some ways deeply paradoxical character of the Algerian revolution. Those who initiated the revolution and on the whole continued to lead it throughout were for the most part to some degree participants in essentially modern roles in the economy of Algeria or of France itself, former N.C.O.s in the French army, like Krim or Ben Bella, occupants of minor professional or white-collar roles, former industrial workers in France. Quite a large proportion in fact came from the Kabyle areas in which, because of the close links between the colonial administration and political leadership, the practice of emigration to France to work was much more highly developed than it was elsewhere in Algeria. The complementary relationship between genuinely modern wage-labour and an elaborate traditional social structure, previously based on forms of subsistence agriculture or of transhumance which were no longer economically viable in fact stabilized and preserved the traditional social structures to a degree found else-where in Algeria only among the Touaregs of the desert or the Mzabites,[43] the sole groups not entrenched upon by *colon* appropriation of the best agricultural land. Participation on a large scale in the most intractably modern economic roles available, those in Marx's terms which were totally devoid of any traditional status, in practice served to preserve and strengthen a traditional social structure and a vigorous local identity to go with it. The Kabyle proletarians were the most traditional, the *least* proletarianized when in Algeria itself, of all Algerians affected by the modern economy. The greater part of the Algerian rural population, which is to say still far the greater part of the Algerian population as a whole, were, as Pierre Bourdieu has insisted, not only economically mar-ginal to a degree to which no member of an industrial work-ing class in employment could in principle become; they were also lodged in a traditional social structure whose adaptive resources had been largely destroyed.[44] Both in the cities and in effect in the countryside the indigenous Algerian population consisted to a large degree of a vast lumpenprole-tariat. If participation in the most modern economic roles enabled the Kabyle tribes to retain a degree of confident and stable cultural imperviousness to the colonial ideology, the situation of the greater part of the Algerian population constituted a far more total denunciation of the colonial economy.

The main fighting soldiers of the F.L.N., the *mujahidin*, were drawn from both groups, the integral tribes and the in-creasingly deracinated peasantry. If at the time of the Moqrani revolt the tribal warriors were known as *mujahidin*, it was because they were fighting under the leadership of their traditional leaders and because their tribes were still integrated Muslim societies. By 1954 the title *mujahidin* merely reflected the fact that while all indigenous Algerians had an enemy to fight against, if they chose to do so, they had for the most part no viable social organization left to fight for, and their common Islamic culture had in consequence to act as a unifying and legitimating interpretation of the goal of their struggle at the mass level where the common coin of ex-colonial national autonomy which the F.L.N. leaders paid out in international negotiation could hardly be clearly intelligible, let alone emotionally current. During the war itself, something like half the Algerian rural population was resettled to facilitate its military control, an operation described accurately enough by Bourdieu as *Déracinement*, uprooting, which served to complete the disruption of Algerian rural society.[45] It is appropriate enough that the most distinguished ideologist of the Algerian revolution, Frantz Fanon, should have been an ideologist of the *déracinés*, the urban and more particularly the rural lumpen-proletariats and the purgation of their souls by the supposedly creative activity of violent destruction.[46] The Algerian revolution was a war more than a revolution, a war, too, fought by men united by little concrete except the common object of their hate, the *colons*, a war of hideous and singularly intimate brutality, a war to avenge the trauma of colonization. It was not a war, in most parts of Algeria at least, fought to preserve damaged but intrinsically viable social and economic structures. Only, rather oddly, in the Kabyle mountains which were in a measure economically integrated with metropolitan France and which *could* remain culturally viable at all just because they were so, could the war be seen as a defensive war, a war to preserve a past still living in the present. For most of Algeria the past was plainly crippled beyond all hope of resuscitation. The Algerian revolution, like the Vietnamese revolution, was a war of national liberation, the belated expulsion of an invading army. But there were some portentous differences between the two. In some ways Algeria was a nation united only, insofar as it was united at all, against the invaders whom it wished to expel. Partly, no doubt, this was a matter of Algeria never having been exactly a nation even before the French arrived: merely a collection of Arab and Berber tribes under the loosest of Turkish suzerainty, not a united kingdom as Vietnam was, for instance, at the beginning of the nineteenth century under Gia Long. But there was another difference, too, a difference in the destructiveness of the invasion. Algerian society was disrupted and rendered unadaptive to a degree which Vietnam never suffered. The murderous internecine faction-fighting during and immediately after the war mirrored the fragmented character of the society itself. The *Damnés de la Terre* of Fanon are a plausible enough object of emotional sympathy, but they are scarcely the most reassuring material on which to build a new and stable national society. It is not altogether surprising that the Algerian successor elite, the leaders of the revolutionary army (especially outside Algeria) and the highly trained French-educated civil servants, should have made so little attempt to put the Fanonist heroes to such use. Wars of national liberation, if militarily successful, leave nations to be organized as viable societies in their wake. Apart from President Ben Bella's acceptance of the peasant seizure of certain French estates and their assignment, together with a few factories, to their occupants to run under a measure of governmental supervision, the policy of *autogestion*,[47] the post-revolutionary Algerian government has not been much given to programmes of radical social change. In the immediate aftermath of the agreements at Evian which brought the war to an end the Algerian economy was in a very bad condition. It has been heavily dependent on foreign aid, particularly French and much more recently Russian, to get itself back into working order. The continued links between France and Algeria have often been tense, particularly over agreements inside the Common Market about wine imports which threatened Algeria with an enormous glut of wine, and about the terms of French–Algerian cooperation in the exploitation of the oil deposits. In these contests Algeria has had some measure of success because of the skill and determination of an extremely modernist civil service, the inheritors in this generation of the mantle of Ferhat Abbas. The international environment, particularly in the case of the oil negotiations has proved rather favourable to the exercise of these skills. But, although in foreign policy under both Ben Bella and Boumedienne it has taken a consistently vigorous anti-colonial line at the level of public pronouncements, the Algerian government, except at one stage and over a specifically Arab issue in 1967, has been reluctant to risk any substantial national commitment at a more pragmatic level. As a revolutionary government it has disappointed a great many of its supporters (as well as shooting a number of others). Inside the society traditional identities and separatist urges survive in some parts, but transmuted today, as Jeanne Favret argues, into the form of desperate efforts not to escape the control of the central government, but rather to involve it in the distribution of more of the modernist facilities, roads, schools, jobs, which alone make possible the very survival of local social units, villages or tribal groups.[48] Only in the Kabyle areas, again, where local insurrections are in a position (because of previous modernist investment in education and national insurrection) to call on tribal assistance within the national political elites, do these forays stand much chance of success. The internal inequalities and much of the social backwardness created by the colonial regime have survived its departure and the successor elites appear to be under little external pressure to alleviate them and to have little unitary will of their own to do so – let alone *idea* of how to do so.[49] It is not difficult to find who were the victims of the Algerian revolution: the *colons*; and it is not difficult to see *when* they were defeated: when they lost control over the political will of the French state. The F.L.N. never defeated the French army and by 1960 the French army had come very close to defeating the F.L.N. conclusively.[50] But by then it had made such chaos in both Algerian society and economy and the very activity of colonial repression had become from a Machiavellian point of view such a naive archaism that the French state had lost the will to go on with the struggle. So Algeria got her freedom, and the vast majority of the Algerian population still break stone.[51] There seems to be little reason to suppose that their future political direction will be very different from other Arab countries under modernist leadership. The Algerian revolution indeed was hardly designed to produce anything more than this. Its aim was simply to expel the *colons* from their position of dominance, economic and political, of Algeria. In this at least it has by and large succeeded. The *colons* have gone in large numbers and those few that remain certainly no longer dominate the country. The infidel invasion is over at last, leaving behind in human terms only a number of Algerians with different pigmentation. The colonial regime is finished; all Algeria has to live with now is neocolonialism, or to put it more clinically the world economy. The French occupation has not left her for the moment in a condition to carry off this cohabitation with much ease. Moreover the actual character of the Algerian revolution does not seem to have done much to assist in making the best of a bad job. A revolution whose most gifted ideologist was Frantz Fanon is perhaps not likely to display stunning skill when it comes to living with the world economy. Today in the eighteenth year of the Algerian revolution[52] it still seems unlikely that the damned will inherit the earth.

At the beginning of the twentieth century the territory which is now Turkey made up the heartland of the Ottoman empire, an Islamic empire which had controlled to some degree, between the sixteenth and nineteenth centuries, a great part of the Mediterranean littoral from Tangier along the North African coast to the east and back along its northern shore as far as the Adriatic. In the sixteenth century up to the battle of Lepanto the Ottomans had threatened the conquest of the whole Mediterranean world in a way in which no Moslem power had done for more than half a millennium. As late as the 1680s Ottoman armies threatened the Hapsburg capital, the city of Vienna. By 1900, though, this expansive vigour was far in the past. Some parts of the empire, particularly Balkan countries like Greece and Serbia, had liberated themselves. One, Egypt, had in effect established its administrative and political independence without in any way deserting the official religious culture of the empire, though it had subsequently come under British military occupation. Yet other sections of the empire, particularly along the North African coast had become colonies or protectorates of one of the western powers. The Ottoman empire, like the other great non-European empire still in existence in 1900, the Chinese empire, had suffered severely from the combined military and economic expansiveness of the European powers from the eighteenth century onwards. Being for geographical and historical reasons much more intimately involved with European civilization, it had suffered in a more direct and a more obviously alarming fashion. The Chinese political class, the leading mandarins of the central and provincial administration, had had trouble with the western barbarians for much of the nineteenth century; but it was only towards the end of that century that any great number of them had difficulty in retaining a firm cultural perspective on the matter. China was the civilized world. The Chinese empire was the political embodiment of Confucian civilization and Confucianism was the universal set of truths which legitimated the Chinese empire.[1] Confucianism had travelled abroad beyond the limits of the empire – or at any rate what were now in the nineteenth century the limits of the empire, for instance to Annam and to Japan. Once arrived there, too, it had sometimes become associated with political forms rather radically different from those of the classic Chinese state. But from a Chinese point of view, at least until the late nineteenth century when Liang Ch'i-Ch'ao and K'ang Yu-Wei began to examine Japan to see whether it might not have a number of lessons to offer for China itself,[2] the fate of Confucianism abroad was not likely to be a topic of oppressive concern for Chinese thinkers. If Confucianism was rather different in a Japanese setting, so much the worse for the status by universal standards of Japanese civilization. Confucian China, the most intricate administrative structure of the largest subject population in the world with a scale of historical continuity which made all European states seem vulgarly parvenu, China was a world sufficient unto itself.[3] The western barbarians might be a damnable nuisance and their steamships might present military problems which were quite beyond imperial resources to deal with,[4] but from the point of view of significant cultural challenge, it was hard to see how they could even enter into consideration. The history of the Chinese empire throughout had been crowded by a succession of barbarian nuisances; wave upon wave of barbarian assault had been survived and absorbed. The Opium Wars and the establishment of rights of extraterritoriality in the Treaty Ports had been undeniable humiliations, excessively disagreeable necessities of state; but in themselves they had hardly constituted a profound existential challenge to the status of Confucian civilization or the state which exemplified it. Confucian civilization furnished answers to questions more pressing in urgency, profoundly deeper in significance and incomparably wider in scope than those of how to keep barbarian traders or missionaries in their place. The latter might, and indeed did, render the literati officials frantic by their provocations; but the literati, as the representatives of Chinese civilization, had little difficulty until the very end of the nineteenth century in remaining culturally blasé in the face of western civilization as such.

For a number of different reasons such poise was not readily available to the Ottoman statesmen of the nineteenth century. One reason, simple geographical propinquity, was obvious enough. The Ottoman empire as a unit was in real danger of dismemberment by western powers throughout the nineteenth century; and many of its outlying provinces were in fact detached from it in one way or another during the course of the century. But the main reason was not simply one of geographical location, though the latter certainly entered into it. The relationship between Islam and Christianity had been intimate in other respects besides the geographical throughout the history of Islam. Even doctrinally Mahomet was the culmination of a religious tradition which explicitly included Jesus Christ. The history of Islam in the west was a history of military confrontation with Christian civilization from the time of the conquest of Syria by the Arabs onwards, one marked throughout by crusades and countercrusades, by wars defined by both parties as holy wars. Islam was a religion much more doctrinally preoccupied with the possession of political power than Christianity, at least in the form in which that doctrine may be conjectured to have left the hands of its original proponent. It is a highly plausible interpretative allegation that the crusade, the infliction of Christian control over non-Christian peoples by force of arms, represents a perversion of the teachings of Christianity. But to attempt to extract the idea of the *jihad,* the holy war, from Islamic thought is not merely a delicate conceptual operation; it is in fact a doctrinal death blow. Military conquest was where Mahomet began. His kingdom was overtly designed to be of this world. The truths of Islam are vindicated by the military triumphs of the holy warriors, those who go on the *jihad.* Military conquest may have been where Christianity ended up; but despite the earlopping doctrinal deviations of Simon Peter, the kingdom claimed by the founder of Christianity, far from being a crusader kingdom was indeed a kingdom 'not of this world'. It was an accident of history that Christianity became associated with organized social power, first with Roman imperial authority and later with the variety of barbarian kingdoms which were to become in the fullness of time the N.A.T.O. powers. It was an accident of *military* success that Islam became the religion of such a large proportion of the globe; but it was not an accident, given that it did become at all widespread, that it should have become widely associated with political authority; rather, it was a doctrinal necessity, a logical consequence of the structure of the religious ideology.

By the nineteenth century, and more particularly by the second half of the nineteenth century, this characteristic of Islam had been rendered more than a little discomfiting by another major historical development, the growth of industrial productivity, military force and consequent political power, in the Christian states of western Europe. It is still – and has been ever since Max Weber – a subject of fierce controversy what relationship, if any, there was between this process of what is now frequently thought of simply as economic and military modernization and the fact that the countries in which it in effect began were in historical formation, if not necessarily any longer in elite intellectual culture, Christian countries. But whether or not the fact that modernity made its first appearance in Christian countries was a historical accident, or whether it was the product of an immanent cultural dynamic, it was from the point of view of the Islamic world a profoundly disturbing matter that modernity should make its first appearance wearing an infidel mask.[5] Inside western societies modernity, insofar as it was a distinctive idea at all, was largely conceived of in practical terms as a change in the level of human control exercised over the natural environment and in cultural terms as a form of secularization, a restriction of the social scope alloted to specifically religious values. Whatever the sociological origins of modernity in the west, the historical process in which it emerged, the human experience over time of secularization, hardly suggested to the participants in this process intimate connections between Christianity and modernity. In the Islamic world, by contrast, the geographical and historical source of modernity made all but the most unequivocally instrumental features of it intrinsically suspicious. Thus modernization in the Islamic world began and remained for some little time overwhelmingly military in purpose. But by the second half of the nineteenth century it was no longer possible for it to remain solely military in effect. At the beginning of the nineteenth century military technology, artillery, rifles and even factories in which these could be manufactured, could be imported wholesale and by themselves. By 1900 as a result of changes in military technology this was no longer so. In the aftermath of the Crimean war a whole series of changes in military technology, listed conveniently by Professor Hurewitz,[6] in artillery, machine guns and rifles, the communication of information and the bulk transport of supplies and in naval construction, revolutionized military industry. The main consequence of these changes for the rulers of Islamic states in the Middle East was that they were no longer in a position to hope to catch up with western military technology.[7] The military apparatus of industrial societies was increasingly impossible for pre-industrial societies to compete with in any serious fashion. Modern weaponry demanded modern armies and modern armies required the modernization of progressively wider segments of society, at first elite educational institutions to provide a modern officer corps, today perhaps mass educational institutions to produce a modern rank and file soldiery, then economic development to enlarge tax revenue for the purchase of increasingly expensive weaponry abroad, eventually industrialization in order to be able to manufacture weapons which are competitive with those of other modern powers and to retain the capacity to do so however the international diplomatic climate towards the country in question may alter. In the first stage military modernization in an Islamic country might in principle still be undertaken as a contribution to an essentially expansive strategy. The Napoleonic invasion of Egypt may have been a necessary condition for the establishment of Mehemet Ali's own unitary political control, but it was far from being a sufficient condition for the degree of expansive military power which he went on to amass and which made it possible for him to occupy Syria and threaten as late as 1840 the Anatolian heartland of the Ottoman empire.[8] But the intervention in 1840–1 of the major European powers with the exception of France made plain the weakness in international, as opposed to inter-islamic terms, of even Mehemet Ali's power. Subsequent Islamic modernization was for some time predominantly military in orientation and instrumental in purpose. It was also, by contrast with Mehemet Ali, for the most part rather limply defensive in character.

Contrasts between the military modernization of the Ottoman empire, the Islamic state which made most persistent efforts at military modernization and that, for instance, of Japan – not to mention the earlier history of Islam – must be explained in strategic terms. Had the Ottoman empire been in an economically more promising and strategically less pressured situation, as was Japan,[9] it might have been possible for the Ottomans to undertake extensive modernization in military, agricultural and industrial organization without to any great degree abandoning existing Islamic values (which were bellicose enough in all conscience) simply in order to generate the military and economic prerequisites for imperial expansion. In these circumstances, such a measure of secularization as ensued in this process would have been a product of the action of elites which were demonstrating their capacity to succeed in terms of a number of traditional values at the same time as they were engaged in modifying these values in practice in other respects. But in the circumstances which actually obtained in the Ottoman empire in the first half of the nineteenth century, the economic constraints on the central government were decidedly fiercer than they were in the Japan of the Meiji restoration, while the opportunity for rapid capital accumulation and accelerated economic development inside the empire and the strategic flexibility of the empire from a military point of view were both so restricted by the invasive pressures of western industry and western military power that there was little opportunity for military modernization to result in a self-reinforcing increase in the government's power to pursue traditionally accredited goals of military expansion. Thus when modernization came to the empire, it could not come in what was even at first a reassuringly insulated and instrumental form, but carried disagreeable secular overtones with it. And whereas secularization in Europe had been the product of a dialogue and a struggle internal to European societies, in the Ottoman empire secularization resulted from a defensive response of increasing urgency to the invasive impact of a traditionally inimical civilization. European secularization resulted from the integral logic of European civilization; but Turkish secularization, or the growth of secularism

inside Islamic society as a whole was a reactive phenomenon, a partial abandonment of identity in the effort to preserve any identity at all. Such a perspective focusses on the
city of Istanbul, the capital of the Ottoman empire, and on
the elite groups resident in it or in relation with it who
could plausibly conceive themselves as having some responsibility for its welfare. The number and membership of these
groups changed substantially between 1800 and the time of
the Kemalist revolution in the aftermath of the First World
War, largely as a result of successive stages in the effort to
modernize the military forces under the control of the central
government or its successor. Their preoccupations at all
points up to 1918 had much in common with the preoccupations of the central political elites, however recruited, of
other great surviving traditional empires of polyethnic composition, increasingly unable to sustain the pressures of great
power politics in an age in which the powers of western
Europe and the United States were engaged in rapid industrialization: the Austro-Hungarian empire of the Hapsburgs,
for instance, as much a casualty of the 1914–18 war as the
Ottoman empire itself, or the Russian empire of the Roman-
ovs, equally destroyed by the war but resurrected by the
triumph of the Bolsheviks. Some aspects of the policies of the
Ottoman central government in the nineteenth century had
some analogies with those of the Austro-Hungarian empire,
in particular the uncomfortable shift towards greater institutional recognition of local nationalist sentiment; and there
are obvious resemblances in the degree of strategic exposure
to foreign military threat experienced by the two empires.
The contrast between the closely encircled character of the
Ottoman and Austro-Hungarian domains and the comparatively unthreatened borders of much of the Russian empire is
instructive. If any one of the three empires was to be revived
as a political unit after its wartime collapse, the Russian empire presented a more viable strategic entity than either of the
other two. As to why exactly the Russian empire did survive,
it is still, despite the attentions of a number of distinguished
historians,[10] hard to be sure which were the crucial factors. But
in this context it is not necessary to offer any clear explanation
of the survival of the great Russian state, it is merely necessary to note the crude geographical and strategic advantages

which it enjoyed in comparison with the Ottoman empire and which made it conceivable that it would survive the cataclysm of the First World War, in a sense in which it is hardly conceivable that the Ottoman empire should have done so.

The unit which did survive the post-war collapse of the Ottoman empire turned out in fact to be the Turkish nation, a geographical unit defined on an ethnic and linguistic basis, a state open to legitimation as the political embodiment of a national group, the Turks. It was not a particularly easy feat to retain the viability in international power political terms, the sheer military defensibility, of even the land area of what is now Turkey. But at this stage in the progressive disintegration of the Ottoman state, a section of the Ottoman political elite under Kemal Ataturk were in a position to restrict their political energies to the protection and reconstruction of a political unit which could, given decisive and skilful leadership, at last *be* defended with success. They were also given in some respects particularly favourable conditions in which to attempt this political reconstitution, the invasion of the Turkish heartland of Anatolia by the armies of what had some time previously been one of the subject nationalities of the empire, the Greeks. The Turks as an ethnic and linguistic group were by no means confined to Anatolia or indeed to the territories of the former Ottoman empire. Indeed there were numerous Turkic groups in Russian central Asia. But the Turks had been, ever since the beginning of the Ottoman empire, the core nationality of the empire and Anatolia, the area invaded by the Greeks in the aftermath of the First World War, was the demographic centre of Turkish settlement in the empire. In these conditions Kemal Ataturk was enabled to lead a movement in circumstances which in many respects constituted a Turkish war of national liberation. A section of the Ottoman political elite set out to defend a residue of the Ottoman state in the guise of a Turkish nation; and it found it a simpler matter to establish the plausibility of such a political entity, as other contenders for national political leadership since have done, when the area over which they were attempting to establish their authority was predominantly inhabited by a single ethnic group, an ethnic group associated in the past with geographically more extensive power, and when this area was being invaded by armies made up of another ethnic group. Kemal and his officers, then, were presented with a peculiarly favourable opportunity when compared with those available to previous segments of the Ottoman elite, though the energy with which they took it is not readily susceptible of neat sociological explanation. Furthermore, while the Turkish nation may have been from a demographic and strategic point of view a unit which *could* with energetic leadership be rendered viable, it is certainly unclear not just that the Kemalists would be successful in establishing its viability but also that if they were successful (or in the effort to achieve success) they would have been *compelled* to establish the particular type of social order which did in the end emerge from the Kemalist revolution. In particular it is not easy to argue that it was the necessities of the situation of Turkey at the beginning of the 1920s (as opposed to the personal will of Mustapha Kemal Ataturk) which meant that Turkish society was so painfully secularized in all its public aspects, nor that it should have been eventually, though somewhat fitfully, transformed into a parliamentary democracy. Indeed the massive social forces which have been at various times devoted to reversing either or both of these transformations – and indeed the mutual tension of the two transformations when an overwhelmingly Islamic and peasant electorate chooses the government of a supposedly secular and 'modernizing' state – hardly suggest that the Kemalist programme was well adapted in all aspects to the historical situation of Turkish society, let alone that it was a logical transposition of its structural imperatives. It is perhaps a more plausible allegation that the failure of the more leftist segments of the Turkish national movement in the face of the Greek invasion, the so-called Green Army and the first champions of a Turkish communism, *did* reflect the continued internal stability and the massive conservatism of Turkish rural society. Turkey had not been subjected to direct and protracted colonial occupation, though the Anatolian economy was naturally not wholly unaffected by the world market. The conditions of the struggle against the Greek invasion plainly failed to provide the conditions for establishing an agrarian radical leadership in the national liberation struggle.

In order to begin to understand the force of the drive

towards secularism which led Ataturk to such extremes it is necessary to understand not just the intimate links in formal ideology between specifically religious values and the archaic constitutional structure of the Ottoman order, but also (and not as a simple functional derivative) the relationship between opposition to secularization and the political power of the traditional status groups which controlled the Ottoman polity. The key to understanding the slow pace of secularization within the Ottoman state is not merely the recognition of the prodigious conceptual distance between the formal theory of the Ottoman order and that of a secular state, it is also the absence for a considerable period of time of any class or powerful status group to provide a political or social basis for reform efforts. The traditional Ottoman order represented in ideological pretension a complete integration of state and religion (*din-ü-devlet*).[11] The position of the Sultan or *Padişah* had certain interpretative prerogatives attached to it, but its status derived solely from it being the formal head of a theocratic order. The norms which governed the activities of the state were laid down in the *Şeriat*, the Arabic *Sharî 'a*, based on the Koran and the body of accredited traditions of the Prophet.[12] Its application to concrete issues was formally the task of the body of *Ulema*, scholars who acted as judges, theologians and educators under the general authority of the *Şeyhul-Islâm*,[13] the supreme religious dignitary of the empire under the *Padişah* (and one who in certain circumstances had the legal authority, if not the executive capacity, to depose the *Padişah*). In addition to the directly religious roles of the *Ulema*, there were two other groups of functionaries, administrative and military, who shared in the control of imperial affairs. The administration under the Grand Vizier, the *Sadrazam*,[14] was a comparatively central and homogeneous body; but the military officials, whether the central corps of Janissaries with their elaborate involvement with metropolitan artisan interests and their increasing military superannuation or the provincial cavalry forces, the *sipahîs*, the holders of imperial benefices, together formed an elaborate and entrenched series of interests, necessarily threatened by any form of military modernization.[15] The provincial benefice system had by the eighteenth century been largely diverted from its original military purpose, producing a series of essentially uncontrollable feudal tenures and contributing to the increasingly disastrous fiscal policy of paying present imperial debts by alienating future imperial revenue. One other feature of the traditional Ottoman system which had initially been a manifestation of considerable political and military assurance, but which was to become with the renewed expansion of European Christendom a major weakness, was the *millet* system.[16] Although the Ottoman empire was an Islamic state, quite large sections of its population did not belong to the community of believing Moslems, the *ümmet,* but were organized instead as largely self-administered religious communities of Latin or Orthodox Christians or Jews, known as the *millets.* The Islamic community of the empire had shown over time decidedly more talent and inclination for maintaining a plural society than the majority of Christian states. When the empire was once again subjected to the military challenge of Christian expansion, the *millets* became metamorphosed into ethnic groups struggling for national liberation.

It is not difficult to see, in looking at this traditional structure, that any very decisive innovation might well risk the appearance of heresy, and that being heretical in a state in which religious dignitaries held such a salient position was an uncomfortable position even for a Sultan.[17] Innovations with an obviously secularizing dimension threatened the political, and in all probability the economic, interests of the official exponents of the imperial ideology. Innovation of a specifically military kind threatened the economic interests of powerful local fief-holders, encouraging efforts to promote a measure of feudal disintegration in the empire, and it threatened the political and economic interests of the military units quartered in Istanbul itself. At the same time many of the pressures from the outside which in the end forced the empire to attempt a measure of military modernization also greatly increased the problems of internal military control which it faced, because of the encouragement which they gave to *millet* separatism. Heresy and opposition on the part of entrenched political interests were sufficiently powerful obstructions to reformist enthusiasm in themselves. When allied, as under the pressures of western expansion they at times came to be, with the charge that dealings with foreign-

ers in the effort to modernize amounted essentially to treasonable cooperation in the infidel assault on the empire, they
guaranteed explosive political resistance to reformist efforts
emanating even from the highest quarter. Until well into the
nineteenth century any substantial level of modernizing reform had to be based politically upon the residue of purely
autocratic power available to the *Padişah* and his chief
minister. As soon as the reformers posed a clear threat to the
interests of the *Ulema* as a whole or to the Janissaries, this
residue of autocratic power was placed in jeopardy. The
palace coup was a recurrent threat in the Ottoman polity. A
reforming *Padişah*, like Selim III in 1807, was in the end an
almost inevitable recipient of this disagreeable favour.[18]

In order to understand where the social basis for large-scale
reform in the empire derived from it is necessary to examine
the early history of modernizing efforts, a history which essentially resulted in the creation of institutions largely independent of the traditional power-holding status groups and
more diverse in the sources of their social recruitment than
these latter had become. It was from the staffs of these novel
institutions, in particular from the officer corps of the modern
army and the instructors in the modern educational institutions, that the protagonists of reform were drawn.

In its earlier period of expansion the Ottoman empire had
been eager and on the whole successful in its attempts to
adopt military or naval innovations by the Christian powers
which seemed likely to be of material advantage.[19] But the
empire's political structure was very much that of a conquest
state; and its administrative apparatus was impossible to
maintain at its early level of excellence inside a fixed or
shrinking defensive perimeter. In the seventeenth and in the
early eighteenth century the efficacy, both military and diplomatic, of the empire wilted and the policies pursued by the
central administration became more conservative, more introverted and more rigid. The beginnings of significant
modernization in the empire came in the first half of the
eighteenth century, usually upon the advice of renegade
Christians. They were commended almost exclusively in
terms of the assistance which they might be able to offer in
confronting the geopolitical threat from the Christian states
in general and from the nascent Russian empire in parti-

cular. The career of Peter the Great was on several occasions held up to the Ottoman government as a fitting model for their emulation.[20] For the first time in 1699 the Ottoman empire had been compelled to sign a peace treaty, the Treaty of Carlowitz, explicitly as a defeated power; and it was obliged to repeat this humiliation a mere nineteen years later in the Treaty of Passarowitz. Shortly after the second date Ottoman ambassadors were despatched on extensive commissions to Vienna and Paris to investigate the opportunities for emulation.[21] Not long afterwards, in 1727, a Hungarian Unitarian refugee Ibrahim Muteferrika was allowed to set up the first printing press in the empire to print works in Turkish, excluding only works of specifically Islamic scholarship, with the official theological blessing of the *Şeyhul-Islâm* and of fifteen other leading *Ulema*.[22] In 1731 Ibrahim published a work of his own entitled *Rational Bases for the Polities of Nations* which set out to answer the question of why it was that 'Christian nations which were so weak in the past compared with Muslim nations begin to dominate so many lands in modern times and even defeat the once victorious Ottoman armies.'[23] He attributed the geopolitical advance of the European Christian powers to a combination of technical military and naval innovations and the establishment of political structures designed to advance the public wealth and power. He even went so far as to point out in a guarded way that the legal codes of European states were now based upon rational principles, while the Ottoman polity was founded upon the *Şeriat*; but he left the issue of what conclusion should be drawn from this particular contrast carefully open.[24] The main thrust of his argument was to urge that the bigoted Ottoman disinterest in the doings of western powers had already brought the empire to a condition of extreme peril and that this peril could only be averted by a systematic attempt to learn from the Christian powers all the skills of military technology and administrative organization of which they currently disposed. Peter the Great, he pointed out, had succeeded in transforming the Russian administration by systematic imitation of western models and had contrived to develop powerful modern armies and navies by importing European military and naval advisers to reorganize and train these forces.[25] The steady military pressure of the Russians, particularly north of the Black Sea, was a persistent preoccupation of the Ottoman government; it was not surprising that the first serious efforts at military modernization should have been initially commended and in the end practically undertaken because of anxiety to contain this threat. In 1734 a school of military engineering, essentially for the training of artillerymen, was set up, probably under a French renegade.[26] Forty years later after a costly six-year war with Russia, French technical assistance made possible the establishment of the first modern military unit organized on European lines, independent of the Janissary system. The Military Engineering School had been re-established with a well-educated Turkish staff in 1769 and in 1776 a Naval Engineering School staffed largely by French officers was also established.[27] A third period of reform, to be followed as in the two earlier cases by a more protracted period of reaction, began in 1792 under the young Sultan Selim III. Efforts were made to establish modern gun foundries and arsenals, together with a complete new army, known significantly as the *Nizam-i-Cedid,* the New Order, wholly independent of the Janissary system. The military engineering school was extended in 1792 and 1795 and numerous European instructors were imported. (Among the unsuccessful candidates from France for a technical post was Napoleon Bonaparte.) In 1793 permanent Ottoman embassies were set up in the leading European capitals: London, Paris, Vienna, Berlin and Madrid.[28] A serious attempt was made by the Sultan to apply the lessons of European civil and military success, described by one envoy in 1791 as resting upon 'a disciplined army, ordered finances, enlightened, honest and patriotic public officials and popular security and prosperity'[29] to the chaotic, corrupt and threatened circumstances of the old Ottoman order. But in many ways the situation hardly offered much hope of success in this Augean labour. The enthusiasm of the French government in the second half of the eighteenth century for offering their services as technical assistants to the Ottoman government, was a product of *French* expansive purposes in the eastern Mediterranean. Driven out by the British in mid-century from their extensive settlements in India and North America, French imperial energies switched to the Middle East in quest of the economic opportunities presented by the decay of Ottoman power, the prizes both strategic and commercial of controlling trade routes from the Red Sea and the Black Sea into the Mediterranean. French military and naval officers engaged in assisting the Ottoman forces were also frequently engaged in systematic military and naval espionage for their own state, on one occasion even going so far as to investigate the possibilities for driving a canal through the Suez isthmus.[30] Selim III himself, whilst heir to the throne, had been discovered to be in correspondence with the French court and his ally the then Grand Vizier had been disposed of in consequence for sedition. Napoleon's invasion of Egypt at the end of the century only confirmed the darkest suspicions of Ottoman reactionaries for several decades. While even Selim's correspondence with Versailles had been innocent enough in fact and while there was in reality no well-grounded reason to suppose that the reformers in the Sultan's entourage were in any way equivocal in their allegiance to the Turkish state, there can be no question but that the French and other European military experts whom they employed were frequently engaged in activity which was directly treasonable in nature from the Ottoman viewpoint. However pure the reformers' intentions under these circumstances it was difficult for their efforts in practice not to be constructively treasonable in effect. Furthermore the combined concentration of both reformers and reactionaries on the purely military threat, particularly from Russia, obscured the reality of another threat which in the long run was to prove at least equally lethal.

The trade of the empire had come to be largely in non-Turkish hands and artisan production, except insofar as it was covertly integrated into the Janissary system,[31] was largely abandoned to traditional guild organizations, rather than considered as a direct and continuing object of state policy.[32] By the early nineteenth century, Ottoman domestic production in the heartlands of the empire was increasingly archaic in character when set against the forces of European economic competition. At the same time the diplomatic energies of European powers had been extensively devoted to enlarging the privileges previously made available in the capitulations and to establishing an effective domination of the empire's domestic markets. The threat identified two centuries earlier, in the face of the price inflation of the sixteenth century, by a number of imperial advisers that the Turkish economy would become essentially a colonial primary producer obliged to purchase industrial goods from the European countries and to exchange its own agricultural products for these on increasingly unfavourable terms of trade had now become actual.[33] The relationship between the economic resources of the empire and its ineluctable military commitments in the sheer struggle to survive made its strategic situation one of crippling weakness. The only powers which were likely to provide any significant measure of assistance were those which had something direct to gain from doing so: still further inroads into Turkish domestic markets or a favourable opportunity to participate in the territorial dismantling of the empire. Only a much greater measure of disintegration in the empire could make possible a reasonably stable preponderance of power of the reforming elements over the reactionary forces. Equally, only a much greater measure of its disintegration could leave the inheritors of the Ottoman state with a national unit susceptible of defence on the basis of its surviving economic resources.

Between the death of Selim III in 1808, murdered because of the threat of an attempt on the part of the reformists to return him to the throne, and the rising of the Young Turks, the Committee of Union and Progress, against the Sultan Abdul Hamid in 1908, there was a crucial shift in the social strata from which reformist impulses derived. In the time of Selim III, either the Sultan himself and his immediate entourage or the traditional political status groups were still in a position to arrest all reform with some success. By 1878, the year in which Abdul Hamid suppressed the reform Constitution of the empire which had been granted in 1876 and reverted to a personal autocracy, the obstructive power of the traditional political status groups had been effectively destroyed. Only the will of the Sultan himself could hold back the tide of reform. Thirty years later not even the autocratic will of the Sultan could continue to do so. The same measures which had made it possible for the Sultan to exert despotic power, whether in a reforming direction or for purely reactionary ends, had during the period from Mahmud II's reign to 1908 created a new social group which was no longer prepared to tolerate a despotic and reactionary order. In a development reminiscent in many ways of certain stages of enlightened absolutism in western Europe, the Sultan Mahmud II had established a much greater degree of centralization in the Ottoman administration than it had known for centuries, by means of a systematic assault on a variety of traditional and localist privileges and the power of the groups which held them.[34] By redeveloping Selim III's modern army, the New Order, he had acquired an instrument which gave him the military capacity to destroy the Janissaries in 1826. Following on this triumph, referred to by the reforming party as 'The Auspicious Incident',[35] he had proceeded to abolish the remaining military fiefs supporting traditional cavalry units and to divert the revenues directly to the imperial treasury. Despite eventually and definitively losing control of Egypt to Mehemet Ali and being compelled by the western powers to accept the independence of the Morea, he had established a much greater measure of control over the remaining provincial governors of the empire. In religious affairs he established a government department to administer properties assigned to religious endowments, a measure which promised some possibility of eventual economic control over the *Ulema*.[36] In 1838 an administrative body established by the Sultan, titled the 'Board of Useful Affairs', even went so far as to propose the establishment of a national system of secular education. But the Board lacked the constitutional power to implement this recommendation and it was a prospect which proved altogether too disquieting for the *Ulema*. A school for providing elementary secular education, employing the Lancastrian monitorial system, was set up by the army to train rank and file soldiers and to furnish basic preparation for courses of instruction for officers.[37] Above the primary level the Board of Useful Affairs established two secondary schools for adolescents, designed to bridge the gap between the traditional Koranic schools and the secular establishments of higher education. The Engineering Schools of Selim III were re-established, a military music school was set up (one of the instructors being Donizetti pasha, a brother of the composer), and a Military Academy, modelled on Saint Cyr was added to these in 1834.[38] Mahmud II in short was a classic modernizing autocrat, attempting to centralize political control and to impose administrative uniformity on a chaotic and particularist traditional society which exemplified in practice to the highest degree Montesquieu's criterion of political liberty, the capacity of one power to obstruct another. But unlike the enlightened despots of western Europe Mahmud did not have any emergent social class in the society at large with which he could cooperate in his efforts. Those who were in the end to carry the effort of modernization significantly further were not generated by the internal development of society itself. In a very direct fashion they were the epigoni of the Ottoman state apparatus, as modernized and centralized by Mahmud II. It was from a military and administrative elite educated in western secular culture in the midst of a traditional rural and urban society whose educational experience, where it possessed any educational experience at all, was restrictedly Islamic in character that the residuary legatees of the Ottoman empire in the end emerged. The officer corps of the army and the civil bureaucracy may in the end have created a class of entrepreneurs, industrial and commercial, even agricultural, but they did so essentially through their own etatist attempts at economic expansion, after rescuing the Turkish state as such, not through the administrative and peace-keeping services which they provided to an existing economic class. Capital accumulation through purely (or even impurely) economic activity was no easy feat for a Turk in the nineteenth or early twentieth centuries. The regime of the capitulations was extended during the nineteenth century under French, British and Russian diplomatic pressure at different times, until the whole foreign trade and much of the internal trade of the empire was in the hands of hundreds of thousands of resident foreigners and the Turkish government had virtually no control over trade flows into or out of the empire. The financial services of foreign banking combines threatened the political autonomy of the imperial administration itself.[39] Tariffs fixed by international treaty at very low rates made it impossible to protect Turkish industry or domestic manufacture. Virtually no modern industry was in consequence established and traditional domestic manufactures decayed. The Young Turks of the Committee of Union and Progress were the first national political leaders to attempt a measure of industrial development to restore this balance.[40] But it required the development of instruments of economic control in the war and the five years of Kemalist insurrection afterwards to create the real possibility of national economic planning, while the sloughing off of the last restrictions from traditional commercial groups inside the society, Greek, Jewish, Armenian in particular and the enormous resettlements of population which this represented, left the Turkish masters of the Turkish state at last in control of the economy. Even then the control which they exercised was hardly a very full one. The Ottoman state, like the Russian and Chinese empires had become heavily indebted to foreign capital during the nineteenth century in the effort to perserve its own political viability. Like China, but unlike Russia, it had been forced to accept a measure of international control over its debt repayments – indeed been obliged to consign up to 30 per cent of its budget to servicing these. Also like China before 1914, and unlike Russia, it had been quite unable to achieve any significant level of industrial development on the basis of these loans. Even public investment in infrastructure, railways, roads and port facilities, was very low. Such railways as there were were mostly uneconomically sited and whatever eventual returns on capital they yielded were re-exported. After the establishment of the Kemalist regime, governmental control of the residual economy was much more extensive; but even after 1923 the Turkish government continued to repay annually on the Ottoman Public Debt a sum which at times reached some 10 per cent of its total annual revenue and it only ceased to do this as late as 1947.[41]

It is a necessarily contentious question how successful the policies of etatism should be judged to be in developing the economy within the limits of freedom open to the Turkish government. There has certainly been substantial development since the Treaty of Lausanne accepted the existence of the modern Turkish state in 1923, both in terms of gross national product, industrial development, agricultural productivity and average per capita income. Equally clearly, rates of population growth and substantial economic incompetence on the part of planning staffs over the decades (and perhaps particularly over the period from 1958 on) have meant that rates of per capita growth have been compara-

tively low and the increase of literacy and welfare facilities in the more backward rural areas still very restricted.
Illiteracy which was nearly 90 per cent in 1927 was still
just over 50 per cent in 1965.[42] Turkish agriculture continues to present grave problems and there seems little
prospect of their being solved from a purely economic point
of view in the near future. In the early 1960s one million
out of the total of three million families engaged in agriculture were partial owners, share-croppers, tenants or landless labourers, while of the two million peasant proprietors
a large proportion were farming essentially uneconomical
units.[43] There have been a number of land-reform measures
passed by the government since 1923, but their implementation has been extensively frustrated by the opposition of
feudal landowners in the south-east and of more modern
capitalist large-scale farmers in the west and north-east.[44] The
rural sector is characterized, as is usually the case with largely
peasant countries, by massive disguised unemployment, and
the rate of expansion of wage-employment in the industrial
sector will clearly not be able to absorb surplus rural labour
within the reasonably near future. Further land reform is
clearly necessary to enable a growing agricultural sub-prole-
tariat to continue to live on the land in tolerable conditions.
But uneconomical settlement patterns and general shortage
of development capital mean that large proportions of the
rural population can hardly contribute materially to the production of marketable agricultural surpluses.[45] Efforts were
made from the 1930s on to improve the position of poorer
peasants by establishing agricultural credit cooperatives; but
these have not enjoyed great success. Ecological factors, a
shortage of development capital and an absence of trained
agronomic personnel: all three combine to make it difficult
for the government to stimulate rapid agrarian development.

The product of the Turkish revolution, the new secular
nation state of Turkey established by Mustapha Kemal in
Anatolia between 1919 and 1923, has certainly not contrived
an economic miracle. But the social basis of its economic
policies was from the beginning a tense balance of a state
bureaucracy, military and civil, committed to national viability and a strongly traditional rural society committed predominantly to being left alone.[46] There was virtually no

Turkish proletariat in 1919 – certainly none in the rural heartland of Anatolia; and the issue of national viability was posed in very direct terms for Turkish rural society, as well as for the members of the modern bureaucratic groups, by the Greek invasion. The joint resistance of the modern military and civil leaders under Ataturk and the traditionalist peasantry was made acceptable to both by this common threat. In order to be left alone, indeed in order to escape the domination of despised traditional foes and inferiors, the Anatolian peasantry were forced to commit themselves to the restoration of a viable national unit within which to live. Hence when the Turkish state had duly been established as a result of this successful resistance, its possessors and manipulators had strong emotional as well as prudential reasons to prevent it from encroaching too drastically upon the perceived interests of Turkish rural society. Kemal Ataturk received significant military and economic assistance from the Bolshevik government during the independence struggle and indeed subsequently. He and his ministers were delighted in the aftermath of the war to pick up from the Soviet Union hints on how to promote economic development and industrialization by means of state action. The etatist programme in effect was simply the Bolshevik industrialization programme detached completely from its ideological moorings and its association with a profound hostility to peasant society as such: electrification without a hint of Soviets or collectivization. Lacking either the economic or the educational prerequisites for massive industrialization or the political predilection for collectivizing the peasantry, the Turkish government were left with a messily pragmatic series of expedients for increasing national power by promoting economic growth. These did something to restrict the havoc inflicted upon Turkey by the Great Depression, while being compatible with the perceived interests of both the major groups, peasants and bureaucrats whose efforts had established the nation. In the absence of either an existing Turkish entrepreneurial group of any size, wealth or experience and of an existing Turkish proletariat and with class stratification little advanced in the villages it is not easy to see what alternative economic course the Kemalist government could reasonably have pursued. Had Ataturk in fact failed to drive out the Greek invaders

and Anatolia been occupied by the Greeks or even partitioned it is conceivable (though not perhaps particularly
probable) that an alternative political elite might eventually
have emerged to lead a more traumatized peasantry in a
national movement based on hostility to class stratification in
the countryside as well as to foreign occupying forces. But in
the forces grouped around Ataturk the Anatolian peasantry
already possessed an effective national political elite with a
strong will to power and an impressive mastery of modern
military and diplomatic skills. The alternatives which did
offer themselves, a variety of Communist and Socialist groups
based on Istanbul, Anatolia or the Russian oil ports of Batum
or Baku, the so-called 'Green Army', Circassian bandit leaders
or discredited former Ottoman generals turned volunteer
leaders of Russian puppet regimes like Enver Pasha, were none
of them of impressive political weight.[47] Ataturk thrashed the
bandits militarily, outmanoeuvred with ease the various political groups (at one point setting up his own Official Communist Party of Turkey, but never officially falling out with
the Bolshevik government) and in the end suppressed them
all with some finality. A ramshackle array of unattached intellectuals and naive and over-ambitious brigands, they had
no significant basis of social support and their foreign affili-
ations and conspiratorial tactics in the military and diplomatic crises of 1919 to 1923 made it easy to brand them as
traitors to the nation. It is important to understand this because the brief history of Communism in Turkey between
1919 and 1923 constitutes in many ways a precise reversal of
the key development of the Chinese revolution. Between
1927 and 1945 Chiang Kai-shek had shown himself to the
aspiring national elites of China to be incapable of defending
the national interests of China, while Mao and the Chinese
Communists had shown themselves brave and effective
national champions. Between 1919 and 1923 in Anatolia a
national bureaucratic elite which did not hold its power
because of its position in the rural class structure and which
had nothing to lose but its power within the residue of the
state which it was attempting to defend proved itself a vigorous and devoted protagonist of the interests of a beleaguered
ethnic group and, in doing so, recreated a nation. In China
the K.M.T. was associated with the oppressiveness of land-

lord power in a rural social order which systematically betrayed the values of its traditional ideology and, as a government, it did not dare to resist the modern armies of Japan
because of the vulnerability of the modern cities which it
held and their almost certain loss in the event of a Japanese
attack. In Anatolia the residue of the Ottoman armies under
a superbly capable leader made a final stand to defend the
interests of the Turks as their traditional empire disinte-
grated, as the Entente powers occupied the imperial capital,
the Greeks invaded Anatolia itself, the Armenians threatened
to secure their independence and the Russians, the most
persistent enemies of the empire for several centuries[48] in-
trigued busily, too, to extend their power inside Turkey. The
greater part of Ataturk's political energies were taken up with
the political forces to his right, the interests committed in
some fashion to the traditional Ottoman order. In the critical
military conditions of 1919 to 1923 it was no very difficult
matter to discredit the disorganized opposition to his left by
disclosing accurate enough information about its very practical commitment to the interests of a traditionally hostile, if
openly practically helpful, foreign power. In a sense Ataturk's
skill, like that of Nasser after him, may perhaps have been
more impressively demonstrated in his capacity to continue
to secure Russian assistance in the midst of suppressing the
local allies and instruments of Moscow, than it was in the
comparatively unexacting task of actually carrying out the
suppression.

Given Ataturk's personal commitment to secularization
and the establishment of a viable national independence for
the Turks, the key to the understanding of the Turkish
revolution is not so much the narrative account of the reforms
which Ataturk contrived to implement once he *had* achieved
power, as it is the more structural explanation of how it was
that anyone of whatever political skill could contrive to
achieve and preserve power within a framework in which this
programme could be implemented. Ataturk's own prodigious
personality gave in practice a slightly artificial clarity of line
to the Turkish revolution. But the years since his death have
consequently served to restore a proper degree of imprecision
to the outlines of what is meant by it. It is possible, even, as
it is with the Russian or Chinese or Cuban revolutions that

nothing closely resembling what we now think of as these events would ever have taken place had the particular charismatic leader himself not appeared when he did. Many political and social structures in the twentieth century have experienced profound crises. Most of them have not experienced anything much resembling a revolution. A novel order is not an easy structure to create and the cult of personality, consequently, not an arbitrary feature of twentieth-century historical experience. But whatever the personal contribution of Ataturk, what it is useful to consider at the level of generality adopted here is merely what it was about the situation in Anatolia in 1919 which made it *possible* for him to exert such a startling impact on the history of his country.

Kemal was an Ottoman officer. He was not, it is true, a member of the Committee of Union and Progress itself, the group which forced the Sultan Abdul Hamid to put into operation the suspended Constitution of 1876; but he made his mark in national politics during the three years following the Committee's move of 1908. Like Enver Pasha, a member of the Committee and of the subsequent imperial ruling triumvirate, he went to Libya to organize resistance to the Italians in 1911. He led the victorious resistance to the Allied invasion of the Dardanelles during the First World War and had himself appointed as Inspector-General of the Ottoman armies in Anatolia in its aftermath. The Committee of Union and Progress itself struggled to establish control over the central administration of the empire from 1908 on with little initial success.[49] The Committee won two massive electoral victories as a result of the wide support which they enjoyed among the younger Ottoman army officers, civilian administrators and modern professional men in general throughout the Turkish areas. But they were not, as the Young Ottomans had been,[50] members of high-status families in the traditional ruling bureaucracies. Their power came from their relationship with military units. But the Sublime Porte, the central administration of the empire, remained largely outside their control; and, quite apart from the intermittent risks of counter-revolutionary coups, like that of 1909, many of the policies pursued by the empire were strongly in conflict with their aims. Those policies which did take some effect often had rather disastrous consequences. The Italian seizure of

Libya had little connection with governmental efforts; but the loss of virtually all the European territories of the empire, and the rising in the Yemen, were all connected with Unionist projects of centralization and the suppression of localist resistance.

Enver Pasha's career as a Pan-islamic or, later Pan-turanian leader was an epitome of the first stage of the young civil and military bureaucrats' campaign: the establishment of a unified, centralized modern regime, constitutional if possible, but militarily effective at all costs. The effects of these policies culminating in the Arab revolt[51] and in the Entente occupation of Istanbul was the total liquidation of the Ottoman empire. As the Greek armies moved into Anatolia in 1919, Kemal Ataturk was left with the opportunity to point up and eventually to transform into effective political reality a very simple contrast. The Sultan and the traditional Ottoman government sat in Istanbul, the prisoner of the Entente powers, signing away in the Treaty of Sèvres virtually all remaining interests of the Turkish people. Kemal at the head of the surviving Turkish armies in Anatolia was able to set up National Assemblies and consolidate the resistance of the Turkish people to the Greek invasion. History forced the Turks to choose between the Sultan and Kemal and it made the choice a simple one. Kemal himself contrived that the choice should amount to a novel but viable national identity, a nation of Turks within a militarily defensible frontier with their own language, a secular law, no Sultan, no Caliph and even, in the end, western hats instead of the fez. The prophet Mahomet himself had allegedly proclaimed: 'The worst things are those that are novelties, every novelty is an innovation, every innovation is an error, and every error leads to Hell-fire.'[52] Kemal, taking him at his word, decided that only complete secularism could make Turkey modern; so he made the Turkish nation, a nation state able to survive in the modern international arena, a secular state. Mahomet had also said that 'He who imitates a people becomes one of them',[53] and Kemal perhaps hoped here too that his prophetic insight would hold good. But although Kemal could and did make the Turkish state into a passable imitation of a western secular state, he had less success plastically with Turkish society, the great bulk of which remains firmly Islamic.

The Turkish revolution was made by the epigoni of a state apparatus and its makers remade a nation state for themselves to rule over. They had no particular desire for the most part – and at least equally limited capacity – to remake a society.

8 *Cuba*

Of all the revolutions of the twentieth century none was quite as surprising when it actually happened as the Cuban revolution. It is still possible, even now, that it may turn out to be the most influential of all the twentieth-century revolutions, and this, not so much because of its merits, as because of its very unexpectedness. All of the other revolutions so far considered took place in overwhelmingly peasant countries. But Cuba not only had an extremely high *average* standard of living in comparison, for instance, with other Latin American countries, it also had more than 50 per cent of its population resident in its urban areas,[1] particularly the great swollen metropolis of Havana. The outbreak of the revolution in Cuba had no very direct connection with participation, or above all defeat, in either of the two world wars of the present century, experiences which were clearly crucial to the forms taken by the Russian, Chinese, Turkish, Yugoslav, Indonesian and even, in a refracted way, Vietnamese revolutions. Cuba, unlike Algeria, Vietnam or Indonesia was not still a colony and it could not be said very accurately to have been under military occupation. There was an American military base on the island, Guantanamo; but its formal status rested on an international treaty between the Cuban and American governments, not on any form of American claim to local sovereignty. It was true that Cuba had *once* been a colony and that the process of decolonization had been for it quite unusually destructive, involving a decade of murderous and unsuccessful struggle and another protracted and bitter war at the end of the century. It was also true that the role of the United States in the final stage of decolonization had been highly equivocal from the viewpoint of Cuba and that the famous Platt amendment giving the United States a legal right of intervention in Cuban internal affairs was a slight on national autonomy particularly humiliating even for Latin America. It is equally true that the United States had a very dominating position in relation to the Cuban economy and that the Cuban government which Fidel Castro overthrew in January 1959 was corrupt, dictatorial and subservient in its fundamental policies to the economic interests of the United States. But both of these last two considerations would have been equally true of numerous other Latin American countries – and indeed, except for the identity of the capitalist power in question, would be true arguably of a great many different countries in other parts of the world too. Hence, if the occurrence of the Cuban revolution is in some ways harder to explain than that of many other revolutions in this century, it was for many none the less welcome for that. With no third world war immediately in sight (and, perhaps more importantly, with the prospect of a third world war becoming harder and harder for the most inexpert or the reddest to face with equanimity), and with colonies becoming in progressively shorter supply, it has been the historical effect of the Cuban revolution, whether justifiably or not, to have resuscitated the plausibility of the revolutionary role as an option for the future and not merely a glorious embellishment of a vanishing phase of history. It has bred a kind of vaudeville of revolution, centred around the glamorous figure of Ché Guevara, and rationalized by a clever French philosopher, a pupil of the stern Althusser, Régis Debray.[2] The content of this interpretation is not intellectually impressive.[3] In it the revolutionary is transmuted into a type of D'Artagnan figure and the more intractable issues of social change and economic order brushed aside for a facile preoccupation with the seizure of power. This is a logical extension, no doubt, of part of the Leninist heritage; but it is a logical extension only of *part* of it, and that the part most insecurely related to the matrix of Socialism. In any case, whatever the internal legitimacy of its genealogy, it seems more illuminating to see this most recent revolution in the revolution as a mirror-image of the counter-insurgency theory developed by the French army in Vietnam and Algeria and since extended in literary bulk and in geographical incidence, if hardly in intellectual force, by the Americans. By choosing the role of international Robin Hood, Guevara kept his hands cleaner than he might have contrived to do inside Cuba; but he scarcely helped to establish the title of the Cuban revolution as the herald of a new and better economic order even in Cuba. The character of his intervention in Bolivia suggests that even the most talented of the Cuban revolutionaries had failed to draw the right lessons from the Cuban experience – perhaps in part because he was not himself a Cuban. The success of the Cuban regime at the very task of establishing a new economic order (which, as time goes by, must necessarily become more salient in proving its title to emulation by others in Latin America or even beyond) is still sufficiently in doubt for a long-time supporter of the regime like the agronomist René Dumont to question seriously whether Cuba is a Socialist country[4] and for Fidel Castro himself to confess a good measure of bafflement at its economic situation.[5] It is plainly more important, here, to understand why it was, in other than semantic terms, that the Cuban revolution took place in *Cuba*, than it is to suggest any great likelihood of anything closely resembling it happening anywhere else in the near future. Indeed, if Dumont is right, it may well be more important also from the point of view of advancing elsewhere the social values which the Cuban revolution is alleged to exemplify to understand just why it was that it happened in *Cuba* and to understand *what* it was that did happen there. This is not to say that we should attempt to remove the element of surprise altogether from what did take place. The inevitability of particular revolutions is strikingly easier to perceive in retrospect than it is to predict in advance. In some ways an analysis of Cuban history and the condition in which it had left Cuban society and the Cuban economy by 1959 makes the Cuban revolution a readily intelligible series of events. But the merest attention to the outlines of the story provides a salutary reminder that what is socially intelligible as a historical outcome is not necessarily at all easy to bring about in the real world. Fidel Castro and his handful of followers in the Sierra Maestra no doubt felt that there were powerful forces working on their behalf; but they were in the best possible position to sense the fragility of any supposedly necessary triumph for the Cuban revolution.

The fact that the handful of survivors from the yacht

Granma did manage to raise an effective guerrilla movement against Batista's substantial and well-equipped army and in the end did succeed in overthrowing the regime, must reveal something about that regime. In particular it suggests that the absence of significant and effective foreign (that is to say, United States) counter-insurgency assistance to the government in the last two years of the revolt may well have been an important factor in assisting (perhaps even a necessary condition for) Castro's success. Equally the development of the 26th July Movement's policies after taking power undoubtedly shows much about the character of the Cuban economy and the difficulty of maintaining its operation in the prevailing manner, once the structure of dictatorial social control had broken down. But it also draws attention to very significant features of the international environment in which those who had secured control of the Cuban state were enabled to make their decision on what they would choose to do with it. The existence of international rivalry for political influence and a measure of political control between the United States and the Soviet Union, together with the simple geographical location of the island of Cuba, at points less than a hundred miles from the American coast,[6] gave to Castro a crucial initial dimension of freedom of action which could hardly have been available to a radical leader even a dozen years before, let alone earlier than that.[7] The Soviet Union was understandably eager to acquire a political, and if possible a military, foothold in a territory so close to the American mainland. It was eager to begin to extend its influence into Latin America and to disrupt American commercial hegemony wherever it existed, partly simply as a component of the general assault on the economic structures of the major capitalist powers and partly in order to improve the international trading situation of its own economy and that of the industrialized countries of eastern Europe which had substantially passed under its economic control.[8] Over the years Cuba has been both an expensive and, in some ways, a politically rather intractable ally for the Russians: René Dumont estimates that they had disbursed some 4,000 million dollars on it by 1969, without including the costs of armaments.[9] But it is no doubt a sufficient recompense for these costs that Cuba in return has more than fulfilled the nightmares of

American policy-makers. In many ways the series of economic policies pursued by the post-revolutionary government has not turned out to be particularly successful.[10] Even with the bounty of the Soviet Union the net effect of the Castro regime after a decade of power is less than stunning in purely economic terms; and, as Dumont points out obviously enough, the Soviet Union would not have the resources to bail out on a comparable scale the government of one of the major Latin American nations, Brazil or Mexico for example, let alone Latin America as a whole.[11] If there was an intimate link between the degree of economic specialization of Cuba under Batista and its bitter political and economic dependence on the United States throughout the twentieth century, there was an equally intimate link between this degree of specialization and the very high *average* standard of living by Latin American standards enjoyed by the Cuban population, deriving from the comparatively well-protected position of the Cuban urban proletariat[12] and of a substantial proportion of the landholding peasantry in sugar production. The same factors which at the level of social structure made it possible to carry out a strikingly popular anti-American national revolution, at the level of economic structure made it extraordinarily difficult to reconstruct the economy and adjust it to new patterns of international trade, without drastically depressing in the long run average living standards.[13] Initially, despite the shifting character of their economic objectives, the revolutionary leadership preserved a good measure of confidence in their handling of economic problems. But, as the years went by, and more blithe projects ended in disaster than came to any very impressive fruition, and as American pressures became more insistent, the arbitrariness and authoritarianism of the political structures became more consolidated. It is quite possible that they would have relaxed little even without the stimulus of these economic perplexities: Cuban history and Cuban society were little marked by experience of democratic structures or understanding of democratic values and the prevailing cultural preoccupation with masculinity and violence fitted readily into an authoritarian political order. But, on the other side, the populist sympathies of the leadership were communicated with histrionic effectiveness and their authenticity was plain enough. At the same time the United States which had cast itself decisively over the preceding seventy years as the symbolic arch-enemy of the Cuban populace, while involving the Cubans extensively in the toils of its own distinctive way of life, played out its role as focus for the projective hostilities of Cuban society with an unerring touch. In case there might begin to arise, in the prevailing aura of economic incompetence, some ambiguity as to just what the Cuban revolution was now about, what net services it was providing and to whom, the Americans contrived to ensure that there should still remain, vividly to the fore, the menace of American imperialism for it to be *against*.[14] An embattled society, with a reliable enemy to make its contestant posture reasonable, has provided in consequence the key image of the Cuban revolution. But, however evocative this image may have been, it was necessarily selective as an interpretation of the social character of the revolution. It fits with suspicious neatness one universalist account of what is at stake in international politics today, the struggle between *Socialist* production, epitomized by the Soviet bloc and more recently by the People's Republic of China, and the forces of world capitalism, in this instance epitomized by what, in the light of the Bay of Pigs to say nothing of a long series of earlier incidents, is quite accurately identified as United States imperialism. Cuba first played a really symbolically salient role in American history during the declining years of Southern slavery, when the planter ideologues urged the acquisition of the island to provide the additional land area which the Southern slave system required in order to expand geographically, the only remaining fashion in which it could retain its economic viability.[15] Genovese's elegant and persuasive neo-Marxist rationale of the economic decline of slavery lends the planter dream of annexing Cuba a decided historical resonance, as the last vain yearning of a doomed civilization. There are strong ideological incentives, particularly for young Latin American radicals – or for North American revolutionaries with their unenviable domestic prospects – to see the Cuban revolution of 1959 and the regime which it has brought into being as playing a comparably definite role in the disintegration of the doomed American empire, the post-war order constructed by the United States to preserve the domination of international capitalism over the national economies of the greater part of the world. But the attempt to explain why it was that events which are now properly titled – both for the better and the worse – the Cuban revolution did take place in Cuba can hardly preserve the reassuring (or as it would be for others disturbing) simplicity of these outlines. To understand the occurrence of the Cuban revolution is certainly not to grasp the inevitable (or perhaps even the probable) end of the American empire within any readily predictable future. In particular the rather complex process which makes up the Cuban revolution lends singularly little plausibility to the idea that a handful of intellectuals and hangers-on, very possibly from another country, taking to the hills to carry out a guerrilla operation will constitute necessarily any sort of serious challenge to the entrenched political and military elites with their fiercely nationalistic modern armies who currently control the governments of almost all other Latin American countries. The sheer physical scale of the island, taken with its comparative wealth, fostered a degree of national integration which could not be matched by other Latin American countries like Mexico or Peru with their massive Indian populations resolutely on the margins of the modern sectors of society and economy or by the sprawling backlands of Brazil. The extent of urbanization in Cuba and the extent to which even the rural population had been proletarianized by their participation in the sugar industry gave Cuba a social structure very unlike that of most other Latin American countries.[16] At the same time the intimacy of the island's links, economic and cultural to say nothing of political, with the United States was much greater than with any other largely urban and proletarian nation of the continent, like Uruguay. This is not to say, of course, that there is not great revolutionary potential in a number of other Latin American countries with very various social structures and current economic problems;[17] but it is to say that an understanding of the Cuban revolution may not be at all a helpful way of approaching the question of which (if any) of them are likely soon to experience a revolution, let alone of what assistance (again, if any) such an experience would be likely to offer to them in facing their economic problems.

To understand the Cuban revolution it is necessary to understand how its distinctive social structure arose, and why its economic dependence upon the United States had become so painfully clear decades before the revolution and lasted virtually unscathed despite the resentment which its clarity evoked in many Cuban circles. It is also necessary to understand why the Batista regime in the end collapsed so ignominiously in the face of a military challenge which in its earlier stages was simply negligible and which indeed never reached more than relatively minor proportions in strictly military terms. The last is not difficult. By the time that Castro took power a combination of internal economic difficulties and increasing repressive brutality had served to alienate a great proportion of the politically concerned populace from Batista. The combination of astonishing and well-demonstrated bravery with a tasteful blurring of political outline which Castro's 26th of July Movement offered (perhaps authentically enough) provided a wide variety of those disaffected with a splendid focus for their contestant aspirations. Much of the literature in the 'Revolution Betrayed' idiom has been mildly fatuous in conception;[18] but there would hardly have been such a spate of this literature had so many and so diverse political groupings not felt such high hopes of Castro's enterprise. There was clearly much arbitrariness to the fact that as many as a dozen men in fact survived the landing from the *Granma*;[19] and even more arbitrariness to the fact that three of these twelve were Fidel Castro, Ché Guevara and Raul Castro (and hence perhaps to the fact that the guerrilla rising was in the end successful). But there was no arbitrariness to the fact that (in a slightly lunatic way) it did make sense to embark on the *Granma* with fewer than a hundred men to go to challenge a dictatorship with a modern and American-equipped army and that Castro had an evocative tradition in the history of Cuba, the tradition above all of José Martí,[20] behind him in setting out to struggle in this way. It is the historical basis of this tradition, a genuinely national tradition in a way in which Peru or Brazil for example could scarcely be said to *have* a national tradition, which must be identified before it is possible to grasp Castro's fidelity to his own revolutionary aims throughout its muddled and intermittently almost pointlessly destructive course.

With most of the revolutions considered here, it has been a key question to ask of them what was the identity of the group on whose behalf the revolution was purportedly made. Who were the Turks in, for example, 1900? Who were the Yugoslavs? Who, even, were the Russians? Was the Russian revolution simply the definitively successful assertion of Great Russian chauvinism? (Probably the Russian revolution was not *simply* anything.) Will the Vietnamese revolution turn out, when the Laotian or Cambodian regimes disappear from view, to represent a final triumph of the Vietnamese empire? Cuba, neatly enough, is an island. Today the Cuban leadership may think on a tri-continental scale; but the scale on which they had to succeed in taking power was merely one rather large island. There is, then, nothing very teasing about the geographical locus of the Cuban revolution. But who exactly, apart simply from those holding Cuban nationality, were the Cubans? They were not any of them any longer for example millennially indigenous inhabitants of the island. The peoples whom the Spaniards found in the island on their arrival at the turn of the century were Arawak Indians – perhaps 60,000 of them, of which a mere 1,000 survived as a separately recorded group by 1544.[21] Since then the remainder has been virtually erased both demographically and culturally. There is, then, no Indian problem in Cuba: one major difference from, for example, Bolivia, as Guevara was later to find out. All Cubans, black, white or varying intermediary shades, are today essentially immigrants and a great many of them are immigrants of the last century and a half. Cuba, especially in the last century of Spanish rule, was 'unquestionably the major slave colony of the Spanish empire'.[22] By 1850, partly through the destructive impact of the revolution in Haiti, it had become a major world sugar producer and by continuing illegal slave importation had built up a very large slave population. Sugar had been introduced into the island as early as the sixteenth century by the Spaniards. Four centuries of negro gang slavery in the cane fields might have created a fearsome heritage of racial hatred for the Cuban nation today. But in practice it was not until the nineteenth century that Cuba became essentially a sugar island and the type of slave system which developed from the sixteenth to the eighteenth cen-

turies under the ideologically concerned and highly centralized administration of the Spanish crown and its lay and
ecclesiastical associates had an important impact upon the
present character of Cuban race relations.[23] If the Southern
states of America had had their way and contrived to annex
Cuba and assimilate it to their own pattern of slave-holding,
one group of Cubans who would certainly have noticed the
difference would have been the Cuban freedman and in all
probability the urban slave population too.

The social relations of the Cuban population were clearly
affected by the fact that a certain percentage of the population were descended from negro slaves. Up to the revolution
(and possibly in a greatly diminished form even today) socially acknowledged coloration and socio-economic situation
were closely aligned. Whiter Cubans tended to be decidedly
richer, though rich Cubans tended (especially inter-genera-
tionally) to be becoming somewhat whiter. The 'coloured'
proportion of the Cuban population has been falling fairly
steadily since 1861 when it formed some 45 per cent of the
population to 1953 when it formed only 26.8 per cent; and
this trend seems to have been due to effective assimilation,
rather than to any more rapid rate of net immigration by
white than by black settlers.[24] The whole history of Cuban
race relations despite the fact that Cuba became a slave
colony almost as soon as the Spanish occupiers arrived has
been in significant contrast with that of North America.
Cuban slave law throughout formally protected the legal
status of the slave as an independent human personality in
a number of ways, recognizing the right to make full Christian
marriages and protecting them in numerous respects once
made, encouraging the development of literacy, providing
strong legal encouragements to manumission and recognizing
a variety of rights to personal security for the slave and his
family for which he had the legal standing to demand the
protection of the royal courts.[25] The effectiveness with which
these laws were enforced naturally varied greatly: it would
be naive to suppose that they constituted much alleviation
of the lot of the slaves in the sugar gangs in the mid-nine-
teenth century. But there did exist royal lay administrators
and ecclesiastical officials who were charged directly with
their enforcement and it is certain that they never simply

lapsed, though the brutalizing of social relations deriving from the sugar boom may have made them a rather insubstantial protection for much of the nineteenth century.[26] But for most of its history not only the legal framework but also the character of Cuban economic development served in some measure to protect the slave population from the level of degradation experienced in North America. After the first gold seams had been worked out, quite early in the Spanish occupation, it was not immediately apparent what economic role the island of Cuba would be usefully able to play in the Spanish imperial economy. No plantation crops were developed with much intensity until the 1760s.[27] The island's economic activities were largely focussed from the mid-sixteenth century until the late eighteenth on small-scale tobacco cultivation, on extensive cattle-ranching to provide hides and tallow for export and on the development of the great city of Havana as harbour for the treasure fleet, with all the subsidiary provisioning services which such a function demanded. Cuban agrarian activities were thus for several centuries largely taken up with raising cattle on open lands and with the raising of tobacco, of fruit and vegetables in the vicinity of the cities, especially Havana. Cuba was an extremely urbanized society by pre-industrial standards. A substantial proportion of the slaves, on (unreliable) official figures up to 50 per cent,[28] were not engaged in agrarian activities at all, but were working in the cities in a wide variety of artisan and labouring roles. In addition to this proportion, there was a substantial free coloured or mulatto population. In 1846 the population of Havana included 62 per cent free or slave negroes or mulattoes,[29] and other Cuban cities had an even larger proportion. The urban and artisan character of much of the slave population led to the development of much freer systems of work regulation than existed on the plantations, in particular to extensive use of a version of the Roman procedure of the *peculium*, whereby skilled slaves hired themselves out for what they could get and paid their masters a fixed sum per week or month, frequently buying themselves out of slavery with the savings which they accumulated from the remainder. There was in consequence a large free coloured population, with its own volunteer military units, with some access to education, and with a vigorous cultural life of its own virtually throughout the period of negro slavery in the island, the numbers of which seldom except in the period between 1817 and 1855 fell much below half of those of the coloured slave population[30] and which were particularly heavily concentrated in the urban areas. The structure of social control for the urban coloured population as a whole was strikingly less hostile than in the southern American states and monetary incentives played an important part in the regulation of labour. At the same time in the first two centuries of Spanish settlement slave-holding in the rural areas was also rendered less oppressive by the very real possibility of physical refuge for the oppressed slave. The Cuban climate and the absence (unlike in a North American colony like Virginia) of a hostile indigenous population on the frontier of effective settlement made it possible for permanent communities of escaped negroes, the *cimarrones* or maroons, to live in freedom in the backwoods, often raiding colonial settlements and cooperating with buccaneers or more conventional military detachments despatched by other colonial powers against the Spanish colonial forces.[31] Despite repeated governmental efforts to destroy them, maroon villages continued to exist in the mountainous regions at either end of the island in Pinar del Rio and above all Oriente from the second of which the leaders of the Cuban war of independence set out in 1868 and from which too Fidel Castro's forces succeeded in overthrowing Batista ninety years later.[32] Cuba is an easy country in which to maintain a modest physical subsistence on the land. It is also eminently well suited to the cultivation of sugar-cane, an activity which, if practised efficiently, requires excessively hard physical labour over one part of the agricultural year. Until the coming of a really massive sugar crop, Cuba was not particularly wealthy and its geographical configurations and legal heritage contrived to keep the oppressiveness of its social relations within reasonable limits, by prevailing historical standards. Havana was a luxury town, almost a tourist town, from the sixteenth century because of its favourable position on the Atlantic crossing. It had, and was to retain for the American trade right up to Castro's revolution, a large population of prostitutes.[33] But Cubans at large certainly did not suffer from this immodest prosperity. It was sugar which brought the real bitterness to

Cuba's social heritage, leaving the gay and decadent cities perhaps no more damaged than those elsewhere in the Caribbean or Latin America,[34] but riveting upon the countryside a brutal labour regime which resulted in a rash of slave revolts. Cuba became rich and populous, but in doing so it also lost the moderating influence of maroon licence. Something like the dynamics of unopposed capitalism began to operate in earnest at last.[35] They were not to be obstructed effectively again until Castro and his followers returned to the old maroon hideaways of the Sierra Maestra to begin the reconquest of Cuba. Since his triumph, three years later, Cuba has contrived to export some surplus and some perhaps not exactly *surplus* population;[36] and it has entirely reorientated its political economy. But it is still unclear how far the wealth can be maintained without a continuing submission to the still savage labour disciplines of the sugar harvest and it has proved easier by far to disrupt the crude constraints of capitalist labour mobilization for this purpose than to provide any reliably institutionalized alternative procedure which is not absurdly wasteful in economic terms.

The creation of the full-scale sugar economy involved a striking increase in the size of the population. The total population of the island was about 170,000 in 1774, with a white majority.[37] By 1804, it had reached 500,000, with a significant coloured majority, including at least 180,000 slaves. It continued to show a coloured majority beyond 1855, by which time the total population was well over a million.[38] The peak slave population, recorded in the early 1840s, amounted to more than 400,000. It seems never to have been the case that the majority of slaves were engaged in sugar cultivation; only some 66,000 out of 260,000 in 1825 for example or 150,000 out of 400,000 in 1860.[39] But even these proportions meant that very large numbers of slaves were engaged in cane cultivation under the most appalling conditions, almost as many slaves by 1860 in fact as the figures for the entire population of the island less than ninety years earlier. The effects of this dramatic expansion in an unskilled and brutalized negro labour force upon the integration of Cuban colonial society were necessarily highly destructive.

However, Castro's revolution was not in itself an instance of Black Power and the aspect of the sugar economy against which it was directed was not confined to the destructive consequences of a labour system whose legal basis was definitively abolished in 1886.[40] It was not so much Cuba as a sugar island, nor even the political structures which this economic role created which gave the Cuban revolution its distinctive direction. Cuba became a sugar island while it was still a Spanish colony. It was still a sugar island when it won its independence from the Spanish crown in a vicious three-year war between 1895 and 1898. What *did* provide the occasion for Castro's revolution sixty years later was the historical relationship which derived from the way in which the war of independence ended, from the military intervention of the United States.[41] Cuban independence from Spain was effected by a peace settlement, the Treaty of Paris, to which no Cuban was even a party. The United States did not recognize the Cuban insurgents as a provisional government and U.S. forces remained in military occupation of the island for four years from 1898 to 1902 and returned to take over executive authority again from 1906 to 1909.[42] The Cuban constitutional convention was forced to accept as a part of the Cuban constitution the famous Platt amendment, which was passed by the United States Senate as a rider to an army appropriation bill.[43] In May 1903 this was incorporated into a treaty between the two countries, signed after the withdrawal of U.S. occupation forces.[44] It required Cuba to sell or lease lands to the United States for naval stations, limited Cuba's treaty-making powers and its capacity to contract public debts, insisted on the Cuban government's introducing sanitation into the cities in a form acceptable to the American government, and gave to that government the right to intervene in Cuba 'for the preservation of Cuban independence' and the maintenance of a government capable of protecting life, liberty and property.[45] Had the Soviet Union had the foresight to get such a clause included in the constitutions of Hungary and Czechoslovakia, many international legal embarrassments might well have been avoided. But while the actual inclusion of such a clause in the constitution was an unusual practice for the United States to require even in a Caribbean country, it had a place within a tradition of political conduct which was well-consolidated both before and after 1902. Besides its exploits in Cuba itself the United States intervened in countries in the

Caribbean area between 1895 and 1933 no less than thirty times,[46] slightly under once a year on average. In 1912 the solicitor of the Department of State, who should presumably have been well placed to know, observed that no nation 'has with more frequency ... used its military forces for the purpose of occupying temporarily parts of foreign countries'.[47] When Theodore Roosevelt attempted to justify the seizure of the Canal Zone of Panama to a meeting of his own cabinet one of its members, Philander Knox, was led to protest acidly: 'Oh, Mr. President, do not let so great an achievement suffer from any taint of legality.'[48] American military power and the contempt for Caribbean nations with which it was deployed evoked powerful hostility in Cuba from the date of independence onwards. Hatred for the United States was a key political emotion in the island and the progressive integration of Cuban sugar production into the United States metropolitan market gave the emotion an increasingly wider and more intimate frame of reference for the great majority of the population.

Cuba did become to a very considerable degree an economic colony of the United States, as Guevara[49] and others complained. It was a prototype for the most offensive style of neo-colonialism, a relationship in which American governments intervened persistently in Cuban internal affairs in order to favour the interests of American citizens. It is not, however, possible to give an adequate analysis of the economic relationship between Cuba and the United States by treating the interests of the American metropolitan economy as unitary and as comprehensively inimical to those of Cuba as a whole. In the extravagantly destructive three-year war of independence, the Cuban economy had been severely damaged. Some 300,000 had died, many as a result of the system of concentration camps established by the Spanish General Weyler.[50] The area under cultivation in 1899 had fallen by about 30 per cent from that of 1895.[51] Both numbers of cattle and production of tobacco had fallen by some 80 per cent and the sugar harvest was a mere 300,000 tons compared with a million tons in 1895.[52] American occupation may have helped to restore a modicum of civil order and economic viability in the wake of the departing Spaniards. It certainly contributed to the re-establishment of the communications network and to the creation of more effective public health measures, specially against yellow fever. Over later decades the inflow of American investments and of loan funds to the chronically indebted government, often in a form which violated the letter as well as the spirit of the Platt Amendment, were all conceived of – and not altogether absurdly in intention – as contributions to the Cuban economy and polity. But the gains never failed to be balanced by rather obvious costs. In return for the gift of American investment capital (by no means an inexpensive gift of which to be on the receiving end) the Cubans also had to accept sustained American complicity in the very fly-blown political structures which served to maintain a level of law and order acceptable to the resident American ambassador, an individual, as one of their number testified in 1961 to a U.S. Senate Committee,[53] always the second most powerful man on the island and often more powerful than the Cuban President himself. It is at least possible, perhaps even probable, that the average per capita wealth of Cuba would have been as low or lower in 1959, had American assets been extensively confiscated in the revolutionary spasms of 1933 to 1934[54] and had American capital not significantly penetrated the economy since that date. What is certain is that if this had been so, there could not have been such an overwhelmingly plausible and powerfully emotive *explanation* of why it was no higher and of why it was distributed in such an inegalitarian fashion. By the 1920s an economic relationship between the two economies had come into existence in which American restrictions of Cuban sugar imports were as provocative from the Cuban point of view as American intervention had been in the past. At this point American failures to exploit Cuba were necessarily as offensive as American exploitation of it. The consolidated tradition of distrust within which all actions of the United States towards Cuba were perceived guaranteed that nothing the United States did would be interpreted favourably. Little which it did do was calculated to help to dissipate this distrust.

American ownership of Cuban sugar land was much increased in the aftermath of the war of independence. In 1896 American investment in Cuba was estimated at some $50 million, chiefly in mining and sugar properties.[55] But with the Cuban–American reciprocity treaty of 1903 the integration

of the two economies increased rapidly. In return for a 20
per cent preferential reduction in the U.S. sugar tariff, Cuba
gave 20–40 per cent tariff reductions for a number of American products. The Cuban share of the American sugar market
which had been 17.6 per cent in 1900 reached over 50 per
cent by 1913 and the value of American exports to Cuba,
$27 million in 1897, reached $200 million by 1914. During
the First World War American capital displaced European in its predominance in Cuba. Preferential access
to the American market facilitated the expansion of the
Cuban sugar industry, much of it owned by American
firms. At the same time preferential access for American
manufactures militated against the establishment of Cuban
domestic industries of an import-substitutive character. After
the First World War American politicans became increasingly sensitive to the dependence of American economic stability on foreign trade.[56] Mayor James Curley of Boston
estimated in 1924 that only seven months per year of American factory production could be absorbed by the domestic
market; the remaining five months worth required to be
exported if it was to be sold. American civilization would
collapse into anarchy if foreign trade were interrupted for
more than a few months, Herbert Hoover observed.[57] Hence
there was heavy American diplomatic pressure to preserve
favoured access to the Cuban market for American manufactures. At the same time American investment in Cuba
rose by more than 500 per cent between 1913 and 1928.[58] By
1929 it had reached more than $500 million, over 27 per cent
of total U.S. investment in Latin America, and American
interests controlled over 70 per cent of the sugar crop. The
world sugar market, though, was not only subject to dramatic
price-fluctuations, it was also increasingly competitive because
of the protected position of beet sugar producers in several
of the wealthy consuming countries, particularly the United
States. American beet sugar secured a steeper tariff against
Cuban sugar in 1922, threatening directly the interests of
American producers of raw or refined sugar in Cuba itself
and indirectly the export opportunities of numerous American manufacturers on the Cuban market. In 1927 the Machado government in Cuba threatened a programme of national
autarky[59] and in 1928 the U.S. Foreign Trade Convention

was warned that if the United States continued to be so careless of Cuban sugar interests in its tariff policies, Cuba would be forced to attempt to industrialize. In 1929 to 1930 there was a massive lobbying battle over the Smoot–Hawley tariff in which American sugar interests in Cuba, American domestic industrial consumers of Cuban sugar and American industrial exporters to Cuba, in conjunction with the Cuban President, Machado, fought the American domestic beet-sugar producers in Congress to restrict a proposed increase in the tariff on Cuban sugar.[60] In 1927, as the Cuban historian Guerra y Sánchez pointed out,[61] the United States government was receiving more than 140 million pesos in excise income on Cuban sugar, almost double the total annual revenues of the government of Cuba. Some of this indeed was even diverted as a direct subsidy to American domestic beet-sugar producers. With the increase in the tariff in 1930 and with growing imports into the United States from its Puerto Rico and Philippines possessions, the Cuban share of the U.S. sugar market declined from 49.4 per cent in 1930 to 25.3 per cent in 1933.[62] In 1934, in 1939 and 1941 Franklin Roosevelt made efforts to improve the tariff position of Cuban sugar in return for corresponding tariff concessions for American imports into Cuba.[63] Despite a substantial decline in total size as a result of revaluation in assets after the sugar crisis, U.S. direct investment in Cuba still ranked third among Latin American countries in 1956, despite the fact that its rate of increase since 1946 had been the lowest of that made in any of the leading Latin American countries.[64] The American share of the sugar industry had fallen: Cuban-owned sugar production in the island in 1955 made up 58.7 per cent of the total, while American interests produced some 40 per cent of raw sugar. But outside the sugar sector matters were not encouraging. U.S. interests owned more than 90 per cent of Cuban public utilities and about half of Cuban public service railways, while 80 per cent of Cuban imports between 1946 and 1950 came from the United States and 73.4 per cent continued to do so even in 1955.[65]

From the American military withdrawal in 1902 until 1959 it had been American policy to secure a Cuban government capable of protecting (and disposed to protect) American investments in Cuba. In a memorandum of 1921 drawn up by the American representatives engaged in vetting the acceptability of the Cuban presidential election, listing six desirable qualities for a Cuban President to possess, 'thorough acquaintance with the desires of this government' headed the list which was rounded off with a further item, 'amenability to suggestions or advice which might be made to him by the American Legation'.[66] The President who met these stringent standards duly broke up strikes and exiled union leaders who had been troubling the American sugar centrals. An American bank loan to the Cuban government in 1923 was marketed, with State Department permission, with a summary of the first three articles of the Platt Amendment printed on the loan prospectus.[67] American marines were moved into Camagüey province in 1917 to protect American railway and sugar properties. By 1921 the pretence that they were engaged in training exercises had worn thin and there was strong Cuban government pressure for their removal to the treaty base of Guantanamo. But an American businessman, the President of the Cuba Company, objected that 'that section of Cuba is a hotbed of Bolshevism. The Bolshevists are inclined to destroy property. The presence of the marines has prevented them' and he succeeded in persuading the U.S. administration to keep them there until next year.[68] Under the dictator Machado, an American bank, the Chase Bank, had at one point loaned over $250,000 to the President in person or to his private business interests and in addition had taken onto their payroll his son-in-law whom they described as 'from any business standpoint ... perfectly useless'.[69] When Machado, after several years of increasingly tyrannical and arbitrary rule, was overthrown in August 1933 by a military revolt, an American envoy of a most unusual sort, 'more a Proconsul than an ambassador',[70] Sumner Welles, who had temporarily deserted the Assistant Secretaryship of State for the assignment,[71] had been in Cuba for some months trying to coerce Machado into a more compliant frame of mind. Disappointed by his exiguous success, Welles had just started reluctantly to negotiate with opposition leaders the replacement to Machado which he had concluded to be necessary.[72] Welles continued to advise the interim Cuban government on how to deal with rising labour unrest and outbreaks of violence. Two American warships were despatched to Havana for their 'moral effect' and the Cuban Secretary of War requested Welles to arrange for American reinforcements to be on hand at Key West and Guantanamo. In September 1933, a month after the first army revolt, a mulatto sergeant stenographer, Fulgencio Batista, with student support took control of the army and set up a new government under the Auténtico leader Grau San Martín.[73] Labour disorders worsened and several sugar mills across the island were seized by their workers. Twenty-nine American naval vessels were ordered to proceed to Cuba or Key West and the Ambassador, Sumner Welles, as well as numerous American businesses on the island, urged intervention on the grounds of dangers to American property. But Roosevelt refused. The San Martín regime was described by Welles as 'ultra-radical' with 'frankly communistic' theories.[74] But it did not take long for Welles to realise that Batista was, as another American observer put it, 'too ambitious to have radical leanings'.[75] The U.S. government decided in consequence not to recognize the nationalistic San Martín government on the grounds of the 'seemingly communistic tendencies' revealed by its passage of a Workman's Compensation Law and decrees affecting electricity rates.[76] They adhered to their resolve, despite pressure by British interests on the island through the British government, to recognise the existing Cuban government. Instead the United States representative succeeded in detaching Batista from the existing government and in January 1934 Batista and the army removed Grau San Martín and replaced him with an administration representing more acceptably the entrenched pro-American political elites, a regime which the United States promptly and cordially recognized as the government of Cuba.

The formal character of the political regime established by this deal varied a certain amount. Batista, for instance, retired from the island in 1944 for some years and settled down in Florida to enjoy the massive fortune which he had accumulated.[77] In his place two Auténtico Presidents held office, Grau San Martín and Prío Socorrás. The levels of corruption exhibited by both of these governments represented little, if any, of an improvement over Batista's own performance.[78] Disgust at the prevailing decadence of the political order led to the creation and expansion of a further political party, the Ortodoxos, for which Fidel Castro stood as a parliamentary candidate in 1952.[79] But shortly before the end of Prío Socorrás's term of office in 1952, Batista once again engineered a military coup and returned to the Presidency, dispensing with the electoral process. As Cuban governments went, Batista's first period of office had been reasonably popular, marked by a certain amount of labour-protective legislation and the establishment of effective control over both labour and producer interests by a combination of bribery of selected individuals and the distribution of carefully chosen benefits. But in the period following his 1952 coup the Cuban economy was in a very difficult situation. There were few economic benefits to distribute and the proportion of coercion to bribery employed in the social control of large groups was decidedly higher than in his earlier period of power. He continued to enjoy what might be politely termed 'realistic' relations with the Cuban Communist Party and there was no organized working-class opposition until Castro had virtually seized power. Even in April 1958, when Castro's 26th July Movement called for a general strike in support of the rebels in the Sierra, the strike was eventually opposed by the Communist Party and was an almost complete failure.[80] It was an extremely miscellaneous assemblage of (mostly rather young) Cubans whom Castro succeeded in leading against Batista, first in 1953 in the assault on the Moncada barracks[81] and then three years later, after their training in Mexico, on the yacht *Granma,* purchased for Castro by the elaborately discredited former President Prío Socorrás.[82] Castro's own political apprenticeship in the corridor gunfights of the University of Havana was not such as to lay emphasis on the finer subtleties of ideological commitment.[83] He knew very clearly what he was against: the whole seedy Cuban political order with its intimate and degrading dependence upon United States power. He knew that it would be no easy feat to destroy it and he did not in consequence take the trouble to spend much time worrying about what exactly he would attempt to create in its place, if the opportunity came. Extravagantly brave and histrionically compelling, he was the perfect leader for a hopeless armed struggle, though his suitability for governing a country was perhaps more marginal. The true slogan of the Cuban revolution is still '*Patria o Muerte*', fatherland or death, a slogan as much in keeping with the suicidal assault on the Moncada barracks as with the assurance with which the Cuban forces repulsed the grotesque American invasion of the Bay of Pigs. Batista showed his judgement of the political significance of the soon to be formed July 26th Movement by allowing Castro to live in Havana for over two months after his release from the rather short prison sentence actually imposed for his part in the Moncada affair.[84] It required a man of Castro's startling personal qualities to fault Batista's practised judgement of what was and what was not, in Cuban political terms, a dangerous threat. Only a man radically detached, whether by his own choice or by force of circumstances, from all interests in the existing order and indeed one ready unhesitatingly at any point to sacrifice his own life to the restitution of national honour could have led a revolt against Batista which did terminate in a social revolution.

Castro (with in due course the ready assistance of the United States government) turned the struggle against Batista and the first years of his successor regime into a desperate battle to restore the tarnished national honour of Cuba. He could hardly have had the nerve to carry out the social revolution which he in the end did carry out, if he had at any point been ready to set the short-run economic interests of the island above what seemed to his bitter vision the effort to win in reality for his country an independence which had never before been more than nominal. '*Patria o Muerte*' is a less than luminously directive slogan for a socialist revolution. But its reckless bravado, and perhaps its mild social myopia too, was a necessary condition for accepting the appalling risks of the course on which he despatched the island and for holding to it insofar as it made any sense at all in spite of (and at times almost because of) the external pressures to which he was subjected.[85] There were, moreover, extremely large potential gains in the long run from the course in question which lent some point to the risks, and there was plainly no very happy future to the economic structures within which Batista or his stand-ins had always chosen to work. Cuban average real income per head (in constant prices) was around $201 in 1903–6. It was still around $200 in 1956–8.[86] In this half century there had been massive immigration of labour, largely unskilled but with some, particularly from Spain, with valuable professional or artisan accomplishments. Its agricultural fertility was startling: sugar grew like a weed[87] and many other crops could be raised successfully with moderate care. But although quite a number of other crops were in fact produced on the island, average yields for most of them were markedly below international standards.[88] Cuba was a capitalist society and many of its problems, from stagnant real income, vast areas of unused farmland, and exotically inefficient agricultural production from the viewpoint of maximizing yields did derive from its position in the international capitalist economy. But it would be a grave error to suppose that these structures derived from the logic of the free market. Indeed many features of the Cuban economy were about as far from the free market as the holders of political power, the sugar centrals, the Cuban political class, the cattle barons, and the labour unions[89] could make them. The product of a vast series of protective pay-offs designed to preserve the profitability of a guaranteed market to all those granted access to it, it systematically sacrificed to this goal all other Cuban economic interests whatever: above all the interest in economic growth. An integrated series of interlocking regulative and producer associations painstakingly redistributed income among each other in order to prevent any of the parties suffering unduly in periods when the sugar quota or crop were unfavourable and to spread the returns widely among the partners in times of prosperity. These arrangements were not, of course, charitable in intent. They resulted from the persistent deployment of political power by groups which could not safely be ignored. Batista's regime in many ways resembled the corporate states and its elaborately cartelized markets and toughly negotiated monopolistic privileges effectively protected the interests of the best *organized* sectors of society, proletarian, agricultural producer or industrial manfacturer. As a regime it possessed a singularly hideous secret police, along with a massive tolerance for gambling, prostitution, and the range of shady semi-criminal and criminal pursuits which cluster round large-scale vice. It was not an edifying regime, though its worst tendencies only began to appear with great frequency and in extreme forms after it had begun to be effectively challenged in 1957 and 1958. It reacted brutally to the Moncada raid, an armed uprising; but most Latin American governments treat armed uprisings in a fairly brusque fashion and Fidel Castro's jail term, given that he had the good fortune to escape getting shot by his captors as many of his companions were, hardly compares in length with the fifteen- to twenty-year terms handed out with some abandon by the present regime for much more elaborately inferential kinds of treason than armed rebellion. Its economic policies, within the confines of the American sugar quota and the protection of major Cuban producers, in fact addressed all the problems which the revolutionaries were later to attempt to solve, in some cases with rather similar techniques. Extensive state investment in industrial plant for import-substitutive manufactures, price stabilization organizations for rice, corn and coffee, a whole series of attempts to provide effective rural credit facilities to assist in agricultural diversification, and a large-scale attack on seasonal unemployment all collectively failed to shake the dominance of sugar over the economy or to enhance the productive efficiency of the sugar sector.[90] They failed to do so because the existing arrangements in the sugar sector provided guaranteed profits for those already enjoying substantial profits and made it economically irrational for them to attempt to maximize production. The Cuban sugar economy was a tightly controlled monopolistic structure designed externally to fulfil the American sugar quota, however large that might be, and internally to provide guaranteed profits for existing Cuban sugar interests, both growers (predominantly Cuban by the 1950s) and refiners (predominantly American), and to pay whatever protection money was necessary to whomever it turned out to be necessary to pay protection money in order to reach these two targets. For the large numbers of Cubans who drew no direct benefits from it this was a profoundly (though perhaps also a rather confusingly) unsatisfactory arrangement. Even for many of those who did draw direct benefits, like the members of the powerful sugar workers union, the costs in terms of low-grade housing, health, education and other social investments, as a result of the stagnation of the economy were in reality very heavy. For much of Cuban rural society these costs were not even balanced by gains. The large numbers of marginal, semi-subsistence peasants, illiterate, living in mud-floored huts, many of them bearing intestinal parasites throughout their lives, men like the poor subsistence peasants around the Sierra Maestra, or the small coffee-growers of eastern Oriente whom Castro and his brother Raul eventually won over,[91] were firmly excluded from such benefits as did flow from Cuba's productive achievements.

Many Cuban political figures had set themselves, usually in sententiously nationalistic accents, to remedy these ills. None had had any great success. Castro in January 1959 or at the time of the attack on the Moncada barracks probably had less understanding of them (though plainly more will to *do* something about them at whatever risk) than, for instance, Batista himself. There seems every reason to take the naiveté of some of his early pronouncements, on descending victoriously from the mountains, as perfectly authentic. As he and Guevara themselves emphasized in later years, the guerrillas were in most respects singularly ignorant and amateurish young men whose hatred for bureaucracy was plainly ideologically more emotive than any taste for the economic rationality of centralized planning. When Castro promised on television in February 1959 that, unless his plans were obstructed, he would in a few years raise the Cuban standard of living above that of the United States and the Soviet Union because both of these invested most of their resources in armaments, there is no reason to suspect that he was making an elaborate joke.[92] Neither he nor Guevara[93] had in 1959 any clear analytical understanding of the economic problems of Cuba. They blamed sugar, a crop, and the United States, a country, for the immobilizing consequences of the whole monopolistic system. Being determined to achieve a level of real and immediate popular benefit from their revolution, they forced a number of immediate actions, particularly in the field of rent reductions, regardless of their economic consequences and set themselves in their first major reform action, the first Agrarian Reform Law, to remedy the most poignant creation of the sugar system, the landless rural labourer, with wage-work for only part of the year.[94] It was in many respects not a particularly radical law, though it became more radical in implementation, perhaps partly because of worker pressure for 'land or work'.[95] But the expropriation of large areas of

American sugar company land and the intervention of a
number of other foreign business enterprises provoked the
Americans, and the difficulties of running the expropriated
properties in a rational manner encouraged more extensive efforts to establish state control of agricultural production. At the same time the political struggle inside the
Cuban government between Castro's personal supporters and
a variety of pre-existing political groupings and holders of
administrative power became much sharper, as internal class
conflict and external danger both increased. It was no more
inevitable that Castro should win this battle than it was that
he should defeat Batista's army. It required extraordinary
energy, will-power and what his biographer called, rather
equivocally, 'toughness'[96] for Castro to win. But, having won,
many issues became much simpler: not technically, of course
– few technical issues in economic organization proved simple
enough for the guerrillas in power for a number of years –
but politically, in terms of goals and of allegiances.

The withdrawal of the American sugar quota by Eisenhower in 1960 and the Bay of Pigs invasion reinforced these
divisions between an old Cuba largely (at least in its
wealthier sections) demographically displaced to Florida and
a new Cuba, much of it deeply devoted to Fidel and to the
new world which he was attempting to create. Real Cuban
liberals never had much chance. There was no powerful
Cuban national bourgeoisie, eager to brave the icy blasts of
competition in order to maximize their profits and ready to
take over the island from the departed Batista, only a small
group of young men who had risked their lives for a number
of years so that Cuba should be quite different and who were
ready cheerfully to dispose of anyone who stood in their way.
Castro made extensive use of the Cuban Communist Party,
a party with a rather impressive history of effective labour
representation, though one which had become perhaps
slightly over-educated to the tawdry realities of Cuba's world
economic situation and internal political structures.[97] It was
in any case the only effective party in Cuba with any sort of
mass following and organization and many of the goals to
which its members were dedicated were shared by Castro.
It is now abundantly clear to all concerned that it is Castro
so far who has made use of the Communist Party, not the

Communist Party which has made use of Castro. In many respects the Cuban revolution today has much achievement to be proud of – particularly in its assaults on the poverty of those sections of Cuba's society about whom no one had been particularly concerned before. In health, in education – the great campaigns against illiteracy[98] – in housing and in average diet, Cuba is for most of those still living there a better place by far than it was at the beginning of 1959 when Castro descended into Havana. In some ways the young guerrillas, now not quite so young, are wiser. Hostility to bureaucracy which was previously often reducible to dislike of sitting at a desk, reading through and understanding complicated files, has moderated. If distrust for the Americans is, understandably, still of hysterical proportions, distrust of the Russians and the Chinese has now attained respectable dimensions. But the triumphs of the guerrillas are still in a sense young men's triumphs, the result of daring long maintained and generosity and sympathy genuinely felt. It is still a faintly bourgeois revolution for all the massive state control of productive resources which it has brought about: wildly patriotic and very much for the masses, but still more than a little uncertain over how to solve the problems of really significantly increasing production. If it fails in this task, it will in the end prove merely the most recent, though by all means the most attractive, of the succession of redistributive lunges in which successive Cuban governments have attempted to release their country from the toils of sugar and Yankee imperialism. The Yankees have now been expelled; but even a triumphant patriotism is not enough to make the position of a sugar island in the world economy an easy road to a Socialist commonwealth.

Conclusion: approaches to the ideological assessment and causal explanation of modern revolutions

In the light of the eight revolutionary experiences just analysed in detail, what insight is gained into the question of
what sort of events revolutions have now become or the issue
of why such revolutions as do occur do in fact take place and
why it should be the case that other in many ways at least
equally eligible territories do not experience them? The
boundary between the question of what exactly a revolution
is and the question of why exactly revolutions take place is a
necessarily conventional one. The categories of historical or
sociological explanation in the case of events of this order of
complexity are inordinately vague. Any reasonably lucid account of what the Mexican revolution is taken to have been
will contain, at least implicitly, sketches of explanations of
many features of it. Even conventional narrative historical
outlines of revolutionary developments can hardly make much
sense without including explanatory terms of a sociological
character. In addition to the logical difficulties which arise
simply over distinguishing what it is that one wishes to explain, the revolutionary *explanandum,* from what is supposed
to explain it, the series of terms aligned together as the *ex-
planans*[1] a further problem characteristic of explanation in
the human sciences arises in the case of revolution in a peculiarly acute form. Revolution is an actor's concept, not a
purely external, naturalistic identification. Not only is it an
actor's concept but it is by practical (though perhaps not
logical)[2] necessity a very highly contested identification. When
the officials of the Central Intelligence Agency in South
Vietnam in 1964 or the officials of the Soviet Security Services
in Budapest in 1956 observed serenely that they really did
not see the revolutions, they were not slyly turning a Nelsonic
blind eye to a prominent series of signals. Nor were they ill-
informed. It can be safely assumed that in terms of discrete

facts the C.I.A. knew vastly more about Vietnam in 1964 and the Russian security services vastly more about Budapest in 1956 than the virtuous persons who deplored the massive military interventions which ensued. The disagreement between the Americans and – slightly earlier than 1964 – President Diem on the one side and the N.L.F. on the other as to what was taking place in South Vietnam was not a simple (or even a peculiarly complex) factual disagreement, though both sides, as is normally the way with revolutions, had accumulated a number of facts which it was desirable from their own point of view to keep hidden. One part of the disagreement between the two sides which could be presented as being ultimately factual in character would be a disagreement about the future. Revolution is in part a teleological concept and many twentieth-century revolutions and an increasing number of twentieth-century revolutionary enterprises have been organized under the banner of a philosophy of history in which the future plays the star part. But even the N.L.F. (or for that matter the government of North Vietnam) has an essentially defensive and pragmatic rhetoric concerned above all, besides the endless struggle for national independence and unity, with the creation of minimal economic security and prosperity for the peasantry.[3] If they have their eyes at all fixedly on the future, it is a very near future indeed; while, on the side of the South Vietnamese government, even in the days of President Diem with his idiosyncratic interpretation of the French *gauchiste* Catholic philosophy of Personalism,[4] it seems a trifle fanciful to ascribe any philosophy at all to the regime, perhaps even any very clear conception of the future. But it is clear that there are very distinct differences of value between the two contestant groups, however various the values to which segments of the groups internally give their allegiance. It is also clear that these differences between the groups extend further than a sharp preference as to what sorts of people end up shot once the victory of one side or the other has been established, though it is also clear that the identity of the victims is one component of the revolutionary or reactionary future which all sides do take equally seriously.

However, expressed in this way, the point is too simple to be accurate. It is not simply a disagreement about future facts of power: which side is going to provide the new political elite. If it was certainly known to the South Vietnamese government that they were going to lose within the next five years (and perhaps still more of it was certainly known to the North Vietnamese government that *they* were going to lose), although many of those now fighting might under these circumstances change sides and although it would make perfectly good sense to do so either way on, it would also make perfectly good sense to choose decisively *not* to do so, but to go on fighting despite the inevitability of defeat. There might, however be a time scale in which this choice would make less unequivocal sense in a universal perspective for Marxist-inspired insurrectionary movements. If it could be known with certainty that the percentage of the human race under capitalist rulership a millennium hence will be twice what it is today, the mood of Marxist-inspired resistance would be substantially more chastened than it is today. But although at the present it would require some delicate rethinking to refurbish the Marxist heritage in the face of this particular discouraging fantasy, there is no conclusive reason why the rethinking could not be done. It is also worth noting that this comparatively exposed character of revolutionary theory to knowledge about the future derives from its structural ineptitude for long-term *cynicism*. Many revolutionaries become highly cynical people, though perhaps more start out as did the young Djilas or Trotsky as the very reverse of cynical. But being a revolutionary cannot be *merely* an exercise in cynicism. Even the ineffable Joseph Stalin had a vision of the distant future under Socialism which seems to have been authentically Utopian – to balance the corrosive cynicism of his immediate social and political vision.[5] Revolutionaries *have* to suppose themselves engaged in creating a better future – that is what being a revolutionary is – while the regimes which they challenge need not expect a future a whit less corrupt or bestial than the present which they are attempting to defend. Accordingly any attempt to reduce the analysis of revolution to the replacement of one ruling class by another (or to be a little less tendentious of one political elite by another) is necessarily politically partisan. Revolutionaries are committed by their proclaimed beliefs to changes not only in the tenure of positions of power but to changes in the social stratification (in some cases even to the eventual disappearance of any such social phenomenon as social stratification), to drastic improvements in social welfare and eventually to decisive changes in ideology (that is: not merely in the ritual proclamation of those political and social values which it is physically prudent to proclaim, but to a transformation in the way in which men's experience of living in their society leads them to perceive and to feel about that society). To confine the analysis of revolution to the study of the technology of the seizure of power (or for that matter to confine the study of resistance to revolution to the study of counter-insurgency theories) is either implicitly to assume the impropriety of the phenomenon studied or else to choose a deliberately politically trivial level of perception. Revolution, as Fidel Castro belatedly discovered,[6] is difficult. There is vastly more to it than seizing power – and this is equally true of anti-revolutionary politics. Any serious analysis of revolution as a political phenomenon must take seriously the question of what it is that revolutions do bring about.

When the F.L.N. in Algeria made a number of assaults on buses or local officials in 1954, the French administration saw themselves as being confronted by an outbreak of brigandage. Eight years later in 1962 the brigands became the government and their status was transmuted internationally into heroes of the Algerian national struggle. To many Frenchmen then (and perhaps for that matter now), they no doubt remained (such of them as have survived the Kabyle mountains and the western European hotels) brigands still. The disagreements were not disagreements of fact; they reflected a change in conventions attendant on a shift in the location of power. Doughty brigands in plenty had lived before Ben Bella and Boudiaf, lacking only the resources of a government propaganda office to tell their praises. Retrospectively endowed with this facility, Algerian brigands back to the days of Moqrani or of Abdel-Kader himself were likewise transformed into heroes of the Algerian national struggle. All who fought the French (and any brigand had necessarily in some sense fought the French, or at least carried arms in defiance of them) were now endowed with the mantle of nationalism. But this euphoric transposition did not survive indefinitely unscathed. It turned out soon enough that brigands, traditional Algerian characters by all means, continued to live on after the triumph of Ben Bella too. Buses could still get shot up and tax collectors assaulted. It might be the case that the motives of localist dissidence in independent Algeria are very different from those of traditional resistance in past decades;[7] but the actions involved might be and at times have been strikingly similar. And since they were now directed against the authority of the national government of free Algeria, they looked exceedingly like the actions of brigands. To the French authorities any Algerian nationalist had been incipiently a brigand throughout the colonial occupation. To the Algerian nationalist insurgents from 1954 on – and indeed often earlier–any brigand was at least incipiently a nationalist. Colonial regime and anticolonial resistance could alike agree for the most part on the use of a single category. Indeed what they fought about could be aptly described as simply what it was that the category meant. But with the coming of independence such simplicity of vision could hardly be maintained. Now once again there are brigands in the mountains and bureaucrats deciding upon the location of national virtue, posted in the cities of the plain.[8] In revolutionary situations many categories can become conflated which in more settled circumstances can hardly avoid being distinguished.

To make the point another way by considering the *intentions* of the agents: one might decide, for the hell of it, to smash the windows of a hotel, or for that matter to tear up the seats of a railway train. In the latter case, many apparently do. Equally one might decide to break the windows of a hotel for the greater glory of God: some people have odd Gods. Equally one might decide to break the windows of a hotel in order to bring on the revolution. From the point of view of most people in this country at the moment, breaking the windows of a hotel is breaking the windows of a hotel is breaking the windows of a hotel. But it does not take a vast reach of the historical imagination to grasp that the same would not necessarily have held true of Petrograd in February 1917 – let alone in late October. Even in Petrograd breaking hotel windows would seldom have been the most efficacious of revolutionary acts, but it would at least have been generally intelligible as such. In part the distinction is essentially a technological one, breaking hotel windows being a technically rational, though hardly optimal, revolutionary move in Petrograd at the right time, but being less effective outside the London Hilton on sundry occasions. But this is a little too simple. It is an open question whether any actions at all could be said to be technically rational from the point of view of revolutionary efficacy in England or perhaps even Great Britain at the moment. (What cannot be brought about, one cannot assist in bringing about.) If any actions are in this sense technically rational here at the moment, they must certainly be the product of a more sensitive social imagination than that which leads people to smash the lamentable embellishments of the London Hilton. But that certainly does not mean that smashing its windows in order to bring on the revolution becomes the same action as smashing them for the hell of it. (For one thing its rationality is much more perilous than that of the latter action which can hardly avoid attaining at least momentary rationality.) In analysing revolutionary actions, whether effective or ineffective, it is necessary always to analyse both what is being attempted and what is actually achieved,[9] to attempt to avoid the fantasies and the mendacities of both revolutionaries and existing authority.

Revolutions are very intricate phenomena and in identifying a given set of events, Mexican national politics between 1910 and 1920, or between 1910 and 1940, Zapata's rising, Lenin's seizure of power in October 1917, as a revolution these events are being regarded in a distinctive way; at the very least as representing somehow a decisive change whether for better or worse in the destinies of a society and its members. But revolutions are not merely natural phenomena like floods or droughts or hurricanes or freak harvests, as all events in the natural order are. They are both the product of, and constituted by, human action. It is possible in a sociological manner to take a group of revolutions and consider them as a set of naturalistically conceived social totalities, inquiring into the necessary and sufficient conditions for their occurrence, in search of natural regularities. Much interest might come out of an inquiry of this sort, though it is only fair to point out that so far not a tremendous amount of interest *has* done so. It is also possible, and at least equally proper, to see revolutions as belonging increasingly in the modern world to a tradition of historical action, Firstly, revolutions are the product of and are constituted by human actions and thus though much about them might be explicable without direct reference to this characteristic and though not all of them can be explained simply by reference to it (they are hardly the *intended* result of most of the actions involved), it is still true that an adequate account of what any particular revolution is (and still more an adequate account of what all revolutions are) must include an adequate account of the character of the wide variety of actions which comprise it. The second consequence is from a practical viewpoint perhaps even more important. Revolutions belong to a tradition of historical action in the strong sense that virtually all revolutions in the present century have imitated – or at least set out to imitate as best they could – other revolutions of an earlier date. The conditions of revolutionary possibility are extensively determined by the understanding held by existing ruling groups of what dangers they have to face and how easy these are to surmount, and by the understanding held by potential revolutionaries of the circumstances in which they might be able to seize power and the uses to which they might put it. Plainly as revolutionary forces wax and wane from decade to decade in one part of the world or another, the morale and repertoire of both revolutionary and counter-revolutionary forces will alter constantly. Revolutions may become possible in conditions in which they would previously have been quite inconceivable. This is indeed largely what has happened in the transformation of Marxism into an ideology of organized peasant rebellion in the period from the late 1920s till today. If the Debray interpretation of the Cuban revolution were adequate,[10] such a shift might equally well come with the rise of the student guerrilla group as an autonomous revolutionary agent in the Latin American backland. But it is at least as probable in compensation – since counter-revolutionaries too can learn – that revolutions will become impossible in conditions in which previously they would have been comparatively simple to bring about.

Revolutions, then, have to be considered as very complex series of actions initiated in highly particular circumstances and at particular points in time. The temptation to conceive of them as simply the collapse of long decrepit social orders, societies irretrievably out of functional equilibrium, is a temptation to ignore their character as performances of great complexity, in favour of a vision drawn from metaphors of natural processes. Functionalist analyses of revolution, like those of Chalmers Johnson,[11] plainly favour this perspective, as, for that matter, did classical pre-Leninist Marxism to some degree. But, in this sense at least, the experience of twentieth-century political revolution is very much of a Leninist rather than a classically Marxist phenomenon, a matter not of plucking the ripe fruits of protracted and ineluctable processes of social development, but rather of contriving not to miss a bus which may well set out only once, if indeed it sets out at all. Creativity of political vision and decisiveness of practical action are both at a high premium in twentieth-century revolutionary experience, an eminently Machiavellian experience, and although these have been combined thus far with a fairly assured expectation on the part of successful revolutionaries that they have access to a privileged understanding of the historical process, it is quite unclear by now that they are correct in this belief. It is the voluntarist component of Leninism, not the pseudo-scientific theory of society which it still incorporates in a gingerly manner which has (insofar as any part of it could be said to have done so) stood the test of twentieth-century revolutionary experience. The serenity of the classical Marxist understanding of revolution was only compatible in the case of Lenin's own understanding of what he was doing, as a result of heroic feats of psychological repression. In the aftermath of his triumph, Marxism, a theory of the potentiality for complete human liberation, has had to convert itself into a legitimatory ideology for a variety of state structures. In consequence, since Lenin's death, all trace of a foundation for serenity has disappeared. No one perhaps is today in much of a position to identify with assurance what the meaning of twentieth-century revolutions will turn out to have been in historical perspective.

But before venturing on the issue of what in the light of twentieth-century experience modern revolutions do in fact mean, it is appropriate to consider briefly the possibilities for explaining causally why they have occurred. In the twentieth century the European revolutionary tradition altered in character in two very decisive ways. For the first time it resulted in the establishment of revolutionary states which were capable of long-term survival within the international state system. But it produced this result, notoriously, not in the highly industrialized societies of western Europe and North America, but in a set of largely pre-industrial societies, many of them colonies or countries in a semi-colonial relationship with western capitalism. Hence the revolutionary seizure of political power became a more elaborate and long-term assignment in which the rewards of success, if not always the penalties for failure, are – or at least may be thought to be – altogether more dramatic in the case of each particular society than they appeared likely to be in the late nineteenth century. This development also gave a certain international status to the idea of being 'revolutionary', and thus created governments whose ambition to change the social structure of their countries was as discreet as that of Metternich eager to lay claim to the epithet. There have been a number of revolutions in the twentieth century which have resulted in part from the degree of success attained by the Russian revolution. But there have been a great many more states which have described themselves as revolutionary than have made themselves revolutionary for this reason. The idea of political revolution has become excessively muddled as a result of these two developments.

Taking the eight revolutionary experiences considered here it could be asked what sort of explanations could be given of them. In the first instance it would plainly be possible to give classic narrative historical explanations of their occurrence, in which all identifiable actions are fitted sequentially together and made intelligible as actions. Every revolution has a story. But narrative explanations of the political development of other non-revolutionary societies, though perhaps more boring, are equally available. Even quite skilful historical narratives may bring little general analytical insight into the concept of revolution in its application to twentieth-century history. If the activity of explanation is to be pressed further, it seems better to begin by separating out three components of the revolutionary process. Firstly it is convenient to take the revolutionary project, held in varying forms and for varyingly sophisticated reasons by a group of revolutionaries. What revolutionaries attempt to do and what they suppose themselves to be bringing about varies with the level of educational or practical experience attained by the revolutionaries, a matter which is in principle susceptible of systematic sociological explanation. But it also, of course, varies with what others have attempted to do and indeed succeeded in doing in the past. The study of changes in these revolutionary projects is a study in intellectual history, sometimes at a vulgar, sometimes at a highly sophisticated level, the intellectual biographies of twentieth-century revolutionaries. It is plainly causally more important in the case of revolutionaries who do attain substantial personal power and at the opposite end of the continuum of revolutionary influence it shades into the second and more resolutely sociological category, the communication of the relevance of this project to the lives of substantial numbers of people. The more intellectual (and historical) end of the continuum is extravagantly difficult to handle in causal terms,[12] but it is far from trivial in the causal understanding of revolutions. What might the history of twentieth-century revolution have been, supposing Lenin (and perhaps Trotsky for good measure) to have died at the age of twenty?

But if the most intellectual component of the revolutionary project is necessarily and importantly historical because it has to do with patterns of foreign travel, diffusion of information, dates and other such matters, the social (or perhaps definitionally anti-social) role in which the project is incarnated is more readily susceptible of sociological treatment. Almost all societies in the twentieth century have had some revolutionaries, certainly all societies which have had universities. Having *some* revolutionaries is not much of a contribution towards experiencing a revolution. In fact it does not seem likely that even having a large number of revolutionaries is anywhere near a sufficient condition. However, how many revolutionaries there are in a society at a particular time, where in the society there is for them to go to (with or without a revolution), and what they feel revolutionary about, are all questions which might plausibly be explained in terms of structural features of their society. It is just exactly what they propose to *do* about feeling revolutionary which cannot readily be explained in this way, and just exactly what they do propose to do about this is arguably often, if not always, a necessary condition not so much for their seizing power (though it might well be this also), but for their succeeding in putting any power which they contrive to seize to authentically revolutionary uses.

The second component of the revolutionary process which requires explanation is the publicly visible relevance of the revolutionary project to the situations of large numbers of men. This is the stage at which it becomes most natural to think of the sequence of events as a revolution (whether only potentially, if an aborted revolution, if social control does not in fact fail, or an actual revolution, if social control *does* collapse). It does not probably have to be the case in all circumstances that the appeal of the revolutionary project is felt with any clarity by a large proportion of the population nor that it should necessarily appeal to its enthusiasts for the same reasons nor that a large proportion should be very deeply committed to it as such. In an important sense no Cubans had much idea of the character of Castro's revolutionary project in December 1958. He could hardly be said to have had *much* idea of its character himself in any detail at that point, except insofar as it was simply the effort to create a very different order from that which currently existed. All revolutions are supported by many who would not have supported them had they had a clear understanding of what the revolutions were in fact to bring about (though it is also importantly true that in the case of the revolutions which do establish viable new orders which can solve many of the problems which their predecessor regimes had failed to solve – in the case of what may tentatively be termed 'successful' revolutions – they are also *not* supported by many of those who would have done so had they had a clear understanding of what the revolutions were in fact going to bring about). In a very important sense what the Yugoslav and Chinese and North Vietnamese governments have to offer their subject populations is Communist government but the revolutionary project which they offered to their societies in order to acquire power and which in fact led to their acquiring power was not usually overtly *Communist* government at all. In the case of both Vietnam and China the offer was much closer at the crucial stage to being simply one of decent government, non-oppressive, non-foreign government which protects the poor from the fear of starvation or gross maltreatment. Communist government as such tends to be something of an acquired taste and one which not all those given the opportunity of acquiring it *do* in the event acquire. But non-oppressive government is as close to an innate preference as is to be discovered among the diversity of human societies. It is perhaps more often the case than not that revolutionary projects which do present themselves to large numbers of people in a form in which they seem clearly and immediately to their advantage, are misunderstood even in the broadest outline. This is not to say that all revolutions are somehow betrayed. But it certainly does imply that the process of garnering effective support in the face of an existing and hostile government for the effort to reconstruct the economy and stratification system of a society, is intrinsically complicated and inelegant and is not likely to admit of neat and comprehensive moralization. Revolutionary seizure of power (as opposed to intra-elite *coups d'état*) usually in the twentieth century takes place by means of protracted civil war. In war, expediency is a very prominent ground of action. The moralities adopted by revolutionaries are uncompromisingly teleological. Victory has to justify a multitude of corpses. But since revolutionaries, like other humans, are fallible, it is not always the case that the performance of victorious revolutionaries does justify any great number of corpses. Indeed it is not always a striking advance on the performance of pre-revolutionary regimes. And even if it had, as a matter of fact, thus far invariably been a prodigious improvement, it is entirely clear that it would not *have* to continue to be so in the future. Human fallibility and the corruptions of power are serious considerations. The supposition that they do not need to be taken into consideration in regimes which disposed of their predecessors by armed assault and which customarily refer to themselves as Socialist, is simply risible. Socialism, even where it has some definite content, is not a talisman which purifies all who touch it. This is important because much of the most sensitive historical writing about revolutionary processes is so fiercely *engagé* that it is incapable of dealing seriously with the question of why, causally, large numbers of people do come to support revolutionary efforts initiated by much smaller groups. Accounts of revolutionary mobilization, pre-

mised essentially on convictions about the rationality or otherwise of revolutionary action, are characteristically written on
an analogy with accounts of religious conversion by fideist
devotees of the religion in question or by inveterate free-
thinkers hysterically averse to all religious conviction. When
the Vietnamese peasantry supported the Vietminh or the
Chinese peasantry supported Mao, there is no need to explain
their adherence by presenting them as having seen a great
light, nor is there the least reason to present them as having
been hoodwinked by a group of power-hungry paranoiacs.

All that is necessary (and all that can be true) is to explain
how the Chinese peasants with their restricted experience of
social and political possibilities would be likely to come to
see the Chinese Communists as a decisive improvement on
the K.M.T. or, later on, the Japanese invaders. Not the least
important ingredient of this explanation is the plain fact that
the Chinese Communists *were* a decisive improvement on
these particular competitors.[13] It is perfectly plain that the
hapless Chinese peasantry had no idea whatsoever in 1940 or
1945 that they were letting themselves in for the Cultural
Revolution – and it is at least possible that they would have
been profoundly indifferent to the information if they had
any such idea, having at the time other altogether more
pressing matters on their mind. The insight that man does
not make his history under conditions of his own choice is
one readily available to any peasant. Whatever the eventual
benefits or costs made available to China by the Cultural Revolution, the Chinese Communist Party was substantially the
best option available for most Chinese in 1940, 1945 or 1949.
If it had not been it would not, in this particular case, have
won power. However it would also not have won power, if
it had not had the determination and on occasion the ruthlessness to reimpose effective central political control over a
country which had not experienced this for almost a century.
Each of these prerequisites for its success requires explanation
and it is not necessarily the case that the correct explanation
of both can be fitted together into an edifying tale of how
the good triumphed. Not all history is edifying and many of
those who triumph under any banner are not particularly
good. Revolutions, like police forces, often offer splendid
opportunities for psychopaths, though it is also true that

psychopaths may often make invaluable cadres (or police officers).

Much of the process of revolutionary mobilization is open to effective sociological explanation. What the revolutionary project, as offered to the populace, means to different sections, and why their different interpretations of it give them differing levels of commitment to the effort of bringing it about, are all dependent in part on the structure of the society. But it was not a fact about the social structure of China that the Comintern had a particular policy in 1925 – and not all protracted revolutionary potentials, even in the twentieth century, find their own Mao (even if many of them now have the chance of becoming hazily acquainted with the reflections of the Chinese people's Mao).

The third component of the revolutionary process, the failure of social control, appears in many ways to be peculiarly amenable to sociological analysis. If societies are considered in the functionalist manner as systems in some sort of equilibrium, the failure of social control may be explained, as characteristically by Chalmers Johnson for example,[14] as a product of disequilibrium in the social system. It is presumably tautological that the seizure of power (or at any rate the removal of power from its current possessors) is a necessary condition for revolution. It is certainly tautological to affirm that the failure of social control is a necessary condition for the seizure of power. But the idea of social control in this sense is a highly equivocal idea. In one of its senses, very crudely, repressive capacity, the failure of social control can in effect be caused by the occurrence of revolution. The Yugoslav revolution (with substantial external assistance in the form of *matériel*) was what expelled the German army from Yugoslavia – though having the *German* army to expel may also have been a necessary condition for its occurrence. Plainly, having a German army of occupation is not a *sufficient* condition for generating a revolution, since many countries enjoyed the former facility without experiencing the latter. But the fact that a large measure of revolutionary mobilization was a prerequisite for expelling the German army does suggest the tendentiousness of taking the inadequacy of social control, in the sense of sheer physical repressive capacity, as being the key element in revolution. Few largely pre-industrial states possess an apparatus of physical repression for purposes of social control which can match a German army of occupation. Massive repressive capacity implies the capacity to repress much opposition, but if allied to sufficient political maladroitness, it may well create even more opposition than it suppresses.

However, the notion of social control as vulgarly used is importantly ambiguous between the notion of an integrated social system (the functionalist dream) and the notion of an effective military and police apparatus. There *may* be some integrated social systems in the sense construed by an American functionalist sociologist like Parsons,[15] but there are certainly few enough of them (and few enough revolutions for that matter) to make their absence an unhelpful explanation of the actual incidence of revolutions. And if what their absence is held to explain is the *possibility* of revolution in a particular society, there is once again a real danger of regression into tautology. The more purely military and police conception is more obviously a necessary condition of an analytically significant sort. If the Russian Provisional government had suppressed the Bolsheviks more thoroughly in June or July of 1917, a measure which any of their successors in the role of bourgeois revolutionaries would be much more likely to take because of what happened in October of that year, the Bolshevik revolution might well never have taken place. The most elegant of revolutionary potentialities do on occasion get slain by ugly little facts in just this way. It may be tautologous that there can be no revolution without a disruption of the coercive capacity of those who have to be displaced, but it is an eminently causally significant tautology to which to draw attention when it comes to practical action. Both the level of purely repressive capacity and the inadequacy of social integration which makes revolutionary mobilization possible can be explained in terms of the structure of the society.

Revolutionaries and the potential failure of social control are widely distributed in the second half of the twentieth century and are quite often to be found in the same country, but large-scale revolutionary mobilization is comparatively rare. Where all three are present the phenomena are likely to receive characterization as a revolution. But the presence of these three attributes is plainly insufficient to constitute in itself the basis of a viable new political order, capable of mastering the problems which the previous regime was unable to solve, along with the multiplicity of new problems which the establishment of a revolutionary regime itself creates. To put this point simply, revolution is no more a practically adequate analytical category than is persistence. *Nouveaux Régimes* are just as liable not to be viable as *Anciens Régimes* and it is perfectly possible, though perhaps not very common, for the only practical tasks at which the revolutionary government is clearly superior to its predecessor to be the art of social control. Governing is a difficult art which although it may employ some of the same qualities as successful guerrilla warfare, also requires others which are not commonly possessed by guerrillas, successful or otherwise.

These very general considerations make it possible to isolate two peculiar difficulties intrinsic to the attempt to explain the occurrence of revolutions. The first is a problem which arises generally in the social sciences, the question of how to separate a class of phenomena for analysis which is sufficiently homogeneous to be susceptible of a significantly common explanatory hypothesis, without being so small in number that the explanatory hypothesis must be essentially historical in character, in that no question of the recurrence of the phenomenon could possibly arise. It is dismally obvious that this difficulty is likely to be more acute in the case of an aspirant sociology of revolution than it is for example in the case of the sociology of the family. Even if the latter is covertly reduced to meaning the sociology of the family in industrial societies, there are, at least, and have been, and will with good fortune continue to be a great many families in industrial societies. However many revolutions there are going to be, there have not, at least in the distinctively twentieth-century sense in which the term has been employed here, been very many so far, and at first sight the discrepancies between their causation are at least as striking as the uniformities. Furthermore, such uniformities as can readily be identified seem on the whole more like lexical preconditions for applying the category 'revolution' at all, than they do empirically discovered attributes of an independently identified natural class of phenomena. The sociology of revolution is persistently in danger of presenting a laborious account of what we mean in calling a set of events a revolution in the mistaken impression that it is thereby disclosing the natural properties of a natural species. This is not, of course, to say that it may not be illuminating to consider seriously, as the years go by and the naming continues, just what it is that we *do* now mean in calling a set of events a revolution. But it does imply that the painful effort to render our categories sufficiently abstract to encompass the increasingly heterogeneous class of developments which we come to entitle 'revolutions' may represent less a profound gain in theoretical insight than a systematic destruction of the descriptive resources of our political language. If the development of a sociology of revolution means the loss of the capacity to tell the difference between a Sierra Leonean military coup and the Chinese revolution, any funds devoted to supporting its development will be money excessively ill-spent.

It would be possible in principle to construct a typology of overt resistance to state authority in all political structures of any scale or at any rate in all nation states. Those who feel that comparative government or comparative politics as these now exist are academic disciplines marked by a high level of intellectual achievement would have every reason to feel optimistic about the possibilities of intellectual achievement available in constructing such a prelude to a sociology of dissidence (comparative disobedience). There is no obvious reason why political action directed against established authority should be any less subject to coherent analysis than political action performed by such authority or political action within the bounds prescribed by such authority. Breaking rules is a form of behaviour just as likely to disclose empirical regularities as keeping them. Why men rebel is certainly no more puzzling a question in *general* than the question of why men obey. Indeed, taking sociologists by and large as well-fed and reasonably well-protected members of western professional groups, it seems appropriate to note that in the more Winchian component of sociological explanation[16] it may be strikingly harder for them to reach any intuitive understanding of why men obey in some parts of the world than it would be for them to understand why men rebel. In any case it would be foolishly optimistic to suppose that even an elaborate presentation of our knowledge of human social existence organized under the category of disobedience would be of any very startling assistance to us in understanding why such revolutions as have so far happened have been caused – let alone what sorts of conditions will generate revolutions in the future. This is partly, as noted before, because in the course of revolutionary attempts to seize power, past regularities are likely to play an extremely prominent part in the taking of present and future decisions both by revolutionaries and by their enemies. This point has been put in a more abstract way, and its implications explored quite elaborately, by philosophers concerned to demonstrate or to refute its incompatibility with a determinist thesis about the universal causal determination of human action. But the status of the point is probably too vulgar and pragmatic, if clearly understood, to bear at all on the issue of determinism. What it does establish is the peculiar unsuitability of revolutions for wholesale incorporation into naively positive causal theories of social integration and disruption. Those searching above all else for regularities in social questions must search for them where they are to be found. Revolution as a category of social interpretation is definitionally a product of highly agonistic behaviour within a framework in which there are markedly few common normative constraints and in which the relationship of the future outcome to past outcomes of similar struggles is explicitly what is at stake for all the most active participants. The three different components of the revolutionary process may be expected to display important regularities. But the crucial feature of even the most abortive revolution is precisely the uniting of these three components, and at this point whatever past regularities have been effectively identified by either side necessarily enter very prominently into the ground of present action.

Furthermore the reason why there exists a separate category of social interpretation, revolution, and why all efforts successful or otherwise to dispose of an existing government by illegal means and largely by the agency of members of the society in question are not simply construed as instances of the well-tried and clearly intelligible category of rebellion or civil war, is in some danger of disappearing. Even such a minimal level of concession to preoccupation with causality as is involved in defining a revolutionary process in a way which does not discriminate between abortive and significantly successful revolutions, poses some threat to the identity of revolution as a discrete category. The reason why revolution is a central concept in the tradition of historical action in twentieth-century history, both for those who favour it and for those who struggle to eliminate it, the reason why the attribute 'revolutionary' is a deeply valued international status symbol for a regime in the second half of the twentieth century – this reason is not adequately recognized in isolating for unitary study the class of all those states of affairs which have exhibited the revolutionary process, ending in the establishment of a new regime. The very grounds for studying revolution at all as a distinctive phenomenon are vitiated by the attempt to amass a collection of exhibits sufficiently extensive to permit the elaboration of plausible causal theories. Revolution remains a highly rationalist as well as a determinedly teleological category. If we edge away from analysing the rationality of the goals pursued, in the effort to identify patterns in the strategies used to pursue them, it will be an understanding of the behaviour of dissidents rather than an understanding of the mechanics of revolution which we shall derive from the enquiries, even if they are optimally successful. The rationalist flavour of the concept of revolution is peculiarly important because its recognition requires the recognition of two further characteristics of revolutions: firstly that the reason why most men support revolutions cannot often be very directly related to what revolutions are going to produce (a view clearly confirmed by the great majority of the revolutions considered here) and secondly that the justification of revolution (as opposed to the ideological marketing of revolution) is necesarily a function of the performance of the post-revolutionary regime. This point is in some danger of generating misunderstanding. Many regimes are so exotically deplorable that any successor regime could hardly fail to represent a change for the better; it would require ingenuity as well as singular dedication to fail to improve on the late President Duvalier. But although the performance of many regimes may be such as amply to justify rebellion, the pretensions of a revolution necessarily extend well beyond those of a justified rebellion. It would be a plausible claim that where there is widespread revolutionary mobilization, it is always the case that rebellion is justified, though there is no reason to assume, as *gauchiste* rhetoric tends to (in peculiar inheritance from Christian providentialist theories) that wherever rebellion is justified, the governors must be wicked and the rebels virtuous: it may simply be the case that the governors are incompetent or feeble and the rebels effective or tough. Conversely, of course, it is certainly not the case that all territories in which there is no revolutionary mobilization somehow enjoy governments which deserve the power which they possess. Power and right are unfortunately not very tidily related in the world.

Initially the revolutionary project arose within the structure of a number of philosophies of history which claimed to identify mechanisms through which power and right could be expected to coalesce more adequately in the future. The most elaborate theory of revolution, that of Karl Marx, provided a clear account of why the proletarian revolution would establish a public order of equality and liberty, after a brief dictatorship of a great majority over a tiny minority. The rationalist account of the mechanics of social development purported to show how justified rebellion and revolution must at last in this instance become identical. Revolutions, however, did not happen in an authentically Marxist manner, as Lenin, for instance, speedily realized. The Leninist model of revolution, elitist, manipulative and unrelentingly opportunist, was both a handy prescription for action and a rather lucid guide to how revolutions in the twentieth century have in fact come about. Increasingly miscellaneous sections of the populace have produced the justified rebellions and a variety of revolutionary groups espousing numerous differing theories have attempted to provide the rationality which converts a justified (and, of course, a *successful*) rebellion into a revolution. The universalist assurance of the revolutionaries (not on the whole a consequence of the glowing aesthetic splendours of the political orders produced elsewhere by their colleagues) naturally leads them to attempt to generate rebellions even where the justification for rebellion is not so oppressively obvious to the majority. But in these cases the populace are less likely to make their indispensable contribution. Even the most justified rebellion in the face of the modern armaments available to every modern state is a venture of desperation. The populace at large does not rebel for fun. Lacking the rationalist assurance of a better order waiting in the future to be grasped, and having invested a lifetime of often highly repressed effort in the struggle to survive at all, most men, particularly in countries in which massive rebellion is at all probable, rebel as a final gesture of misery, not as an expression of optimism about the future. Those who subscribe to the Leninist philosophy of history presumably suppose that the effort to produce revolution is justified almost everywhere – everywhere where there has not already been a Leninist revolution: the revolutionary elite can meaningfully offer its services on a universal basis. But in the actual mechanics of revolution there are effective impediments to the realization of this universal fantasy. Where the desperate act of rebellion does not appear justifiable to the great majority there will not be a revolution. Even if revolutions must now be recognized as divided irrevocably into the relatively blind and reflex rebellion of the masses and the relatively open-eyed and rationalist reach for power by a revolutionary elite, there remains one rationalist link between the two: the nature of the existing regime. There can be no revolutions, however abortive, except where the previous regime, whether by its weakness or by its viciousness, has lost the right to rule.

Nevertheless many revolutions are more than a little abortive, not only in the sense that they fail to fulfil their promises, a characteristic shared to the full with them by non-revolutionary regimes, but in the decisively more important sense that they prove quite incapable of governing well the societies over which they have taken power. It is, of course, eminently probable that some revolutionary governments (as it is certainly true of quite a number of non-revolutionary governments) do not particularly wish to govern their societies well. What constitutes governing a given society well is a highly disputable matter; indeed it would be possible in pursuit of a misplaced theory of ethical relativism to construe whatever the ruling elites of particular societies feel comfortable with in the way of governmental behaviour as good government for that society. But although the question *is* morally complex, this can hardly be a reason for believing that it is morally without meaning, let alone for believing the ludicrous Panglossian theory that every individual or class or ruling class's moral insensitivity determines the content of morality for him or it. The perception that the issue is morally complicated is in itself the realization that it is an issue of real moral substance. All revolutionary regimes commit themselves to putting the concentration of political power in the society which they in part control and in part serve to decisively better uses than their predecessors. Any understanding of the meaning of revolution as a phenomenon in the modern world must necessarily attend to the question of how far different revolutionary regimes discharge this commitment with success and to the very intricate issue of what are the connections between the ways in which the revolutions come about and the levels of success which they achieve and the diversity of strategies which they adopt in discharging this commitment. Anyone who felt (rather than claimed for political purposes to feel) much assurance about these matters currently would either be something of a fool or else be strikingly ignorant. The more clearly we recognize the place of revolution in the tradition of historical action, as opposed to the political sociologist's (or ideologist's) conceptual tool-bag, the clearer it becomes that the crucial dilemma of revolutionary experience from an intellectual point of view is the question of just what the rationalist component of revolutionary action, its promise to elicit a new order which is clearly superior from the ruins of the old, does now depend upon. In thinking about this question there are numerous competing forms of closure to experience vociferously on offer at the moment; but in the face of these dizzy perplexities it would show a more appropriate humility to refuse to divide the map of the world up at a glance into moral segments – the good and the bad. Some regimes in the world are passable and some are very bad. Survival is no very adequate index of virtue, nor is revolutionary victory. The actual distribution of different varieties of governmental achievement remains eminently open to investigation.

What, then, in outline does it make sense, in view of the character of the revolutions which have taken place in the twentieth century, to mean by the idea of revolution? Why does it seem likely that there will be many more revolutions and why should this be neither a ground for dejection nor a ground for expecting the world to become a decisively better place? One point which will be apparent from the treatment of the eight revolutions discussed earlier is that the relationship between nationalism and internationalism is today much more equivocal in revolutionary action than it was construed as being either in the universalist rhetoric of the First French Republic or in the theoretical system of classical Marxism. This point is partly simply definitional (what a revolution is is the displacement of the government of a state and the establishment of a new political order representing previously unrepresented social interests and recognized as an independent nation state under international law). But it is also in part all too glumly empirical: notions of power politics are no less analytically essential for making sense out of the economic and political relationships between countries of the *soi-disant* Socialist camp than they are for doing so in the case of those of a purely capitalist persuasion. For ideological purposes this anomaly is normally explained (where it is recognized at all) by the fact that the delinquent is not truly a Socialist nation any more (Oh for good old Joe) – or, in extreme cases, after all perhaps it never was one. If 'Socialist' means 'guaranteed to behave in an altruistic manner on all occasions', then there is no reason to quarrel with such an explanation. But in this sense it seems fair comment that no one has yet elaborated at all a plausible account of how a modern state could be made – and more importantly could be *kept* – Socialist. Both the liberal internationalism of Free Trade in the nineteenth century and the supposedly Socialist internationalism of countries with state-owned productive resources in the twentieth century, although advertised as paths to international order and justice have in fact been extensively adorned with the use of international violence. There is no obvious means which could ensure that the use of the concentrated power, economic, political or military of one nation state will never be used against the interests of another nation state of lesser strength. The formal creation of citizen equality in either liberal or Socialist states does not preclude the persistence of vast inequalities of power in all existing societies. Equally the existence of international organizations – either world-wide like the United Nations or confined to the Socialist bloc – in which all member states are notionally equal does not remove the vast discrepancies in resources between different nations. Inequalities of power over time usually get put to use.

Thus the fact that what successful revolutions create is new national regimes is of central importance in identifying what criteria are involved in assessing the extent to which a revolution is abortive. It is certainly not an accident that among the revolutionary governments considered earlier those with the most unequivocal achievements to their credit have communists or at least extensively state capitalist governments. All successful twentieth-century revolutions have taken place in countries which were integrated into the international capitalist economy (insofar as they were integrated at all into an order of non-subsistence economic relationships) in a way which disrupted traditional economic adaptations or made future economic progress excessively difficult to achieve. That is the core of truth in the Leninist theory of imperialism. Marxism-Leninism identified imperialist economic structures as the focus of the economic and social problems of the great majority of societies in the world and it offered a confident solution to these problems: world Socialist revolution. Marxist-Leninists (particularly of the amateurish stamp to be found in Cuba) may often have made in the short run a fairly uproarious mess out of the economic structures of the countries in which they obtained power. But at least they had – or at least had acquired by the time of the Second World War – a reasonably clear notion of the sort of economy which ought to be created in order for their country to become modern, and a fairly inflexible determination to create such a structure, if given the opportunity to make the attempt. In 1971 these simple verities have been not a little muddied. The creative projects have become more difficult to outline with assurance, and economic strategies have diverged very widely. The Russian style of battleship diplomacy, allied on their frontier with China with what the Chinese observe as openly racist xenophobia,[17] is sufficiently unattractive in its resonances to make the common enemies seem a rather fragile bond.

As Marx noted over a hundred and twenty years ago the creation of the world economy has been a vastly destructive as well as an exceedingly creative process. Some of its most destructive aspects furthermore did not appear prominently until the present century. Modern medicine has created rates of population growth which require extraordinarily rapid and effective adaptation of economic structures in order to prevent real economic regression. At the same time the environmental conditions in the world economy within which the economic structures of less developed societies have been compelled to attempt to adapt are in many ways increasingly exacting. It is notorious that the gap between the wealth of the rich countries and that of the poor countries in the world has not been narrowing in recent years and it may be still widening today. The extraordinary difficulties of producing a more even distribution of productive resources between the regions of a Socialist country like Yugoslavia, even where the government is committed to this aim and is prepared to sacrifice some little economic growth to attain it, make it very obvious why it is so difficult for poor countries to improve their terms of trade with rich countries.[18] Equally there are still today probably more countries than not governed by men with a deeper interest in the preservation of a variety of different national or international structures than they have in maximizing the economic growth of their countries (not necessarily for unedifying reasons). Under earlier demographic conditions such preferences might often, however corrupt in motivation, have formed the basis of wise and humane statecraft. But in the second half of the twentieth century they are a perilous luxury for any society. A minimal condition for real revolutionary achievement is the capacity to use state power to protect the economic interests and expand the productive resources of the society in which the revolution has occurred. Both the elite and the mass contribution to revolutionary action contain a crucial component of economic nationalism. Since Leninism as a doctrine (whatever its internal coherence) does focus rather fiercely on this aspect of revolutionary potential in the second half of the twentieth century, it is not particularly surprising at an elite level that it should continue to exert great appeal especially in countries which in Lenin's phrase 'cannot go on any longer in the old way'.[19] But since it is ludicrous to suppose that international economic maltreatment or international political oppression is confined to the world capitalist nations, it is equally absurd to suppose that the meaning of twentieth-century revolution can be clearly identified within the corpus of Marxist theory. There are perhaps empirical reasons for supposing that countries which today need a revolution (of which there are not a few) would be best advised to entrust their destinies to decidedly Marxist political elites and ones which (other things being equal) are better the better organized they are. The historical record of twentieth-century revolution suggests that if your country is in a really dismal way a Communist government (of your own creation) may be an eminently rational investment (which is, of course, not to say that it is necessarily at all a real possibility). The reason, however, why a Communist government might be an eminently rational investment in many countries is certainly not because Marxism-Leninism is in any sense true. Indeed it is precisely because of the total fatuity of the expectations indicated in Lenin's *State and Revolution,* one of the canonical works, that Communist governments do on occasion provide such indefeasible services. It is because the locus of revolution is a nation state in which the concentration of political power and the will to put this to effective use have together proved inadequate to protect the national society from elaborate damage from the impact of the world economy, that the post-revolutionary regime requires still greater concentration of power and substantially firmer will to restore the viability. In order for a revolutionary regime to prove effective in the excessively taxing conditions in which revolutionary regimes are at all likely to arise today it is necessary for it, however populist its rhetoric or authentic its concern for an egalitarian distribution of social welfare, to maintain a highly concentrated distribution of political power. The least withered state apparatuses in the modern world have been created by revolutions.

Furthermore – and this is, if anything, even more important – the universalist claims of Marxism-Leninism are such that they may in perfectly good faith set it in conflict on occasion with the bases of authentically revolutionary mobilization in present conditions. In the nineteenth century western liberal states (as well as western illiberal states) conceived themselves as entrusted by the historical process with a destiny, a *mission civilisatrice*, to bring the benefits of modernity, religious or otherwise, to the benighted areas of the globe, the white man's burden. There is a conceptual continuity between the gunboat diplomacy of nineteenth-century imperialism and the battleship diplomacy of the Soviet Union today (or – at least equally, of course – with the battleship diplomacy of the United States today). The universal distribution of 'Socialist' economic structures is not just a goal of Soviet foreign policy, it is also in theory, if not always in practice, a theoretical obligation of the Soviet state and of Marxist-Leninists in all countries, a universal remedy, though not necessarily a complete remedy, for the historical political and economic ills of mankind. A civilized state is a Socialist state. The consequence of this identification is a sort of Red Man's Burden, which makes it as dangerous from the point of view of national independence to live inside the ancient limits of Chinese suzerainty or the territory 'protected' by the Warsaw Pact as it is to do so within the geographical domain to which the Monroe Doctrine applies. Bringing civilization to barbarians, and to barbarians inside the supposedly traditional boundaries of the realm is as apt a description of the Chinese reconstruction of Tibet as it was of the English dominion over Southern Ireland. Stamping out feudalism in Tibet and keeping the Papists in their place plainly belong to very different philosophies of history; and the end product of the occupation in Tibet might in the event turn out decisively more beneficial than it did in Southern Ireland. But that does not alter the point that military occupation by the armed forces of a modern state in order to extend the benefits of civilization as conceived by those who control the state apparatus is an intrinsically colonial enterprise. Exporting revolution on the bayonets of a modern army may mean exporting some of the capacities which a post-revolutionary regime needs to display if it is to prove effective, but it is at least as likely to promote revolutionary mobilization against the invaders as on their behalf. Colonial regimes have historically provided many different benefits to many different places, as well as exacted rather more benefits for themselves from most places in return. But colonial regimes in Czechoslovakia or Tibet are morally equivocal in just the same way as traditional European colonies were morally equivocal. The presence of armies of occupation suggests all too clearly the reality of indigenous scepticism that the colonial power is doing them a favour. When in receipt of favours like this, what nation needs oppressors? Communist regimes have tended to be extremely difficult to dislodge (at any rate since Béla Kun), however colonial they may be in character. But so too over long periods of time up to the Second World War did traditional colonial regimes prove. Except for the crucial failure of social control (which was as far away in pre-war Vietnam as in Czechoslovakia today), the components of a modern revolution, perhaps sometimes even one conducted under Socialist auspices, may well be present in countries enjoying a Communist government. How easy it would in fact be in these countries to improve on the performance of their present regimes is a difficult question to answer, though in some cases the possibility of greater freedom with only the same extent of economic inefficiency may be very real. But, as emphasized before, justified rebellion does not necessarily produce a successful post-revolutionary regime. There are certainly Communist governments which might be – and even which have been – the targets of eminently justified rebellions. So, if it makes sense for Marxist-Leninists to export revolution on the bayonets of modern armies which they happen to command, it is also necessary to realize that one day there may be real and successful modern revolutions directed against regimes with Marxist-Leninist titles and formal political organization.

Simply because styles of integration of national economies and societies into the world economy are experienced for the great majority of nations in the world today (including many in the 'Socialist' bloc) as essentially inimical to the maintenance of local identities and the preservation of local interests, there are going to go on being revolutions. In the case of all the revolutions analysed (with the partial exception of the Mexican revolution) the revolutions came because elite groups in the societies concerned came to adopt notions of how power could be acquired and how, once acquired, it could be used to preserve the currently neglected interests of the majorities of their populations. The most helpful social situation for lending mass plausibility to the promises of the revolutionary elites is the colonial situation or the situation of temporary enemy occupation. It is not an accident that so many of the political revolutions which have involved really massive popular mobilization have been wars of national liberation, often liberation from the colonial yoke. The process of decolonization, linked with the establishment of international legal institutions like the United Nations which effectively define the achievement of revolutionary success, provided for a time particularly favourable conditions of mass revolutionary potential and international protection for an established revolutionary regime. This produced an important and genuine, if elusive, shift in international conceptions of legitimate authority. The best-accredited revolutionary movements today, in Mozambique or Portuguese Guinea or South Africa in effect enjoy the residue of this historical shift. But all of the regimes which have experienced successful revolutions in the twentieth century have belonged among the states whose situation in the world economy is either colonial or neo-colonial. It is, plausibly, more difficult to focus popular distress in neo-colonial countries around the salvationary offers of revolutionary elites. The intricate dependences of the world market form a less incisive projective field than the notably direct experiences of classical colonialism. But the need for political elites better capable of defending the economic interests of these societies on the world market may well be almost as urgent as in the case of colonial regimes themselves. Here is a case, perhaps, in which the direction of historical development is running rather against the probability of easy revolutionary success, but in which revolutionary success *might* on occasion represent as striking a real improvement as it did at the time perhaps in Yugoslavia or North Vietnam.

What is left, then, of the concept of revolution as it has in fact applied to real historical developments in this century? Firstly, it is suggested, a notion of revolutionary achievement; not one of a very Utopian kind, promising a transcendently better human world within a future anyone but a fool could claim clearly to imagine, but a notion, nevertheless, of brusque and intractable authority. It is, for better or worse, false, that the *'malheureux sont les puissances de la terre'*.[20] But that power can be torn on occasion by the hands of those who can minister to the desperation of their needs from the hands of those who cannot or who do not wish to, the history of twentieth-century revolution does show, perhaps most grandly in the case of China. If all revolutions definitionally include a process of popular mobilization which constitutes in essence a justified rebellion, it is not difficult to grasp the pathos of revolution, its delicate availability for world-wide moral fantasy – identification with the weak (and hopefully good) against the strong and (sometimes irrefutably) bad. But if all successful revolutions establish (and must as of today establish) effective modern state powers, capable of operating among the taxing disciplines of modernity, it is easy to see how the pathos of revolution should readily evaporate from the post-revolutionary regimes. As Benjamin Schwartz puts it nicely, 'The mystique of revolution belongs to history as a moral political drama, rather than to history as a technico-economic process.'[21] The enduring revolutionary grandeur of Chairman Mao is linked directly to the Chinese government's failure to publish serious economic statistics for many a long year.

What is left of the concept of revolution is essentially a metaphor (which is, after all, what the concept of revolution began as) – a metaphor of the recapture of control by the virtuous over an inimical destiny. We may think of it aptly in terms of an individual riding the breakers, triumphantly poised at the crest of a surging wave. In the economic, political and military structures of the modern world, most nation states seldom achieve any very decisive degree of control over the development of their nation. The poorer the nation is, the more this is true. For most regimes the experience of political enterprise escapes chaos merely by the determination with which most of the interests supposedly in their charge are ignored. Most regimes are pounded helplessly on the sands, or tossed vertiginously under the great waves. Even when, occasionally, quite small groups of political actors can contrive to articulate these massive energies and direct them, as they hope, to the establishment of an entirely new order, the metaphor is aptly discouraging. Breakers cannot be ridden for ever; the pace slackens, the board dips and the balance and mastery are gone. The establishment of such a degree of freedom and control in such a testing environment is at best a brief triumph of political athleticism. But that does not show that surfing is impossible or revolution devoid of meaning.

The difference between before and after is not a difference between this world and another world. Post-revolutionary states too are often brutal, corrupt, tyrannical and incompetent. But it is at times a very real and an extraordinarily important difference nevertheless. What revolutionaries offer themselves and their own societies is above all else an image of power, control, certainty and purpose in a world in which impotence, incomprehension and the terror of sheer meaninglessness are permanent threats. It is a very rationalist offer – and only insofar as it *is* a very rationalist offer is it any more than the most trivial of *actes gratuits*, the veriest idiocy. No doubt there is something permanently exposed in all rationalist political interpretation. The variety of values at stake in the accumulation and exercise of political power is so enormous, and the selective mechanisms involved in any interpretation of the meaning of what is taking place are so decisive, that the possibility that any interpretation will appear in retrospect the most besotted of delusions is always pressing. Certainly the air of fleeting mastery, of the decisive impact of the human will on the processes of history, which does cling around the great revolutionary crises is liable to a very sad evanescence. But the powerful grounds for such scepticism are always in the end potentially nihilist. There is much reason to see the calm and purposeful maintenance of ancient political orders today, conservative political rationalism, as an enactment of a fantasy every bit as historically exotic as that of the revolutionaries: consider the career of Winston Churchill or that of Charles de Gaulle. Any political action, the meaning of which depends on achieving a determinate future for a national political unit is open to the same dismissive sneer. The key Machiavellian insight that the grandest of political achievements are such fragile gestures in the face of such a final menace is as vivid and as persuasive as ever it was. And yet the starvation and butchery of millions and the desperation of ten of millions are the most naturalistic of realities and they will continue to make their claims. Revolution is in many ways a feeble remedy for their ills – and it is no remedy at all for many of them. Also it is a remedy the distribution of which is much affected by factors which are extremely arbitrary from the point of view of the suffering society. But weak though it may be as a remedy and capricious though the conditions of its supply are likely to remain, it is still today, for those states and societies which can no longer go on in the old way, often the only remedy there is.

Notes

Preface

1. 'There must be formed a sphere of society which claims no *traditional* status but only a human status, a sphere which is not opposed to particular consequences but is totally opposed to the assumptions of the German political system; a sphere, finally, which cannot emancipate itself without emancipating itself from all other spheres of society, without, therefore, emancipating all these other spheres, which is, in short, a *total loss* of humanity and which can only redeem itself by a *total redemption of humanity*. This dissolution of society, as a particular class, is the *proletariat*.' (Karl Marx, *Contribution to the Critique of Hegel's Philosophy of Right*, in T. B. Bottomore (ed.), *Karl Marx: Early Writings*, pb. ed. New York 1964, 58.) Marx's own emphases.

2. 'Working Men of all Countries, Unite!' Conclusion of Karl Marx and Friedrich Engels, *Manifesto of the Communist Party*, London, February 1848 (Karl Marx and Friedrich Engels, *Selected Works*, 2 vols, Moscow 1958, Vol. 1, 65).

Introduction

1. The question of whether it is possible to produce value-neutral social or political science (a logical question in the philosophy of the social sciences) and the question of how far it would be desirable to do so, even if it were possible (a question of substantive morality), are both very complex issues. I assert, rather than argue, a position here. For a very helpful introduction see W. G. Runciman, *Social Science and Political Theory*, Cambridge 1963, especially chapters 1 and 8. See also, Charles Taylor, 'Neutrality in Political Science', in P. Laslett and W. G. Runciman (eds), *Philosophy, Politics and Society*, 3rd Series, Oxford 1967, chapter 2; and especially Alasdair Macintyre, 'The Idea of a Social Science', in B. R. Wilson (ed.), *Rationality*, Oxford 1970, chapter 6.

2. For the application to the philosophy of action of Aristotle's idea of the practical syllogism, see e.g.: G. E. M. Anscombe, *Intention*, 2nd ed., Ithaca, N.Y. 1963, 57–78.

3. This does not mean that rational discussion of the values at stake is impossible nor that any prejudice goes. Indeed one premise of the argument is the crucial significance of the category of rationality in social interpretation.

4. G. Lichtheim, *A Short History of Socialism*, London 1970, 123–4.

5. The clearest and most interesting account of the growing incoherence of this tradition is G. Lichtheim, *Marxism: An Historical and Critical Study*, 2nd ed. pb. London 1964. For a stimulating introductory account see his *A Short History of Socialism*.

6. Arthur Hatto, '"Revolution": An Enquiry into the Usefulness of an Historical Term', *Mind*, new series, LVIII, 232 (Oct. 1949), 495–517. Karl Griewank, *Der Neuzeitliche Revolutionsbegriff*, 2nd ed. Frankfurt 1969, is the most extensive discussion of the historical origins of the concept.

7. Hatto, *op. cit.*, 505; and Vernon F. Snow, 'The Concept of Revolution in Seventeenth Century England', *The Historical Journal*, V, 2 (1962), 167–74.

8. But cf. Hannah Arendt, *On Revolution*, London 1963, 40–1.

9. For a particularly clear presentation see George Lichtheim, *The Origins of Socialism*, London 1969.

10. Cf. the Confucian perspective on rebellion: 'There is nothing evil in human nature ... the people are not born to rebel; but if the people are not nourished and are not taught, rebellion results.' (Mary C. Wright, *The Last Stand of Chinese Conservatism*, pb. ed. New York 1966, 143.)

11. See especially Chalmers Johnson, *Revolution and the Social System*, Stanford 1964; and, more elaborately, Chalmers Johnson, *Revolutionary Change*, pb. ed. London 1968.

12. For millennarianism in general see Sylvia L. Thrupp (ed.), *Millennial Dreams in Action: Essays in Comparative Study* (*Comparative Studies in Society and History*, Supplement 2, The Hague 1962); and K. Burridge, *New Heaven, New Earth*, Oxford 1969. For studies of cargo cults see particularly Peter Worsley, *The Trumpet Shall Sound*, pb. ed. London 1970, and K. O. L. Burridge, *Mambu: A Melanesian Millennium*, London 1960. For millennarianism as a more general response to colonialism see especially Vittorio Lanternari, *The Religions of the Oppressed: A Study of Modern Messianic Cults*, pb. ed. New York 1965; and Georges Balandier, *The Sociology of Black Africa*, London 1970.

13. In real historical situations these two possibilities are far from being mutually exclusive. Most revolutions incorporate both features in some of their aspects.

14. This is not a tautology. The reactionary supposition that a belief in the possibility of a new order today must be essentially religious is false.

15. Christopher Hill, *Puritanism and Revolution*, pb. ed. London 1962, chapter 3, 'The Norman Yoke'.

16. See Caroline Robbins, *The Eighteenth Century Commonwealthman*, Cambridge, Mass. 1969, 369–70; F. D. Cartwright, *Life and Correspondence of Major Cartwright*, 2 vols, London 1826; E. P. Thompson, *The Making of the English Working Class*, London 1963, especially 82–8.

17. There is still no satisfactory study of the development of the idea of progress. For a classic introduction, see J. B. Bury, *The Idea of Progress*, pb. ed. New York 1955. For a more elaborate treatment

of some of the non-Marxist nineteenth-century thinkers associated with discussion of the idea of progress, see Frank Manuel, *The Prophets of Paris*, Cambridge, Mass. 1962. For a critical analysis of the concept of social development as such see Robert A. Nisbet, *Social Change and History*, pb. ed. London 1969.

18. J. Egret, *La Pré-Révolution française*, Paris 1962. G. Lefebvre, *The Coming of the French Revolution*, pb. ed. New York 1957.

19. M. Dommanget, *Babeuf et la Conjuration des Égaux*, Paris 1970 ed.; and M. Dommanget, *Sur Babeuf et la Conjuration des Égaux*, Paris 1970. For a hostile view see J. L. Talmon, *The Origins of Totalitarian Democracy*, pb. ed. London 1961, 168–247.

20. Condorcet, *Esquisse d'un tableau historique des progrès de l'esprit humain*, O. H. Prior (ed.), Paris 1933, 199.

21. Albert Soboul, *The Parisian Sans-Culottes and the French Revolution 1793–4*, Oxford 1964. Cf. A. Cobban, *The Social Interpretation of the French Revolution*, Cambridge 1964, chapter XI.

22. Karl Marx, *Pre-capitalist Economic Formations*, ed. E. J. Hobsbawm, London 1964, 127–9.

23. Marx, *op. cit.* 78. This view was essentially shared by Lenin and by Trotsky, see e.g. Trotsky, quoting Lenin, 'The city inevitably leads the village', in Hélène Carrère d'Encausse and Stuart R. Schram, *Marxism and Asia*, London 1969, 242.

24. Marx, *op. cit.* 129. This view might be slightly qualified by modern studies, but the central point about the relative scales of urban and rural revolt would remain valid.

25. For a lucid account of Marx's own thought as essentially non-determinist in character see Shlomo Avineri, *The Social and Political Thought of Karl Marx*, pb. ed. Cambridge 1970. For the comparatively positivist position of Engels, see Z. A. Jordan, *The Evolution of Dialectical Materialism*, London 1967; and Lichtheim, *Marxism*, 237–243.

26. In Marx's own case it would perhaps be more natural to say that he began with what was undesirable – the systematic ideology of classical liberal economics. What is crucial is that he began with categories which were in fact normative and his commentary upon them was focussed in normative terms.

27. Marx and Engels, *Selected Works*, Vol. 2, 168.

28. Karl Marx, *The Eighteenth Brumaire of Louis Napoleon* (in Marx and Engels, *Selected Works*, Vol. 1, 247).

29. Avineri, *op. cit.* 217.

30. Friedrich Engels, 'On Authority' (in Marx and Engels, *Selected Works*, Vol. 1, 638).

31. G. W. F. Hegel, *The Philosophy of Right*, Oxford 1942, 12.

32. This is a post-1917, rather than pre-1917, characteristic of Leninist revolutionary theory, a consequence of the advantages in a revolutionary situation of possessing the instrument for the creation of which Lenin argued in *What is to be Done?* It is not a consequence advertised in that work or indeed one probably imagined by Lenin himself when he wrote it.

33. This is not intended as a general explanation of the motivation

of revolutionaries which, as in the case of other men, varies widely. Many revolutionaries are clearly more directly drawn to one face than than to the other. Some are drawn by the peculiar appeal of the combination. Cf. E. Victor Wolfenstein, *The Revolutionary Personality: Lenin, Trotsky, Gandhi*, Princeton 1967; Fred Weinstein and Gerald M. Platt, *The Wish to be Free: Society, Psyche and Value Change*, Berkeley 1969, chapter 4; Harold Lasswell, *Psychopathology and Politics*, pb. ed. New York 1960.

34. See the memorable portraits in F. Dostoevsky, *The Possessed*, and Joseph Conrad, *The Secret Agent*.

35. See particularly the sections from the projected second volume of *L'Ancien régime et la révolution française*, translated by John Lukacs as A. de Tocqueville, *The European Revolution and Correspondence with Gobineau*, pb. ed. Garden City 1959, 31–172.

36. Quoted by Lenin in *'Left-wing' Communism, an Infantile Disorder* in *Selected Works*, 2 vols, Moscow 1947, 2, 607.

37. Lenin, *Left-wing Communism* in *Selected Works*, 2, 629.

38. An indispensable qualification.

39. Lenin, *op. cit.* 2, 621.

40. See note 12 to this chapter.

41. Mao Tse-tung, *Selected Military Writings*, Peking 1963, 224–5.

42. John Hospers, *An Introduction to Philosophical Analysis*, London 1956, 51–2. This is a pragmatic point, not an observation about the theory of meaning.

43. Cf. George McT. Kahin, *Nationalism and Revolution in Indonesia*, Ithaca, N.Y. 1952, with Jan M. Pluvier, *Confrontations: A Study in Indonesian Politics*, London 1965. After the events of 1965 the failure of the Soekarno regime is scarcely open to dispute.

44. The Fanonist claim is that non-revolutionary decolonization is insufficiently disruptive to destroy the oppressive inequalities of colonial structures (Frantz Fanon, *The Wretched of the Earth*, London 1965). But Algeria itself could hardly have been more effectively disrupted (Pierre Bourdieu and Abdelmalek Sayad, *Le Déracinement*, Paris 1964), while its present condition is hardly that to which Fanon aspired.

45. Cf. Michael Oakeshott, *Rationalism in Politics*, London 1962, 8–10, 24–6, 111–36 (especially 119–20). The twentieth century has been the great age of political cookbooks precisely because the traditions of most countries no longer provide very illuminating intimations on how to cope with daily political reality.

46. Lenin, *The State and Revolution* in *Selected Works*, 2, 143, 213–24. For Kautsky's own thought see the forthcoming study by Richard Geary.

47. Lenin, *op. cit.* in *Selected Works*, 2, 169–71, 194, 206–11. See also Herbert Marcuse, *Soviet Marxism: A Critical Analysis*, New York 1958.

48. A. de Tocqueville, *The European Revolution*, 161.

49. S. M. Lipset, *Political Man*, London 1960, 403. (The chapter title is 'The End of Ideology'.)

50. It is hard to know which is the more successful in this respect.

The last days of Stalin and the second Eisenhower administration disclose striking limitations in each.

51. Contrast e.g. Paul Baran, *The Political Economy of Growth*, pb. ed. New York 1968. A. G. Frank, *Latin America: Underdevelopment or Revolution*, London 1970; Gunnar Myrdal, *An Asian Drama*, pb. ed. New York 1968; H. Myint, *The Economics of Developing Countries*, London 1964; R. Dumont and M. Mazoyer, *Développement et Socialismes*, Paris 1969.

52. This does not seem to have been true of China since the beginning of the Cultural Revolution because of the Rousseauist moral preoccupations of Mao Tse-tung. (See e.g. Benjamin I. Schwartz, 'China and the West in the "Thought of Mao Tse-Tung"', in Ping-ti Ho and Tang Tsou, *China in Crisis*, Chicago 1969, Vol. 1, Bk. 1, 365–379.) But there is a real possibility that it will become, or even has become, so again.

1. Russia

1. This refers, of course, to the October Bolshevik seizure of power, not to the revolution of February 1917. Much of the support of the Bolshevik coup itself could not be said to be 'Marxist' as such.

2. Isaac Deutscher, *The Unfinished Revolution: Russia 1917–67*, pb. ed. London 1969.

3. How long can it be meaningfully said that a 'revolutionary' process persists? If the battered bureaucrats of the Kremlin are still honorary revolutionaries may there not be hope even for Richard Nixon?

4. Eduard Bernstein, *Evolutionary Socialism*, pb. ed. New York 1961; Peter Gay, *The Dilemma of Democratic Socialism*, pb. ed. New York 1962.

5. Whether or not Marx's analysis of capitalist–proletarian polarization was intended to be a concrete sociological prediction, it is perfectly clear from the *Communist Manifesto* (Marx and Engels, *Selected Works*, 1, 34–45) that at a crucial point in his intellectual development he did expect overt conflict between the two to increase and the proportional power of the two to alter with it.

6. Gay, *Dilemma of Democratic Socialism*, 250.

7. For a chronology of the revolution, see R. V. Daniels, *Red October: The Bolshevik Revolution of 1917*, London 1967, 233–43.

8. See e.g. Theodore H. Von Laue, 'Of the Crises in the Russian Polity' (in John S. Curtiss (ed.), *Essays in Russian and Soviet History*, Leiden 1965, 303–22). Cf. George Kennan, 'The Breakdown of the Tsarist Autocracy', in R. Pipes (ed.), *Revolutionary Russia*, London 1968, 1–15 with H. Seton-Watson, 'Comment on Kennan', *op. cit.* 15–22; A. Gerschenkron, *Economic Backwardness in Historical Perspective*, London 1962, chapter 6.

9. For the major study of the purges see Robert Conquest, *The Great Terror*, London 1968. For a cool brief discussion of their more rational dimension see J. P. Nettl, *The Soviet Achievement*, London 1967, 139–49. For a more histrionic presentation see I. Deutscher, *Stalin*, pb. ed. London 1961, chapter 9.

10. L. Kochan, *Russia in Revolution. 1890–1918*, pb. ed. London 1970, 19.

11. This was not to say that it was not making progress in a number of dimensions: educational, see Kennan, in Pipes (ed.), *Revolutionary Russia*, 5 but cf. *ibid*. 16–17: agrarian, see George L. Yaney, 'The Concept of the Stolypin Land Reform', *Slavic Review*, XXIII, 2 (June 1964), 275–93: or even in some respects towards social integration in general, see George L. Yaney, 'Social Stability in Pre-revolutionary Russia: A Critical Note', *Slavic Review*, XXIV, 3 (Sept. 1965), 521–7. But a greater measure of social integration might accentuate rather than reduce the dangers of Russian internal social relations.

12. There was not, however, as there was in China a direct incompatibility between the type of professionalism of skill required in the modern officer and the status demands of the roles from which the officer corps could alone be recruited. (Cf. Mary C. Wright, *The Last Stand of Chinese Conservatism*, pb. ed. New York, 201, 220.)

13. Even George Yaney seems to acknowledge this in his article 'The Concept of the Stolypin Land Reform', *Slavic Review*, XXIII (1964), 279–81. Increased social interaction and greater articulation of local communities with the state structure may well have been precisely what was most dangerous for the autocracy.

14. Yaney, *op. cit.*; G. T. Robinson, *Rural Russia under the Old Regime*, pb. ed. Berkeley 1967, chapter XI.

15. L. Kochan, *Russia in Revolution*, 27.

16. George Katkov, *Russia 1917: The February Revolution*, pb. ed. London 1969, and George Katkov, 'German Political Intervention in Russia during World War I', in Pipes (ed.), *Revolutionary Russia*, 63–88.

17. Only 12.6 per cent of the population was recorded as urban in the 1897 census (Peter I. Lyashchenko, *History of the National Economy of Russia to the 1917 Revolution*, New York 1949, 273), though the rate of growth of the proletariat was considerable from the 1880s on (Lyashchenko, *op. cit.* 503–5); R. Portal, 'The Industrialization of Russia in H. J. Habbakuk and M. Postan (eds.), *Cambridge Economical History of Europe*, VI, 2, 808, 826, 845.

18. Kochan, *Russia in Revolution*, 35–6; Lyashchenko, *op. cit.* 530–2, 538–45.

19. See the classic statement in *Capital*, Vol. 1. chapter XXXII, Moscow 1961, especially 763.

20. T. H. Von Laue, 'Russian Peasants in the Factory 1892–1904', *Journal of Economic History*, XXI (March 1961); G. V. Rimlinger, 'Autocracy and the Factory Order', *Journal of Economic History*, XX (March 1960).

21. Lenin, *State and Revolution* in *Selected Works*, 2, 174: '*We ourselves*, the workers, will organize large-scale production on the basis of what capitalism has already created, relying on our own experience as workers ... The united workers will hire their own managers and technicians and pay them *all*, as, indeed *all* "state" officials in general, ordinary workmen's wages.'

22. Ezra Mendelsohn, *Class Struggle in the Pale*, Cambridge 1970; Allan K. Wildman, *The Making of a Workers' Revolution*, Chicago 1967, especially 38–48, 173–8.

23. H. Seton-Watson, *The Russian Empire 1801–1917*, Oxford 1967, 564, 598; Kochan, *Russia in Revolution*, 48–50, 86-92.

24. On the failure of the Mensheviks before 1905, see Wildman, *The Making of a Workers' Revolution*. For an intelligent study of the outstanding Menshevik leader, see I. Getzler, *Martov: A Political Biography of a Russian Social Democrat*, Cambridge 1967. For Menshevik hopes and their disappointment between 1905 and 1912 see Leopold Haimson, 'The Problem of Social Stability in Urban Russia 1905–17 (Part 1)', *Slavic Review*, XXIII, 4 (Dec. 1964), especially 624-6, 629–32.

25. Haimson, *Slavic Review*, XXIII, 4; and XXIV, 1.

26. Haimson, *Slavic Review*, XXIII, 634-6; Robinson, *Rural Russia under the Old Regime*, 208–42, especially 219, 238–9; George L. Yaney, *Slavic Review*, XXIII, 2, 292. (But Yaney's whole article, *op. cit.* 275–93, is an important corrective to the common account of the Stolypin reforms as an act of external violence committed upon the mass of the peasantry from above.

27. Haimson, *Slavic Review*, XXIII, 630–5.

28. Haimson, *Slavic Review*, XXIII, 631.

29. Haimson, *Slavic Review*, XXIV, 18, 51, 54.

30. Alexander Kerensky, *Russia and History's Turning Point*, New York 1965 (or in a more chastened vein, Paul Miliukov, *Political Memoirs 1905–17*, ed. A. P. Mendel, Ann Arbor 1967).

31. A. Walicki, *The Controversy over Capitalism*, Oxford 1969, 185–94; Maximilien Rubel, 'The Relationship of Bolshevism to Marxism', in R. Pipes (ed.), *Revolutionary Russia*, 300–23 (especially 300–5).

32. Walicki, *op. cit.* 119–26, 132–94.

33. Walicki, *op. cit.* 9–13; A. Gerschenkron, *Economic Backwardness in Historical Perspective*, 167–71; Martin Malia, *Alexander Herzen and the Birth of Russian Socialism*, New York 1965.

34. It was able to finance rapid industrialization before 1909 only by heavy state subsidies dependent on massive governmental borrowing from western European financiers, borrowing which could only be serviced by state exports of grain wrung from a heavily taxed peasantry. Even with these subsidies and with the protection of high external tariffs much of the resulting industrial capacity was foreign-owned. See T. H. Von Laue, *Sergei Witte and the Industrialization of Russia*, New York 1963. Even when a more balanced form of industrial growth became possible, partly as a result of the Stolypin reforms, dependence on foreign capital remained heavy. See Roger Portal, 'The Industrialization of Russia', in H. J. Habbakuk and M. Postan (eds), *Cambridge Economic History of Europe*, VI, 2, 801–74, especially 845–51.

35. Walicki, *op. cit.* 178.

36. On Struve, see Richard Kindersley, *The First Russian Revisionists; A Study of 'Legal Marxism' in Russia*, Oxford 1962. On

Plekhanov, see Samuel H. Baron, *Plekhanov: The Father of Russian Marxism*, pb. ed. Stanford 1966.

37. For Marx's comment see Karl Marx and Friedrich Engels, *Selected Correspondence*, 379. I have followed the translation in Walicki, *op. cit.* 186.

38. Marx and Engels, *Selected Correspondence*, 379.

39. Not however in its actual membership, organization or discipline. It was a party which spoke for the peasantry but, precisely for this reason, it was not an effective political organization. See H. Seton-Watson, *The Russian Empire*, 560. For studies of the Social Revolutionaries before and during 1917, see O. H. Radkey, *The Agrarian Foes of Bolshevism*, New York 1958; and Radkey, *The Sickle under the Hammer*, New York 1963.

40. Franco Venturi, *The Roots of Revolution*, pb. ed. New York 1966, 498–506.

41. Walicki, *op. cit.* 84.

42. See Adam B. Ulam, *Lenin and the Bolsheviks*, pb. ed. London 1969, chapter III, and page 16.

43. George Lichtheim, *Marxism: An Historical and Critical Study*, 278–300; Peter Gay, *The Dilemma of Democratic Socialism*, pb. ed. New York 1962; and cf. V. I. Lenin, *What is to be Done?*, ed. S. V. Utechin, Oxford 1963.

44. Allan K. Wildman, *The Making of a Workers' Revolution*, Chicago 1967.

45. See Wildman, *op. cit. passim*. Proletarian organization was focussed on the factory rather than the trade union. The unit of representation in both the Petrograd Soviet in 1906 and in the Duma was the factory (Kochan, *op. cit.* 115).

46. H. Seton-Watson, *The Russian Empire*, 474–80, 640. Kochan, *op. cit.* 73.

47. V. I. Lenin, *Collected Works*, London 1964, Vol. 23, 253. A speech delivered on 9 January 1917 at the Zurich People's House.

48. Leon Trotsky, *The History of the Russian Revolution*, London 1934, 343. A finely reasoned passage of historical analysis.

49. All accounts of the revolution make clear the astonishment, and indeed near incredulity, in the ranks of the Bolsheviks themselves which greeted Lenin's proclamation on his arrival in Petrograd of the April Theses (*Selected Works*, Vol. 2, 17–22). It required enormous effort to keep even the Bolshevik Party (a party committed to organizational unity above almost any other instrumental value) acting as a united group in the period of the insurrectionary struggle; and even Lenin's own efforts did not suffice to keep Zinoviev and Kamenev under party control at the crucial time.

50. See Shlomo Avineri, in Pipes (ed.), *Revolutionary Russia*, 326–8; Marx and Engels, *Manifesto of the Communist Party* in *Selected Works*, Vol. 1, 53–4.

51. D. Geyer, in Pipes (ed.), *Revolutionary Russia*, 179. Geyer's whole account of the Bolshevik leadership of the Petrograd rising is outstanding.

52. L. Schapiro, *The Origin of the Communist Autocracy*, pb. ed. New York 1965, chapter 6.

53. A process gloomily but effectively chronicled by Schapiro, *op. cit.*

54. The majorities of the white Russian armies naturally came from inside the former empire. Allied intervention never touched the lives of most Russians directly. The only real war which the Bolsheviks had to win in order in practice to survive was civil war. But Lenin was not to know this in March 1918 – and his anxieties were eminently realistic. (Ulam, *Lenin and the Bolsheviks*, 535–6.)

55. See especially note 9 above.

56. M. Lewin, *Russian Peasants and Soviet Power: A Study of Collectivization*, London 1968.

57. Ulam, *Lenin and the Bolsheviks*, 646.

58. This claim is not intended to be more than tautologous. It is not independently explanatory. There is some reason to believe that the land reforms were quite effective, under pressures less violent than those of 1917: Yaney, *Slavic Review*, xxiii, 275–93; Alexander Gerschenkron, 'Agrarian Policies and Industrialization 1861–1917' in Habbakuk and Postan, *Cambridge Economic History of Europe*, vi, 2, especially 783–800

59. Cf. Yaney, *Slavic Review*, xxiii, 275–93, with G. T. Robinson, *Rural Russia under the Old Regime*; Eric Wolf, *Peasant Wars of the Twentieth Century*, New York 1969, chapter 2.

60. Robinson, *Rural Russia*, 87–8.

61. This probably represents an overestimate, see Robinson, *op. cit.* 244.

62. A. Leroy-Beaulieu, *The Russian Peasant*, Sandoval, N. Mexico, 1962, 137–8.

63. Robinson, *op. cit.* 260–1. Lyashchenko, *History of the National Economy of Russia*, 730–7. This failure was significantly influenced by governmental tax policies and it might well have been decisively reversed had the First World War not intervened: Gerschenkron, in Habbakuk and Postan (eds), *Cambridge Economic History of Europe*, vi, 2, 767–8, 798–800.

64. Robinson, *op. cit.* 144.

65. Robinson, *op. cit.* chapter xi.

66. Robinson, *op. cit.* 189.

67. Robinson, *op. cit.* 216.

68. Robinson, *op. cit.* chapter viii, especially 130–1.

69. Kochan, *op. cit.* 143.

70. Lenin, *Two Tactics of Social Democracy* in *Selected Works*, Vol. 1, 367 (see also 352, 361–70, 395, 413–14).

71. Z. A. B. Zeman and W. B. Scharlau, *The Merchant of Revolution: The Life of Alexander Israel Helphand (Parvus) 1867–1924*, London 1965, especially 110–12.

72. Leon Trotsky, *The Permanent Revolution* and *Results and Prospects*, London 1962, 237.

73. Ulam, *Lenin and the Bolsheviks*, 432.

74. Ulam, *op. cit.* 622. (Speech to 10th party congress. March 1921.)

75. L. Trotsky, *History of the Russian Revolution*, 343. Kochan, *op. cit.* chapter 15, 'Lenin Arrives'.

76. Kochan, *op. cit.* 212.

77. Ulam, *op. cit.* 714 (notes for speech – never delivered – to 11th party congress of March 1922).

2. Mexico

1. How long the Russian revolution is judged to have lasted depends usually on which features of it are thought admirable or causally decisive. The causal explanations or moral assessments of the transformation tend in practice to influence the specification of just what is to be explained or assessed. But at least October 1917 provides a powerful focus for *any* definition of what the revolution was.

2. Stanley R. Ross, *Is the Mexican Revolution Dead?*, pb. ed. New York 1966.

3. Quoted by Adam B. Ulam, *Lenin and the Bolsheviks*, pb. ed. London 1969, 652.

4. For an illuminating analysis see Pablo G. Casanova, *Democracy in Mexico*, New York 1970. For a more extensive investigation of political institutions see R. Scott, *Mexican Government in Transition*, Urbana, Ill. 1959. Also, peering through a rather odder lens, G. Almond and S. Verba, *The Civic Culture*, Princeton 1963.

5. Jean A. Meyer, 'Les ouvriers dans la révolution mexicaine: les Bataillons Rouges', *Annales: Économies, Sociétés, Civilisations*, xxv, 1 (Jan.–Feb. 1970), 32.

6. For the early period see James D. Cockcroft, *Intellectual Precursors of the Mexican Revolution, 1900–13*, Austin 1968, chapters 3–5.

7. See James W. Wilkie, *The Mexican Revolution: Federal Expenditure and Social Change since 1910*, Berkeley 1967, especially 136–9, 153, 157–61; Howard F. Cline, *Mexico: From Revolution to Evolution 1940–60*, London 1962, especially 33–4, 211–13; F. Chevalier, 'The *Ejido* and Political Stability in Mexico', in Claudio Veliz (ed.), *The Politics of Conformity in Latin America*, London 1967, 158–91. For the relationship between Cardenas's decisions and the political pressures upon him see Joe C. Ashby, *Organised Labor and the Mexican Revolution under Lazaro Cardenas*, Chapel Hill 1967.

8. For a spirited account of the 1810 rising and its ironic conclusion see Charles C. Cumberland, *Mexico: The Struggle for Modernity*, pb. ed. London 1968, chapter 6.

9. Wilbert H. Timmons, *Morelos of Mexico: Priest, Soldier, Statesman*, El Paso 1963, 16–29.

10. Timmons, *op. cit.* 101–2.

11. Timmons, *op. cit.* 103.

12. Raymond Carr, *Spain 1808–1939*, Oxford 1966, 143–5.

13. Cumberland, *op. cit.* 217–20. Cockcroft, *op. cit.* 14–18.

14. Cumberland, *op. cit.* 232–3. Cockcroft, *op. cit.* 13–26.

15. For Russia see T. H. Von Laue, *Sergei Witte and the Industrialization of Russia*, New York 1963, and 'A Secret Memorandum of Sergei Witte on the Industrialization of Imperial Russia', *Journal of*

Modern History, XXVI, 1 (March 1954), 60–74. In Mexico, the government had little difficulty in maintaining its solvency, see Cumberland, *op. cit.* 232.

16. Cumberland, *op. cit.* 227; Cockcroft, *op. cit.* 18–19. The metallurgical industry which did exist was preponderantly in foreign hands: Eric R. Wolf, *Peasant Wars of the Twentieth Century*, New York 1969, 23.

17. See Geroid T. Robinson, *Rural Russia under the Old Regime*, pb. ed. Berkeley 1967, especially 130, 251–2.

18. For the background to this process see especially François Chevalier, *Land and Society in Colonial Mexico: The Great Hacienda*, pb. ed. Berkeley 1970, pt. 2.

19. On the labour force of the haciendas and its sources see Chevalier, *Land and Society*, 69, 277–8, 294–5.

20. Robinson, *op. cit.* 61.

21. For the key differences in background see especially François Chevalier, 'Survivances seigneuriales et présages de la révolution agraire dans le nord du Mexique (Fin du XVIIIe et XIXe siècle)', *Revue Historique*, CCXXII (1959), 1–18; and François Chevalier, 'Un facteur décisif de la révolution agraire au Mexique: le soulèvement de Zapata (1911–1919)', *Annales*, XV, 1 (Jan.–Feb. 1961), 66–82.

22. For the extent to which the geographical factors behind this pattern have survived the impact of modern technology cf. Chevalier, *Land and Society*, frontispiece map with Cumberland, *op. cit.* map at pages 12–13.

23. For the importance of this, see Chevalier, *op. cit. Revue Historique* (1959), 2–5.

24. See Chevalier, *op. cit. Revue Historique* (1959), 9–16.

25. See Morfi's formulation (Chevalier, *op. cit. Revue Historique* (1959), p. 10) that the regime of the hacienda created a civil economy which rendered many families 'useless to the state'.

26. George M. McBride, *The Land Systems of Mexico*, New York 1923, chapter IV, 96, 102.

27. Chevalier, *op. cit. Revue Historique*, 16–18. For the context of the Cristero revolt see briefly Cumberland, *op. cit.* 275–87.

28. Wolf, *op. cit.* 36.

29. John Womack Jr, *Zapata and the Mexican Revolution*, London 1969, 196–7. Womack's study is an outstanding piece of narrative history.

30. The best study of one of these, also from Chihuahua, is Michael C. Meyer, *Mexican Rebel: Pascual Orozco and the Mexican Revolution*, Lincoln, Nebraska 1967. For the importance of the more cosmopolitan and modernist experience available for the formation of Obregon's political judgement see briefly but illuminatingly Wolf, *op. cit.* 38–9.

31. Robert E. Quirk, *The Mexican Revolution: The Convention of Aguascalientes, 1914–15*, Bloomington 1960, 213.

32. It is not possible to estimate at all precisely how many lives it did cost in fact. For two recent figures see Cumberland, *op. cit.* 244–6; and Casanova, *op. cit.* viii.

33. For an indication of the extent of Mexican economic growth see conveniently the table printed by Raymond Carr, 'Mexican Agrarian Reform, 1910–60', in E. L. Jones and S. J. Woolf (eds), *Agrarian Change and Economic Development: The Historical Problems*, London 1969, 167.

34. The degree of cultural distinctness was much less than that of the Tarascan village studied by Paul Friedrich, *Agrarian Revolt in a Mexican Village*, pb. ed. Englewood Cliffs 1970. See page 9 on language usage.

35. Womack, *op. cit.* 71n. Cf. the figures for Nahuatl-speaking in Tepoztlan as late as 1940 given by Oscar Lewis, *Life in a Mexican Village: Hepoztlan Restudied*, pb. ed. Urbana 1963, 33–4. My whole discussion of Morelos follows Womack closely.

36. Chevalier, *Annales*, 1961, 75.

37. Womack, *op. cit.* 71n.

38. Womack, *op. cit.* 302.

39. Chevalier, *Annales*, 1961, 69–70.

40. Womack, *op. cit.* 70–1.

41. The Madero family had one of the ten largest fortunes in Mexico in 1910, Cockcroft, *op. cit.* 61.

42. For two useful studies of Madero in English see Charles C. Cumberland, *Mexican Revolution: Genesis under Madero*, Austin, Texas 1952; and Stanley R. Ross, *Francisco I. Madero: Apostle of Mexican Democracy*, New York 1955.

43. Cockcroft, *op. cit.* 159. Cockcroft's study contains much interesting information, but its analytical categories are extremely crude.

44. Womack, *op. cit.* 105–28.

45. Womack, *op. cit.* 43.

46. Womack, *op. cit.* 43.

47. Womack, *op. cit.* 48–9.

48. Womack, *op. cit.* 48.

49. Womack, *op. cit.* 47–8.

50. Womack, *op. cit.* 49–50.

51. Womack, *op. cit.* chapter 1. For the continuity of the revolution with the mass component of the first attempt at a Mexican revolution, see the battle cry, '*Mueran los gachupines*': Womack, *op. cit.* 33; and Cumberland, *Struggle for Modernity*, 113.

52. Chevalier, *Annales* 1961, 67.

53. Womack, *op. cit.* 197–8.

54. Chevalier, *Annales* 1961, 81.

55. Womack, *op. cit.* 357–70.

56. Chevalier, *Annales* 1961, 69.

57. Womack, *op. cit.* 126, and appendix B, *passim*. (For full text of Plan of Ayala, see pages 400–4.)

58. Article 6: Womack, *op. cit.* 402.

59. Article 7: Womack, *op. cit.* 402–3.

60. Article 8: Womack, *op. cit.* 403.

61. For the development of Diaz Soto y Gama's attitudes see especially Cockcroft, *op. cit.* 71–7, 217–32. Chevalier, *Annales* 1961, 79. Antonio Diaz Soto y Gama should not be confused with the agrono-

mist Ignacio Diaz Soto y Gama who helped to organize the surveying of Morelos under Zapata (Womack, *op. cit.* 231).

62. Womack, *op. cit.* 227–35, 240.

63. Chevalier, *Annales* 1961, 78.

64. Chevalier, *Annales* 1961, 79. On the lawyer Cabrera's land reform ambitions and his attempt to unite Carranza and Zapata on them see Womack, *op. cit.* 154, 207–11, 218.

65. Chevalier, *Annales* 1961, 79.

66. See crudely Cockcroft, *op. cit.* 50–1, on the contrast between Zapata and Obregon in their attitudes to capitalist agriculture; and Cumberland, *Struggle for Modernity*, 296, for Obregon's performance over land reform as President.

67. For the conditions under which the constitutional Convention was selected and came to its decisions see Cumberland, *Struggle for Modernity*, 259–72.

68. See Chevalier article in Veliz (ed.), *Politics of Conformity*, 164. This article contains an outstanding brief survey of the effect of the Mexican agrarian reform.

69. Chevalier, *Politics of Conformity*, 168.

70. Chevalier, *Politics of Conformity*, 188–90.

71. See the very hostile judgement of René Dumont, *Living Lands*, London 1965, chapter 6.

72. See especially, Casanova, *op. cit.*

73. Chevalier, *Politics of Conformity*, 180. The menace to the commercially unsophisticated Indian community presented by the impact of *mestizo* capitalist energies and skills is brought out very vividly in the story of Naranja as told by Paul Friedrich, *op. cit.*

74. Chevalier, *Politics of Conformity*, 177.

75. This is a conservative estimate. Womack estimates two-fifths, *op. cit.* 370.

76. I am following in this discussion the argument of Jean Meyer in his forceful article, 'Les ouvriers dans la révolution mexicaine', *Annales* (1970), 30–55.

77. Jean Meyer, *op. cit.* 31. Factual materials in the remainder of this chapter are taken from this article, unless otherwise mentioned.

78. See especially Cockcroft, *op. cit.* chapter 6.

79. For doubts on the radical credentials of De La Huerta's heterogeneous support see Cumberland, *Struggle for Modernity*, 242, 244. More tartly, Frank Tannenbaum, *Peace by Revolution: Mexico after 1910*, pb. ed. New York 1966, 147. For the rather contingently radical meaning of *Delahuertismo* in a particular local area see Friedrich, *op. cit.* 105–12.

80. For the Casa and the general spread of Anarchosyndicalist ideas in Mexico in this period see, in addition to Jean Meyer, Cockcroft, *op. cit.* especially 223–9.

81. For an interesting account of this first attempt at a revolutionary settlement see Robert E. Quirk, *op. cit.*

82. Cockcroft, *op. cit.* 138–40.

83. For an extended account of the role of union pressure in these moves see Joe C. Ashby, *op. cit.*

84. There was in a sense good Marxist authority for such an alliance, both universal (The city against the countryside: Karl Marx, *Precapitalist Economic Formations*, London 1964, 78) and particular (Marx called the Mexicans 'Les derniers des hommes' and was at one point prepared to applaud their being conquered by the Americans because of the superior economic dynamism of the latter: Horace B. Davis, *Nationalism and Socialism: Marxist and Labor Theories of Nationalism to 1917*, New York 1967, 61–3.)

85. The perils of an indefinite reliance on this political balance are stated eloquently in Casanova, *op. cit.*

3. China

1. Barrington Moore, *Social Origins of Dictatorship and Democracy*, Boston 1966, 207–14.

2. Mary C. Wright, 'Introduction: The Rising Tide of Change', in Mary C. Wright (ed.), *China in Revolution: The First Phase 1900–13*, New Haven 1968, 1–63.

3. Wright, *op. cit.* 9. Joseph R. Levenson, *Liang Ch'i-Ch'ao and the Mind of Modern China*, pb. ed. Berkeley 1967, 30, 197.

4. Wright, *op. cit.* 5–8. For an illuminating account of Chinese relations with Tibet at an earlier period see John K. Fairbank (ed.), *The Chinese World Order*, Cambridge, Mass. 1968, 180–97.

5. Wright, *op. cit.* 14–15.

6. Wright, *op. cit.* 11–14.

7. Wright, *op. cit.* 27, 35–6, 365–418. Ralph L. Powell, *The Rise of Chinese Military Power 1895–1912*, Princeton 1955.

8. Wright, *op. cit.* 50, 55–8.

9. Wright, *op. cit.* 17–19, 32–42.

10. Wright, *op. cit.* 16–19. The central place of the railway issue in sparking off the Revolution of 1911 itself and the lengths to which the revolutionaries were ready to go in the effort to avoid provoking foreign reactions should be noted (Wright, *op. cit.* 50, 55–6).

11. Wright, *op. cit.* 10, 37–8; Jean Chesneaux, *The Chinese Labor Movement, 1919–27*, Stanford 1968.

12. Lionel Kochan, *Russia in Revolution 1890–1918*, pb. ed. London 1970, 118–19; G. T. Robinson, *Rural Russia under the Old Regime*, pb. ed. Berkeley 1967, 190.

13. Wright, *op. cit.* 15.

14. For very tart judgements on the limited social achievements of the Japanese modernization see Moore, *Social Origins of Dictatorship and Democracy*, chapter 5; and Masao Maruyama, *Thought and Behaviour in Modern Japanese Politics*, pb. ed. London 1969, 1–155.

15. Moore, *Social Origins of Dictatorship and Democracy*, especially 267–86. It is highly significant in this light that, as Mary Wright herself observes, in the period from 1900–13 'there was a drive to change almost everything except land tenure' in China (Wright, *op. cit.* 24).

16. Mary C. Wright, *The Last Stand of Chinese Conservatism*, pb. ed. New York 1966, 210–15, 238–47 (The case of Japan acted as a direct incentive, see *ibid.* 239); Benjamin I. Schwartz, *In Search of*

Wealth and Power: Yen Fu and the West, pb. ed. New York 1969, 15.

17. Joseph R. Levenson, *Confucian China and its Modern Fate*, 3 vols, London 1958–64, Vol. 2, *The Problem of Monarchical Decay*, London 1964, 20.

18. Cf. Wright, *The Last Stand of Chinese Conservatism*, chapter 4; and Levenson, *Confucian China and its Modern Fate, passim* (the Levenson work is particularly outstanding in its intelligence and sensitivity) with Moore, *Social Origins of Dictatorship and Democracy*, 162–74 and Étienne Balázs, *Political Theory and Administrative Reality in Traditional China*, London 1965, 50–74.

19. Though it is clear that it *is* how the gentry did become outstandingly rich: see Moore. *op. cit.* 164–71 and Chung-li Chang, *The Income of the Chinese Gentry*, Seattle 1962.

20. Schwartz, *In Search of Wealth and Power*, 162.

21. Cf. Franklin L. Ford, *Robe and Sword: The Regrouping of the French Aristocracy after Louis XIV*, Cambridge, Mass. 1953, especially chapter 12.

22. Chalmers Johnson, *Peasant Nationalism and Communist Power*, London 1963.

23. Levenson, *Confucian China and its Modern Fate*, vol. 2, 146.

24. See especially Harold Isaacs, *The Tragedy of the Chinese Revolution*, pb. ed. New York 1966. Robert C. North, *Moscow and Chinese Communists*, Stanford 1953.

25. See Schwartz, *In Search of Wealth and Power*.

26. Levenson, *Confucian China and its Modern Fate*, Vol. 1, 115.

27. Schwartz, *In Search of Wealth and Power*, 232.

28. James Thomson, *While China Faced West*, Cambridge, Mass. 1969, 12.

29. Thomson, *op. cit.* 6–20 and chapter 7. Cf. Wright, *The Last Stand of Chinese Conservatism*, chapter 12.

30. Ping-ti Ho, *Studies in the Population of China, 1368–1953*, Cambridge, Mass. 1959, 278.

31. Ho, *Studies in the Population of China*, 275.

32. But cf. the argument of Dwight H. Perkins, *Agricultural Development in China 1368–1968*, Chicago 1969, chapter 2, especially page 32, that except in the first half of the nineteenth century global rises in grain production roughly kept pace with population growth. The evidential basis for any conclusion on this subject on a national scale is very sketchy.

33. R. H. Tawney, *Land and Labour in China*, London 1932, 86; Perkins, *Agricultural Development in China*, chapter 7.

34. Tawney, *op. cit.* 88.

35. Tawney, *op. cit.* 74.

36. Tawney, *op. cit.* 50.

37. There are a number of studies of villages during and after the period of Communist takeover, of varying care and plausibility; C. K. Yang, *A Chinese Village in Early Communist Transition*, Cambridge, Mass. 1959; David and Isobel Crook, *Revolution in a Chinese Village*, London 1959; Jan Myrdal, *Report from a Chinese Village*, pb. ed.

Harmondsworth 1967; William Hinton, *Fanshen: A Documentary of Revolution in a Chinese Village*, New York 1966. Hinton's book, though fiercely partisan, is by far the most illuminating in the picture which it gives of the relationship between the internal social conflicts of the village and the interventions of the Communist cadres from the outside.

38. Tawney, *op. cit.* 77. For a general survey of Chinese agriculture in the 1930s see J. L. Buck, *Land Utilization in China*, New York 1964 reprint (1st ed. Nanking 1937). For a modern analysis which argues strongly against seeing an increase in tenancy as a major factor in the widespread peasant distress of the first half of this century see Dwight Perkins, *Agricultural Development in China*, chapter 5.

39. Tawney, *op. cit.* 46, 48.

40. Tawney, *op. cit.* 84.

41. Thomson, *While China Faced West*, 257.

42. For a brief but balanced summary see Perkins, *Agricultural Development in China*, 189–91. For a discussion of the social obstacles to the development of a coherent economic strategy see John W. Lewis, 'The Study of Chinese Political Culture', *World Politics*, xviii, 3 (April 1966), 503–24. For a survey of approaches to raising agricultural productivity see Anthony M. Tang, 'Policy and Performance in Agriculture', in A. Eckstein, W. Galenson and T. C. Liu (eds), *Economic Trends in Mainland China*, Chicago 1968. For a study of the economy as a whole see Nai-Ruenn Chen and Walter Galenson, *The Chinese Economy under Communism*, Edinburgh 1969.

43. The comparison with Mexico is illuminating. Many Mexican villages were Indian communities invaded by *mestizo* agricultural entrepreneurs (see e.g. Paul Friedrich, *Agrarian Revolt in a Mexican Village*, Englewood Cliffs, N.J. 1970). But although Chinese villages might be affected by an influx of merchant capital near the major cities, even there the relationship would be less one of polar opposition between community and intruder than in the Mexican case. There was no ethnic differentiation between town and country as such and the rural communities were less solidarist in their communal organization than in Mexico. Chinese intellectuals with Populist leanings, like Li Ta-Chao, future co-founder of the Chinese Communist Party, were unable to point to any institutions of peasant communalism, like the Russian *mir*, which could form the basis for building Socialism (see Maurice Meisner, *Li Ta-Chao and the Origins of Chinese Marxism*, Cambridge, Mass. 1967, especially 85–6).

44. Balázs, *Political Theory and Administrative Reality*, 50–74.

45. For some comments on the relationship between theory and practice in this matter see Wright, *Last Stand of Chinese Conservatism*, 79–89, 127–33, 173–4; and Ping-ti Ho, *The Ladder of Success in Imperial China*, New York 1962.

46. Chung-li Chang, *The Chinese Gentry*, pb. ed. Seattle 1967, 165–209; Wright, *Last Stand of Chinese Conservatism*, 80.

47. Wolfgang Franke, *The Reform and Abolition of the Traditional Chinese Examination System*, Cambridge, Mass. 1963; Wright (ed.), *China in Revolution*, 39, 185, 189, 206, 240, 299–304.

48. There had, of course, always been some tension between the moral ideology associated with the mandarin role and the economic opportunities, the exploitation of which made it such an eminently desirable one. Cf. E. Balázs, *Chinese Civilization and Bureaucracy: Variations on a Theme*, New Haven 1964; and Chung-li Chang, *The Income of the Chinese Gentry*, Seattle 1962.

49. See especially Edgar Snow, *Red Star over China*, London 1937, *passim*; and the reporting of Agnes Smedley and Nym Wales.

50. Tawney, *Land and Labour in China*, 74.

51. Stuart R. Schram, *The Political Thought of Mao Tse-tung*, pb. ed. Harmondsworth 1969, 53 n2, 252.

52. Leon Trotsky, *Problems of the Chinese Revolution*, pb. ed. Ann Arbor 1967; Harold Isaacs, *The Tragedy of the Chinese Revolution*, pb. ed. New York 1966. See also Allen S. Whiting, *Soviet Policies in China 1917–24*, New York 1954; Conrad Brandt, *Stalin's Failure in China 1924–27*, Cambridge, Mass. 1958; Robert C. North, *Moscow and the Chinese Communists*, Stanford 1953; Benjamin I. Schwartz, *Chinese Communism and the Rise of Mao*, pb. ed. New York 1967.

53. Of which perhaps the most eloquent expression is Harold Isaacs, *op. cit.*

54. Jean Chesneaux, *The Chinese Labor Movement*, 42. Total industrial labour force was less than $1\frac{1}{2}$ million in 1919. Albert Feuerwerker, 'The Chinese Economy 1912–49', *Michigan Papers in Chinese Studies*, 1, 1968, 7. Total factory and mine employment was less than 2 million in 1933 in a population of 500 million. Cf. Lyashchenko, *History of the National Economy of Russia*, New York 1949, 504–5, 542–5.

55. Chesneaux, *Chinese Labor Movement*, 408.

56. See e.g. Robert J. Lifton, *Thought Reform and the Psychology of Totalism*, pb. ed. Harmondsworth 1967.

57. See especially Franz Schurmann, *Ideology and Organization in Communist China*, pb. ed. Berkeley 1968.

58. Schram, *The Political Thought of Mao Tse-tung*, 53–6, 250–9; Mao Tse-tung, *Selected Works*, Peking 1967, Vol. 1, 23–59.

59. Roy Hofheinz Jr, 'The Ecology of Chinese Communist Success: Rural Influence Patterns 1932–45', in A. D. Barnett (ed.), *Chinese Communist Politics in Action*, pb. ed. Seattle 1969, 3–77.

60. Chalmers Johnson, *Peasant Nationalism and Communist Power*, London 1963.

61. Hofheinz in Barnett (ed.), *Chinese Communist Politics in Action*, 26–7, 46–52.

62. Shanti Swarup, *A Study of the Chinese Communist Movement 1927–34*, Oxford 1966, 258–66; Edward Snow, *Red Star over China*, London 1937.

63. The purposes of the Communists were of course very different from those of the warlords.

64. This is perhaps controversial. But cf. the contemporary judgement of the very sympathetic Edgar Snow: *Red Star over China*, 238, 436.

65. Thomson, *While China Faced West*, 26.

66. Thomson, *op. cit.* 16.
67. John Israel, *Student Nationalism in China 1927–37*, Stanford 1966, 136.
68. Israel, *op. cit.* 181.
69. See note 49 above.
70. See e.g. Hofheinz in Barnett (ed.), *Chinese Communist Politics in Action*, 77.
71. Johnson, *Peasant Nationalism and Communist Power*, 58.
72. Johnson, *op. cit.*
73. Schurmann, *Ideology and Organization in Communist China*, especially 17–104, 503–92.

4. Yugoslavia

1. It is no doubt improper from some points of view to term its behaviour 'unpredictable'. But, by the 1960s, both Russians and Americans had been strikingly wrong in their predictions of its prospective behaviour. From the perspective considered here the fact that the Russians could be so mistaken in their predictions about a Communist country establishes the sense in which the behaviour was unpredictable.
2. Chalmers Johnson, *Peasant Nationalism and Communist Power*, London 1963. This was probably an incidental felicity of Chalmers Johnson's insight, not a direct intention behind the organization of his research.
3. H. Carrère d'Encausse and Stuart R. Schram, *Marxism and Asia*, London 1969, 330–5.
4. Johnson, *op. cit.* chapter 2, especially pages 55–8.
5. Johnson, *op. cit.* chapter 6.
6. For a sharp criticism of this judgement in relation to China itself see Donald G. Gillin, '"Peasant Nationalism" in Chinese Communism', *Journal of Asian Studies*, XXIII, 2 (Feb. 1964), 269–89.
7. Paul Shoup, *Communism and the Yugoslav National Question*, New York 1968, Appendix A, table 3, 268 (figures for 1961).
8. Shoup, *op. cit.* 2.
9. Shoup, *op. cit.* 30–3.
10. George D. Jackson Jr, *Comintern and Peasant in East Europe, 1919–1930*, New York 1966, 100–12; Shoup, *op. cit.* 34.
11. Shoup, *op. cit.* 5–6; Jackson, *op. cit.* 216. For interesting materials on the differing cultural and social backgrounds of different areas see D. Warriner (ed.), *Contrasts in Emerging Societies: Readings in the social and economic history of south-eastern Europe in the nineteenth century*, London 1965; and Charles and Barbara Jelavich (eds), *The Balkans in Transition: Essays on the Development of Balkan Life and Politics since the Eighteenth Century*, Berkeley 1963.
12. Harold Isaacs, *The Tragedy of the Chinese Revolution*, 2nd ed. pb. New York 1966; or, with more balance, Charles B. McLane, *Soviet Strategies in Southeast Asia; An Exploration of Eastern Policy under Lenin and Stalin*, Princeton 1966, 3–64. The peasants were allotted an indispensable instrumental role throughout, but it was the purposes of the national bourgeoisie that they were to be instru-

mental to, in the short run. But some leading members of the Chinese party, including its future founder Li Ta-Chao as early as 1919, had realized the need to appeal predominantly and authentically to the peasantry for their mass following (Maurice Meisner, *Li Ta-Chao and the Origins of Chinese Marxism*, Cambridge, Mass. 1967, 75, 80–8).

13. Frederick F. Liu, *A Military History of Modern China 1924–49*, Princeton 1956, chapter 2; Isaacs, *Tragedy of the Chinese Revolution*, 82–3 and *passim*.

14. Shoup, *op. cit.* 14, 22–7. For Bauer's work and its significance see George Lichtheim, *Marxism: An Historical and Critical Study*, London 1961, 306–11; and for a more jaundiced (and less lucid) view in relation to nationalism particularly, Horace B. Davis, *Nationalism and Socialism: Marxist and Labor Theories of Nationalism to 1917*, New York 1967, 149–63.

15. Shoup, *op. cit.* 14–15. Cf. Davis, *op. cit.* 163–5.

16. Shoup, *op. cit.* 247–60.

17. For a general survey see Jackson, *op. cit.* On the Radic alliance and its débâcle see especially 100–12; and Ivan Avakumović, *History of the Communist Party of Yugoslavia*, Vol. 1, Aberdeen 1964–, 72–5.

18. Avakumović, *op. cit.* 15–16; Shoup, *op. cit.* 17. For rather different reasons the section of the Irish nationalist movement led by James Connolly also refused to support the war effort of Great Britain (noted by Davis, *op. cit.* 125).

19. Jackson, *op. cit.* 105.

20. Shoup, *op. cit.* 37 and n.

21. On the Béla Kun regime see Rudolf L. Tökes, *Béla Kun and the Hungarian Soviet Republic*, New York 1967.

22. Shoup, *op. cit.* 19; Jackson, *op. cit.* 216; Avakumović, *op. cit.* 25–32, 43–4.

23. R. V. Burks, *The Dynamics of Communism in Eastern Europe*, Princeton 1961, 66–7, 71–2.

24. Burks, *op. cit.* 78–9, 226; Jackson, *op. cit.* 216–17.

25. Jackson, *op. cit.* tables 4 and 5 on pp. 12–13.

26. Jackson, *op. cit.* especially chapter XII.

27. Jackson, *op. cit.* 112–13, 224.

28. See Avakumović, *op. cit* 30–59 for an account of the ban (the *Obznana*) and the political developments which led up to it.

29. Jackson, *op. cit.* 106–7.

30. For an extremely interesting analysis of the problems of economic development which Bukharin was attempting to resolve by his 'alliance with the middle peasants' and a balanced assessment of his and his main opponents' success in resolving them see Alexander Erlich, *The Soviet Industrialization Debate, 1924–1928*, 2nd ed. Cambridge, Mass. 1967.

31. E.g. Jackson, *op. cit.* 114–15.

32. Stuart R. Schram, *Mao Tse-tung*, pb. ed. Harmondsworth 1966, 139–43. But the interpretation of the precise relationship between the positions of Mao, Li and the Comintern remains fiercely controversial. For a much more nuanced account, emphasizing the difficulties of the material and the problems of communication for all parties involved

see Shanti Swarup, *A Study of the Chinese Communist Movement, 1927–34*, Oxford 1966, especially chapter VII.

33. Avakumović, *op. cit.* chapter 4.

34. Avakumović, *op. cit.* 95–7. (But see 97 n24 on doubts about the circumstances of Djaković's death.)

35. See conveniently Avakumović, *op. cit.* appendix A, 185. Also, for a critical period, Phyllis Auty, *Tito: A Biography*, London 1970, 131, 267.

36. There are a large number of accounts of this process, many by participants, varying in their degree of sympathy with Četniks or Partisans. For a clear and interesting brief treatment see Shoup, *op. cit.* chapter 2. For a good recent presentation of Tito's part in the process see Auty, *op. cit.* Part 3. Tito's autobiography, edited by Vladimir Dedijer, *Tito Speaks; His Self Portrait and Struggle with Stalin*, London 1954, has some vivid material. There is no satisfactory extended account of the Četnik viewpoint, but for a brief account of the origins of the Četnik/Partisan conflict which is as hostile to the Partisans as anyone could wish see Branko Lazitch, *Tito et la révolution yougoslave, 1937–56*, Paris 1957, 67–104 (especially 71).

37. Burks, *op. cit.* 108.

38. Burks, *op. cit.* 107–9, and appendix B, 226.

39. Burks, *op. cit.* 226.

40. Jackson, *op. cit.* 7, 9.

41. Jozo Tomasevich, *Peasants, Politics, and Economic Change in Yugoslavia*, Stanford 1955, 212, 321–4, and chapter 24, especially 551–6. Tomasevich's study, although a little unwieldy, is by far the most elaborate and careful discussion available in English of Yugoslav social and economic development between 1900 and 1941.

42. Tomasevich, *op. cit.* 702, and see chapter 28 *passim*.

43. Lorraine Barić, 'Traditional Groups and New Economic Opportunities in Rural Yugoslavia', in Raymond Firth (ed.), *Themes in Economic Anthropology (A.S.A. Monographs 6)*, pb. ed. London 1970, 257.

44. Barić, in Firth (ed.), *op. cit.* 253–78, especially 276.

45. For two recent sympathetic and undoctrinaire, if brief, Western discussions see Robert A. Dahl, *After the Revolution?: Authority in a Good Society*, New Haven 1970, 130–40; Carole Pateman, *Participation and Democratic Theory*, Cambridge 1970, chapter 5 and literature cited in these.

46. His mother was in fact a Slovene and he was brought up partly in Slovenia; for his family background and early life see Auty, *op. cit.* chapter 1.

47. Avakumović, *op. cit.* 125–37; Auty, *op. cit.* 128–31.

48. See Avakumović, *op. cit.* 103–17, 142–73 for a detailed but very sardonic account of these efforts. An interesting comparison is the situation in Vietnam between 1945 and the beginning of the French war of reconquest.

49. See especially Milovan Djilas, *Land Without Justice: An Autobiography of his Youth*, London 1958, 21–50.

50. Avakumović, *op. cit.* 120; Auty, *op. cit.* 114.

51. Avakumović, *op. cit.* 159.

52. Avakumović, *op. cit.* 161n, 174.

53. Quoted by Lazitch, *op. cit.* 32.

54. Auty, *op. cit.* 131.

55. For the undignified reversals necessitated by the Pact and its aftermath see Lazitch, *op. cit.* 36–52, and Auty, *op. cit.* 149, 153. Also Avakumović, *op. cit.* chapter 7. But cf. his insistence, on page 175, that these measures posed no disciplinary problems for the party leadership.

56. Shoup, *op. cit.* 44.

57. Shoup, *op. cit.* 47 n86.

58. Avakumović, *op. cit.* 108–11.

59. For the political background to this move see J. B. Hoptner, *Yugoslavia in Crisis, 1934–41*, New York 1962. For the coup itself see Dragiša N. Ristić, *Yugoslavia's Revolution of 1941*, London, Penn. 1966.

60. Ristić, *op. cit.* 75. Mihailović had also held this view, Lazitch, *op. cit.* 53–4.

61. Shoup, *op. cit.* 63–4, 66–70, 95n, and see Burks, *op. cit.* 121–6.

62. Auty, *op. cit.* 173; Shoup, *op. cit.* 63.

63. Shoup, *op. cit.* 67–8; Auty, *op. cit.* 200–2.

64. Auty, *op. cit.* 194–5, 203, 213–14.

65. Auty, *op. cit.* 165–6, 188–9. For the Japanese purpose in invading China and their response to Chinese resistance see Johnson, *op. cit. passim.*

66. Auty, *op. cit.* 249–51; Shoup, *op. cit.* chapter 3; Milovan Djilas, *Conversations with Stalin*, pb. ed. Harmondsworth 1963, 133–42.

67. See Adolf Sturmthal, *Workers Councils: A Study of Workplace Organization on both Sides of the Iron Curtain*, Cambridge, Mass. 1964, especially chapter 4; P. Blumberg, *Industrial Democracy: The Sociology of Participation*, London 1968; Jiri Kolaja, *Workers Councils: The Yugoslav Experience*, London 1965; A. Meister, *Socialisme et Autogestion: L'expérience Jougoslave*, Paris 1964; and especially D. Riddell, 'Social Self-Government: The Background of Theory and Practice in Yugoslav Socialism', *British Journal of Sociology*, XIX, 1 (March 1968), 47–75.

5. *Vietnam*

1. For a particularly tart anti-Communist sharing this assumption see Samuel P. Huntington, *Political Order in Changing Societies*, pb. ed. New Haven 1968, 8, especially 'the one thing Communist governments can do is to govern', etc.

2. On the revolution see George M. Kahin, *Nationalism and Revolution in Indonesia*, Ithaca 1952. On the Indonesian Communist Party see especially Ruth T. McVey, *The Rise of Indonesian Communism*, Ithaca 1965 (for the early period); and Donald R. Hindley, *The Communist Party of Indonesia, 1951–63*, Berkeley 1964.

3. For an illuminating analysis of Indonesian society and its national potential see W. F. Wertheim, *Indonesian Society in Transition: A Study in Social Change*, 2nd ed. The Hague 1964.

4. See briefly Jan M. Pluvier, *Confrontations: A Study in Indonesian Politics*, London 1965.

5. For the main economic changes in the traditional sector see Charles Robequain, *The Economic Development of French Indochina*, London 1944, chapter 6; John T. McAlister, *Vietnam: The Origins of Revolution*, London 1969, 74–8; Joseph T. Buttinger, *Vietnam: A Dragon Embattled*, 2 vols, London 1967, Vol. 1, 162–74, 460–68 (and especially study by Pierre Gourou cited on pages 530–1 which I have been unable to see). The major work on Vietnamese rural society under the French is Pierre Gourou, *The Peasants of the Tonkin Delta* (2 vols), New Haven 1955.

6. It would, for example, have made sense in Yugoslavia to see as the representative agency of *Croat* national liberation, Pavelić's Fascist Ustaši.

7. McAlister, *op. cit.* 193; Bernard B. Fall, *The Two Vietnams: A Political and Military Analysis*, 2nd ed. London 1967, 207–9.

8. For the taxation of Vietnamese peasants see Buttinger, *op. cit.* Vol. 1, 23–6, 42–3 (on establishment of the tax regime), 53, 55, 216. On peasant revolt see Paul Isoart, *Le phénomène national vietnamien: de l'indépendance unitaire a l'indépendance fractionée*, Paris 1961, 285, 288–90. For the rather different peasant economic problems of Java see especially Clifford Geertz, *Agricultural Involution: The Process of Ecological Change in Indonesia*, Berkeley 1963; and Wertheim, *op. cit.* chapters 5 and 9.

9. See Harry J. Benda, *The Crescent and the Rising Sun: Indonesian Islam under the Japanese Occupation*, The Hague 1958, and Wertheim, *op. cit.* chapter 8. For an admirable study of the character of Indonesian Islam as a highly syncretistic way of life see Clifford Geertz, *The Religion of Java*, pb. ed. Glencoe 1964.

10. For a brief general survey of the impact of Japanese conquest on South-east Asian nationalism see Willard H. Elsbree. *Japan's Role in Southeast Asian Nationalism*, 1940–45, 2nd ed. New York 1970. For a particularly clear account of the effect of the Japanese occupation on Vietnam see McAlister, *op. cit.* pt. IV, 109–82, which seems to be in strong tension with the author's claim (106, 185, etc.) that there would have been a revolution in Vietnam even without the Japanese occupation.

11. See especially McAlister, *op. cit.* 112, 114. Besides the authoritative account of this period by P. Devillers in his *Histoire du Vietnam de 1940 à 1952*, Paris 1952, there is an extensive treatment in English by Ellen J. Hammer, *The Struggle for Indochina 1940–55*, pb. ed. Stanford 1966.

12. In Indonesia those, like Sjahrir, who refused resolutely to collaborate with the Japanese occupation were, as subsequent political competition proved, simply too Western (and perhaps democratic) in their thinking to have any real mass political appeal. See Kahin, *op. cit.* 92–3, 319–22 (written in 1952). Bruce Grant, *Indonesia*, pb. ed. Harmondsworth 1967, 62–3.

13. The resistance of even the Communists was not very extensive. It was not until less than three months before the Japanese finally

disposed of the colonial administration that Giap began to organize a military force, and this force only totalled about a thousand men when the Japanese acted (McAlister, *op. cit.* 153–4).

14. For the circumstances in which this first struggle concluded see especially Philippe Devillers and Jean Lacouture, *End of a War: Indochina 1954*, London 1969.

15. See especially John T. McAlister Jr, 'Mountain Minorities and the Vietminh: A Key to the Indochina War', in P. Kunstadter (ed.), *Southeast Asian Tribes, Minorities, and Nations*, Princeton 1967 (2 vols), vol. 2, 771–844.

16. On the sects see especially Bernard B. Fall, 'The Political-Religious Sects of Vietnam', *Pacific Affairs*, XVIII, 3 (Sept. 1955), 235–53. For their more recent political activities see, incidentally, D. Pike, *Viet Cong: The Organization and Techniques of the National Liberation Front of South Vietnam*, Cambridge, Mass. 1966 (fiercely hostile but full of interesting information on N.L.F. propaganda). Some useful information appears in the major works by Devillers, McAlister and Fall and in Jean Lacouture, *Vietnam between Two Truces*, pb. ed. New York 1966. For a more parochial level see Gerald C. Hickey, *Village in Vietnam*, pb. ed. New Haven 1967.

17. On Vietnamese history see Le Thành Khôi, *Le Viêt Nam: Histoire et Civilisation*, Paris 1955. There is a history of Vietnam in English by Joseph Buttinger, *The Smaller Dragon*, New York 1958. McAlister, *Vietnam: The Origins of Revolution*, emphasizes the localist and disintegrative features of this historical tradition in his explanation of the course of the revolution. There is a certain parochialism (not without its current ideological convenience) in this perspective. All countries exhibit substantial localist sentiment which is open to political exploitation. In the perspective of the societies of South-east Asia or indeed of Asia as a whole (excluding China), it is the extent of past national integration, both culturally and politically, which stands out.

18. Fall, *The Two Vietnams*, 64.

19. For the text of the dissolution see I. Milton Sacks, 'Marxism in Vietnam', in Frank N. Trager (ed.), *Marxism in Southeast Asia*, Stanford 1959, 158. For indications of its lack of organizational meaning see McAlister, *Vietnam*, 235.

20. For an account of the background to Dienbienphu see McAlister in Kunstadter (ed.), *op. cit.*; Bernard B. Fall, *Street without Joy: Indochina at War 1946–54*, Harrisburg, Penn. 1961; and *Hell in a very small Place: The Siege of Dien Bien Phu*, Philadelphia 1967. The *political* impact of the military victory was decisive, although the Vietminh were in no position even after it to expel the French by direct military force.

21. On this rising, see Fall, *The Two Vietnams*, 155–7. For the revolutionary background of the province see Tran Huy Lieu, *Les Soviets du Nghe-Tinh (de 1930–1931) au Viet Nam*, Hanoi 1960; McAlister, *Vietnam*, 93–100; Jean Lacouture, *Hồ Chi Minh*, Paris 1967, 5–11.

22. On the historical relationship between Vietnam and China see

especially (in addition to the general works cited in note 17 above): Hisayuki Miyakawa, 'The Confucianization of South China', in Arthur F. Wright (ed.), *The Confucian Persuasion*, Stanford 1960, 21–46; A. B. Woodside, 'Early Ming Expansionism (1406–27): China's abortive conquest of Vietnam', *Harvard Papers on China*, XVII (Dec. 1963); Truong Buu Lam, 'Intervention versus Tribute in Sino-Vietnamese Relations, 1788–1790', in John K. Fairbank (ed.), *The Chinese World Order*, Cambridge, Mass. 1968, 165–79. There is a useful study of the relationship during the Second World War and up to the Geneva Conference in King C. Chen, *Vietnam and China 1938–54*, Princeton 1969.

23. P. Devillers, 'The Struggle for the Unification of Vietnam', *China Quarterly*, 9 (Jan.–March 1962). J. Lacouture, *Vietnam between Two Truces*, pb. ed. New York 1966, Part II.

24. For a tart presentation of this point see Fall, *Two Vietnams*, 12–19.

25. Fall, *Two Vietnams*, 6.

26. See Jean Chesneaux, 'Stages in the Development of the Vietnam National Movement 1862–1940', *Past and Present*, 7 (1955), 63–75. For the initial resistance in Cochin China see Milton E. Osborne, *The French Presence in Cochinchina and Cambodia: Rule and Response*, Ithaca 1969, 60–4, and 299–300 (n41), 301 (n2), 303–4 (n13), 304 (n17).

27. The process is described particularly well in McAlister, *Vietnam*, though the causal analysis advanced is far less convincing.

28. Chesneaux, *Past and Present*, 7, 65. More of the text is translated in Osborne, *op. cit.* 303–4. The original was first published in an article by Admiral Reveillère, 'Patriotisme annamite', in the *Revue Indo-Chinoise*, 190 (2 June 1902), 515–17 which I have not seen.

29. Sacks, in Trager (ed.), *op. cit.* 124–7; Chesneaux, *Past and Present*, 7; McAlister, *Vietnam*, 87–100.

30. Chesneaux, *Past and Present*, 7.

31. For the effect of the United Front policy adopted by the Comintern see especially Sacks, in Trager (ed.), *op. cit.* 137–40. On the effect of the Popular Front government in France itself see *ibid.* 140–3.

32. Hélène Carrère d'Encausse and Stuart R. Schram, *Marxism and Asia*, London 1969, 249–50 (and for his later position see also 322 and n). Sacks, in Trager (ed.), *op. cit.* 157.

33. Sacks, in Trager (ed.), *op. cit.* 157.

34. Jean Chesneaux, *Le Vietnam: Études de politique et d'histoire*, Paris 1968, 48–9. For the importance of Confucianism among the mandarins see Osborne, *op. cit.* 22–3, 161–2, 264–5.

35. See e.g. Le Van Ho, 'Introduction à l'ethnologie du Dinh', *Revue du sud-est asiatique*, 1962, 2, 85–122, especially 116–18; Kenneth P. Landon, *Southeast Asia: Crossroad of Religions*, Chicago 1949, chapter 2, especially 33 and 60. For the character of these beliefs in a single South Vietnamese village today see Hickey, *op. cit.* chapter 3.

36. See especially works cited in note 22 of this chapter.

37. Joseph R. Levenson, *Liang Ch'i-Ch'ao and the Mind of Modern China*, pb. ed. Berkeley 1967.

38. Buttinger, *Vietnam: A Dragon Embattled*, Vol. 1, 50.

39. Chesneaux, *Past and Present*, 7; Isoart, *op. cit.* 228–9; Buttinger, *Vietnam: Dragon Embattled*, Vol. 1, 50, 455–6, 458; McAlister, *Vietnam*, 57–60.

40. Levenson, *op. cit.* 178.

41. Buttinger, *Vietnam: Dragon Embattled*, Vol. 1, 206–9; McAlister, *Vietnam*, 87–94.

42. Mary C. Wright, 'From Revolution to Restoration: The Transformation of Kuomintang Ideology', *Far Eastern Quarterly*, XIV, 4 (1955), 515–32 (and in her *The Last of Chinese Conservatism*, pb. ed. New York 1966, chapter XII).

43. Levenson, *op. cit.* 197.

44. Osborne, *op. cit.* chapter 7.

45. Buttinger, *Vietnam: Dragon Embattled*, Vol. 1, 165–6.

46. Chesneaux, *Past and Present*, 7 (1955), 71; Robequain, *op. cit.* 144.

47. See especially Sacks in Trager (ed.), *op. cit.* 127–43; Buttinger, *Vietnam: Dragon Embattled*, Vol. 1, 223–5; Chesneaux, *Past and Present*, 7, 73–4.

48. McAlister appears implicitly to deny this: *Vietnam*, 106, 185 – but nothing in his own factual analysis supports the denial and he appears less than completely decided about the issue elsewhere (e.g. page 218).

49. Certainly the Algerian rebels never attained a level of military success remotely resembling that of the Vietminh and it is hard to imagine French revulsion from the repression reaching the proportions which it did without the previous failure in Vietnam.

50. For the clearest outline in English see McAlister, *Vietnam*, chapters 12–18.

51. Sacks in Trager (ed.), *op. cit.* 150. See especially McAlister in Kunstadter (ed.), *op. cit.* Vol. 2, 791–5.

52. For the impressive career of Ho Chi Minh see the (rather slight) biography by Jean Lacouture, Paris 1967. For accounts of the first struggle see especially the works by Bernard Fall cited in note 20 to this chapter, and Buttinger, *Vietnam: Dragon Embattled*, Vol. 2.

53. For the importance of the Vichy regime in this context see e.g. McAlister, *Vietnam*, 112, 114; Sacks in Trager (ed.), *op. cit.* 148–9, etc.

54. On the context in which Ho Chi Minh was obliged to operate in China see especially Chen, *Vietnam and China*, 55–85. Also Lacouture, *Hô Chi Minh*, 68–9; Fall, *Two Vietnams*, 98–100; Sacks in Trager (ed.), *op. cit.* 146–7, 149; and on the consequences of the actual Chinese occupation of North Vietnam to receive the Japanese surrender, not discussed in the text, McAlister, *Vietnam*, Part 6.

55. Chen, *op. cit.* 55–60.

56. Chen, *op. cit.* 83–4. For the essential correctness of this judgement inside Vietnam as proved in the occupation see McAlister, *Vietnam*, 231–7.

57. Buttinger, *Vietnam: Dragon Embattled*, Vol. 1, 437; McAlister, *Vietnam*, 40.

58. Buttinger, *Vietnam: Dragon Embattled*, Vol. 1, 437; McAlister, *Vietnam*, 57.

59. Chesneaux, *Past and Present*, 7 (1955), 63, 65.

6. Algeria

1. A. Humbaraci, *Algeria: A Revolution that Failed*, London 1966, 33; M. K. Clark, *Algeria in Turmoil: A History of the Rebellion*, New York 1959, chapters 1, 16; Robert Aron *et al.*, *Les Origines de la Guerre d'Algérie*, Paris 1962, 319–20. Clark's hostile journalistic account contains much interesting detail. For a clear, but limited account from the purely military point of view see E. O'Ballance, *The Algerian Insurrection 1954–62*, London 1967.

2. Germaine Tillion, *L'Afrique bascule vers l'avenir*, Paris, 1960, especially 95–6.

3. Charles-Robert Agéron, *Les Algériens musulmans et la France 1871–1919*, Paris 1968, Vol. 2, 769. And see the defence of this claim against Yacono's challenge in C.-R. Agéron, 'Les Algériens Musulmans et la France 1871–1919', *Revue Historique*, 494 (April–June 1970).

4. Aron, *op. cit.* 232; A. Nouschi, *La Naissance du nationalisme algérien 1914–54*, Paris 1962, 43–4, 107–9; Samir Amin, *The Maghreb in the Modern World*, pb. ed. Harmondsworth 1970, 36; H. Isnard, *La Vigne en Algérie*, 2 vols, Gap 1951–4; Michel Launay, *Paysans algériens*, Paris 1963, 13–109.

5. Agéron, *Les Algériens musulmans et la France*, Vol. 1, 24–6.

6. Agéron, *op. cit.* Vol. 1, 101.

7. Agéron, *op. cit.* Vol. 1, 67–8.

8. Agéron, *op. cit.* Vol. 1, 68–76. For an introduction to pre-colonial Algerian society and economy see Lucette Valensi, *Le Maghreb avant la prise d'Alger*, Paris 1969, chapters 2 and 3.

9. David C. Gordon, *The Passing of French Algeria*, London 1966, 52.

10. Agéron, *op. cit.* Vol. 1, 3n.

11. Agéron, *op. cit.* Vol. 1, 6.

12. Agéron, *loc. cit.*

13. See especially Aron, *op. cit.* Part 2; Nouschi, *op. cit.* 141–3; Gordon, *op. cit.* 53–4.

14. The best general account of the progress of all three Maghrib states to independence is Roger le Tourneau, *Évolution Politique de l'Afrique du Nord Musulmane 1920–61*, Paris 1962.

15. See X. Yacono, 'La France et les Algériens Musulmans 1871–1919', *Revue Historique*, 493 (Jan.–March 1970); C.-R. Agéron, 'Les Algériens Musulmans et la France 1871–1919', *Revue Historique*, 494 (April–June 1970).

16. Agéron, *Les Algériens musulmans et la France*, Paris 1968, Vol. 1, 8, 37–43 on Napoleon's concern for indigenous interests and its lack of appeal to the *colons*.

17. Agéron, *op. cit.* Vol. 1, 450–4, and index sub Ferry, Jules, *passim*.

18. Agéron, *op. cit.* (=*Publications de la Faculté des Lettres et Sciences Humaines de Paris-Sorbonne, Série, Recherches*, 44).

19. Agéron, *op. cit.* Vol. 2, 1165. See the whole chapter, 1140–89,

for an admirable account of the impact of the war upon the Muslim population.

20. See Yacono, *op. cit. Revue Historique*, 493 (Jan.–March 1970).

21. Yacono, *op. cit.*

22. Valensi, *op. cit.* chapter 3.

23. Bernard Lewis, *The Middle East and the West*, London 1964, 95.

24. Le Tourneau, *op. cit.* 315n.

25. Gordon, *op. cit.* 25.

26. Gordon, *op. cit.* 25.

27. Agéron, *op. cit.* Vol. 2, 1087.

28. See John T. McAlister Jr, *Viet Nam: The Origins of Revolution*, London 1969, 9; and John T. McAlister Jr, 'Mountain Minorities and the Vietminh: A Key to the Indochina War', in P. Kunstadter (ed.), *South East Asian Tribes, Minorities and Nations*, Vol. 2, Princeton 1967, 774; W. B. Quandt, *Revolution and Political Leadership: Algeria 1954–68*, Cambridge, Mass. 1969, 78; Gordon, *op. cit.* 239 claims that some 10,000 *harkis* may have been killed at independence.

29. Le Tourneau, *op. cit.* 329.

30. Aron, *op. cit.* 296.

31. Le Tourneau, *op. cit.* 314.

32. Gordon, *op. cit.* 52.

33. Gordon, *op. cit.* 21. For his earlier exploits see Agéron, *Les Algériens musulmans et la France*, Vol. 2, 1050–2 and his article 'L'Emir Khaled fut-il le premier nationaliste algérien?', *Revue de l'occident musulman*, 2, 2 (1966).

34. For a good introduction see W. Cantwell Smith, *Islam in Modern History*, Princeton 1957, chapter 2. Much the fullest account of the Islamic reform movement in Algeria is now Ali Merad, *Le Réformisme musulman en Algérie de 1925 à 1940* (Paris 1967).

35. Ali Merad, 'L'Enseignement politique de Mohammed 'Abduh aux Algériens (1903)', *Orient*, 28 (1963), 75–123. For a useful study of 'Abduh's ideas see Malcolm H. Kerr, *Islamic Reform; The Political and Legal Ideas of Mohammed 'Abduh and Rashid Rida*, Berkeley 1966.

36. Gordon, *op. cit.* 41–3; Merad, *Le Réformisme musulman*, 412–15.

37. Gordon, *op. cit.* 26n.

38. Gordon, *op. cit.* 42–3.

39. Karl Marx, *Contribution to the Critique of Hegel's Philosophy of Right*, in T. Bottomore (ed.), *Karl Marx: Early Writings*, pb. ed. New York 1964, 58.

40. I. Milton Sacks in F. Trager (ed.), *Marxism in Southeast Asia*, Stanford 1959, 118. For extensive discussion of Franco-Algerian relations by the Comintern see H. Carrère d'Encausse and Stuart Schram, *Marxism and Asia*, London 1969, 60–1, 63, 196–8, 201–2; and cf. 249–51. On the role of the Communist Party in Algeria see also especially, Aron, *op. cit.*

41. Carrère d'Encausse and Schram, *op. cit.* 322.

42. *Op. cit.* note 2 of this chapter.

43. On the Mzabites see especially Pierre Bourdieu, *Sociologie de l'Algérie*, 3rd ed. Paris 1963, chapter 3.

44. See especially Pierre Bourdieu and Abdelmalek Sayad, *Le Déracinement: La Crise de l'agriculture traditionelle en Algérie*, Paris 1964.

45. Bourdieu, *op. cit.*; and see at greater length, Pierre Bourdieu *et al.*, *Travail et travailleurs en Algérie*, Paris 1963.

46. See especially Frantz Fanon, *The Wretched of the Earth*, London 1965.

47. See especially D. and M. Ottaway, *Algeria: The Politics of a Socialist Revolution*, Berkeley 1970, chapter 3. The essential structural triviality of these reforms is an assumption of Samir Amin's gloomy analysis in *The Maghreb in the Modern World*, pb. ed. Harmondsworth 1970, chapters 4, 7 and 8 (especially page 141).

48. Jeanne Favret, 'Le traditionalisme par excès de modernité', *Archives Européennes de Sociologie*, VIII, 1, 1967.

49. Cf. Favret, *op. cit.*; Amin, *op. cit.*; Quandt, *op. cit.*; Ottaway, *op. cit.*

50. O'Ballance, *op. cit.* especially 208–10.

51. W. B. Yeats, *Collected Poems*, New York 1964, 'Parnell', 309.

52. Cf. Fanon's most illuminating study of Algerian society in rebellion, *L'An V de la révolution algérienne*, Paris 1959 (translated as *Studies in a Dying Colonialism*, New York 1965).

7. Turkey

1. See especially Joseph Levenson, *Confucian China and its Modern Fate*, 3 vols, London 1958–64.

2. Joseph Levenson, *Liang Ch'i-Ch'ao and the Mind of Modern China*, pb. ed. Berkeley 1967, 24, 30, 50–1, 64, 117–18.

3. See e.g. Maurice Meisner, *Li Ta-Chao and the Origins of Chinese Marxism*, Cambridge, Mass. 1967, 18, for a particularly overt statement of this perspective in 1915.

4. See especially John K. Fairbank, *Trade and Diplomacy on the China Coast: The Opening of the Treaty Ports 1842–54*, pb. ed. Stanford 1969.

5. See e.g. W. Cantwell Smith, *Islam in Modern History*, Princeton 1957, especially chapters 1 and 2.

6. J. C. Hurewitz, *Middle East Politics: The Military Dimension*, New York 1969, 44.

7. Cf. the extent of Mehemet Ali's efforts at military modernization (Hurewitz, *op. cit.* 30–3) with the extent of economic transformation completed by Japan in order for it to match the military efforts of Russia in the early twentieth century (see William W. Lockwood (ed.), *The State and Economic Enterprise in Japan*, Princeton 1965, especially chapter 3).

8. Hurewitz, *op. cit.* 32.

9. There is a convenient summary of the basis of Japanese economic modernization in Barrington Moore's *Social Origins of Dictatorship and Democracy*, Boston 1966, chapter 5. See more extensively Wil-

liam W. Lockwood, *The Economic Development of Japan: Growth and Structural Change 1868–1938*, Princeton 1954; Henry Rosovsky, *Capital Formation in Japan 1868–1940*, Glencoe 1961; Thomas C. Smith, *The Agrarian Origins of Modern Japan*, pb. ed. New York 1966.

10. See especially E. H. Carr, *The Bolshevik Revolution 1917–23*, Vol. 1, London 1960, Part 3, and Vol. 3, chapters 26, 31–4 etc.; Richard Pipes, *The Formation of the Soviet Union: Communism and Nationalism 1917–23*, revised ed. Cambridge, Mass. 1964.

11. Niyazi Berkes, *The Development of Secularism in Turkey*, Montreal 1964, 10. The introduction to Berkes's book is a very lucid presentation of the essentials of the Ottoman traditional order and the book as a whole displays a rich and sophisticated understanding of the uncomfortable process of westernization.

12. Berkes, *op. cit.* 9. For a clear discussion of the *Shari'a* see Joseph Schacht, *An Introduction to Islamic Law*, Oxford 1964. For a more nuanced treatment of the position of the *Ulema*, see Uriel Heyd, 'The Ottoman 'Ulemā, and Westernization in the time of Selīm III and Mahmūd II', *Scripta Hierosolymitana*, ix (ed. Heyd) Jerusalem 1961, 63–96.

13. Berkes, *op. cit.* 15–16.

14. Berkes, *op. cit.* 10.

15. See especially Berkes, *op. cit.* 14, 56, 71, 89–92. These issues are also helpfully discussed in Bernard Lewis, *The Emergence of Modern Turkey*, London 1961, chapters 1 and 4.

16. Berkes, *op. cit.* 9, 11, etc. For a discussion of the place of one very important *millet* in the Ottoman system, see Avedis K. Sanjian, *The Armenian Communities in Syria under Ottoman Dominion*, Cambridge, Mass. 1965, chapter 2; and for its incipient transformation into a modern nationalist movement see Louise Nalbandian, *The Armenian Revolutionary Movement: The Development of Armenian Political Parties through the Nineteenth Century*, Berkeley 1963. For a general view of the *millet* system see H. A. R. Gibb and Harold Bowen, *Islamic Society and the West*, Vol. 1, *Islamic Society in the Eighteenth Century*, Part 2, London 1957, chapter 14. For some observations on the system's impact in European territories see the chapters by Shaw, Vucinich and Stoianovich in Charles and Barbara Jelavich (eds), *The Balkans in Transition*, Berkeley 1963.

17. Berkes, *op. cit.* 9, 13–14.

18. Lewis, *Emergence of Modern Turkey*, 69–70; Berkes, *op. cit.* chapter 3.

19. Lewis, *op. cit.* 41.

20. Lewis, *op. cit.* 101; Berkes, *op. cit.* 45.

21. Lewis, *op. cit.* 45–6.

22. Berkes, *op. cit.* 39–41.

23. Berkes, *op. cit.* 42.

24. Berkes, *op. cit.* 44–5.

25. Berkes, *op. cit.* 45.

26. Berkes, *op. cit.* 48.

27. Berkes, *op. cit.* 58–60.

28. Berkes, *op. cit.* 77.

29. Berkes, *op. cit.* 77.

30. Berkes, *op. cit.* 66.

31. Berkes, *op. cit.* 56.

32. Lewis, *op. cit.* 33-5.

33. Lewis, *op. cit.* 28.

34. Berkes, *op. cit.* chapter 4; Lewis, *op. cit.* chapter 4.

35. Lewis, *op. cit.* 78.

36. Lewis, *op. cit.* 91-2. For the political significance of this reform see Berkes, *op. cit.* 61-3.

37. Berkes, *op. cit.* 102-4.

38. Lewis, *op. cit.* 83.

39. See especially F. S. Rodkey, 'Ottoman Concern about Western Economic Penetration in the Levant, 1849-56', *Journal of Modern History*, XXX, 4 (Dec. 1958), 348-53 and the blithe assurance of Stratford Canning (348) that no nation had ever lost its independence through the demands of foreign capitalists. Cf. the basis of Sergei Witte's confidence in the capacity of the Russian state to turn the Russian economy from a colonial to a metropolitan economy (T. H. Von Laue, 'A Secret Memorandum of Sergei Witte on the Industrialization of Imperial Russia', *Journal of Modern History*, XXVI, 1 (March 1954), 66). For an account of the remarkable legal institutions protecting resident aliens see Nasim Sousa, *The Capitulatory Regime of Turkey: its History, Origins and Nature (John Hopkins University Studies in Historical and Political Science*, N.S.18), Baltimore 1933.

40. Peter F. Sugar, 'Economic and Political Modernization: Turkey', in Robert E. Ward and Dankwart Rustow (eds), *Political Modernization in Japan and Turkey*, Princeton 1964, 160.

41. Sugar in Ward and Rustow (eds), *op. cit.* 165.

42. Z. Y. Hershlag, *Turkey: The Challenge of Growth*, Leiden 1968, 308.

43. Hershlag, *op. cit.* 209.

44. Hershlag, *op. cit.* 209.

45. Hershlag, *op. cit* 297-8, 211-13.

46. See the anthropologist Paul Stirling's judgement (*Turkish Village*, pb. ed. New York 1966, 13) that Kemal's reforms survived because most country-dwellers neither knew, understood nor cared what the government was doing. This picture is certainly supported by Richard D. Robinson, *The First Turkish Republic: A Case Study in National Development*, Cambridge, Mass. 1963.

47. See e.g. George S. Harris, *The Origins of Communism in Turkey*, Stanford 1967; or the political narrative in Lord Kinross, *Ataturk: The Birth of a Nation* (London 1965).

48. European dismemberment of the empire began to be a pressing danger in Ottoman eyes with the Russian seizure of the Crimea. See, conveniently, Alan W. Fisher, *The Russian Annexation of the Crimea 1772-1783*, Cambridge 1970, especially chapters 1, 7 and 8.

49. The best account of the Young Turks' rather unsuccessful attempt to control the imperial bureaucracy is now Feroz Ahmad, *The Young Turks: The Committee of Union and Progress in Turkish Politics 1908-14*, Oxford 1969.

50. S. Mardin, 'Libertarian Movements in the Ottoman Empire 1878–95', *Middle East Journal*, XVI, 2 (1962), 178–82.

51. Ahmad, *op. cit.* especially 133–40, 153, 156; and Zeine N. Zeine, *Arab-Turkish Relations and the Emergence of Arab Nationalism*, Beirut 1958.

52. Lewis, *op. cit.* 106.

53. Lewis, *op. cit.* 98.

8. *Cuba*

1. Wyatt MacGaffey and Clifford R. Barnett, *Cuba: its People, its Society, its Culture*, New Haven 1962, 39, 44.

2. Régis Debray, *Révolution dans la révolution; lutte armée et lutte politique en amérique latine*, Paris 1967; and Régis Debray, *Strategy for Revolution*, ed. Robin Blackburn, London 1970.

3. See particularly, for a lucid judgement in the same intellectual tradition as that of Debray, E. J. Hobsbawm, 'Guerrillas in Latin America', in Ralph Miliband and John Saville (eds), *The Socialist Register, 1970*, London 1970, 51–61.

4. René Dumont, *Cuba, est-il socialiste?*, Paris 1970.

5. See 26th July speech 1970 (reprinted e.g. in *New York Review of Books*, Vol. XV, 5 (24 Sept. 1970), and numerous later public statements as reported for example in *Le Monde*.

6. For the importance of this to America see Hanson W. Baldwin, 'A Military Perspective', in John Plank (ed.), *Cuba and the United States: Long-Range Perspectives*, Washington D.C. 1967, 200–22, especially 206, and the statement by Henry L. Stimson in 1927, quoted by Raymond Carr, 'The Cold War in Latin America', in Plank (ed.), *op. cit.* 159.

7. The U.S.S.R. was not even particularly interested in Latin America until the 1950s: see Carr, in Plank (ed.), *op. cit.* 159–60.

8. Cf. U.S. and western-European commercial relations with Yugoslavia.

9. Dumont, *op. cit.* 12.

10. My understanding of the economic problems facing Cuba and of the difficulties found by the government in resolving these is taken directly from the very important unpublished research of Brian Pollitt which is clearly superior to any published studies. But he would probably disagree with virtually all the political judgements implied here and must not be held in any way responsible for any of them.

11. Dumont, *op. cit.* 13.

12. On the attitudes of the proletariat see Maurice Zeitlin, *Revolutionary Politics and the Cuban Working Class*, Princeton 1967; Hugh Thomas, *Cuba, or the Pursuit of Freedom*, London 1971, chapters LX and XCVI; and, most helpfully, James O'Connor, *The Origins of Socialism in Cuba*, Ithaca 1970, *passim*.

13. In the short run the political problems presented by these difficulties could be surmounted triumphantly by redistributing much wealth from the rich, many of whom simply left the island, to the poorer (see e.g. Zeitlin, *op. cit.* 274n). But this possibility could not be repeated indefinitely.

14. For a balanced study of the American response to the Cuban revolution see Manuela Semidei, *Les États-Unis et la révolution cubaine 1959–64 (Cahiers de la Fondation Nationale des Sciences Politiques, Relations Internationales*, 166), Paris 1968. At much greater length see also Hugh Thomas, *op. cit.* and works there cited.

15. Eugene D. Genovese, *The Political Economy of Slavery: Studies in the Economy and Society of the Slave South*, 2nd printing New York 1966, 249–50, 263; and Thomas, *op. cit.* chapters XVII and XVIII. The judgement about economic viability is still controversial. But the discussion in Genovese seems on balance persuasive.

16. There is no systematic study of Cuban social structure. See, besides works cited in note 12 of this chapters, Lowry Nelson, *Rural Cuba*, Minneapolis 1950, and Dudley Seers (ed.), *Cuba: The Economic and Social Revolution*, Chapel Hill 1964.

17. See especially Hobsbawm's observations on revolutionary movements, *loc. cit. The Socialist Register, 1970*. For a more abstract and rationalist approach in terms of the indispensability of revolution for economic growth, see Andre G. Frank, *Latin America: Underdevelopment or Revolution: Essays on the Development of Underdevelopment and the Immediate Enemy*, New York 1969.

18. The most analytical presentation of this perspective is to be found in some of the writings on Cuba of Theodore Draper, the most plangent, unsurprisingly, in the works of Cubans who participated in the post-revolutionary regime for some time and then left.

19. For doubts as to exactly how many men did survive the landing and how many eventually arrived in the Sierra, see Thomas, *op. cit.* 901 n53.

20. On Martí see Thomas, *op. cit.* chapter XXV. A brief account of his life and ideas and a study of his role as a symbol in Cuban political rhetoric is Richard B. Gray, *José Martí, Cuban Patriot*, Gainesville, Florida 1962.

21. Herbert S. Klein, *Slavery in the Americas: A Comparative Study of Virginia and Cuba*, Chicago 1967, 139 and n. This is a very crude summary. For a much fuller, more careful and more interesting treatment, see Thomas, *op. cit.* Appendix 3.

22. Klein, *op. cit.* viii.

23. On slavery in Cuba, see Thomas, *op. cit* 33–40 and chapters XII–XIV. At greater length see Klein, *op. cit.* which stresses the difference between the legal character of slavery in the United States and Cuba (following Frank Tannenbaum, *Slave and Citizen: The Negro in the Americas*, pb. ed. New York 1963, and Stanley J. Elkins, *Slavery: A Problem in American Institutional and Intellectual Life*, pb. ed. New York 1963). For a critical commentary on Tannenbaum's general argument, see David Brion Davis, *The Problem of Slavery in Western Culture*, Ithaca 1966, chapter 8. For some telling points about Cuba in particular see Sidney W. Mintz's review of Elkins in *American Anthropologist*, 63 (June 1961), 579–87, especially 582–3. For information on the present character of Cuban race relations, see Zeitlin, *op. cit.* chapter 3. For an account of the position of the negro population on the eve of the revolution, see Thomas, *op. cit.* chapter XC.

24. Klein, *op. cit.* 260.
25. See especially Klein, *op. cit.*
26. Thomas, *op. cit.* 182.
27. See Thomas, *op. cit.* 61 for the beginnings of rapid expansion in sugar production.
28. Klein, *op. cit.* 151–2. But Thomas argues that the proportion must have been much lower – under 25 per cent (Thomas, *op. cit.* 169 and n).
29. Klein, *op. cit* 189–90. This is a slightly higher proportion than that recorded in the 1827 census (Thomas, *op. cit.* 109 n3).
30. Klein, *op. cit.* 202. On the significance of the position of the freedmen, see Klein, *op. cit. passim* and Thomas, *op. cit.* 171–3.
31. Klein, *op. cit.* 69–72, 155–7. For a less romantic view see Thomas, *op. cit.* 37–8. On maroons in general see Yvan Debbasch, 'Le marronage: Essai sur la désertion de l'esclave antillais', *L'Année Sociologique*, 3rd series (1961), 1–112; 1962, 117–95; Roger Bastide, 'Nègres marrons et nègres libres', *Annales; Économies, Sociétés, Civilisations*, xx, 1 (Jan.–Feb. 1965), 169–74 (a review of Debbasch); Roger Bastide, *Les Amériques Noires: Les Civilisations Africaines dans le nouveau monde*, Paris 1967, especially chapter III.
32. Klein, *op. cit.* 72n.
33. Thomas, *op. cit.* 12, 287, 1097 and n.
34. But cf. the treatment meted out to the free negro population after the slave revolts of 1843–44. Thomas, *op. cit.* 205.
35. Stanley Elkins and Eric McKitrick, 'Institutions and the Law of Slavery: The Dynamics of Unopposed Capitalism', *American Quarterly*, ix, 1 (Spring 1957), 3–21. Elkins, *Slavery*, chapter II, 2, pages 37–52. For the effects in Cuba, see Thomas, *op. cit.* Bk. II, 174–77, 182–3. It had been the opportunity, not the will, which had previously been lacking on the part of the landowners (Thomas, *op. cit.* 38).
36. Cf. Richard Fagen, *The Transformation of Political Culture in Cuba*, Stanford 1969, 27–8, and references there cited.
37. Klein, *op. cit.* 202. For an introduction to Cuban sugar growing see Ramiro Guerra y Sánchez, *Sugar and Society in the Caribbean: An Economic History of Cuban agriculture*, New Haven 1964 (and the foreword by Sidney W. Mintz).
38. Thomas, *op. cit.* 168–9; Klein, *op. cit.* 202.
39. Klein, *op. cit.* 151; Thomas, *op. cit.* 168.
40. Arthur F. Corwin, *Spain and the Abolition of Slavery in Cuba 1817–1886*, Austin 1967, 311.
41. For the U.S. military occupation see David F. Healy, *The United States in Cuba 1898–1902: Generals, Politicians and the Search for a Policy*, Madison 1963. For a spirited account of the war and its immediate aftermath see Thomas, *op. cit.* XXVII–XXXVIII.
42. Allan Reed Millett, *The Politics of Intervention: The Military Occupation of Cuba 1906–09*, Columbus, Ohio 1968.
43. Healy, *op. cit.* 178, 162–4.
44. Henry Wriston, 'A Historical Perspective', in Plank (ed.), *Cuba and the United States*, 13.
45. For text of the Platt amendment, see Healey, *op. cit.* 163–4.

46. Wriston, in Plank (ed.), *op. cit.* 20.

47. Quoted by Wriston in Plank (ed.), *op. cit., loc. cit.*

48. Quoted by Wriston in Plank (ed.), *op. cit.* 21.

49. Ernesto Ché Guevara, 'The Cuban Economy: Its Past, and its Present Importance', *International Affairs*, 40, 4 (October 1964), 589–99, especially 589–91.

50. A sympathetic account of Weyler's tactics is given by Thomas, *op. cit.* chapters xxviii–xxx. For the overall effect of the war see chapter xxxv and especially pages 357 and 423–4.

51. Thomas, *op. cit.* 424.

52. Boris Goldenberg, *The Cuban Revolution and Latin America*, London 1965, 100.

53. Quoted by Herbert L. Matthews, *Castro*, pb. ed. Harmondsworth 1970, 47.

54. The best account in English of these events and their outcome is now Thomas, *op. cit.* chapters li–lix. But even this, though extremely vivid, is not as analytical as it might be.

55. Robert F. Smith, *The United States and Cuba: Business and Diplomacy 1917–60*, New York 1960, 24. Smith's work is a most instructive treatment of one of the main themes in modern Cuban history, essential for an understanding of the background to the revolution. I have relied on it for most of the following discussion.

56. For what follows, see Smith, *op. cit.* 33–41, 195–6 (especially 33–4).

57. Smith, *op. cit.* 41.

58. Smith, *op. cit.* 29.

59. Smith, *op. cit.* 50.

60. Smith, *op. cit.* chapter iv.

61. Guerra y Sánchez, *op. cit.* 113.

62. Smith, *op. cit.* 70.

63. Smith, *op. cit.* 158, 161, 167.

64. Smith, *op. cit.* 166–7.

65. Smith, *op. cit.* 166–7.

66. Smith, *op. cit.* 87.

67. Smith, *op. cit.* 94.

68. Smith, *op. cit.* 104–7.

69. Smith, *op. cit.* 128–9.

70. Thomas, *op. cit.* 607.

71. Smith, *op. cit.* 144. Roosevelt had asked for his recognition as a 'special envoy', but despite Smith, *loc. cit.* Machado had declined to accept him as anything more than a normal ambassador (Thomas, *op. cit.* 606).

72. Smith, *op. cit.* 149; Thomas, *op. cit.* chapters li and lii.

73. For this move and its aftermath see Smith, *op. cit.* 149–51; Thomas, *op. cit.* chapters liv–lix.

74. Smith, *op. cit.* 149.

75. Smith, *op. cit.* 152.

76. Smith, *op. cit.* 155.

77. A retirement regretted by the Communists: Thomas, *op. cit.* 736. He had returned to Cuba by 1949: Thomas, *op. cit.* 762.

78. Thomas, *op. cit. chapters* LXIII–LXV.

79. Thomas, *op. cit.* 820.

80. Thomas, *op. cit.* chapter LXXXI.

81. Thomas, *op. cit.* appendix XI.

82. Matthews, *Castro*, 89.

83. For a jaundiced account see Andrés Suárez, *Cuba: Castroism and Communism 1959–66*, Cambridge, Mass. 1967, 12–18; Thomas, *op. cit.* 810–13, etc.

84. Thomas, *op. cit.* 862–7. It is clear that Castro might well have been killed after the Moncada raid and quite possible (Thomas, *op. cit.* 867) that he would have been assassinated had he remained much longer in Havana on his release. But he was released under a *general* amnesty and his behaviour on release was certainly highly provocative.

85. The story of the post-revolutionary regime has been told many times at varying levels. Thomas's treatment is extensive and interesting, though a little diffuse. Matthews, *Castro*, is sympathetic but analytically jejune. An interesting but very hostile account up to 1966 is Suárez, *op. cit.* A very sympathetic and intelligent account of the early transformation of the economy is O'Connor, *op. cit.* – over-optimistic about the short-term gains.

86. O'Connor, *op. cit.* 17.

87. O'Connor, *op. cit.* 35.

88. O'Connor, *op. cit.* chapter IV.

89. Real wages in Cuban manufacturing in 1957 compared favourably with levels in western Europe (O'Connor, *op. cit.* 185–6).

90. O'Connor, *op. cit.* 77–89.

91. O'Connor, *op. cit.* 43; Thomas, *op. cit.* 1555–6. The geography of Oriente explains confusion in nomenclature (northern/south-eastern) of the area in which Raul Castro was operating (see map in Thomas, *op. cit.* XXVI–XXVII).

92. Matthews, *op. cit.* 134.

93. Guevara, *International Affairs*, 1964, 593.

94. On the beginnings of agrarian reform see O'Connor, *op. cit.* chapter V, and Juan Martínez-Alier, 'The Peasantry and the Cuban Revolution from the Spring of 1959 to the end of 1960', in Raymond Carr. (ed.), *St Antony's Papers, 22, Latin American Affairs*, London 1970, 137–57, and the very important unpublished work by Brian Pollitt referred to in note 10 of this chapter.

95. Martínez-Alier, *op. cit.* emphasizes that the first Agrarian Reform Law, if implemented strictly, would have been of very little use to the landless labourer.

96. Matthews, *op. cit.* 144, etc.

97. For the accommodation to the international economic situation see Suárez, *op. cit.* 61. For the accommodation to internal political structures see Thomas, *op. cit.* chapters LX–LXII, 793, 847.

98. Fagen, *op. cit.* chapter 3.

Conclusion

1. For an introduction to the developing analysis of historical explanation see Carl G. Hempel, 'The Function of General Laws in

History', *Journal of Philosophy*, 1942 (reprinted in P. Gardiner (ed.), *Theories of History*, Glencoe 1959, 344–56); Patrick Gardiner, *The Nature of Historical Explanation*, Oxford 1952; Arthur C. Danto, *Analytical Philosophy of History*, Cambridge 1965.

2. For the sense in which it might be argued that it is logically a contested concept see W. B. Gallie, *Philosophy and the Historical Understanding*, London 1964, chapter 8.

3. See G. Chaliand, *The Peasants of North Vietnam*, pb. ed. Harmondsworth 1969, especially 140, 143, 229.

4. Bernard B. Fall, *The Two Vietnams: A Political and Military Analysis*, 2nd ed. London 1967, 246–52.

5. See e.g. Milovan Djilas, *Conversations with Stalin*, pb. ed. 1969, 71–3, 76, 87–8, 111–12.

6. See especially his 26th of July speech 1970 (reprinted conveniently in *New York Review of Books*, 24 Sept. 1970).

7. Jeanne Favret, 'Le Traditionalisme par excès de modernité', *Archives Européennes de Sociologie*, VIII, 1 (1967), 71–93.

8. Though whether the ancient cycle identified by Ibn Khaldun will be repeated yet once more in due course is still a question to keep in mind.

9. This is of course equally true of the behaviour of conservative politicians or that of the adherents of primitive religions.

10. R. Debray, *Revolution in the Revolution?*, pb. ed. Harmondsworth 1968; cf. the admirable observations of E. J. Hobsbawm, 'Guerrillas in Latin America', in Ralph Miliband and John Saville (eds), *The Socialist Register, 1970*, London 1970, 51–61; and more diffusely the views in Leo M. Huberman and Paul M. Sweezy (eds), *Régis Debray and the Latin American Revolution*, New York 1968.

11. Chalmers Johnson, *Revolution and the Social System*, Stanford 1964; and *Revolutionary Change*, pb. ed. London 1968.

12. This is true of all attempts at causal explanation in the history of sophisticated thinking: John Dunn, 'The Identity of the History of Ideas', *Philosophy*, XLIII, 164 (April 1968), 85–104.

13. Cf. Alasdair Macintyre, 'The Idea of a Social Science', in Bryan R. Wilson (ed.), *Rationality*, Oxford 1970, 129. It is plainly a crucial question how far (if at all) revolutions are in this sense irreproachably rational performances.

14. Johnson, *Revolutionary Change*, chapter 4.

15. Talcott Parsons, *The Social System*, pb. ed. New York 1964, 151–200, 480–535; Talcott Parsons and Edward A. Shils (eds), *Toward a General Theory of Action*, pb. ed. New York 1962, 219–21. It is not easy to be clear how the theoretical postulate of a social system relates to the actual character of a society. The interpretations advanced by interpreters of Parsons like Chalmers Johnson seem very crude when set against the balanced opacities of *The Social System*. However, any doubt as to Parsons's own sense of the concrete character of the processes of integration in actual societies can be readily dissipated by consulting the more concrete essays: e.g. *Essays in Sociological Theory*, pb. ed. New York 1964, 295–6.

16. See especially his insistence on the need for an effort at con-

ceptual identification, rather than the technological preoccupation with prediction in his 'Understanding a Primitive Society', in Bryan R. Wilson (ed.), *Rationality*, 78–111.

17. Hélène Carrère d'Encausse and Stuart R. Schram, *Marxism in Asia*, London 1969, 322. 'Having used up all their magic weapons for opposing the national-liberation movements, the leaders of the C.P.S.U. are now reduced to seeking help from racism, the most reactionary of all imperialist theories.'

18. Paul Shoup, *Communism and the Yugoslav National Question*, New York 1968, chapter 6. There are of course numerous other purely external reasons why the terms of trade remain so unfavourable.

19. Lenin, *Selected Works*, Moscow 1947, II, 621.

20. Speech of 8th ventôse 1793, Albert Soboul, *Les Sans-culottes Parisiens en l'An II*, Paris 1962, 419.

21. Benjamin I. Schwartz, 'China and the West in the "Thought of Mao Tse-tung"', in Ping-ti Ho and Tang Tsou (eds), *China in Crisis*, Chicago 1968, 1, 1,371.

Bibliography: a guide to further reading

The bibliography is intended not as a reference list of works cited, but as an aid in further study. It is designed to be used in conjunction with the analysis advanced in the text and is thus arranged historically and topically, *not* alphabetically. The authority for statements made in the text may be examined in the notes, where full bibliographical details are given in the first citation of each work in every chapter. The bibliography itself does not stand in any justificatory relationship to the text. It does not contain all the works on subjects relevant to the argument which I have consulted and it contains a number of items (mostly journal articles) which I have not even contrived myself to see at all, but which trustworthy authorities suggest may be of value. What it is intended to provide is an extensive guide to the literature on matters relevant to the revolutions discussed. In the case of the particular revolutions the coverage given is as extensive as I can imagine might be useful to any significant numbers of readers. In other sections the coverage is much more selective. It is not a bibliography for specialists in the history of any of the countries considered. With a single arbitrary exception it includes only works in English or French.

Works marked *, **, or *** are of particular merit of interest.
Works marked † are suitable for introductory reading.

1. RUSSIA

The political and economic background to the revolution

V. Kluychevsky, *Peter the Great*, pb. ed. New York 1961.

Marc Raeff, *Origins of the Russian Intelligentsia; the eighteenth century nobility*, pb. ed. New York 1966.

Hugh Seton-Watson, *The Russian Empire, 1801–1917*, Oxford 1967.

* Jerome Blum, *Lord and Peasant in Russia from the ninth to the nineteenth century*, pb. ed. New York 1965.

Michel Confino, *Domaines et seigneurs en Russie vers la fin du xviiie siècle; étude de structures agraires et de mentalités économiques*, Paris 1963.

Michel Confino, *Systèmes agraires et progrès agricole. L'assolement triennal en Russie au xviiie–xixe siècles; étude d'économie et de sociologie rurales*, Paris 1969.

Lazar Volin, 'The Russian Peasant and Serfdom', *Agricultural History*, XVII, 1943.

Lazar Volin, 'The Peasant Household under the Mir and the Kolkhoz in Modern Russian History' in Caroline F. Ware (ed.), *The Cultural Approach to History*, New York 1940.

A. Leroy-Beaulieu, *The Russian Peasant*, Sandoval, New Mexico 1962.

John Maynard, *The Russian Peasant, and other studies*, 2 vols, London 1942.

* Geroid T. Robinson, *Rural Russia under the Old Regime*, pb. ed. Berkeley 1967.

Donald W. Treadgold, *The Great Siberian Migration: Government and Peasant in Resettlement from the Emancipation to the First World War*, Princeton 1957.

François-Xavier Coquin, *La Sibérie: peuplement et immigration paysanne au xixe siècle*, Paris 1969.

* Lazar Volin, *A Century of Russian Agriculture: From Alexander II to Khruschev*, Cambridge, Mass. 1970.

Wayne S. Vucinich (ed.), *The Peasant in Nineteenth-Century Russia*, pb. ed. Stanford 1968.

Sir Donald Wallace, *Russia*, London 1912.

Peter I. Lyashchenko, *History of the National Economy of Russia to the 1917 Revolution*, New York 1949.

* Alexander Gerschenkron, *Economic Backwardness in Historical Perspective; a book of essays*, Cambridge, Mass. 1962.

Alexander Gerschenkron, 'Agrarian Policies and Industrialization: Russia 1861–1917', in H. J. Habbakuk and M. M. Postan (eds), *Cambridge Economic History of Europe*, VI, 2, Cambridge 1965, 706–800.

Alexander Gerschenkron, *European History in the Russian Mirror*, Cambridge 1970.

Herbert J. Ellison, 'Economic Modernization in Imperial Russia; purposes and achievements', *Journal of Economic History*, XXV, 4 Dec. 1965), 523–40.

Theodore H. Von Laue, *Sergei Witte and the Industrialization of Russia*, New York 1963.

Theodore H. Von Laue, 'Russian Labor between Field and Factory', *California Slavic Studies*, III 1964.

Theodore H. Von Laue, 'A Secret Memorandum of Sergei Witte on the Industrialization of Imperial Russia', *Journal of Modern History*, XXVI, 1 (March 1954), 60–74.

Theodore H. Von Laue, 'Russian Peasants in the Factory, 1892–1904', *Journal of Economic History*, XXI, 1 (March 1961).

Roger Portal, 'The Industrialization of Russia', in Habbakuk and Postan (eds), *Cambridge Economic History of Europe*, VI, 2, Cambridge 1965, 801–72.

G. V. Rimlinger, 'Autocracy and the Factory Order', *Journal of Economic History*, XX, 1 (March 1960), 67–92.

G. V. Rimlinger, 'The Expansion of the Labor Market in Capitalist Russia, 1861–1917', *Journal of Economic History*, XXI (1961).

G. V. Rimlinger, 'The Management of Labor Protest in Tsarist

Russia, 1870–1905', *International Review of Social History*, 5, 2 (1960), 226–48.

† Cyril E. Black (ed.), *The Transformation of Russian Society; aspects of social change since 1861*, Cambridge, Mass. 1960.

Martin Malia, *Alexander Herzen and the Birth of Russian Socialism*, pb. ed. New York 1965.

* Franco Venturi, *The Roots of Revolution: a history of the Populist and Socialist movements in nineteenth-century Russia*, pb. ed. New York 1966.

** Andrzej Walicki, *The Controversy over Capitalism; studies in the social philosophy of the Russian Populists*, Oxford 1969.

Arthur P. Mendel, *Dilemmas of Progress in Tsarist Russia: Legal Marxism and Legal Populism*, Cambridge, Mass. 1961.

James H. Billington, *Mihailovsky and Russian Populism*, Oxford 1958.

Richard E. Pipes, '*Narodnichestvo*: A Semantic Inquiry', *Slavic Review*, XXIII (1963).

Paul Avrich, *The Russian Anarchists*, Princeton 1967.

Jonathan Frankel (ed.), *Vladimir Akimov on the Dilemmas of Russian Marxism, 1895–1903*, Cambridge 1969.

Samuel H. Baron, *Plekhanov; the Father of Russian Marxism*, pb. ed. Stanford 1966.

Richard Kindersley, *The First Russian Revisionists; a study of Legal Marxism in Russia*, Oxford 1962.

Leopold H. Haimson, *The Russian Marxists and the Origins of Bolshevism*, pb. ed. Boston 1966.

John L. H. Keep, *The Rise of Social Democracy in Russia*, Oxford 1963.

Richard E. Pipes, *Social Democracy and the St. Petersburg Labor Movement, 1885–97*, Cambridge, Mass. 1963.

** Allan K. Wildman, *The Making of a Workers' Revolution: Russian Social Democracy, 1891–1903*, Chicago 1967.

Fedor Il'ich Dan, *The Origins of Bolshevism*, London 1964.

James F. Brennan, 'The Origin and Nature of Economism in St. Petersburg', *Canadian Slavic Studies*, 4, 2 (Summer 1970), 162–82.

Ezra Mendelsohn, *Class Struggle in the Pale. The formative years of the Jewish Workers' Movement in Tsarist Russia*, Cambridge 1970.

* David Lane, *The Roots of Russian Communism; a social and historical study of Russian Social Democracy, 1898–1907*, Assen 1969.

Solomon M. Schwarz, *The Russian Revolution of 1905. The Workers' Movement and Formation of Bolshevism and Menshevism*, Chicago 1967.

† Theodore H. Von Laue, 'Of the Crises in the Russian Polity', in John S. Curtiss (ed.), *Essays in Russian and Soviet History*, Leiden 1963, 303–22.

† Lionel Kochan, *Russia in Revolution, 1890–1918*, pb. ed. London 1970.

Theodore H. Von Laue, *Why Lenin? Why Stalin? a reappraisal of the Russian Revolution, 1900–30*, London 1966.

** Leopold H. Haimson, 'The Problems of Social Stability in Urban

Russia, 1905–17', *Slavic Review*, XXIII, 4 (Dec. 1964), 619–42; XXIV, 1 (March 1965), 1–22, 47–56.

Theodore H. Von Laue, 'The Chances for Liberal Constitutionalism', *Slavic Review*, XXIV, 1 (March 1965), 34–46.

Arthur P. Mendel, 'Peasant and Worker on the Eve of the First World War', *Slavic Review*, XXIV, 1 (March 1965), 23–33.

George L. Yaney, 'Social Stability in Pre-revolutionary Russia: a critical note', *Slavic Review*, XXIV, 3 (Sept. 1965), 521–7.

* George L. Yaney, 'The Concept of the Stolypin Land Reform', *Slavic Review*, XXIII, 2 (June 1964), 275–93.

The revolutions of 1917 and their consequences

George Katkov, *Russia 1917. The February Revolution*, pb. ed. London 1969.

** Marc Ferro, *La révolution russe de 1917; la chute du tsarisme et les origines d'octobre*, Paris 1967–.

* Alexander Rabinowitch, *Prelude to Revolution; the Petrograd Bolsheviks and July 1917 uprising*, Bloomington, Ind. 1968.

William G. Rosenberg, 'The Russian Municipal Duma Elections of 1917; a preliminary computation of returns', *Soviet Studies*, XXI, 2 (Oct. 1969), 131–63.

** Marc Ferro, 'Le soldat russe en 1917; indiscipline, patriotisme, pacifisme et révolution', *Annales; Économies, Sociétés, Civilisations*, 26, 1 (Jan.–Feb. 1971), 14–39.

* Leon Trotsky, *The History of the Russian Revolution*, London 1934.

* Nikolai Sukhanov, *The Russian Revolution, 1917; a personal record*, London 1955.

* Richard E. Pipes (ed.), *Revolutionary Russia*, London 1968.

† John Reed, *Ten Days that Shook the World*, pb. ed. New York 1960.

Oliver H. Radkey, *The Agrarian Foes of Bolshevism; promise and default of the Russian Socialist Revolutionaries, February to October 1917*, New York 1958.

Bertram D. Wolfe, *Three who made a Revolution; a biographical history*, pb. ed. Harmondsworth 1966.

Robert V. Daniels, *Red October: The Bolshevik Revolution of 1917*, London 1967.

Adam B. Ulam, *Lenin and the Bolsheviks*, pb. ed. London 1969.

Louis Fischer, *The Life of Lenin*, New York 1964.

David Shub, *Lenin; a biography*, pb. ed. Harmondsworth 1966.

Alfred G. Meyer, *Leninism*, Cambridge, Mass. 1957.

Leonard B. Schapiro and Peter Reddaway (eds), *Lenin: the man, the theorist, the leader; a reappraisal*, London 1967.

** V. I. Lenin, *Selected Works*, 2 vols, Moscow 1947 (especially *What is to be Done?* [pb. ed. (ed. S. V. Utechin) London 1970]; *Imperialism; Two Tactics of Social Democracy. The State and Revolution; Left-wing Communism: an infantile disorder*).

* Isaac Deutscher, *Trotsky: The Prophet Armed. The Prophet Unarmed. The Prophet Outcast*, 3 vols, pb. ed. New York 1965.
* Leon Trotsky, *The Permanent Revolution*, and *Results and Prospects*, London 1962.
Leon Trotsky, *The Defence of Terrorism: Terrorism and Communism; a reply to K. Kautsky*, 2nd ed. London 1935.
Leon Trotsky, *The Revolution Betrayed: What is the Soviet Union and where is it going?*, London 1937.
Isaac Deutscher, *Stalin; a political biography*, pb. ed. London 1961.
** Edward H. Carr, *A History of Soviet Russia*, 9 vols to date, London 1950–.
† Isaac Deutscher, *The Unfinished Revolution, Russia 1917–67*, pb. ed. London 1969.
† John P. Nettl, *The Soviet Achievement*, pb. ed. London 1967.
Alexander Nove, *An Economic History of the U.S.S.R.*, London 1969.
Maurice Dobb, *Soviet Economic Development since 1917*, pb. ed. London 1966.
William H. Chamberlin, *The Russian Revolution, 1917–21*, 2 vols, London 1935.
† James H. Billington, 'Six Views of the Russian Revolution', *World Politics*, XVIII, 3 (April 1966), 452–73.
Oliver H. Radkey, *The Election to the Russian Constituent Assembly of 1917*, Cambridge, Mass. 1950.
Voline (=Eikhenbaum), *Nineteen Seventeen: The Russian Revolution Betrayed*, London 1954.
Voline (=Eikhenbaum), *The Unknown Revolution: Kronstadt 1921, Ukraine 1918–21*, London 1955.
* Israel Getzler, *Martov; a political biography of a Russian Social Democrat*, Cambridge 1967.
Oliver H. Radkey, *The Sickle under the Hammer; the Russian Socialist Revolutionaries in the early months of Soviet Rule*, New York 1963.
Leonard B. Schapiro, *The Communist Party of the Soviet Union*, pb. ed. New York 1964.
* Leonard B. Schapiro, *The Origin of the Communist Autocracy; political opposition in the Soviet State; first phase, 1917–1922*, pb. ed. New York 1965.
* Robert V. Daniels, *The Conscience of the Revolution; Communist opposition in Soviet Russia*, Cambridge, Mass. 1960.
Paul Avrich, *Kronstadt*, Princeton 1970.
David Footman, *Civil War in Russia*, London 1961.
* Richard E. Pipes, *The Formation of the Soviet Union; Communism and Nationalism, 1917–23*, 2nd ed. Cambridge, Mass. 1964.
Moshe Lewin, *Lenin's Last Struggle*, London 1969.
N. Bukharin and E. Preobrazhensky, *The A.B.C. of Communism* (ed. E. H. Carr), pb. ed. Harmondsworth 1969.
* Alexander Erlich, *The Soviet Industrialization Debate, 1924–1928*, 2nd ed. Cambridge, Mass. 1967.
Barrington Moore, *Soviet Politics: The Dilemma of Power; the role of ideas in social change*, pb. ed. New York 1965.

D. J. Male, 'The Village Community 1924–30', *Soviet Studies*, XIV, 3 (Jan. 1963), 225–48.

D. J. Male, *Russian Peasant Organisation before Collectivisation; a study of Commune and Gathering, 1925–1930*, Cambridge 1971.

* Moshe Lewin, *Russian Peasants and Soviet Power; a study of collectivisation*, London 1968.

Alexander Nove, 'History, Hierarchy and Nationality; some observations on the Soviet social structure', *Soviet Studies*, XXI (July 1969), 71–92.

Merle Fainsod, *Smolensk under Soviet Rule*, London 1959.

Merle Fainsod, *How Russia is Ruled*, rev. ed. Cambridge, Mass. 1963.

Adam B. Ulam, *Expansion and Coexistence; the history of Soviet Foreign Policy*, London 1968.

Robert Conquest, *The Great Terror; Stalin's Purge of the Thirties*, pb. ed. Harmondsworth 1971.

2. MEXICO

Social and economic background to the revolution

** François Chevalier, *Land and Society in Colonial Mexico: The Great Hacienda*, pb. ed. Berkeley 1970.

George M. McBride, *The Land Systems of Mexico*, New York 1923.

François Chevalier, 'Survivances seigneuriales et présages de la révolution agraire dans le nord du Mexique (Fin du xviiie et xixe siècle)', *Revue Historique*, CCXXII (1959), 1–18.

Oscar Lewis, *Life in a Mexican Village: Tepoztlan Restudied*, pb. ed. Urbana 1963.

† Oscar Lewis, *Pedro Martínez: A Mexican Peasant and his Family*, pb. ed. New York 1967.

* Paul Friedrich, *Agrarian Revolt in a Mexican Village*, pb. ed. Englewood Cliffs 1970.

Eric R. Wolf, *Sons of the Shaking Earth*, Chicago 1959.

The revolution and its political antecedents

† Charles C. Cumberland, *Mexico: The Struggle for Modernity*, pb. ed. London 1968.

Wilbert H. Timmons, *Morelos of Mexico: Priest, Soldier, Statesman*, El Paso 1963.

Carleton Beals, *Porfirio Díaz: Dictator of Mexico*, Philadelphia 1932.

Alfred P. Tischendorf, *Great Britain and Mexico in the Era of Porfirio Díaz*, Chapel Hill 1961.

* James D. Cockcroft, *Intellectual Precursors of the Mexican Revolution, 1900–13*, Austin 1968.

*** John Womack Jr, *Zapata and the Mexican Revolution*, London 1969.

William H. Beezley, 'State Reform during the Provisional Presidency: Chihuahua, 1911', *Hispanic American Historical Review*, L, 3 (August 1970), 524–37.

François Chevalier, 'Un facteur décisif de la révolution agraire au

Mexique: Le soulèvement de Zapata, 1911–19'; *Annales; Économies, Sociétés, Civilisations*, XVI, 1 (Jan.–Feb. 1961), 66–82.

Charles C. Cumberland, *Mexican Revolution: Genesis under Madero*, Austin, Texas 1952.

Stanley R. Ross, *Francisco I. Madero; Apostle of Mexican Democracy*, New York 1955.

Michael C. Meyer, *Mexican Rebel: Pascual Orozco and the Mexican Revolution, 1910–15*, Lincoln, Nebraska 1967.

Robert E. Quirk, *The Mexican Revolution: The Convention of Aguascalientes, 1914–15*, Bloomington 1960.

Ronald Atkin, *Revolution 1910–20*, London 1969.

Lowell Blaisdell, *The Desert Revolution: Baja California, 1911*, Madison 1962.

* Eric R. Wolf, *Peasant Wars of the Twentieth Century*, New York 1969.

** Jean Meyer, 'Les ouvriers dans la révolution mexicaine: Les Bataillons Rouges', *Annales; Économies, Sociétés, Civilisations*, XXV, 1 (Jan.–Feb. 1970), 30–55.

The consequences of the revolution

* Clark W. Reynolds, *The Mexican Economy: Twentieth Century Structure and Growth*, New Haven 1970.

† Frank Tannenbaum, *Peace by Revolution: Mexico after 1910*, pb. ed. New York 1966.

Frank Tannenbaum, *Mexico: The Struggle for Peace and Bread*, London 1965.

†Stanley R. Ross, *Is the Mexican Revolution Dead?*, pb. ed. New York 1966.

† Howard F. Cline, 'Mexico: A Matured Latin-American Revolution', *Annals of the American Academy of Political and Social Science*, 334 (March 1961), 84–94.

Frank Brandenburg, *The Making of Modern Mexico*, 4th ed. Englewood Cliffs 1966.

James W. Wilkie, *The Mexican Revolution: Federal Expenditure and Social Change since 1910*, Berkeley 1967.

Howard F. Cline, *Mexico: From Revolution to Evolution, 1940–60*, London 1962.

Robert E. Scott, *Mexican Government in Transition*, 2nd ed. Urbana, Ill. 1962.

Gabriel Almond and Sidney Verba, *The Civic Culture*, Princeton 1963.

** Pablo G. Casanova, *Democracy in Mexico*, 2nd ed. New York 1970.

Marjorie Clark, *Organized Labor in Mexico*, Chapel Hill 1934.

Joe C. Ashby, *Organized Labor and the Mexican Revolution under Lazaro Cardenas*, Chapel Hill 1967.

Wilbert E. Moore, *Industrialization and Labor*, Ithaca 1951.

Raymond Vernon, *The Dilemma of Mexico's Development*, Cambridge, Mass. 1963.

Raymond Vernon (ed.), *Public Policy and Private Enterprise in Mexico*, Cambridge, Mass. 1964.

Manning Nash, 'Economic Nationalism in Mexico' in Harry G. John-son (ed.), *Economic Nationalism in Old and New States*, London 1968, 71–84.

** François Chevalier, 'The *Ejido* and Political Stability in Mexico', in Claudio Veliz (ed.), *The Politics of Conformity in Latin America*, London 1967, 158–91.

Eyler N. Simpson, *The Ejido: Mexico's Way Out*, Chapel Hill 1937.

Nathan L. Whetten. *Rural Mexico*, Chicago 1948.

† René Dumont, *Living Lands*, London 1965.

René Dumont, *Problèmes agraires; réforme agraire et modernisation de l'agriculture au Mexique*, Paris 1969.

T. Schwartz, 'L'usage de la terre dans un village à ejido de Mexique', *Études Rurales*, 10 (July–Sept. 1963), 37–49.

Eric R. Wolf, 'Types of Latin American Peasantry: A preliminary discussion', *American Anthropologist*, 57, 3 (i) (June 1955), 452–71.

* Eric R. Wolf, 'Aspects of Group Relations in a Complex Society: Mexico', *American Anthropologist*, 58, 6 (Dec. 1956), 1065–78.

† Raymond Carr, 'Mexican Agrarian Reform 1910–60', in E. L. Jones and S. J. Woolf (eds), *Agrarian Change and Economic Development: The Historical Problems*, London 1969, 151–68.

Marnie W. Mueller, 'Changing Patterns of Agricultural Output and Productivity in the Private and Land Reform Sectors in Mexico, 1940–60', *Economic Development and Cultural Change*, 18, 1 (Jan. 1970), 252–66.

R. S. Weckstein, 'Evaluating Mexican Land Reform', *Economic Development and Cultural Change*, 18, 2 (April 1970), 391–409.

3. CHINA

The Confucian Order

Ping-ti Ho, *Studies in the Population of China. 1368–1953*, Cambridge, Mass. 1959.

*** Joseph C. Levenson, *Confucian China and its Modern Fate*, 3 vols, London 1958–65.

Ping-ti Ho, *The Ladder of Success in Imperial China; aspects of social mobility, 1368–1911*, New York 1962.

Wolfram Eberhard, *Social Mobility in Traditional China*, Leiden 1962.

Robert M. Marsh, *The Mandarins: the circulation of elites in China, 1600–1900*, New York 1961.

Yung-teh Chow, *Social Mobility in China: Status Careers among the gentry in a Chinese community*, New York 1966.

† Hsiao-tung Fei, *China's Gentry: Essays in rural-urban relations*, pb. ed. Chicago 1968.

Kung-ch'üan Hsiao, *Rural China: Imperial control in the nineteenth century*, Seattle 1960.

Karl A. Wittfogel, *Oriental Despotism: A comparative study of total power*, pb. ed. New Haven 1963.

Wolfram Eberhard, *Conquerors and Rulers: social forces in mediaeval China*, 2nd ed. Leiden 1965.

* Chung-li Chang, *The Chinese Gentry: Studies on their role in nine-teenth-century Chinese society*, pb. ed. Seattle 1967.
Chung-li Chang, *The Income of the Chinese Gentry: A sequel to the Chinese Gentry*, Seattle 1962.
T'ung-tsu Ch'ü, *Local Government in China under the Ch'ing*, Cambridge, Mass. 1962.
* Étienne Balázs, *Chinese Civilization and Bureaucracy: variations on a theme*, New Haven 1964.
* Étienne Balázs, *Political Theory and Administrative Reality in Traditional China* (School of Oriental and African Studies), London 1965.
† Ping-ti Ho, 'The Significance of the Ch'ing Period in Chinese History', *Journal of Asian Studies*, 26, 2 (Feb. 1967), 189–95.
Max Weber, *The Religion of China: Confucianism and Taoism*, pb. ed. New York 1964.
* John K. Fairbank (ed.), *The Chinese World Order*, Cambridge, Mass. 1968.
Mark Mancall, *Russia and China: Their Diplomatic Relations to 1728*, Cambridge, Mass. 1971.
Alexander B. Woodside, *Vietnam and the Chinese Model: A comparative study of Nguyên and Ch'ing civil government in the first half of the nineteenth century*, Cambridge, Mass. 1971.
Maurice Freedman, *Lineage Organization in Southeastern China*, 2nd ed. London 1965.
* Maurice Freedman, *Chinese Lineage and Society: Fukien and Kwangtung*, London 1966.
Martin M.-C. Yang, *Chinese Social Structure; a historical study*, Taipei 1969.
Olga Lang, *Chinese Family and Society*, New Haven 1946.
* Dwight H. Perkins, *Agricultural Development in China, 1368–1968*, Chicago 1969.
G. William Skinner, 'Marketing and Social Structure in Rural China', *Journal of Asian Studies*, 24, 1–3 (Nov. 1964–May 1965), 3–43, 195–228, 363–99.

Internal crisis and the impact of the west
** John K. Fairbank, *Trade and Diplomacy on the China Coast: The opening of the Treaty Ports, 1842–1854*, pb. ed. Stanford 1969.
** Mary C. Wright, *The Last Stand of Chinese Conservatism: The T'ung-Chih Restoration, 1862–1874*, pb. ed. New York 1966.
Ssǔ-yü Têng and John K. Fairbank (eds), *China's Response to the West; a documentary survey, 1839–1923*, Cambridge, Mass. 1954.
Yen-P'ing Hao, *The Comprador in nineteenth-century China: Bridge between East and West*, Cambridge, Mass. 1970.
*** Philip A. Kuhn, *Rebellion and its Enemies in Late Imperial China: Militarization and Social Structure, 1796–1864*, Cambridge, Mass. 1970.
* Franz Michael, *The Taiping Rebellion. History and Documents*, Vol. 1, Seattle 1966.

Vincent Y.-C. Shih, *The Taiping Ideology: Its Sources, Interpretations and Influences,* Seattle 1967.

Frederic E. Wakeman, *Strangers at the Gate; social disorder in South China, 1839–61,* Berkeley 1965.

Siang-tseh Chiang, *The Nien Rebellion,* 2nd ed. Seattle 1967.

Wen-djang Chu, *The Moslem Rebellion in Northwest China (Central Asiatic Studies,* v), The Hague 1966.

James P. Harrison, *The Chinese Communists and Chinese Peasant Rebellions: a study in the rewriting of history,* London 1970.

Jean Chesneaux (ed.), *Mouvements populaires et sociétés secrètes en Chine aux XIXe et XXe siècles,* Paris 1971.

Albert Feuerwerker, *China's Early Industrialization: Sheng Hsuan-huai (1844–1916) and mandarin enterprise,* pb. ed. New York 1970.

John E. Schrecker, *Imperialism and Chinese Nationalism: Germany in Shantung,* Cambridge, Mass. 1971.

** Mary C. Wright (ed.), *China in Revolution: The First Phase, 1900–1913,* New Haven 1968 (especially editor's introduction).

Ralph Powell, *The Rise of Chinese Military Power, 1895–1912,* Princeton 1955.

Mary Backus Rankin, *Early Chinese Revolutionaries: Radical Intellectuals in Shanghai and Chekiang, 1092–1911,* Cambridge, Mass. 1970.

* Harold Z. Schiffrin, *Sun Yat-sen and the Origins of the Chinese Revolution,* pb. ed. Berkeley 1970.

** Benjamin I. Schwartz, *In Search of Wealth and Power: Yen Fu and the West,* pb. ed. New York 1969.

** Joseph R. Levenson, *Liang Ch'i-ch'ao and the Mind of Modern China,* pb. ed. Berkeley 1967.

Y. C. Yang, *Chinese Intellectuals and the West, 1872–1949,* Chapel Hill 1966.

Michael Gasster, *Chinese Intellectuals and the Revolution of 1911; the birth of modern Chinese radicalism,* Seattle 1969.

Wolfgang Franke, *The Reform and Abolition of the Traditional Chinese Examination System,* Cambridge, Mass. 1963.

From 1911 to the Communist triumph: society, economy, government
** R. H. Tawney, *Land and Labour in China,* London 1932.

John L. Buck, *Chinese Farm Economy: a study of 2866 farms in seventeen localities and seven provinces in China,* Chicago 1930.

* John L. Buck, *Land Utilization in China,* 3rd ed. New York 1968 (a larger survey).

Hsiao-tung Fei, *Peasant Life in China: A Field Study of country life in the Yangtze Valley,* London 1939.

Hsiao-tung Fei and Chang Chih-i, *Earthbound China: A Study of rural economy in Yunnan,* London 1948.

Institute of Pacific Relations, *Agrarian China: Selected source materials from Chinese authors,* London 1939.

Ramon H. Myers, *The Chinese Peasant Economy: Agricultural Development in Hopei and Shantung, 1890–1949,* Cambridge, Mass. 1970.

Sidney D. Gamble, *North China Villages: social, political and economic activities before 1933*, Berkeley 1963.

Sidney D. Gamble, *Ting Hsien: A North China rural community*, Stanford 1968.

Martin M.-C. Yang, *A Chinese Village: Taitou, Shantung Province*, London 1947.

Morton H. Fried, *Fabric of Chinese Society: a study of the social life of a Chinese county seat*, London 1956.

Marion J. Levy Jr, *The Family Revolution in Modern China*, pb. ed. New York 1968.

Albert Feuerwerker, 'The Chinese Economy 1912-49', *Michigan Papers in Chinese Studies*, No. 1, Ann Arbor 1968.

John K. Chang, *Industrial Development in Pre-communist China: A quantitative analysis*, Edinburgh 1969.

Ping-ti Ho and Tang Tsou (eds), *China in Crisis*, Vol. 1, Parts 1 and 2: *China's Heritage and the Communist Political System*, Chicago 1968.

Jack Gray (ed.), *Modern China's Search for a Political Form*, London 1969.

† Lucien Bianco, *Les origines de la révolution chinoise, 1915–1949*, Paris 1967.

Ch'ien Tuan-sheng, *The Government and Politics of China, 1912–49*, Harvard 1950.

George T. Yu, *Party Politics in Republican China, 1912–1924*, Berkeley 1966.

Donald G. Gillin, *Warlord: Yen Hsi-shan in Shansi Province, 1911–49*, Princeton 1967.

James E. Sheridan, *Chinese Warlord: The Career of Feng Yü-hsiang*, Stanford 1966.

Frederick F. Liu, *A Military History of Modern China. 1924–49*, Princeton 1956.

Akira Iriye, *After Imperialism: The Search for a new order in the Far East, 1921–31*, pb. ed. New York 1969.

James C. Thomson Jr, *While China Faced West: American reformers in nationalist China, 1928–37*. Cambridge, Mass. 1969.

* Jean Chesneaux, *The Chinese Labor Movement, 1919–27*, Stanford 1968.

Richard B. Landis, 'The Origins of Whampoa Graduates who served on the Northern Expedition', *Studies on Asia*, Vol. 5 (1964), 149–63 (University of Nebraska).

Robert C. North and I. de Sola Pool, 'Kuomintang and Chinese Communist Elites', in Harold Lasswell and Daniel Lerner (eds), *World Revolutionary Elites: Studies in coercive ideological movements*, pb. ed. Cambridge, Mass. 1966, 319–455.

* Mary C. Wright, 'From Revolution to Restoration: The Transformation of Kuomintang Ideology', *Far Eastern Quarterly*, XIV, 4 (1955), 515–32.

* Chow Tse-tsung, *The May Fourth Movement: Intellectual Revolution in Modern China*, pb. ed. Stanford 1967.

** Jerome B. Grieder, *Hu Shih and the Chinese Renaissance: Liberalism in the Chinese Revolution, 1917–37*, Cambridge, Mass. 1970.

The rise of the Communist Party

* Hélène Carrère d'Encausse and Stuart R. Schram, *Marxism and Asia: An Introduction with readings*, London 1969.
* Maurice Meisner, *Li Ta-chao and the Origins of Chinese Marxism*, Cambridge, Mass. 1967.

Maurice Meisner, 'Leninism and Maoism: some Populist perspectives on Marxism-Leninism in China', *China Quarterly*, 45 (Jan.–March 1971), 2–36.

* Harold R. Isaacs, *The Tragedy of the Chinese Revolution*, pb. ed. New York 1966.

Leon Trotsky, *Problems of the Chinese Revolution*, pb. ed. Ann Arbor 1967.

Allen S. Whiting, *Soviet Policies in China, 1917–24*, New York 1954.

Robert C. North, *Moscow and the Chinese Communists*, Stanford 1953.

Conrad Brandt, *Stalin's failure in China, 1924–27*, Cambridge, Mass. 1958.

Charles B. McLane, *Soviet Policy and the Chinese Communists, 1931–46*, New York 1958.

Charles B. McLane, *Soviet Strategies in Southeast Asia: An exploration of Eastern policy under Lenin and Stalin*, Princeton 1966.

Xenia J. Eudin and Robert C. North, *Soviet Russia and the East: a documentary survey*, Stanford 1957.

Conrad Brandt, Benjamin I. Schwartz and John K. Fairbank (eds), *A Documentary History of Chinese Communism*, London 1952.

* Stuart R. Schram, *Mao Tse-tung*, pb. ed. Harmondsworth 1966.
* Stuart R. Schram, *The Political Thought of Mao Tse-tung*, pb. ed. Harmondsworth 1969.

Jerome Ch'en, *Mao and the Chinese Revolution*, pb. ed. London 1967.

Arthur A. Cohen, *The Communism of Mao Tse-tung*, Chicago 1964.

* Benjamin I. Schwartz, *Chinese Communism and the Rise of Mao*, pb. ed. New York 1967.

The Selected Works of Mao Tse-tung, 4 vols, Peking 1967. (These texts are subject to frequent emendation. For some cautions see Schram, *Political Thought of Mao*.)

Karl Wittfogel, 'The Legend of Maoism', *China Quarterly*, nos. 1, 2 and 4: Jan.–March 1960, 72–86; April–June 1960, 16–34; Oct.–Dec. 1960, 88–96.

Robert C. North and Xenia J. Eudin (eds), *M. N. Roy's Mission to China: The Communist-Kuomintang split of 1927*, Berkeley 1963.

Tso-liang Hsiao, *The Land Revolution in China, 1930–34; a study of documents*, Seattle 1969.

Tso-liang Hsiao, *Power Relations within the Chinese Communist Movement, 1930–34; a study of documents*, 2 vols, Washington 1961–7.

John E. Rue, *Mao Tse-tung in Opposition, 1927–35*, Stanford 1966.

† Edgar Snow, *Red Star over China*, London 1937.

Nym Wales (=Helen Snow), *Inside Red China*, New York 1939.
Nym Wales (=Helen Snow), *Red Dust: autobiographies of Chinese Communists*, Stanford 1952.
Anna Louise Strong, *China's Millions*, New York 1935.
Agnes Smedley, *The Great Road: The Life and Times of Chu Teh*, London 1958.
* Shanti Swarup, *A Study of the Chinese Communist Movement, 1927– 34*, Oxford 1966.
John Israel, *Student Nationalism in China, 1927–1937*, Stanford 1966.
* Lyman P. Van Slyke, *Enemies and Friends: The United Front in Chinese Communist History*, Stanford 1967.
* Arthur Doak Barnett (ed.), *Chinese Communist Politics in Action*, Seattle 1969 (especially Roy Hofheinz, 'The Ecology of Chinese Communist Success').
Robert W. McColl, 'A Political Geography of Revolution in China, Vietnam and Thailand', *Journal of Conflict Resolution*, xi, 2 (July 1967), 153–67.
Robert W. McColl, 'The Oyuwan Soviet Area, 1927–32', *Journal of Asian Studies*, 27, 1 (Nov. 1967), 41–60.
Mark Seldon, 'The Guerrilla Movement in Northwest China: The Origins of the Shensi-Kansu-Ninghsia Border Region', *China Quarterly*, 28 (Oct.–Dec. 1966) and 29 (Jan.–March 1967).
Eto Shinkichi, 'Hai-lu-feng – The First Chinese Soviet Government', *China Quarterly*, 8 (Oct.–Dec. 1961), 160–83 and 9 (Jan.–March 1962), 149–81.
Roy Hofheinz Jr, 'The Autumn Harvest Insurrection', *China Quarterly*, 32 (Oct.–Dec. 1967), 37–87.
Donald W. Klein and Anne B. Clark, *Biographical Dictionary of Chinese Communism, 1921–1965*. 2 vols, Cambridge, Mass. 1971.
* Chalmers Johnson, *Peasant Nationalism and Communist Power*, London 1963.
Donald G. Gillin, '"Peasant Nationalism" in the History of Chinese Communism', *Journal of Asian Studies*, xxiii, 2 (Feb. 1964), 269–89.
Arthur Doak Barnett, *China on the Eve of Communist Takeover*, London 1963.

Communist China

* Ch'ing K'un Yang, *A Chinese Village in Early Communist Transition*, Cambridge, Mass. 1959.
** William Hinton, *Fanshen: A Documentary of Revolution in a Chinese Village*, New York 1966.
David and Isabel Crook, *Revolution in a Chinese Village: Ten Mile Inn*, London 1959.
Jan Myrdal, *Report from a Chinese Village*, pb. ed. Harmondsworth 1967.
John W. Lewis, 'The Study of Chinese Political Culture', *World Politics*, xviii, 3 (April 1966), 503–24.
Ch'ing K'un Yang, *The Chinese Family in the Communist Revolution*, Cambridge, Mass. 1959.

Ch'ing K'un Yang, *Religion in Chinese Society: A Study of Contemporary Social Functions of Religion and some of their Historical Factors*, Berkeley 1961.

Donald W. Treadgold (ed.), *Soviet and Chinese Communism: Similarities and Differences*, Seattle 1967.

*** Franz Schurmann, *Ideology and Organization in Communist China*, 2nd ed. pb. Berkeley 1968.

Thomas P. Bernstein, 'Leadership and Mass Mobilisation in the Soviet and Chinese Collectivisation Campaigns of 1929–30 and 1955–56', *China Quarterly*, 31 (July–Sept. 1967), 1–47.

Robert J. Lifton, *Thought Reform and the Psychology of Totalism*, pb. ed. Harmondsworth 1967.

Rensselaer W. Lee III, 'The *Hsia Fang* System: Marxism and Modernisation', *China Quarterly*, 28 (Oct.–Dec. 1966), 40–62.

Lucien W. Pye, *The Spirit of Chinese Politics: A Psychological Study of the Authority Crisis in Chinese Development*, Cambridge, Mass. 1968.

* Nai-Ruenn Chen and Walter Galenson, *The Chinese Economy under Communism*, Edinburgh 1969.

James R. Townsend, *Political Participation in Communist China*, Berkeley 1967.

John W. Lewis, *Leadership in Communist China*, Ithaca 1966.

Arthur Doak Barnett and Ezra Vogel, *Cadres, Bureaucracy and Political Power in Communist China*, New York 1967.

John W. Lewis (ed.), *Party Leadership and Revolutionary Power in China*, pb. ed. Cambridge 1970.

Alexander L. George, *The Chinese Communist Army in Action; the Korean War and its aftermath*, New York 1967.

John Gittings, *The Role of the Chinese Army*, London 1967.

Peter Van Ness, *Revolution and Chinese Foreign Policy: Peking's Support for Wars of National Liberation*, Berkeley 1970.

Dwight H. Perkins, 'Economic Growth in China and the Cultural Revolution (1960–April 1967)', *China Quarterly*, 30 (April–June 1967), 33–48.

Robert J. Lifton, *Revolutionary Immortality: Mao Tsé-tung and the Chinese Cultural Revolution*, London 1969.

Hélène Carrère d'Encausse and Stuart R. Schram, *L'URSS et la Chine devant les révolutions dans les sociétés pré-industrielles*, Paris 1971.

Ezra F. Vogel, *Canton under Communism: Programs and Politics in a Provincial Capital, 1949–1968*, Cambridge, Mass. 1969.

Donald S. Zagoria, *The Sino-Soviet Conflict, 1956–61*, Princeton 1961.

William E. Griffith, *The Sino–Soviet Rift*, London 1964.

William E. Griffith, *Sino–Soviet Relations, 1964–65*, Cambridge, Mass. 1967.

John Gittings, *Survey of the Sino–Soviet Dispute: A commentary and extracts from the recent polemics, 1963–67*, London 1968.

† Jan Myrdal and Gun Kessle, *China: The Revolution Continued*, London 1971.

4. YUGOSLAVIA

Wayne S. Vucinich, 'The Yugoslav Lands in the Ottoman Period; post-war Marxist interpretations of indigenous and Ottoman institutions', *Journal of Modern History*, XXVII, 3 (Sept. 1955), 287–305.

Philip Moseley, 'The Peasant Family; the *Zadruga* or Communal Joint Family in the Balkans and its recent Evolution', in Caroline F. Ware (ed.), *The Cultural Approach to History*, New York 1940.

Charles and Barbara Jelavich (eds), *The Balkans in Transition; essays on the development of Balkan life and politics since the eighteenth century*, Berkeley 1963.

Charles Jelavich, *Tsarist Russia and Balkan Nationalism; Russian influence in the internal affairs of Bulgaria and Serbia, 1879–1896*, Berkeley 1958.

Doreen Warriner (ed.), *Contrasts in Emerging Societies; readings in the social and economic history of south-eastern Europe in the nineteenth century*, London 1965.

Charles Jelavich, 'Serbian Nationalism and the Question of Union with Croatia in the nineteenth century', *Balkan Studies*, 3, 1 (1962), 29–42.

Hermann Wendel, 'Marxism and the Southern Slav Question', *Slavonic Review*, 11, 5 (Dec. 1923), 289–307.

Carole Rogel, 'The Slovenes and Political Yugoslavism on the Eve of of World War I', *East European Quarterly*, IV, 4 (Jan. 1971), 408–18.

Milovan Djilas, *Land without Justice: An autobiography of his youth*, London 1958.

From the First World War to the Second World War
* Hugh Seton-Watson, *Eastern Europe between the Wars, 1918–1941*, 3rd ed. pb. New York 1967.

Vladko Maček, *In the Struggle for Freedom*, University Park, Penn. 1968.

J. B. Hoptner, *Yugoslavia in Crises, 1934–41*, New York 1962.

Ruth Trouton, *Peasant Renaissance in Yugoslavia, 1900–50; a study of the development of Yugoslav peasant society as affected by education*, London 1952.

* Jozo Tomasevich, *Peasants, Politics and Economic Change in Yugoslavia*, Stanford 1955.

P. Joussa, *Les tendances des réformes agraires dans l'Europe centrale, l'Europe orientale et l'Europe méridionale 1918-24*, Niort 1925.

R. M. Brašić, *Land Reform and Ownership in Yugoslavia, 1919–53*, New York 1954.

* Ivan Avakumović, *History of the Communist Party of Yugoslavia*, vol. 1, Aberdeen 1964.

* Phyllis Auty, *Tito: a biography*, London 1970.

* George D. Jackson, *Comintern and Peasant in Eastern Europe, 1919–30*, New York 1966.

** Paul Shoup, *Communism and the Yugoslav National Question*, New York 1968.

Anton Ciliga, *The Russian Enigma*, London 1940.
Anton Ciliga, *Dix ans derrière le rideau de fer*, vol. I, *Au pays du mensonge déconcertant*, Paris 1950.
Guenther Nollau, *International Communism and World Revolution; history and methods*, London 1961.
M. Drachovitch and B. Lazitch (eds), *The Comintern; Historical Highlights; essays, recollections, documents*, New York 1969.
Kermit E. McKenzie, *Comintern and World Revolution 1928–43; the shaping of a doctrine*, London 1964.
* R. V. Burks, *The Dynamics of Communism in Eastern Europe*, Princeton 1961.

The Second World War and the Partisan victory
Dragiša N. Ristić, *Yugoslavia's Revolution of 1941*. London, Penn. 1966.
A. Djonlagic *et al.*, *Yugoslavia in the Second World War*, Belgrade 1967.
† Chalmers Johnson, *Peasant Nationalism and Communist Power*, London 1963.
Michael E. Howard, *The Mediterranean Strategy in the Second World War*, London 1968.
John Ehrman, *Grand Strategy*, vols v and vi, London 1956, in Sir James R. M. Butler (ed.), *History of the Second World War. United Kingdom Military Series*.
* Vladimir Dedijer (ed.), *Tito Speaks; his self-portrait and struggle with Stalin*, London 1954.
Vladimir Dedijer, *With Tito through the War; Partisan diary 1941–4*, London 1951.
Milovan Djilas, *Conversations with Stalin*, pb. ed. Harmondsworth 1963.
F. W. Deakin, *The Brutal Friendship* and *The Last Days of Mussolini*, 2 vols, pb. ed. Harmondsworth 1966.
* R. Čolaković, *Winning Freedom*, London 1962.
† Branko M. Lazitch, *Tito et la révolution yougoslave, 1937–56*, Paris 1957.
* *The Trial of Dragoljub-Draža Mihailović; stenographic record*, Belgrade 1946.
William Jones, *Twelve Months with Tito's Partisans*, Bedford 1946.
Christie Lawrence, *Irregular Adventure*, London 1947.
Lindsay S. Rogers, *Guerrilla Surgeon*, London 1957.
Basil Davidson, *Partisan Picture*, Bedford 1946.
Fitzroy Maclean, *Eastern Approaches*, London 1949.
Jasper Rootham, *Miss Fire; the chronicle of a British mission to Mihailovich, 1943–4*, London 1946.
Stephen H. Clissold, *Whirlwind; an account of Marshal Tito's rise to power*, London 1949.
Julian Amery, *Sons of the Eagle; a study in guerrilla war*, London 1948 (especially on Albania).
C. Fotitch, *The War we Lost; Yugoslavia's tragedy and the failure of the West*, New York 1948.

David Martin, *Ally Betrayed; the uncensored story of Tito and Mihailovitch*, New York 1946.

D. A. Tomasič, 'Nationality Problems and Partisan Yugoslavia', *Journal of Central European Affairs*, VI (1946).

Yugoslavia since the Partisan victory
Hugh Seton-Watson, *The East European Revolution*, 3rd ed. London 1956.

Robert L. Wolff, *The Balkans in our Time*, Cambridge, Mass. 1956.

Robert J. Kerner (ed.), *Yugoslavia*, Berkeley 1949.

Milovan Djilas, *The New Class; an analysis of the Communist system*, London 1957.

Ernest Halperin, *The Triumphant Heretic; Tito's Struggle against Stalin*, London 1958.

Adam B. Ulam, *Titoism and the Cominform*, Cambridge, Mass. 1952.

Josef Korbel, *Tito's Communism*, Denver 1951.

Charles P. McVicker, *Titoism: pattern for international Communism*, New York 1957.

Fred W. Neal, *Titoism in Action; the reforms in Yugoslavia after 1948*, Berkeley 1958.

D. A. Tomasič, *National Communism and Soviet Strategy*, Washington 1957.

Paul Shoup, 'Yugoslavia's National Minorities under Communism', *Slavic Review*, 22 (1963).

J. Frankel, 'Communism and the National Question in Yugoslavia', *Journal of Central European Studies*, XV (April 1955).

D. A. Tomasič, 'The New Class and Nationalism', *Journal of Croatian Studies*, 1 (1960).

Evangelos Kofos, *Nationalism and Communism in Macedonia*, Institute for Balkan Studies, Thessalonike 1964.

Jorjo Tadić (ed.), *Dix années d'historiographie yougoslave, 1945–55*, Belgrade 1955.

Nicolas Spulber, *The Economics of Communist Eastern Europe*, Cambridge, Mass. 1957.

R. Bicanic, 'Interaction of macro- and micro-economic decisions in Yugoslavia 1954–57', in G. Grossman (ed.). *Value and Plan; economic calculation and organization in Eastern Europe*, Berkeley 1960, 346–59.

R. Bicanic, 'Economic growth under centralized and decentralized planning: Yugoslavia; a case study', *Economic Development and Cultural Change*, VI (1957–8), 63–74.

B. McFarlane, 'Yugoslavia's Crossroads', in Ralph Miliband and John Saville (eds), *The Socialist Register, 1966*, London 1966, 114–31.

Branko Horvat, *An Essay on Yugoslav Society*, White Plains, New York 1968.

† J. Djordjevic, 'Political Power in Yugoslavia', *Government and Opposition*, 2, 2 (Jan.–April 1967), 206–17.

Viktor Meier, 'Yugoslav Communism', in W. Griffith (ed.), *Communism in Europe; continuity, change and the Sino-Soviet Dispute*, vol. 1, Oxford 1967, 19–84.

M. George Zaninovich, *The Development of Socialist Yugoslavia*, Baltimore 1968.

* Wayne S. Vucinich (ed.), *Contemporary Yugoslavia*, Berkeley 1969.

George W. Hoffman and F. W. Neal, *Yugoslavia and the New Communism*, New York 1963.

John C. Campbell, *Tito's Separate Road; America and Yugoslavia in World Politics*, New York 1967.

Jack C. Fisher, 'The Yugoslav Commune', *World Politics*, xvi, 3 (April 1964), 418–44.

Jack C. Fisher, *Yugoslavia; a multi-national state; regional difference and administrative response*, San Francisco 1966.

* Ghiţa Ionescu, *The Politics of the European Communist States*, pb. ed. London 1969.

* D. Riddell, 'Social Self-Government; the background of theory and practice in Yugoslav Socialism', *British Journal of Sociology*, xix, 1 (March 1968), 47–75.

Adolf Sturmthal, *Workers Councils: A Study of Workplace Organization on both sides of the Iron Curtain*, Cambridge, Mass. 1964.

P. Blumberg, *Industrial Democracy: the sociology of participation*, London 1968.

Jiri Kolaja, *Workers Councils: The Yugoslav Experience*, London 1965.

Albert Meister, *Socialisme et Autogestion: l'expérience Jougoslave*, Paris 1964.

Wayne E. Leeman, 'Syndicalism in Yugoslavia', *Economic Development and Cultural Change*, 18, 2 (Jan. 1970), 230–9.

Oleg Mandič, 'La stratification sociale en Yougoslavie et la notion de classe', *Cahiers Internationaux de Sociologie*, xxxix (July–Dec. 1965), 171–84.

Radomir D. Lukic, 'L'Influence de l'autogestion ouvrière sur la structure de classe de la société yougoslave', *Cahiers Internationaux de Sociologie*, xxxix (July–Dec. 1965), 185–96.

* Lorraine Barić, 'Traditional Groups and New Economic Opportunities in Rural Yugoslavia', in R. Firth (ed.), *Themes in Economic Anthropology* (*A.S.A. Monographs*, 6), pb. ed. London 1970, 253–78.

V. St. Erlich, *Family in Transition; a study of 300 Yugoslav Villages*, Princeton 1966.

* Joel M. Halpern, *A Serbian Village*, pb. ed. New York 1967.

Joel M. Halpern, 'Farming as a Way of Life; Yugoslav Peasant Attitudes', in Jerzy F. Karcz (ed.), *Soviet and East European Agriculture*, Berkeley 1967, 356–81.

5. VIETNAM

Vietnam before the French

† Joseph Buttinger, *The Smaller Dragon*, New York 1958.

* Le Thành Khôi, *Le Viêt-Nam: Histoire et Civilisation*, Paris 1955.

† André Masson, *Histoire du Vietnam*, Paris 1960.

Jean Chesneaux, *Contribution à l'histoire de la nation vietnamienne*, Paris 1955.

Charles B. Maybon, *Histoire moderne du pays d'Annam, 1592–1820*, Paris 1919.

Jean Chesneaux, *Le Vietnam: Études de politique et d'histoire*, Paris 1968.

Hisayuki Miyakawa, 'The Confucianization of South China', in Arthur F. Wright (ed.), *The Confucian Persuasion*, Stanford 1960, 21–46.

Alexander B. Woodside, 'Early Ming Expansionism (1406–27): China's abortive conquest of Vietnam, *Papers on China (Harvard)*, XVII (Dec. 1963), 1–37.

* Alexander B. Woodside, *Vietnam and the Chinese Model: A Comparative Study of Nguyên and Ch'ing civil government in the first half of the 19th century*, Cambridge, Mass. 1971.

* Michael G. Cotter, 'Toward a Social History of the Vietnamese Southward Movement', *Journal of Southeast Asian History*, IX, 1 (March 1968), 12–24.

Alastair Lamb, *The Mandarin Road to Old Hue; Narrative of Anglo-Vietnamese diplomacy from the 17th century to the eve of the French conquest*, London 1970.

Truong Buu Lam, 'Intervention versus Tribute in Sino-Vietnamese Relations, 1788–1790', in John K. Fairbank (ed.), *The Chinese World Order*, Cambridge, Mass. 1968, 165–79.

Kenneth P. Landon, *Southeast Asia: Crossroad of Religions*, Chicago 1949.

Le Van Ho, 'Introduction à l'ethnologie du Dinh', *Revue du sud-est asiatique*, 2 (1962), 85–122.

The establishment of the French colonial regime and its impact on Vietnamese society and economy

Truong Buu Lam, *Patterns of Vietnamese Response to Foreign Intervention: 1858–1900 (Monograph Series No. 11, South East Asian Studies, Yale)*, New Haven 1967.

Henri Brunschwig, *French Colonialism, 1871–1914: Myths and Realities*, London 1966.

John F. Cady, *The Roots of French Imperialism in Eastern Asia*, 2nd ed. Ithaca 1967.

Stephen H. Roberts, *History of French Colonial Policy, 1870–1925*, 2 vols, London 1929.

Raymond F. Betts, *Assimilation and Association in French Colonial Theory, 1890–1914*, New York 1961.

* Milton E. Osborne, *The French Presence in CochinChina and Cambodia: Rule and Response*, Ithaca 1969.

* Paul Isoart, *Le Phénomène national vietnamien: de l'indépendance unitaire à l'indépendance fractionée*, Paris 1961.

Charles Robequain, *The Economic Development of French Indochina*, London 1944.

** Pierre Gourou, *The Peasants of the Tonkin Delta: a study of human geography*, 2 vols, New Haven 1955.

Pierre Gourou, *Land Utilization in French Indochina*, New York 1941.

Joseph Buttinger, *Vietnam: A Dragon Embattled*, 2 vols, London 1967 (an enormous but uneven work. For an abridged version see Buttinger, *A Political History of Vietnam*).

Roy Jumper, 'Mandarin Bureaucracy and Politics in South Viet Nam', *Pacific Affairs*, XXX, 1 (March 1957), 47–58.

Roy Jumper and Nguyen Thi Hue, *Notes on the Political and Administrative History of Vietnam, 1802–1962*, Saigon 1962.

† Paul Mus, 'The Role of the Village in Vietnamese Politics', *Pacific Affairs*, XXII, 3 (Sept. 1949), 265–72.

Virginia M. Thompson, *French Indochina*, London 1937.

Virginia M. Thompson, *Labor Problems in Southeast Asia*, New Haven 1947.

André Dumarest, *La Formation des classes sociales en pays annamite*, Lyon 1935.

H. Lanoue, 'Vietnam: Bases économiques et sociales des sectes', *Cahiers Internationaux*, 65 (April 1955), 75–88.

Bernard B. Fall, 'The Political-Religious Sects of Vietnam', *Pacific Affairs*, XXVIII, 3 (Sept. 1955), 235–53.

Nguyen Huu Khang, *La Commune Annamite: étude historique, juridique et économique*, Paris 1946.

The rise of Vietnamese nationalism and the end of French colonial rule

* Bernard B. Fall, *The Two Vietnams: A Political and Military Analysis*, 2nd ed. London 1967.

† Jean Chesneaux, 'Stages in the Development of the Vietnam National Movement, 1862–1940', *Past and Present*, 7 (1955), 63–75.

* John T. McAlister, Jr, *Vietnam: The Origins of Revolution*, London 1969.

Tran Huy Lieu, *Les Soviets du Nghe-Tinh (de 1930–1931) au Vietnam*, Hanoi 1961.

Pierre Varet, *Au pays d'Annam: les dieux qui meurent*, Paris 1932.

William M. Ball, *Nationalism and Communism in East Asia*, Melbourne 1956.

Jack H. Brimmell, *Communism in South East Asia; a political analysis*, London 1959.

* I. Milton Sacks, 'Marxism in Vietnam', in Frank N. Trager (ed.), *Marxism in Southeast Asia*, Stanford 1959, 102–70.

Frank N. Trager, 'The Impact of Marxism' in Frank N. Trager (ed.), *Marxism in Southeast Asia*, Stanford 1959, 240–99.

Arthur Doak Barnett (ed.), *Communist Strategies in Asia: a comparative analysis of governments and parties*, London 1963.

Virginia Thompson and Richard Adloff, *The Left Wing in South East Asia*, New York 1950.

Charles B. McLane, *Soviet Strategies in South East Asia: an exploration of eastern policy under Lenin and Stalin*, Princeton 1966.

R. J. O'Neill, 'Regional Influences on Vietnamese Political Parties', *Politics*, IV, 1 (May 1969), 1–19.

† Jean Lacouture, *Hô Chi Minh*, Paris 1967.

Ho Chi Minh (ed. Bernard B. Fall), *Ho Chi Minh on Revolution: Selected Writings 1920-66*, pb. ed. New York 1968.

Truong Chinh, *Primer for Revolt: The Communist Takeover in Vietnam*, ed. Bernard B. Fall, New York 1963.

** Philippe Devillers, *Histoire du Vietnam de 1940 à 1952*, 3rd ed. Paris 1952.

Willard H. Elsbree, *Japan's Role in Southeast Asian Nationalist Movements, 1940-45*, 2nd ed. New York 1970.

* John T. McAlister Jr, 'Mountain Minorities and the Vietminh: A Key to the Indochina War' in P. Kunstadter (ed.), *South East Asian Tribes, Minorities and Nations*, 2 vols, Princeton 1967, vol. 2, 771-844.

Robert L. Solomon, 'Boundary Concepts and Practices in Southeast Asia', *World Politics*, XXIII, 1 (Oct. 1970), 1-23.

King C. Chen, *Vietnam and China 1938-54*, Princeton 1969.

Donald Lancaster, *The Emancipation of French Indochina*, London 1961.

Ellen J. Hammer, *The Struggle for Indochina, 1940-55*, pb. ed. Stanford 1966.

* Paul Mus, *Viêt-Nam: Sociologie d'une guerre*, Paris 1952.

George K. Tanham, *Communist Revolutionary Warfare: From the Vietminh to the VietCong*, 2nd ed. New York 1967.

Edgar O'Ballance, *The Indochina War 1945-54: A Study in Guerrilla Warfare*, London 1964.

Bernard B. Fall, *Street without Joy: Indochina at War 1946-54*, 2nd ed. London 1964.

* Bernard B. Fall, *Le Viet-Minh: La République Démocratique du Viet-Nam 1945-60*, Paris 1960.

Bernard B. Fall, *Hell in a very small place: The Siege of Dien Bien Phu*, Philadelphia 1967.

* Philippe Devillers and Jean Lacouture, *End of a War: Indochina 1954*, London 1969.

The continuing struggle
* Philippe Devillers, 'The Struggle for the Unification of Vietnam', *China Quarterly*, 9 (Jan.–March 1962), 2-23.

Bernard B. Fall, *Vietnam Witness, 1953-66*, London 1966.

Wilfred G. Burchett, *The Furtive War: the United States in Vietnam and Laos*, New York 1963.

Wilfred G. Burchett, *Vietnam: Inside story of the guerrilla war*, New York 1965.

Lucien Bodard, *The Quicksand War: prelude to Vietnam*, London 1967.

Sir Robert Thompson, *Defeating Communist Insurgency; Experiences from Malaya and Vietnam*, London 1966.

Roger Trinquier, *Modern Warfare; a French view of counter-insurgency*, New York 1964.

Vo Nguyen Giap, *People's War, People's Army; the Viet Cong Insurrection Manual for Underdeveloped Countries* (ed. Bernard Fall), New York 1962.

R. J. O'Neill, *General Giap; politician and strategist*, North Melbourne 1969.

Dennis J. Duncanson, *Government and Revolution in Vietnam*, London 1968.

John T. McAlister Jr and Paul Mus, *The Vietnamese and their Revolution*, pb. ed. New York 1970.

Le Chau, *La révolution paysanne du Sud Viet Nam*, Paris 1966.

† Jean Lacouture, *Vietnam between two truces*, pb. ed. New York 1966.

Nghiem Dang, *Vietnam: Politics and Public Administration*, Honolulu 1966.

Edward J. Mitchell, 'Inequality and Insurgency: a statistical study of South Vietnam', *World Politics*, xx, 3 (April 1968), 421–38.

Eric H. Jacoby, *Agrarian Unrest in South East Asia*, Bombay 1961.

* Jeffery M. Paige, 'Inequality and Insurgency in Vietnam: A Reanalysis', *World Politics*, xxiii, 1 (Oct. 1970), 24–37.

* Douglas Pike, *Viet Cong: The organization and techniques of the National Liberation Front of South Vietnam*, Cambridge, Mass. 1966.

Robert Shaplen, *The Lost Revolution*, New York 1965.

* Gerald C. Hickey, *Village in Vietnam*, pb. ed. New Haven 1967.

Robert Scigliano, 'The Electoral Process in South Vietnam: Politics in an underdeveloped state', *Midwest Journal of Political Science*, iv (May 1960), 138–61.

Robert Scigliano, *South Vietnam: Nation under stress*, pb. ed. Boston 1964.

Franz Schurmann, Peter D. Scott and Reginald Zelnik, *The Politics of Escalation in Vietnam*, pb. ed. Greenwich, Conn. 1966.

Victor Bator, *Vietnam, a Diplomatic Tragedy; Origins of U.S. involvement*, London 1967.

Hoang Van Chi, *From Colonialism to Communism: a case history of North Vietnam*, New York 1964.

J. P. Gittinger, 'Communist Land Policy in North Vietnam', *Far Eastern Survey*, xxvii, August 1959.

T. Shabad, 'Economic Developments in North Vietnam', *Pacific Affairs*, xxxi, 1 (March 1958), 36–53.

Patrick J. Honey, *Communism in North Vietnam: its role in the Sino-Soviet Dispute*, Cambridge, Mass. 1963.

Patrick J. Honey (ed.), *North Vietnam Today; profile of a Communist satellite*, New York 1962.

† Gérard Chaliand, *The Peasants of North Vietnam*, pb. ed. Harmondsworth 1969.

Le Chau, *Le Viet Nam socialiste: une économie de transition*, Paris 1966.

6. ALGERIA

Lucette Valensi, *Le Maghreb avant la prise d'Alger*, Paris 1969.

R. Galcissot and Lucette Valensi, 'Le Maghreb pré-colonial; mode de

production archaïque ou mode de production féodal?', *La Pensée*, 142 (1968), 57–93.
* Charles A. Julien, *A History of North Africa from the Arab Conquest to 1830*, London 1970.
Mostefa Lacheraf, *L'Algérie: nation et société*, Paris 1965.
Yves Lacoste, André Nouschi and André Prenant, *L'Algérie passé et présent; le cadre et les étapes de la constitution de l'Algérie actuelle*, Paris 1960.

The colonial regime
* Charles A. Julien, *Histoire de l'Algérie contemporaine*, vol. 1, 1827–1871, Paris 1964.
X. A. Yacono, *La Colonisation des Plaines du Chelif*, 2 vols, Algiers 1955.
André Nouschi, *Enquête sur le niveau de vie des populations rurales Constantinoises de la conquête jusqu'en 1919; essai d'histoire économique et sociale*, Paris 1961.
** Charles-Robert Agéron, *Les Algériens Musulmans et la France, 1871–1919*, 2 vols, Paris 1968.
† X. Yacono, 'La France et les Algériens Musulmans, 1871–1919', *Revue Historique*, 493 (Jan.–March 1970).
† Charles-Robert Agéron, 'Les Algériens musulmans et la France, 1871–1919', *Revue Historique*, 494 (April–June 1970).
Yvonne Turin, *Affrontements culturels dans l'Algérie coloniale*, Paris 1971.
C. M. Andrew and A. S. Kanya-Forstner, 'The French "Colonial Party"; its Composition, Aims and Influence, 1885–1914', *The Historical Journal*, XIV, 1 (March 1971), 99–128.
Charles-Robert Agéron, 'L'Emir Khaled, petit-fils d'Abd el-Kader, fut-il le premier nationaliste algérien?', *Revue de l'occident musulman*, 2 (1966).
Charles-Robert Agéron, 'La politique kabyle sous le Second Empire', *Revue française d'histoire d'Outremer*, 190–1, Sept. 1967.
Ali Merad, 'L'Enseignement politique de Mohammed Abduh aux Algériens (1903)', *Orient* (1963), 4, 75–122.
W. Cantwell Smith, *Islam in Modern History*, Princeton 1957.
Albert Hourani, *Arabic Thought in the Liberal Age, 1798–1939*, pb. ed. London 1970.
* Ali Merad, *Le Réformisme musulman en Algérie de 1925 à 1940*, Paris 1967.
J. Carret, 'L'Association des Ouléma réformistes d'Algérie', *L'Afrique et l'Asie* (1958), 3.
Émile Dermenghem, *La culte des saints dans l'Islam maghrébin*, 3rd ed. Paris 1954.
Pierre J. André   *Contribution à l'étude des confréries religieuses musulmanes*, Algiers 1956.
Pessah Shinar, 'Ibāḍiyya and Orthodox Reformism in Modern Algeria', *Scripta Hierosolymitana*, IX (ed. Heyd), Jerusalem 1961, 97–120.

* Roger Le Tourneau, *Évolution politique de l'Afrique du Nord musulmane, 1920–61*, Paris 1962.

Mahfoud Kaddache, *La vie politique à Alger de 1919 à 1939*, Algiers 1971.

Jean Paul Charnay, *La vie musulmane en Algérie d'après la jurisprudence de la première moitié du xxe siècle*, Paris 1965.

† André Nouschi, *La naissance du nationalisme algérien, 1914–54*, Paris 1962.

* Jacques Berque, *French North Africa; The Maghrib between two World Wars*, London 1967.

Ferhat Abbas, *La nuit coloniale*, Paris 1962.

† David C. Gordon, *The Passing of French Algeria*, London 1966.

Manfred Halpern, 'The Algerian Uprising of 1945', *Middle East Journal*, 2, 2 (April 1948), 191–202.

† Pierre Bourdieu, *The Algerians*, Boston 1962 (= *Sociologie de l'Algérie*, 3rd ed. Paris 1963).

H. Isnard, *La Vigne en Algérie*, 2 vols, Gap 1951–4.

† Germaine Tillion, *L'Afrique bascule vers l'avenir*, Paris 1960.

Germaine Tillion, *France and Algeria; Complementary Enemies*, New York 1961.

† Roger Murray and Tom Weingraf, 'The Algerian Revolution', *New Left Review*, 22 (Dec. 1963), 14–65.

* Robert Aron *et al. Les origines de la guerre d'Algérie*, Paris 1962.

Michael K. Clark, *Algeria in Turmoil: a history of the rebellion*, New York 1959.

Charles-Henri Favrod, *Le F.L.N. et l'Algérie*, Paris 1962.

Edgar O'Ballance, *The Algerian Insurrection, 1954–62*, London 1967.

Hocine Ait Ahmed, *La guerre et l'après-guerre*, Paris 1964.

* Michel Launay, *Paysans algériens*, Paris 1963.

Pierre Bourdieu *et al. Travail et travailleurs en Algérie*, Paris 1963.

* Pierre Bourdieu and Abdel Malek Sayad, *Le Déracinement: la crise de l'agriculture traditionelle en Algérie*, Paris 1964.

* Frantz Fanon, *Studies in a Dying Colonialism* (= *L'An V de la révolution algérienne*), New York 1965.

Frantz Fanon, *The Wretched of the Earth*, London 1965.

The post-revolutionary regime

David and Marina Ottaway, *Algeria: The Politics of a Socialist Revolution*, Berkeley 1970.

William B. Quandt, *Revolution and Political Leadership: Algeria, 1954–68*, Cambridge, Mass. 1969.

* Samir Amin, *L'Économie du Maghreb*, 2 vols Paris 1966.

† Samir Amin, *The Maghreb in the Modern World*, pb. ed. Harmondsworth 1970.

* Jeanne Favret, 'Le traditionalisme par excès de modernité', *Archives Européennes de Sociologie*, VIII, 1 (1967), 71–93.

P. J. Vatikiotis, 'Tradition and Political Leadership: The Example of Algeria', *Middle Eastern Studies*, 2, 4 (July 1966), 330–66.

Jacques Berque, *La Dépossession du monde*, Paris 1964.

Gérard Chaliand, *L'Algérie est-il socialiste?*, Paris 1964.

René Dumont and Marcel Mazoyer, *Développement et socialismes*, Paris 1969.

Charles Debbasch *et al. Pouvoir et administration au Maghreb; études sur les élites maghrébines* (C.N.R.S.), Paris 1970.

Arslan Humbaraci, *Algeria: a Revolution that failed; a political history since 1954*, London 1966.

Jean Dresch (ed.), *Réforme agraire au Maghreb*, Paris 1963.

Jean Morizot, *L'Algérie kabylisée*, Paris 1962.

Cvetko Kostić, 'Transformation des communautés rurales en Yougoslavie et en Algérie', *Cahiers Internationaux de Sociologie*, XLIII, new series (July–Dec. 1967), 109–22.

François Perroux (ed.), *Problèmes de l'Algérie indépendante*, Paris 1963.

Dorothy M. Pickles, *Algeria and France: From Colonialism to Cooperation*, London 1963.

Leon C. Brown (ed.), *State and Society in Independent North Africa*, Washington 1966.

Manfred Halpern, *The Politics of Social Change in the Middle East and North Africa*, pb. ed. Princeton 1965.

Bernard Lewis, *The Middle East and the West*, London 1964.

* Anouar Abdel-Malek, *La pensée politique arabe contemporaine*, Paris 1970.

Gérard Viratelle, *L'Algérie algérienne*, Paris 1971.

7. TURKEY

The Ottoman empire and the west before 1800

* Bernard Lewis, *The Emergence of Modern Turkey*, London 1961.

** Niyazi Berkes, *The Development of Secularism in Turkey*, Montreal 1964.

* W. Cantwell Smith, *Islam in Modern History*, Princeton 1957.

Paul Wittek, 'Le rôle des tribus turques dans l'empire ottoman', *Mélanges Georges Smets*, Brussels 1952, 665–76.

F. A. Belin, 'Étude sur la propriété foncière en pays musulmans et spécialement en Turquie', *Journal Asiatique*, Oct.–Nov. 1861, 390–431; Feb.–March 1862, 156–212; April–May 1862, 257–358.

* Hamilton A. R. Gibb and Harold Bowen, *Islamic Society and the West*, vol. 1, Parts 1 and 2, London 1950–7.

Franklin L. Baumer, 'England, the Turk and the Common Corps of Christendom', *American Historical Review*, 5, 1 (Oct. 1944), 26–48.

Alan W. Fisher, *The Russian Annexation of the Crimea, 1772–1783*, Cambridge 1970.

Stanford J. Shaw, 'The Origins of Ottoman Military Reform: The Nizam-I Cedid Army of Sultan Selim III', *Journal of Modern History*, XXXVII, 3 (Sept. 1965), 291–305.

Uriel Heyd, 'The Ottoman 'Ulemā and Westernization in the time of Selīm III and Mahmūd II', *Scripta Hierosolymitana*, IX (ed. Heyd.), Jerusalem 1961, 63–96.

The nineteenth century

Robert E. Ward and Dankwart A. Rustow (eds). *Political Modernization in Japan and Turkey*, Princeton 1964.

Vernon J. Puryear, *Napoleon and the Dardanelles*, Berkeley 1951.

William R. Polk and R. L. Chambers (eds), *Beginnings of Modernization in the Middle East; the nineteenth century*, Chicago 1968.

J. C. Hurewitz, 'The Beginnings of Military Modernization in the
Middle East: A comparative analysis', *Middle East Journal*, XXII,
2 (Spring 1968), 144–58 (reprinted in *Middle East Politics* cited
next).

J. C. Hurewitz, *Middle East Politics: The Military Dimension*, New
York 1969.

William Miller, *The Ottoman Empire and its Successors, 1801–1927*,
4th ed. Cambridge 1936.

Frank E. Bailey, *British Policy and the Turkish Reform Movement;
a study in Anglo-Turkish Relations, 1826–53*, Cambridge, Mass.
1942.

Harold W. V. Temperley, 'British Policy towards Parliamentary Rule
and Constitutionalism in Turkey (1830–1914', *Cambridge Historical
Journal*, IV, 2 (1933), 156–91.

Roderic H. Davison, 'Turkish Attitudes concerning Christian–
Muslim Equality in the Nineteenth Century', *American Historical
Review*, LIX, 4 (July 1954), 844–64.

Harold W. V. Temperley, *England and the Near East: The Crimea*,
London 1936.

Şerif A. Mardin, *The Genesis of Young Ottoman Thought*, Princeton
1962.

Robert Devereux, *The First Ottoman Constitutional Period; a study
of the Midhat Constitution and Parliament*, Baltimore 1963.

* Roderic H. Davison, *Reform in the Ottoman Empire, 1856–76*,
Princeton 1963.

Nasim Sousa, *The Capitulatory Regime of Turkey: Its history, origin
and nature*, Baltimore 1933.

Donald C. Blaisdell, *European Financial Control in the Ottoman
Empire*, New York 1929.

Vernon J. Puryear, *International Economics and Diplomacy in the
Middle East: a study of British commercial policy in the Levant,
1834–53*, Stanford 1935.

Leland J. Gordon, *American Relations with Turkey 1830–1930: An
economic interpretation*, Philadelphia 1932.

F. S. Rodkey, 'Ottoman Concern about Western Economic Penetration in the Levant, 1849–56', *Journal of Modern History*, 30, 4 (Dec.
1958), 348–53.

E. Z. Karal, 'La transformation de la Turquie d'un empire oriental
en un état moderne et national', *Journal of World History*, IV, 2
(1958), 426–45.

Kerim K. Key, *Origins of the Young Turk Movement, 1839–1908*,
Washington 1955.

Şerif A. Mardin, 'Libertarian Movements in the Ottoman Empire,
1878–95', *Middle East Journal*, XVI, 2 (Spring 1962), 169–82.

Wilbur W. White, *The Process of Change in the Ottoman Empire*, Chicago 1937.

Arshag O. Sarkissian, *History of the Armenian Question to 1885*, Urbana, Ill. 1938.

Avedis K. Sanjian, *The Armenian Communities in Syria under Ottoman Dominion*, Cambridge, Mass. 1965.

Louise Nalbandian, *The Armenian Revolutionary Movement: the development of Armenian Political Parties through the nineteenth Century*, Berkeley 1963.

Leften S. Stavrianos, *Balkan Federation: a history of the movement towards Balkan Unity in modern times*, Northampton, Mass. 1944.

From the Young Turks to the revolution

Ernest E. Ramsaur, *The Young Turks: Prelude to the Revolution of 1908*, Princeton 1957.

* Feroz Ahmad, *The Young Turks: The Committee of Union and Progress in Turkish Politics 1908–14*, Oxford 1969.

Herbert Feis, *Europe, the World's Banker 1870–1914; an account of European foreign investment*, New Haven 1930.

Edward M. Earle, *Turkey, the Great Powers and the Bagdad Railway: a study in imperialism*, London 1923.

Ulrich Trumpener, *Germany and the Ottoman Empire 1914–18*, Princeton 1968.

A. A. Cruickshank, 'The Young Turk Challenge in Postwar Turkey', *Middle East Journal*, XXII, 1 (Winter 1968), 17–28.

* (Lord) John P. D. B. Kinross, *Ataturk: The Rebirth of a Nation*, London 1964.

Elaine D. Smith, *Turkey: Origins of the Kemalist Movement and the Government of the Grand National Assembly (1919–1923)*, Washington 1959.

† Dankwart A. Rustow, 'The Army and the Founding of the Turkish Republic', *World Politics*, XI, 4 (July 1959), 513–52.

Zeine N. Zeine, *Arab–Turkish Relations and the Emergence of Arab Nationalism*, Beirut 1958.

Richard G. Hovanissian, *Armenia on the Road to Independence, 1918*, Berkeley 1967.

Abraham H. Hartunian, *Neither to Laugh nor to Weep; a memoir of the Armenian Genocide*, Boston 1968.

* Kemal Ataturk, *A Speech delivered by Ghazi Mustapha Kemal, President of the Turkish Republic: October 1927*, Leipzig 1929.

George S. Harris, *The Origins of Communism in Turkey*, Stanford 1967.

Charles W. Hostler, *Turkism and the Soviets: the Turks of the world and their political objectives*, London 1957.

Harish Kapur, *Soviet Russia and Asia 1917–27; a study of Soviet policy towards Turkey, Iran and Afghanistan*, London 1966.

Guenther Nollau and H. J. Wiehe, *Russia's Southern Flank; Soviet operations in Iran, Turkey and Afghanistan*, London 1963.

Demetrio Boersner, *The Bolsheviks and the National and Colonial Question 1917–28*, Geneva 1957.

Hélène Carrère d'Encausse and Stuart R. Schram, *Marxism and Asia: an introduction with readings*, London 1969.

Ziya Gökalp (ed. Niyazi Berkes), *Turkish Nationalism and Western Civilization*, London 1959.

Uriel Heyd, *Foundations of Turkish Nationalism. The Life and Teachings of Ziya Gökalp*, London 1950.

Post-revolutionary Turkey

Dankwart A. Rustow, 'Politics and Islam in Turkey 1920–55', in Richard N. Frye (ed.), *Islam and the West*, The Hague 1957, 69–107.

Andreas M. Kazamias, *Education and the Quest for Modernity in Turkey*, London 1966.

* Kemal H. Karpat, *Turkey's Politics: The Transition to a Multiparty System*, Princeton 1959.

Richard D. Robinson, *The First Turkish Republic: a case study in national development*, Cambridge, Mass. 1963.

Frederick W. Frey, *The Turkish Political Elite*, Cambridge, Mass. 1965.

* Joseph F. Szyliowicz, 'Elite Recruitment in Turkey: the role of the Mülkiye', *World Politics*, XXIII, 3 (April 1971), 371–98.

International Bank for Reconstruction and Development, *The Economy of Turkey*, Baltimore 1951.

Zvi Y. Hershlag, *An Introduction to the Modern Economic History of the Middle East*, Leiden 1964.

* Zvi Y. Hershlag, *Turkey: The Challenge of Growth*, 2nd ed. Leiden 1968.

Edwin J. Cohn, *Turkish Economic, Social, and Political Change; the development of a more prosperous and open society*, New York 1970.

Wolfram Eberhard, 'Nomads and Farmers in Southeastern Turkey; Problems of Settlement', *Oriens*, 6, 1, 1 (June 1953), 32–49.

Wolfram Eberhard, *Settlement and Social Change in Asia (Collected Papers*, Vol. 1), New York 1968.

Daniel Lerner, *The Passing of Traditional Society; Modernizing the Middle East*, pb. ed. New York 1964.

* Paul Stirling, *Turkish Village*, pb. ed. New York 1966.

Joseph S. Szyliowicz, 'The Political Dynamics of Rural Turkey', *Middle East Journal*, XVI, 4 (Autumn 1962), 430–42.

Joseph S. Szyliowicz, *Political Change in Rural Turkey: Erdemli*, The Hague 1966.

C. A. O. van Nieuwenhuijze, 'The Near Eastern Village: A Profile', *Middle East Journal*, XVI, 3 (Summer 1962), 295–308.

Halil Inalcik, 'Land Problems in Turkish History', *Muslim World*, XLV, 3 (July 1955), 221–8.

O. L. Barkan, 'La Loi sur la distribution des terres aux agriculteurs et les problèmes essentielles d'une réforme agraire en Turquie', *Revue de la Faculté des Sciences Économiques de l'Université d'Istanbul*, 1944–45.

8. CUBA

General

** Hugh Thomas, *Cuba, or the Pursuit of Freedom*, London 1971 (vast and very well documented and indexed, but slightly blurred in analytical outline).

The colonial development of Cuba

* Fernando Ortiz, *Cuban Counterpoint; Tobacco and Sugar*, New York 1947.
* Herbert S. Klein, *Slavery in the Americas: A Comparative Study of Cuba and Virginia*, Chicago 1967.

Roger Bastide, *Les Amériques noires: les civilisations africaines dans le nouveau monde*, Paris 1967.

Yvan Debbasch, 'Le marronage: essai sur la désertion de l'esclave antillais', *L'Année Sociologique*, 3rd series, 1961, 1–112; 1962, 117–95.

Sidney W. Mintz, review of Stanley J. Elkins, *Slavery, American Anthopologist*, 63 (June 1961), 579–87.

Eugene D. Genovese, *The Political Economy of Slavery: studies in the economy and society of the Slave South*, New York 1965.

Arthur F. Corwin, *Spain and the Abolition of Slavery in Cuba, 1807–1886*, Austin 1967.

R. Guerra y Sánchez, *Sugar and Society in the Caribbean: An Economic History of Cuban Agriculture*, New Haven 1964.

Richard B. Gray, *José Martí, Cuban Patriot*, Gainesville, Florida 1962

The United States and independent Cuba: background to the revolution

Ernest R. May, *Imperial Democracy: The emergence of America as a great power*, New York 1961.

Ernest R. May, *American Imperialism: a speculative essay*, New York 1968.

Walter Lafeber, *The New Empire: an interpretation of American expansion, 1860–1898*, Ithaca 1963.

Philip S. Foner, *A History of Cuba and its Relationship with the United States*, Vols 1 and 2 (1492–1895), New York 1962–3.

Lester D. Langley, *The Cuban Policy of the United States: A Brief History*, New York 1968.

Russell H. Fitzgibbon, *Cuba and the United States, 1900–1935*, New York 1964 (reprint of 1935 edition).

David H. Healy, *The United States in Cuba 1898–1902: Generals, Politicians and the Search for a Policy*, Madison 1963.

Allan R. Millett, *The Politics of Intervention: The military occupation of Cuba, 1906–09*, Columbus, Ohio 1968.

* Robert F. Smith, *The United States and Cuba: Business and Diplomacy 1917–60*, New York 1960.

John Plank (ed.), *Cuba and the United States: Long-range perspectives*, Washington 1967.

Wilfrid H. Calcott, *The Caribbean Policy of the United States 1898–1920*, Baltimore 1942.

† Robert F. Smith (ed.), *Background to Revolution: The Development of Modern Cuba*, pb. ed. New York 1966.

† Ramon E. Ruiz, *Cuba: The making of a revolution*, Amherst, Mass. 1968.

Robin Blackburn, 'Prologue to the Cuban Revolution', *New Left Review*, 21 (Oct. 1963), 52–91.

* Henry C. Wallich, *Monetary Problems of an Export Economy: The Cuban experience 1914–47*, Cambridge, Mass. 1950.

J. Fred Rippy, 'Sugar in Inter-American Relations', *Inter-American Economic Affairs*, 9, 4 (Spring 1956), 50–64.

Jonathan V. Levin, *The Export Economies: Their Pattern of Development in Historical Perspective*, Cambridge, Mass. 1960.

International Bank for Reconstruction and Development: *The Cuban Economy*, Baltimore 1951.

Lowry Nelson, *Rural Cuba*, Minneapolis 1950.

*Wyatt MacGaffey and Clifford R. Barnett, *Cuba: Its People, its Society, its Culture*, New Haven 1962.

Castro's rebellion and the transformation of Cuban society

Hugh Thomas, 'Middle-class Politics and the Cuban Revolution', in Claudio Veliz (ed.), *The Politics of Conformity in Latin America*, London 1967, 249–77.

* Ernesto Ché Guevara, *Reminiscences of the Cuban Revolutionary War*, pb. ed. Harmondsworth 1969.

Ernesto Ché Guevara, *Guerrilla Warfare*, pb. ed. Harmondsworth 1969.

Ernesto Ché Guevara, *Selected Works*, ed. R. E. Monachea and Nelson P. Valdes, Cambridge, Mass. 1969.

G. C. Alroy, 'The Peasantry in the Cuban Revolution', *Review of Politics*, 29, 1 (Jan. 1967), 87–99.

Régis Debray, *Revolution in the Revolution?*, pb. ed. Harmondsworth 1968.

Régis Debray, *Strategy for Revolution*, ed. Robin Blackburn, London 1970.

Leo Huberman and Paul M. Sweezy (eds), *Régis Debray and the Latin American Revolution*, New York 1968.

** Eric J. Hobsbawm, 'Guerrillas in Latin America', in Ralph Miliband and John Saville (eds), *The Socialist Register, 1970*, London 1970, 51–61.

† Herbert L. Matthews, *Castro; a political biography*, pb. ed. Harmondsworth 1970.

Lee Lockwood, *Castro's Cuba, Cuba's Fidel*, New York 1967.

* Andrés Suaréz, *Cuba: Castroism and Communism, 1959–66*, Cambridge, Mass. 1967.

Theodore Draper, *Castro's Revolution: Myths and Realities*, London 1962.

Theodore Draper, *Castroism: Theory and Practice*, London 1965.

Robert Scheer and Maurice Zeitlin, *Cuba: An American Tragedy*, pb. ed. Harmondsworth 1964.

Leo Huberman and Paul M. Sweezy, *Cuba: Anatomy of a Revolution*, London 1961.

William A. Williams, *The United States, Cuba and Castro*, New York 1962.

Boris Goldenberg, *The Cuban Revolution and Latin America*, London 1965.

Seymour M. Lipset and Aldo Solari (eds), *Elites in Latin America*, pb. ed. New York 1967.

* Rufo Lopez Fresquet, *My Fourteen Months with Castro*, New York 1966.

J. P. Morray, *Cuba: The Second Revolution*, New York 1962.

Manuela Semidei, *Les États-Unis et la révolution cubaine, 1959–64*, Paris 1968.

Richard R. Fagen, Richard A. Brody and Thomas J. O'Leary, *Cubans in Exile: Disaffection and the Revolution*, Stanford 1968.

† Ernesto Ché Guevara, 'The Cuban Economy: Its Past and its Present Importance', *International Affairs*, 40, 4 (Oct. 1964), 589–99.

** James O'Connor, *The Origins of Socialism in Cuba*, Ithaca 1970.

D. Bruce Jackson, *Castro, the Kremlin and Communism in Latin America*, Baltimore 1969.

* J. Martínez-Alier, 'The Peasantry and the Cuban Revolution from the Spring of 1959 to the end of 1960', in Raymond Carr (ed.), *St. Antony's Papers*, 22, *Latin American Affairs* (London 1970), 137–57.

Dudley Seers (ed.), *Cuba: The Economic and Social Revolution*, Chapel Hill 1964.

René Dumont, *Cuba: Socialisme et Développement*, Paris 1964.

† René Dumont, *Cuba, est-il socialiste?*, Paris 1970.

Leo Huberman and Paul M. Sweezy, *Socialism in Cuba*, New York 1969.

Maurice Zeitlin, *Revolutionary Politics and the Cuban Working Class*, Princeton 1967.

Michel Gutelman, *L'agriculture socialisée à Cuba*, Paris 1967.

Sergio De Santis, 'The Economic Debate in Cuba', *International Socialist Journal*, 2, 10 (August 1965).

Richard R. Fagen, *The Transformation of Political Culture in Cuba*, Stanford 1969.

K. S. Karol, *Les Guérrilleros au pouvoir*, Paris 1970.

Carmelo Mesa-Lago, 'Le débat socialiste sur les stimulants économiques et moraux à Cuba', *Annales: Économies, Sociétés, Civilisations*, 26, 2 (March–April 1971), 434–55.

9. THE ANALYSIS OF REVOLUTIONARY PHENOMENA

† Crane Brinton, *The Anatomy of Revolution*, pb. ed. New York 1965.

George S. Pettee, *The Process of Revolution*, New York 1938.

Lyford P. Edwards, *The Natural History of Revolution*, 2nd ed. New York 1965.

Ted R. Gurr, *Why Men Rebel*, Princeton 1970.

† Henry Bienen, *Violence and Social Change; a review of current literature*, Chicago 1968.

† Chalmers Johnson, *Revolution and the Social System*, Stanford 1964.

* Chalmers Johnson, *Revolutionary Change*, pb. ed. London 1968.

H. H. Eckstein (ed.), *Internal War: problems and approaches*, New York 1964.

H. H. Eckstein, 'On the Etiology of Internal War', *History and Theory*, IV, 2 (1965), 133–63.

David Willer and George K. Zollschan, 'A Theory of Revolution', in George K. Zollschan and Walter Hirsch (eds), *Explorations in Social Change*, London 1964, 124–51.

Jean Baechler, *Les phénomènes révolutionnaires*, Paris 1970.

Jules Monnerot, *Sociologie de la révolution*, Paris 1969.

H. Janne, 'Une modèle théorique du phénomène révolutionnaire?', *Annales: Économies, Sociétés, Civilisations*, XV, 6 (Nov.–Dec. 1960), 1138–54.

Peter A. R. Calvert, *A Study of Revolution*, Oxford 1970.

Peter A. R. Calvert, 'Revolution: The Politics of Violence', *Political Studies*, XV, 1 (Feb. 1967), 1–11.

† Lawrence Stone, 'Theories of Revolution', *World Politics*, XVIII, 2 (Jan. 1966), 159–76.

Carl J. Friedrich (ed.), *Nomos*, Vol. VIII, *Revolution*, New York 1963.

Sir Dennis W. Brogan, *The Price of Revolution*, London 1951.

Rex D. Hopper, 'The Revolutionary Process', *Social Forces*, XXVIII (March 1950), 270–9.

Peter Amann, 'Revolution: a redefinition', *Political Science Quarterly*, LXXVII, 1 (March 1962), 36–53.

Dale Yoder, 'Current Definitions of Revolution', *American Journal of Sociology*, XXXII, 3 (Nov. 1926), 433–41.

Louis Gottshalk, 'Causes of Revolution', *American Journal of Sociology*, L, 1 (July 1944), 1–8.

† James C. Davies, 'Towards a Theory of Revolution', *American Sociological Review*, XXVII, 1 (Feb. 1962), 5–13.

James C. Davies, 'Political Stability and Instability; some manifestations and causes', *Journal of Conflict Resolution*, XIII, 1 (March 1969), 1–17.

† Mancur Olson, 'Rapid Growth as a Destabilizing Force', *Journal of Economic History*, 23, 4 (Dec. 1963), 529–52.

† Raymond Tanter and Manus Midlarsky, 'A Theory of Revolution', *Journal of Conflict Resolution*, XI, 3 (Sept. 1967), 264–80.

Ivo K. and Rosalind L. Feierabend, 'Aggressive Behaviors within Polities 1948–62; a cross-national study', *Journal of Conflict Resolution*, X, 3 (Sept. 1966), 249–71.

Frank H. Denton and Warren Phillips, 'Some Patterns in the History of Violence', *Journal of Conflict Resolution*, XII, 2 (June 1968), 182–95.

Raymond Tanter, 'Dimensions of Conflict Behavior within and between Nations 1958–60', *Journal of Conflict Resolution*, x, 1 (March 1966), 41–64.

Rudolph J. Rummel, 'Dimensions of Conflict Behavior within Nations, 1946–59', *Journal of Conflict Resolution*, x, 1 (March 1966), 65–73.

Rudolph J. Rummel, 'Dimensions of Conflict within and between Nations', *General Systems*, VIII (1963), 1–50.

E. Feit, 'Insurgency in Organizations; a theoretical analysis', *General Systems*, XIV (1969), 157–68.

* Neil J. Smelser, *Theory of Collective Behavior*, London 1962.

** Barrington Moore, *Social Origins of Dictatorship and Democracy; Lord and Peasant in the Making of the Modern World*, Boston 1966.

* Samuel Huntington, *Political Order in Changing Societies*, pb. ed. New Haven 1969.

James N. Rosenau (ed.), *International Aspects of Civil Strife*, Princeton 1964.

Charles Tilly and James Rule, *Measuring Political Upheaval*, Princeton 1965.

Andrew C. Janos, *The Seizure of Power; a study of force and popular consent*, Princeton 1964.

Feliks Gross, *The Seizure of Political Power in a Century of Revolutions*, New York 1958.

Edward Luttwak, *Coup d'État; a practical handbook*, pb. ed. Harmondsworth 1969.

Katharine C. Chorley, *Armies and the Art of Revolution*. London 1943.

Carl Leiden and K. M. Schmitt, *The Politics of Violence; revolution in the modern world*, pb. ed. Englewood Cliffs, N.J. 1968.

Samuel Huntington, 'Patterns of Violence in World Politics', in Samuel Huntington (ed.), *Changing Patterns of Military Politics*, New York 1962.

Ruth First, *The Barrel of a Gun: political power in Africa and the coup d'état*, London 1970.

Nathan Leites and Charles Wolf Jr, *Rebellion and Authority; an analytical essay on insurgent conflicts*, Chicago 1970.

* Eric R. Wolf, *Peasant Wars of the Twentieth Century*, New York 1969.

Hamza Alavi, 'Peasants and Revolution', in Ralph Miliband and John Saville (eds), *The Socialist Register, 1965*, London 1965, 244–77.

G. C. Alroy, *The Involvement of Peasants in Internal Wars*, Princeton 1966.

† V. G. Kiernan, 'The Peasant Revolution', in Ralph Miliband and John Saville (eds), *The Socialist Register, 1970*, London 1970, 9–37.

D. Hindley, 'Political Conflict Potential, Politicization and the Peasantry in Underdeveloped Countries', *Asian Studies*, 3 (1965), 470–89.

Bruce Russett, 'Inequality and Instability; The Relation of Land Tenure to Politics', *World Politics*, xvi, 3 (April 1964), 442–54.

H. Mendras and Y. Tavernier, *Terre, paysans et politique: structures agraires, systèmes politiques et politiques agricoles*, Vol. 1, Paris 1969.

Teodor Shanin, 'Peasantry as a Political Factor', *Sociological Review*, 14, 1 (1966), 5–27.

** Eric J. Hobsbawm, *Primitive Rebels; studies in archaic forms of social movement in the 19th and 20th centuries*, Manchester 1959.

† Karl Deutsch, 'Social Mobilization and Political Development', *American Political Science Review*, lv, 3 (Sept. 1961), 493–514.

* Cyril E. Black, *The Dynamics of Modernization; a study in comparative history*, pb. ed. New York 1967.

David E. Apter, *The Politics of Modernization*, Chicago 1965.

John P. Nettl, *Political Mobilization; a sociological analysis of methods and concepts*, London 1967 (virtually unintelligible).

† Ira W. Zartman, 'Revolution and Development: Form and Substance', *Civilisations*, xx, 2 (1970), 181–97.

Ghiţa Ionescu and Ernest Gellner (eds), *Populism; Its Meanings and National Characteristics*, London 1969.

Peter Worsley, *The Third World*, 2nd ed. London 1967.

Clifford Geertz (ed.), *Old Societies and New States; the quest for modernity in Asia and Africa*, New York 1963.

Richard Sklar, 'Political Science and National Integration; a radical approach', *Journal of Modern African Studies*, v, 1 (1967), 1–11.

Paul Baran, *The Political Economy of Growth*, pb. ed. New York 1968.

Hla Myint, *The Economics of the Developing Countries*, pb. ed. London 1969.

Harry G. Johnson (ed.), *Economic Nationalism in Old and New States*, London 1968.

Ernest Gellner, *Thought and Change*, London 1964.

Cyril E. Black and Thomas P. Thornton (eds), *Communism and Revolution; the strategic uses of political violence*, pb. ed. Princeton 1965.

Robert C. Tucker, *Paths of Communist Revolution*, Princeton 1968.

Daniel Lerner and Harold Lasswell (eds), *World Revolutionary Elites; studies in coercive ideological movements*, pb. ed. Cambridge, Mass. 1966.

Guenther Nollau, *International Communism and World Revolution; history and methods*, London 1961.

Samuel P. Huntington and Clement H. Moore (eds), *Authoritarian Politics in Modern Society; the dynamics of established one-party systems*, New York 1970.

Adam B. Ulam, *The Unfinished Revolution; an essay on the sources of influence of Marxism and Communism*, New York 1960.

H. Wolpe, 'Some Problems concerning Revolutionary Consciousness' in Ralph Miliband and John Saville (eds), *The Socialist Register, 1970*, London 1970, 251–80.

Ralf Dahrendorf, *Class and Class Conflict in Industrial Society*, London 1959.

Ralf Dahrendorf, *Essays in the Theory of Society*, London 1968.

Stanislaw Ossowski, *Class Structure in the Social Consciousness*, London 1963.

Leo Kuper, 'Race Structure in the Social Consciousness', *Civilisations*, xx, 1 (1970), 88–103.

* Leo Kuper, 'Theories of Revolution and Race Relations', *Comparative Studies in Society and History*, 13, 1 (Jan. 1971), 87–107.

Martin Oppenheimer, *Urban Guerrilla*, pb. ed. Harmondsworth 1970.

E. Victor Wolfenstein, *The Revolutionary Personality: Lenin, Trotsky, Gandhi*, Princeton 1967.

Fred Weinstein and Gerald M. Platt, *The Wish to be Free; society, psyche and value change*, Berkeley 1969.

* Peter Worsley, *The Trumpet Shall Sound; a study of 'cargo' cults in Melanesia*, pb. ed. London 1970.

† Anthony F. C. Wallace, 'Revitalization Movements', *American Anthropologist*, 58, 2 (April 1956), 264–81.

† Kenelm O. L. Burridge, *New Heaven, New Earth; a study of millenarian activities*, pb. ed. Oxford 1969.

Kenelm O. L. Burridge, *Mambu: a Melanesian Millennium*, London 1960.

Vittorio Lanternari, *The Religions of the Oppressed; a study of modern messianic cults*, pb. ed. New York 1965.

Sylvia L. Thrupp (ed.), *Millennial Dreams in Action (Comparative Studies in Society and History, Supplement, 11)*, The Hague 1962.

Max Gluckman, *Order and Rebellion in Tribal Africa*, London 1963.

Max Gluckman, *Custom and Conflict in Africa*, pb. ed. Oxford 1965.

James H. Meisel, *Counter-Revolution: How Revolutions Die*, New York 1966.

Kalman H. Silvert, *The Conflict Society: Reaction and Revolution*, pb. ed. New York 1968.

Kenneth N. Waltz, *Man, the State and War; a theoretical analysis*, pb. ed. New York 1965.

Raymond Aron, *Peace and War; a theory of international relations*, London 1966.

Hans J. Morgenthau, *Politics among Nations: The Struggle for Power and Peace*, 3rd ed. New York 1961.

10. HISTORY OF THE UNDERSTANDING OF REVOLUTION

Thucydides, *History of the Pelonnesian War*, 2 vols, Oxford 1900.

Aristotle, *The Politics* (ed. Barker), Oxford 1946.

Puritanism and Liberty (=The Putney Debates), ed. A. S. P. Woodhouse, 3rd ed. London 1965.

Thomas Hobbes, *Leviathan* (ed. Oakeshott), Oxford 1946.

Thomas Hobbes, *Behemoth, or the Long Parliament* (ed. F. Tönnies), London reprint 1969.

Edward Hyde, Earl of Clarendon, *The History of the Rebellion and Civil Wars in England* (ed. W. D. Macray), 6 vols, Oxford 1888.

John Locke, *Two Treatises of Government* (ed. P. Laslett), 2nd ed. Cambridge 1967.

Jean-Jacques Rousseau, *The Political Writings* (ed. C. E. Vaughan), 2 vols, 2nd ed. Oxford 1962 (especially *Discours sur l'origine et les fondements de l'inégalité parmi les hommes* and *Du Contrat Social, ou principes du droit politique*).

Edmund Burke, *Reflections on the Revolution in France* (ed. C. C. O'Brien), pb. ed. Harmondsworth 1969.

Thomas Paine, *The Rights of Man*, Everyman, London 1915.

Marquis de Condorcet, *Esquisse d'un tableau historique des progrès de l'esprit humain*, Paris 1933.

Saint-Just, *L'Esprit de la Révolution*, Paris 1963.

Robespierre, *Discours et Rapports à la Convention*, Paris 1965.

Joseph de Maistre, *Selected Works* (ed. Jack Lively), New York 1965.

G. W. F. Hegel, *The Phenomenology of Mind*, tr. Baillie, London 1910.

G. W. F. Hegel, *The Philosophy of History*, pb. ed. New York 1956.

G. W. F. Hegel, *The Philosophy of Right*, tr. Knox, Oxford 1942.

Alexis de Tocqueville, *L'Ancien Régime et la Révolution Française*, Oxford 1904.

Alexis de Tocqueville, *The European Revolution* and *Correspondence with Gobineau* (ed. J. Lukacs), pb. ed. Garden City 1959.

Alexis de Tocqueville, *Recollections*, pb. ed. New York 1959.

Alexander Herzen, *My Past and Thoughts*, 4 vols, London 1968.

Karl Marx, *Critique of Hegel's Philosophy of Right* (ed. O'Malley), Cambridge 1970.

Karl Marx, *Early Writings* (ed. Bottomore), pb. ed. New York 1964.

Karl Marx and Friedrich Engels, *Selected Works*, 2 vols, Moscow 1958.

Karl Marx, *Capital*, 3 vols, Moscow 1961.

Karl Marx, *Grundrisse* (ed. McLellan), London 1971.

Karl Marx, *Pre-capitalist Economic Formations* (ed. Hobsbawm), London 1964.

Pierre-Joseph Proudhon, *Qu'est-ce que la propriété?*, Paris 1966.

Pierre-Joseph Proudhon, *Philosophie de la misère* (selections), Paris 1964.

Lorenz von Stein, *The History of the Social Movement in France, 1789–1850*, Totowa, N.J. 1964.

The Political Philosophy of Bakunin (ed. Maximoff), pb. ed. New York 1964.

J. A. Hobson, *Imperialism: A Study*, 6th ed. London 1961.

K. Peter Kropotkin, *Selected Writings on Anarchism and Revolution* (ed. Miller), Cambridge, Mass. 1970.

Georges Sorel, *Reflections on Violence*, pb. ed. New York 1961.

V. I. Lenin, *Selected Works*, 2 vols, Moscow 1947.

Rosa Luxemburg, *The Mass Strike*, pb. ed. New York. 1971.

Rosa Luxemburg, *The Russian Revolution and Leninism or Marxism*, pb. ed. Ann Arbor 1961.
Georg Lukács, *History and Class Consciousness*, London 1971.
Karl Kautsky, *The Dictatorship of the Proletariat*, pb. ed. Ann Arbor 1964.
Robert Michels, *Political Parties*, pb. ed. New York 1959.
Karl von Clausewitz, *On War* (ed. Maude), 3 vols, London 1966.
Antonio Gramsci, *The Modern Prince and other writings*, pb. ed. New York 1967.
Karl Mannheim, *Ideology and Utopia*, pb. ed. London 1960.
Mao Tse-tung, *Selected Works*, 4 vols, Peking 1967.
See also under particular revolutions.
C. B. Macpherson, *The Political Theory of Possessive Individualism*, Oxford 1962.
Quentin Skinner, 'The Ideological Context of Hobbes's Political Thought', *The Historical Journal*, IX, 3 (1966), 286–317.
John Dunn, *The Political Thought of John Locke*, Cambridge 1969.
John Dunn, 'The Politics of Locke in England and America in the Eighteenth Century' in John W. Yolton (ed.), *John Locke: Problems and Perspectives*, Cambridge 1969, 45–80.
Bernard Bailyn, *The Ideological Origins of the American Revolution*, Cambridge, Mass. 1967.
Gordon S. Wood, *The Creation of the American Republic 1776–87*, Williamsburg, Va. 1969.
Franco Venturi, *Utopia and Reform in the Enlightenment*, Cambridge 1971.
Peter Gay, *The Enlightenment: An Interpretation*, 2 vols, London 1966–70.
Peter Gay, *Voltaire's Politics: The Poet as Realist*, Princeton 1959.
Daniel Mornet, *Les origines intellectuelles de la Révolution Française*, 5th ed. Paris 1954.
Judith N. Shklar, *Men and Citizens: a study of Rousseau's Social Theory*, Cambridge 1969.
Maxime Leroy, *Histoire des idées sociales en France (de Montesquieu à Proudhon)*, 3 vols, Paris 1946–50.
J. L. Talmon, *Origins of Totalitarian Democracy*, pb. ed. London 1961.
J. B. Bury, *The Idea of Progress*, pb. ed. New York 1955.
Robert A. Nisbet, *Social Change and History: aspects of the western theory of development*, pb. ed. London 1970.
Guido de Ruggiero, *The History of European Liberalism*, pb. ed. Boston 1959.
Hans Kohn, *The Idea of Nationalism*, pb. ed. New York 1961.
Robert A. Nisbet, *The Sociological Tradition*, pb. ed. London 1970.
Frank Manuel, *The Prophets of Paris*, Cambridge, Mass. 1962.
George Lichtheim, *A Short History of Socialism*, pb. ed. London 1970.
** George Lichtheim, *The Origins of Socialism*, pb. ed. London 1970.
Maurice Dommanget, *Babeuf et la Conjuration des Égaux*, 2nd ed. Paris 1970.

Maurice Dommanget, *Sur Babeuf et la Conjuration des Égaux*, Paris 1970.

Elizabeth L. Eisenstein, *The First Professional Revolutionist; Filippo Michele Buonarroti (1761–1837)*, Cambridge, Mass. 1959.

S. Bernstein, *Auguste Blanqui*, Paris 1969.

A. B. Spitzer, *The Revolutionary Theories of Louis Auguste Blanqui*, New York 1957.

Herbert Marcuse, *Reason and Revolution: Hegel and the Rise of Social Theory*, 2nd ed. New York 1954.

Frank E. Manuel, *The New World of Henri Saint-Simon*, Cambridge, Mass. 1956.

David McLellan, *The Young Hegelians and Karl Marx*, London 1969.

* David McLellan, *Marx before Marxism*, London 1970.

Shlomo Avineri, *The Social and Political Thought of Karl Marx*, pb. ed. Cambridge 1970.

** George Lichtheim, *Marxism: An Historical and Critical Study*, pb. ed. London 1964.

Louis Althusser, *Pour Marx*, Paris 1966.

Georges Gurvitch, *Proudhon. Sa vie, son oeuvre*, Paris 1965.

James Joll, *The Anarchists*, pb. ed. London 1969.

Pierre Ansart, *Naissance de l'anarchisme: Esquisse d'une explication sociologique du proudhonisme*, Paris 1970.

Edward H. Carr, *Michael Bakunin*, pb. ed. New York 1961.

Leopold Labedz (ed.), *Revisionism: essays on the history of Marxist ideas*, London 1962.

Peter Gay, *The Dilemma of Democratic Socialism: Eduard Bernstein's Challenge to Marx*, pb. ed. New York 1962.

J. L. Talmon, *Political Messianism; The Romantic Phase*, London 1960.

Robert C. Tucker, *The Marxian Revolutionary Idea: Marxist thought and its impact on radical movements*, pb. ed. London 1970.

H. B. Davis, *Nationalism and Socialism: Marxist and Labor Theories of Nationalism to 1917*, New York 1967.

Tom Kemp, *Theories of Imperialism*, London 1967.

* George Lichtheim, *Imperialism*, London 1971.

H. Stuart Hughes, *Consciousness and Society; the reconstruction of European social thought, 1890–1930*, pb. ed. New York 1961.

Z. A. B. Zeman and W. B. Scharlau. *The Merchant of Revolution: The life of Alexander Israel Helphand (Parvus) 1867–1924*, London 1965.

John P. Nettl, *Rosa Luxemburg*, 2 vols, London 1966.

John M. Cammett, *Antonio Gramsci and the Origins of Italian Communism*, pb. ed. Stanford 1969.

David Mitrany, *Marx against the Peasant: A Study in Social Dogmatism*, London 1951.

George Lichtheim, *Marxism in Modern France*, New York 1966.

Alain Touraine, *Le mouvement de mai ou le Communisme utopique*, Paris 1968.

Arthur Hatto, "Revolution"; 'an Enquiry into the Usefulness of an Historical Term', *Mind*, new series, 58, 232 (Oct. 1949), 495–517.

Karl Griewank, *Der Neuzeitliche Revolutionsbegriff*, 2nd ed. Frankfurt 1969.

Hannah Arendt, *On Revolution*, London 1964.

11. HISTORICAL BACKGROUND

Norman Cohn, *The Pursuit of the Millennium; revolutionary messianism in the middle ages and its bearing on modern totalitarian movements*, pb. ed. London 1962.

Jacques Goff (ed.), *Hérésies et sociétés dans l'Europe pré-industrielle 11e–18e siècles*, Paris 1968.

Michel Mollat and Philippe Wolff, *Ongles Bleus, Jacques et Ciompi; les révolutions populaires en Europe aux xiv-xve siècles*, Paris 1970.

Trevor Aston (ed.), *Crisis in Europe, 1560–1660*, London 1965.

Robert Forster and Jack P. Greene (eds), *Preconditions of Revolution in Early Modern Europe*, Baltimore 1970.

John H. Elliott, 'Revolution and Continuity in Early Modern Europe', *Past and Present*, 42 (Feb. 1969), 35–56.

Alexandra D. Lublinskaya, *French Absolutism; the Crucial Phase 1620–29*, Cambridge 1968.

Boris H. Porshnev, *Les soulèvements populaires en France de 1623 à 1648*, Paris 1963.

Madeleine Foisil, *La révolte des Nu-Pieds et les révoltes normandes de 1639*, Paris 1970.

Roland Mousnier, *Fureurs paysannes; les paysans dans les révoltes du xvii siècle* (France, Russie, Chine), Paris 1967.

Robert Mandrou, 'Vingt ans après, ou une direction de recherches fécondes; les révoltes populaires en France au xviie siècle', *Revue Historique*, CCXLII (July–Sept. 1969), 29–40.

Michael Walzer, *The Revolution of the Saints; a study in the origins of radical politics*, London 1966.

Ivan A. Roots, *The Great Rebellion, 1642–60*, London 1966.

Pierre Goubert, *L'Ancien Régime*, Vol. 1, Paris 1969.

Keith Thomas, *Religion and the Decline of Magic*, London 1971.

E. P. Thompson, 'The Moral Economy of the English Crowd in the Eighteenth Century', *Past and Present*, 50 (Feb. 1971), 76–136.

John T. Alexander, *Autocratic Politics in a National Crisis; The Imperial Russian Government and Pugachev's Revolt, 1773–1775*, London 1970.

R. R. Palmer, *The Age of the Democratic Revolution: a political history of Europe and America, 1760–1800*, 2 vols, London 1959–64.

Jacques Godechot, *The Taking of the Bastille July 14th 1789*, London 1970.

Georges Lefebvre, *The Coming of the French Revolution, 1789*, pb. ed. 1957.

Georges Lefebvre, *La Grande Peur*, Paris 1932.

Georges Lefebvre, *The French Revolution*, 2 vols, London 1962–4.

Alfred Cobban, *The Social Interpretation of the French Revolution*, Cambridge 1964.

George Rudé, *The Crowd in the French Revolution*, Oxford 1959.

Jeffry Kaplow (ed.), *New Perspectives on the French Revolution; readings in historical sociology*, New York 1965.

Albert Soboul, *The Parisian Sans-culottes and the French Revolution, 1793–4*, Oxford 1964.

Gwyn A. Williams, *Artisans and Sans-culottes; popular movements in France and Britain during the French Revolution*, London 1968.

E. P. Thompson, *The Making of the English Working Class*, London 1963.

Richard Cobb, *The Police and the People; French popular protest, 1789–1820*, London 1970.

Charles Tilly, *The Vendée*, London 1964.

Georges Lefebvre. *Napoleon*, 2 vols, London 1969.

Eric J. Hobsbawm, *The Age of Revolution: Europe 1789–1848*, London 1962.

C. L. R. James, *The Black Jacobins, Toussaint L'Ouverture and the San Domingo Revolution*, 2nd ed. pb. New York 1963.

R. A. Humphreys and John Lynch (eds), *The Origins of the Latin American Revolutions, 1808–1826*, pb. ed. New York 1965.

M. M. Postan and H. J. Habbakuk (eds), *The Cambridge Economic History of Europe*, VI, *The Industrial Revolutions and after*, Cambridge 1965.

Jacques Droz, *Europe between Revolutions, 1815–48*, pb. ed London 1967.

Louis Chevalier, *Classes laborieuses et classes dangereuses à Paris pendant la première moitié du xixe siècle*, Paris 1958.

Georges Duveau, *1848, the Making of a Revolution*, London 1967.

William L. Langer, *The Revolutions of 1848*, pb. ed. New York 1971.

Sir Lewis Namier, *1848; The Revolution of the Intellectuals*, London 1947.

Eric Stokes, 'Traditional Resistance Movements and Afro-Asian Nationalism: the context of the 1857 Mutiny Rebellion in India', *Past and Present*, 48 (August 1970), 100–18.

Roger L. Williams, *The French Revolution of 1870–71*, London 1969.

Jacques Rougerie, *Procès des Communards*, Paris 1970.

Julius Braunthal, *History of the International (1864–1943)*, 2 vols, London 1966–7.

Henry Collins and Chimen Abramsky, *Karl Marx and the British Labour Movement; Years of the first International*, London 1965.

James Joll, *The Second International, 1889–1914*, London 1955.

Hartmut Pogge von Strandmann, 'Domestic Origins of Germany's Colonial Expansion under Bismarck', *Past and Present*, 42 (Feb. 1969), 140–59.

Hans-Ulrich Wehler, 'Bismarck's Imperialism 1862–1890', *Past and Present*, 48 (August 1970), 119–55.

William L. Langer, *The Diplomacy of Imperialism, 1890–1902*, 2 vols, New York 1935.

Guenther Roth, *The Social Democrats in Imperial Germany; A Study in Working Class Isolation and National Integration*, Totowa, N.J. 1963.

Carl E. Schorske, *German Social Democracy, 1905–17; the development of the great schism*, Cambridge, Mass. 1955.

Fritz Fischer, *Germany's Aims in the First World War*, London 1967.

Marc Ferro, *La Grande Guerre*, Paris 1968.

Arno J. Mayer, *Politics and Diplomacy of Peacemaking; containment and counter-revolution at Versailles 1918–19*, London 1968.

A. J. Ryder, *The German Revolution of 1918; a study of German Socialism in war and revolt*, Cambridge 1967.

Francis L. Carsten, *The Rise of Fascism*, London 1967.

Arnold J. Toynbee (ed.), *The Impact of the Russian Revolution, 1917–67; the impact of Bolshevism on the world outside Russia*, London 1967.

David Schoenbaum, *Hitler's Social Revolution; class and status in Nazi Germany, 1933–39*, London 1967.

Franz Neumann, *Behemoth; The Structure and Practice of National Socialism*, London 1942.

Ernest Nolte, *Three Faces of Fascism*, pb. ed. New York 1969.

S. J. Woolf (ed.), *The Nature of Fascism*, pb. ed. New York 1969.

S. J. Woolf (ed.), *European Fascism*, pb. ed. New York 1969.

Gabriel Jackson, *The Spanish Republic and the Civil War, 1931–39*, Princeton 1965.

Victor Serge, *Memoirs of a Revolutionary, 1901–41*, pb. ed. London 1967.

Edward H. Carr, *Conditions of Peace*, London 1942.

Gabriel Kolko, *The Politics of War; allied diplomacy and the world crisis of 1943–45*, London 1969.

Sigmund Neumann, *Permanent Revolution: totalitarianism in the age of international civil war*, 2nd ed. London 1965.

Richard J. Barnet, *Intervention and Revolution: The United States in the Third World*, New York 1968.

Richard Lowenthal, *World Communism; the disintegration of a secular faith*, New York 1964.

David Horowitz, *Imperialism and Revolution*, London 1969.

Index